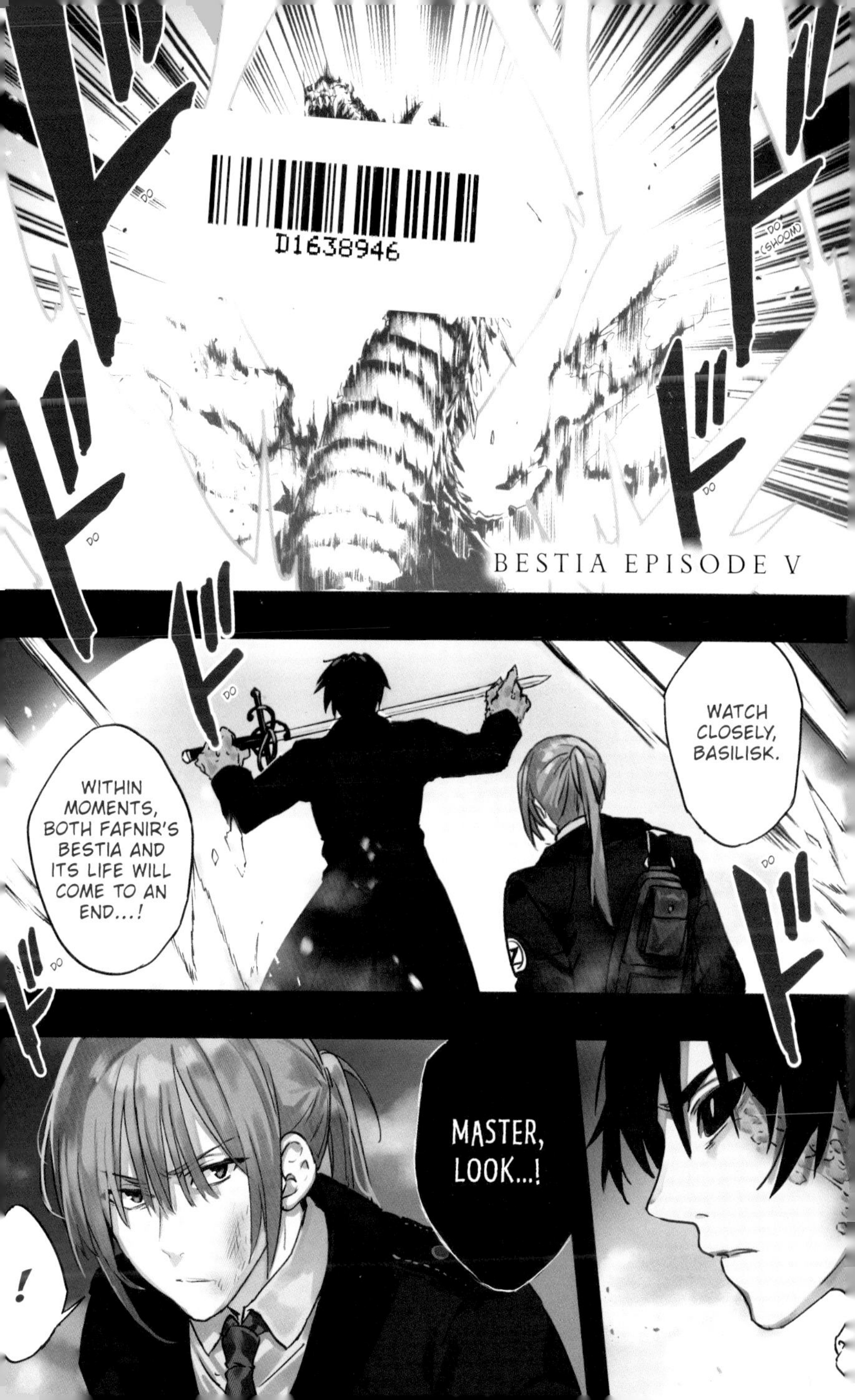
DO
(SHOOM)
DO
DO
DO
BESTIA EPISODE V
DO
WATCH CLOSELY, BASILISK.
WITHIN MOMENTS, BOTH FAFNIR'S BESTIA AND ITS LIFE WILL COME TO AN END...!
DO
DO
MASTER, LOOK...!
!

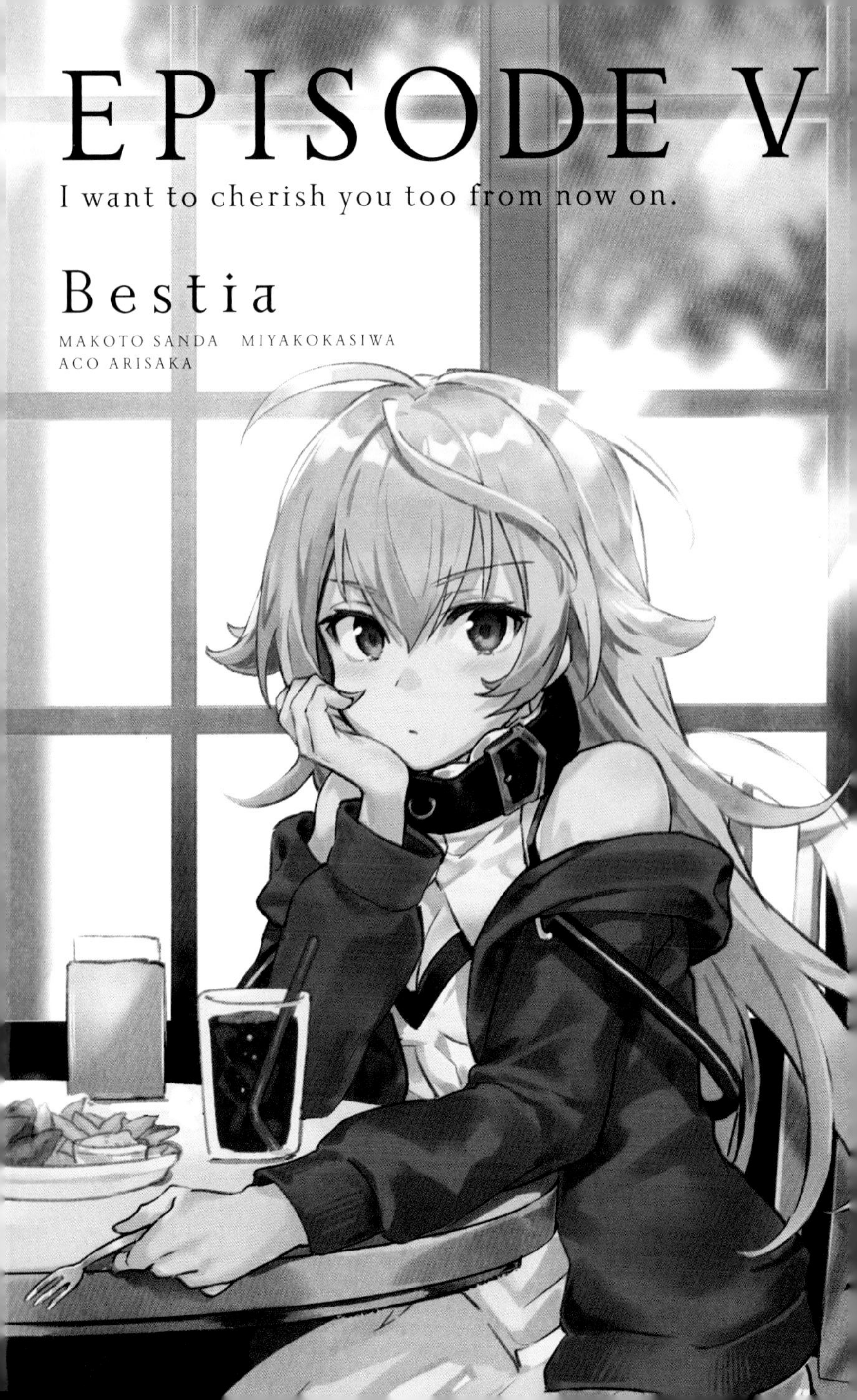
EPISODE V
I want to cherish you too from now on.
Bestia
MAKOTO SANDA MIYAKOKASIWA
ACO ARISAKA

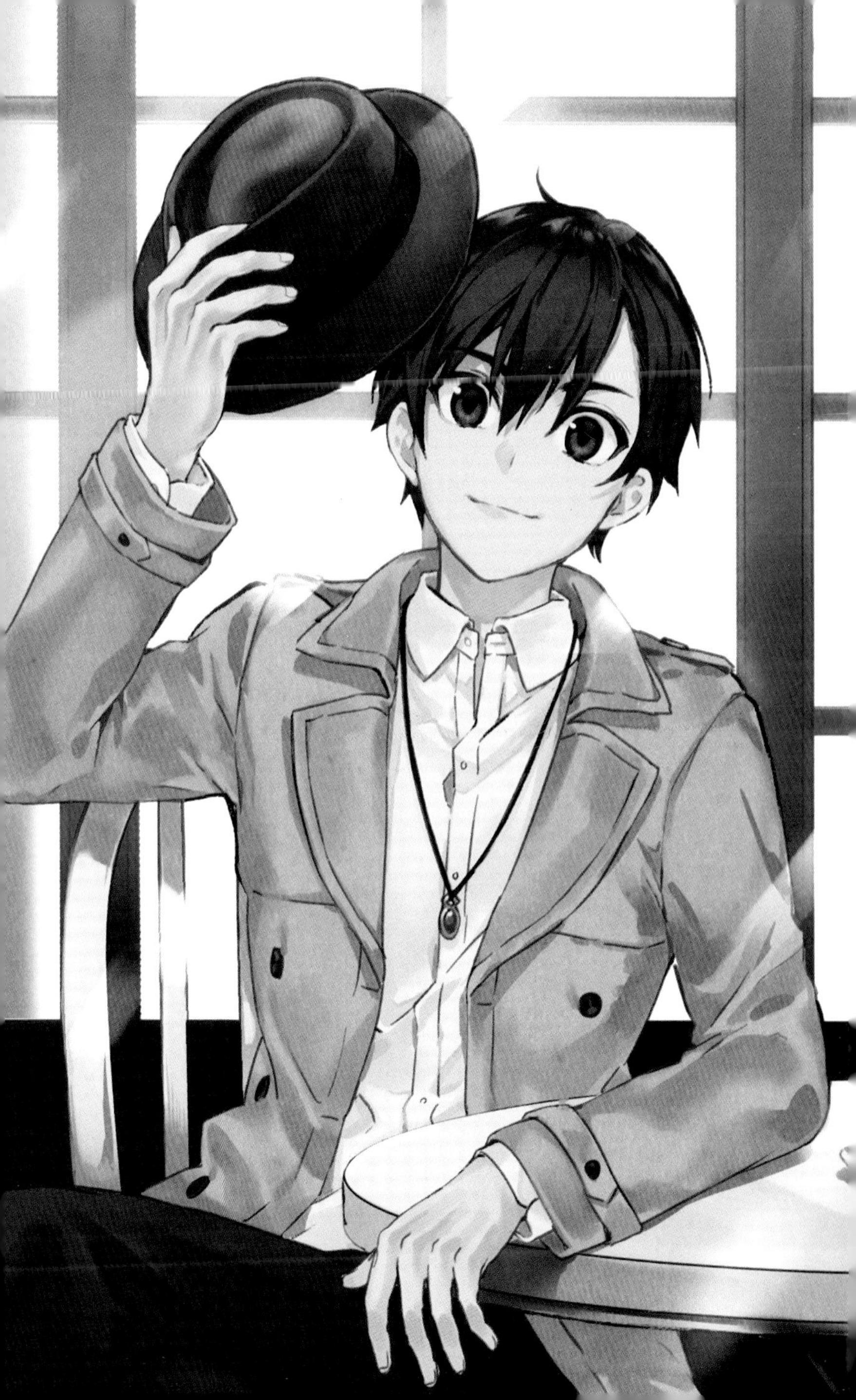

BESTIA 2

MAKOTO SANDA MIYAKOKASIWA ACO ARISAKA

CONTENTS

STORY

Asuka Tsukasa has come to study aboard in his birthplace, London, in the hopes of finding both his missing mother and the girl he knows only from faint memories. He quickly finds himself reunited with the latter—a cryptid named Edgar.

Meanwhile, something is turning swathes of the city to gold. The ZOO operative known as Oldman explains that the cryptid Fafnir has sensed the presence of Asuka, its former master's son, which causes its Bestia abilities to rage out of control. Asuka and Edgar race to the scene to stop Fafnir, only to run into another handler named Rodney and his cryptid, Basilisk. This new pair's merciless attacks turn the battle into a gruesome affair, and in the midst of the fighting, Asuka somehow hears Fafnir's grief-stricken cries. Is there any hope of stopping Fafnir's suicidal rampage......!?

CHARACTERS

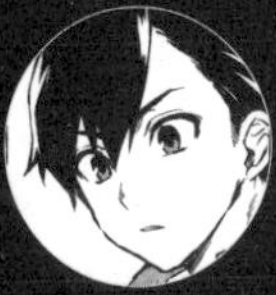

Asuka Tsukasa

Protagonist. Encountering Edgar has led him to become a cryptid handler.

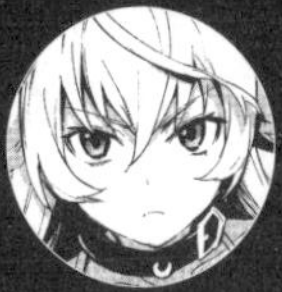

Edgar (Black Dog)

A cryptid who has formed a contract with Asuka. Her Bestia, "Crack," lets her manipulate lightning.

Alistair Reno Gruworth

A distant relative of Asuka's. Unlike him, Alice loves animals.

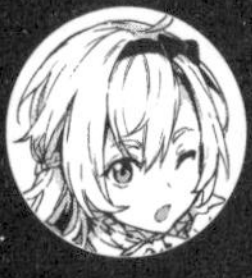

Rodney McGrath

A cool-headed handler who is more than willing to kill cryptids if the mission calls for it.

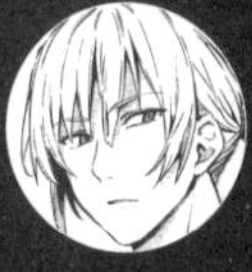

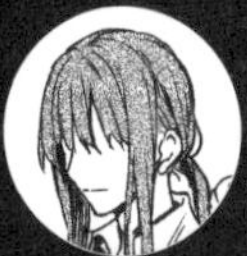

Honoka Tsukasa

Asuka's mother. She was a powerful handler who vanished one day.

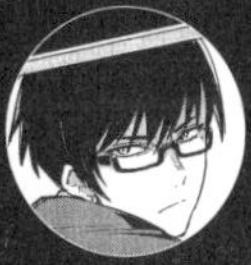

Nameless (Basilisk)

The cryptid who formed a contract with Rodney.

Fafnir (Golden Dragon)

A cryptid once kept by Honoka. Its Bestia is raging out of control.

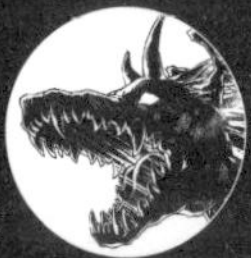

Oldman

Operative for the secret organization known as ZOO.

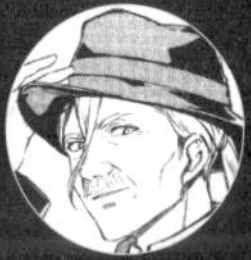

Bestia

MAKOTO SANDA MIYAKOKASIWA

ACO ARISAKA

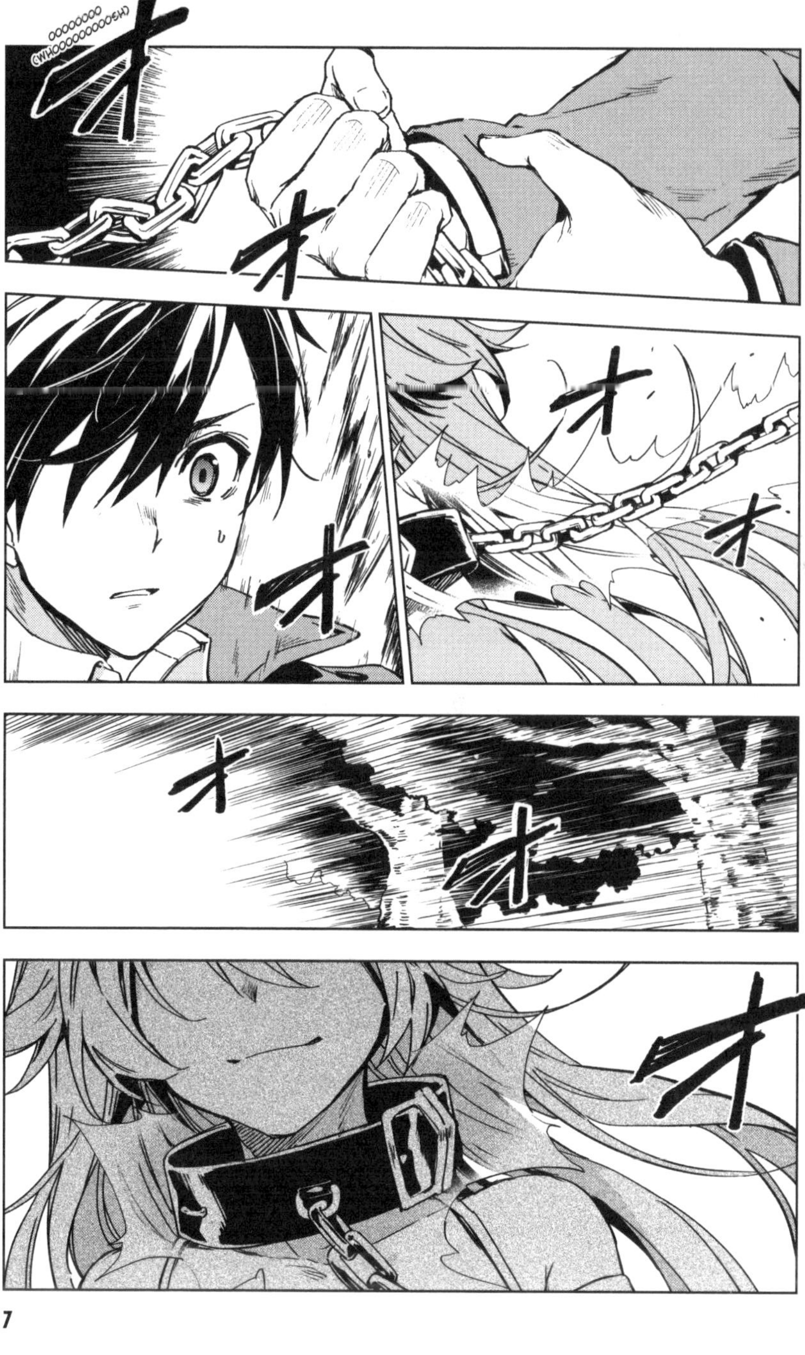
OOOOOOOO
(WHOOOOOOOOOOSH)

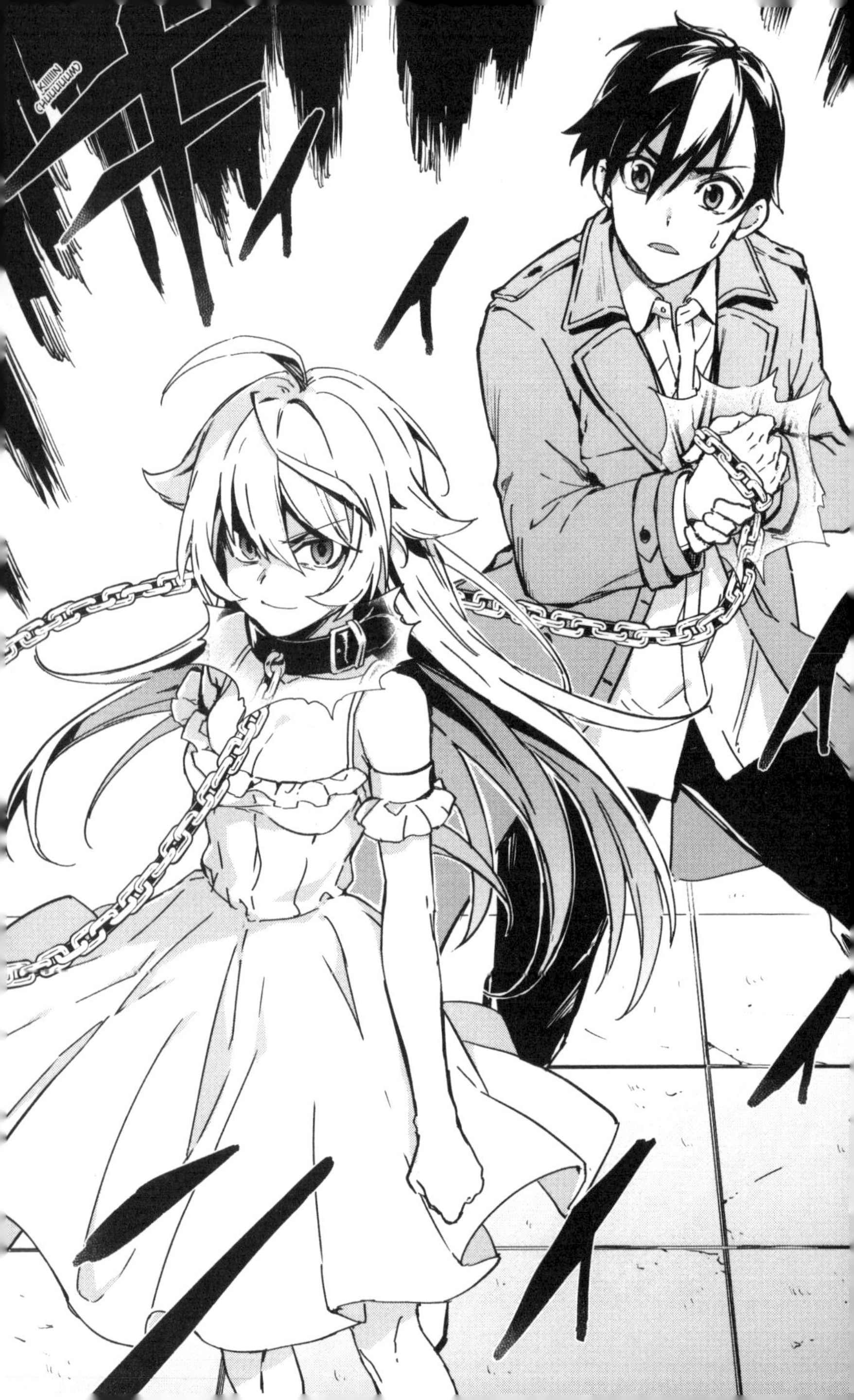
KIIIIIIN
CHUUUUUM

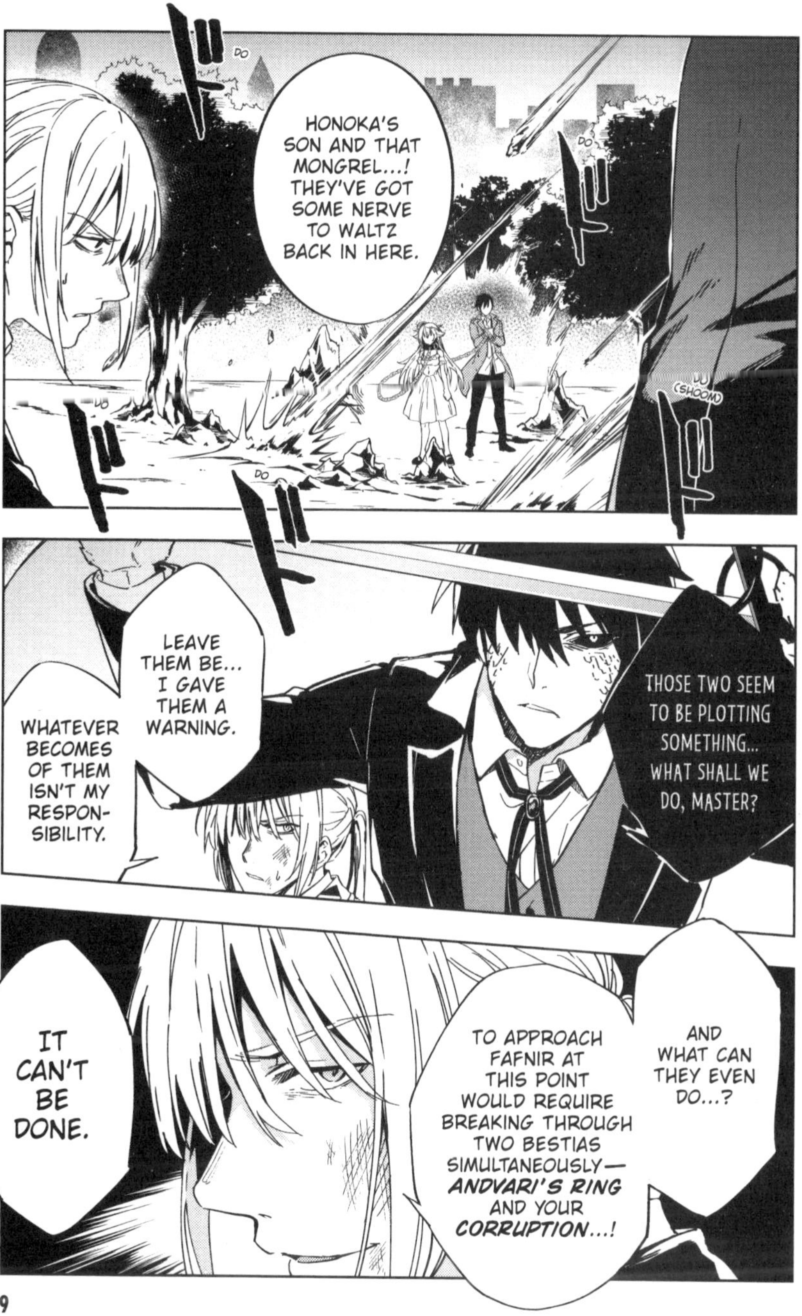
DO
DO
(SHOOM)
HONOKA'S SON AND THAT MONGREL...! THEY'VE GOT SOME NERVE TO WALTZ BACK IN HERE.
DO
DO
THOSE TWO SEEM TO BE PLOTTING SOMETHING... WHAT SHALL WE DO, MASTER?
LEAVE THEM BE... I GAVE THEM A WARNING.
WHATEVER BECOMES OF THEM ISN'T MY RESPON-SIBILITY.
AND WHAT CAN THEY EVEN DO...?
TO APPROACH FAFNIR AT THIS POINT WOULD REQUIRE BREAKING THROUGH TWO BESTIAS SIMULTANEOUSLY—***ANDVARI'S RING*** AND YOUR ***CORRUPTION***...!
IT CAN'T BE DONE.

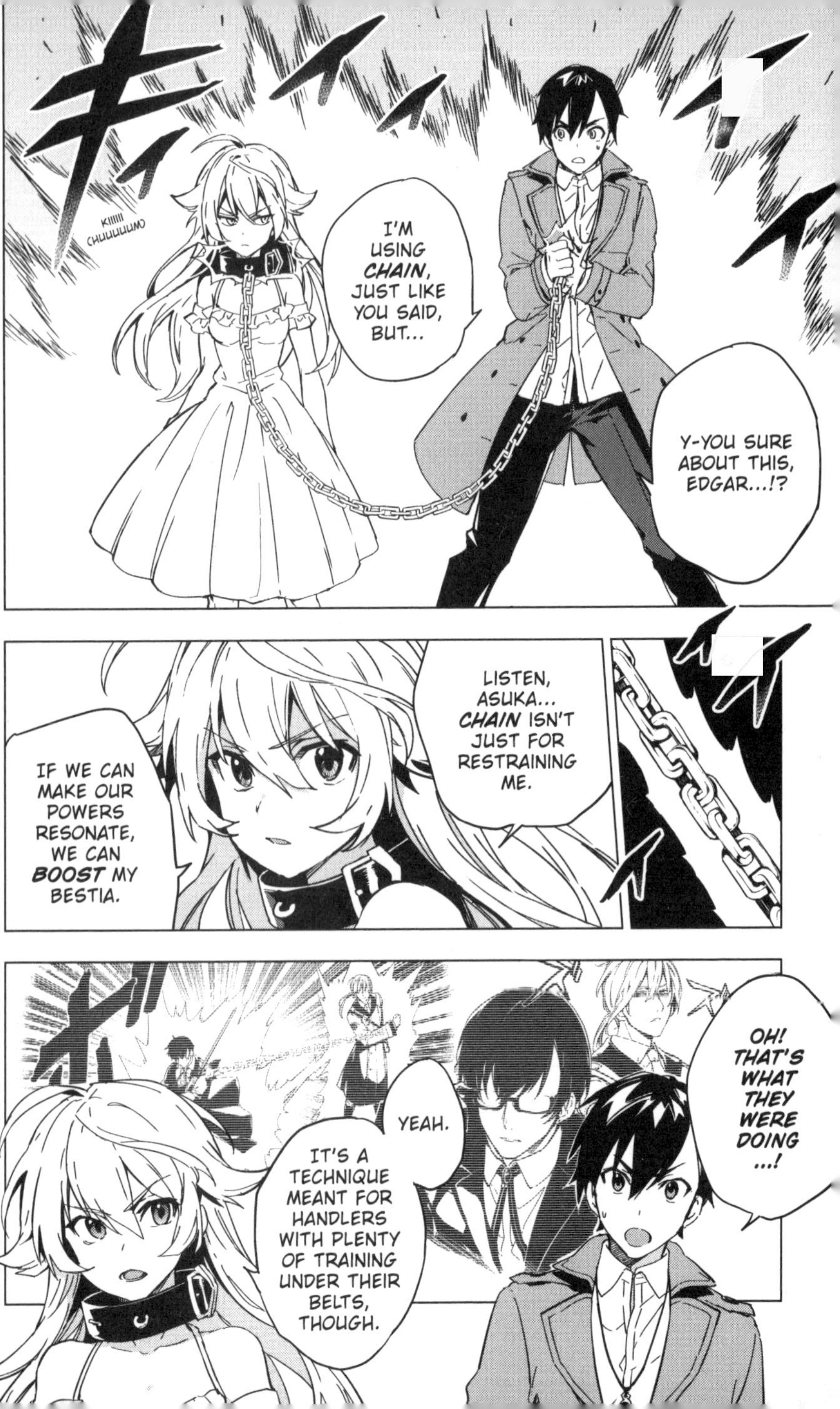
KIIIIII (CHUUUUUUM)
I'M USING **CHAIN**, JUST LIKE YOU SAID, BUT...
Y-YOU SURE ABOUT THIS, EDGAR...!?
LISTEN, ASUKA... **CHAIN** ISN'T JUST FOR RESTRAINING ME.
IF WE CAN MAKE OUR POWERS RESONATE, WE CAN **BOOST** MY BESTIA.
OH! THAT'S WHAT THEY WERE DOING...!
YEAH.
IT'S A TECHNIQUE MEANT FOR HANDLERS WITH PLENTY OF TRAINING UNDER THEIR BELTS, THOUGH.

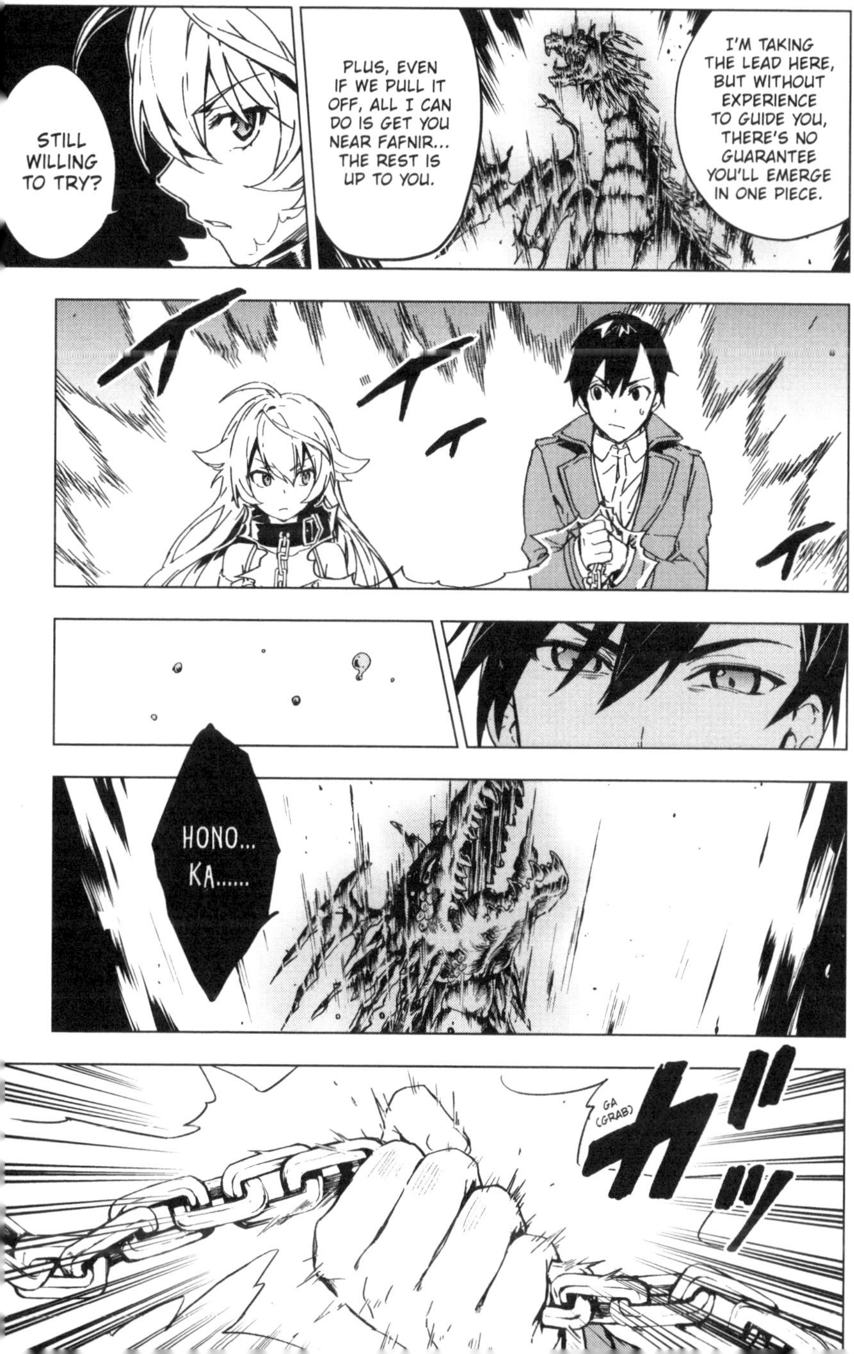
I'M TAKING THE LEAD HERE, BUT WITHOUT EXPERIENCE TO GUIDE YOU, THERE'S NO GUARANTEE YOU'LL EMERGE IN ONE PIECE.
PLUS, EVEN IF WE PULL IT OFF, ALL I CAN DO IS GET YOU NEAR FAFNIR... THE REST IS UP TO YOU.
STILL WILLING TO TRY?
HONO... KA......
GA (GRAB)

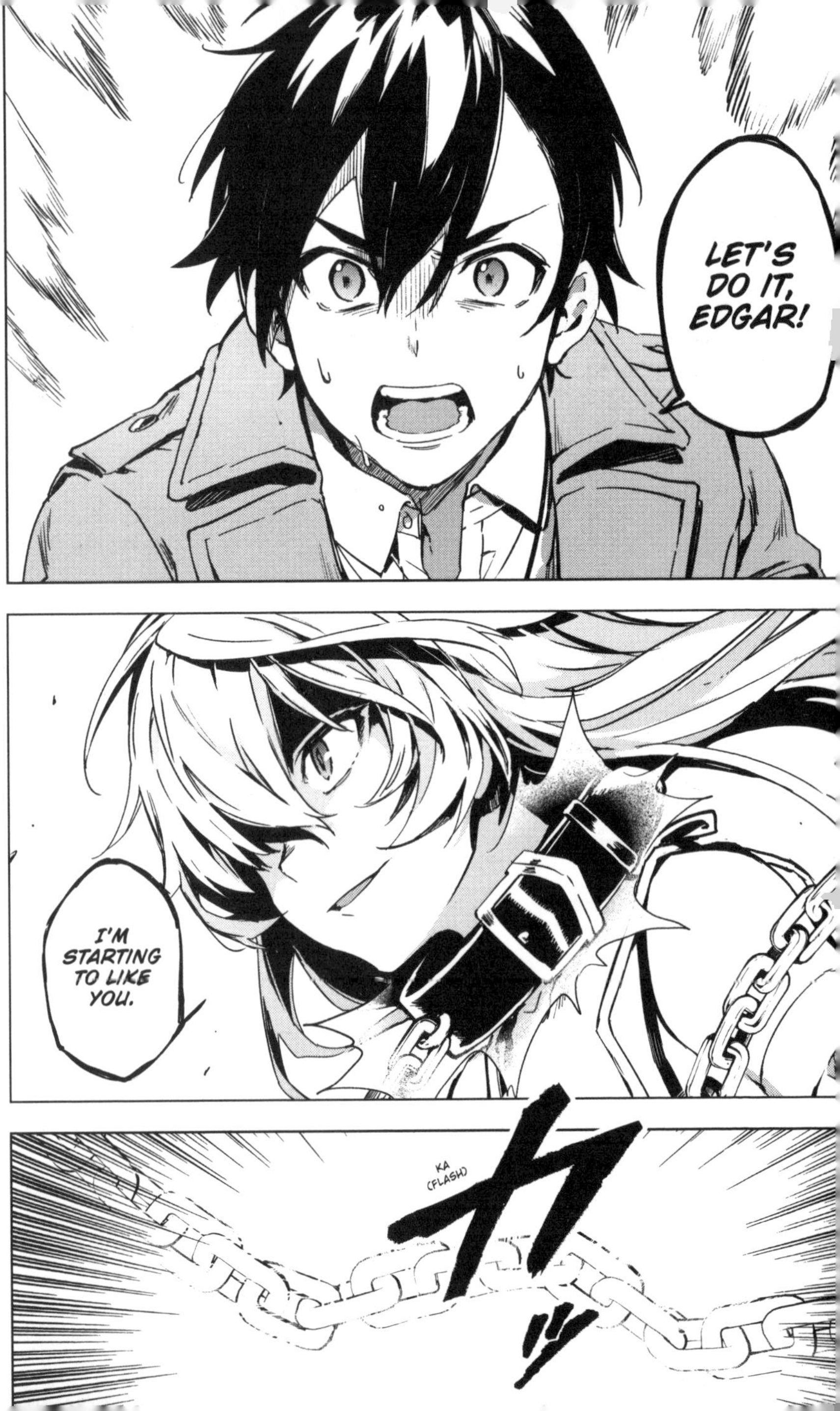
LET'S DO IT, EDGAR!
I'M STARTING TO LIKE YOU.
KA (FLASH)

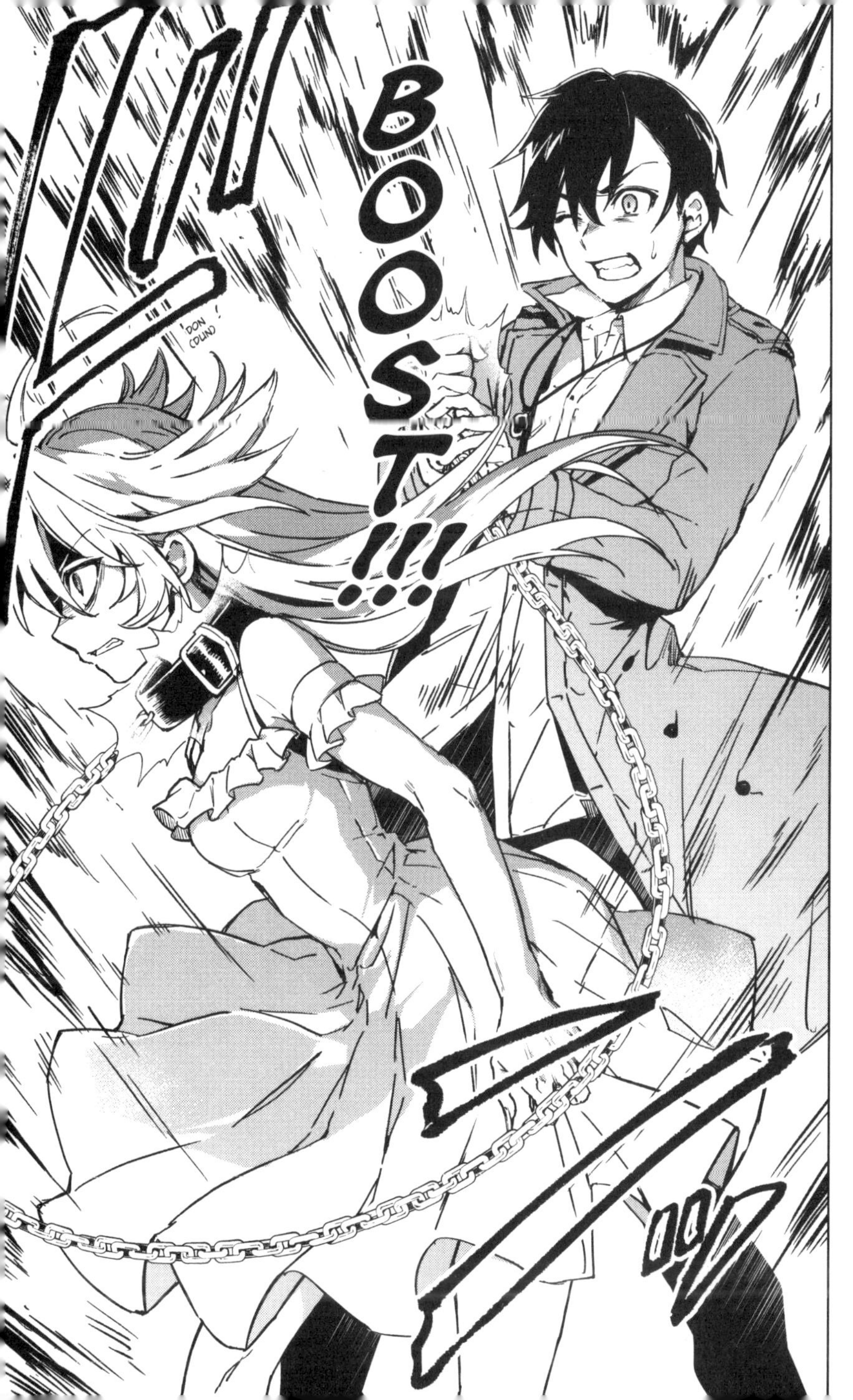
BOOST!!!
DON (DUN)

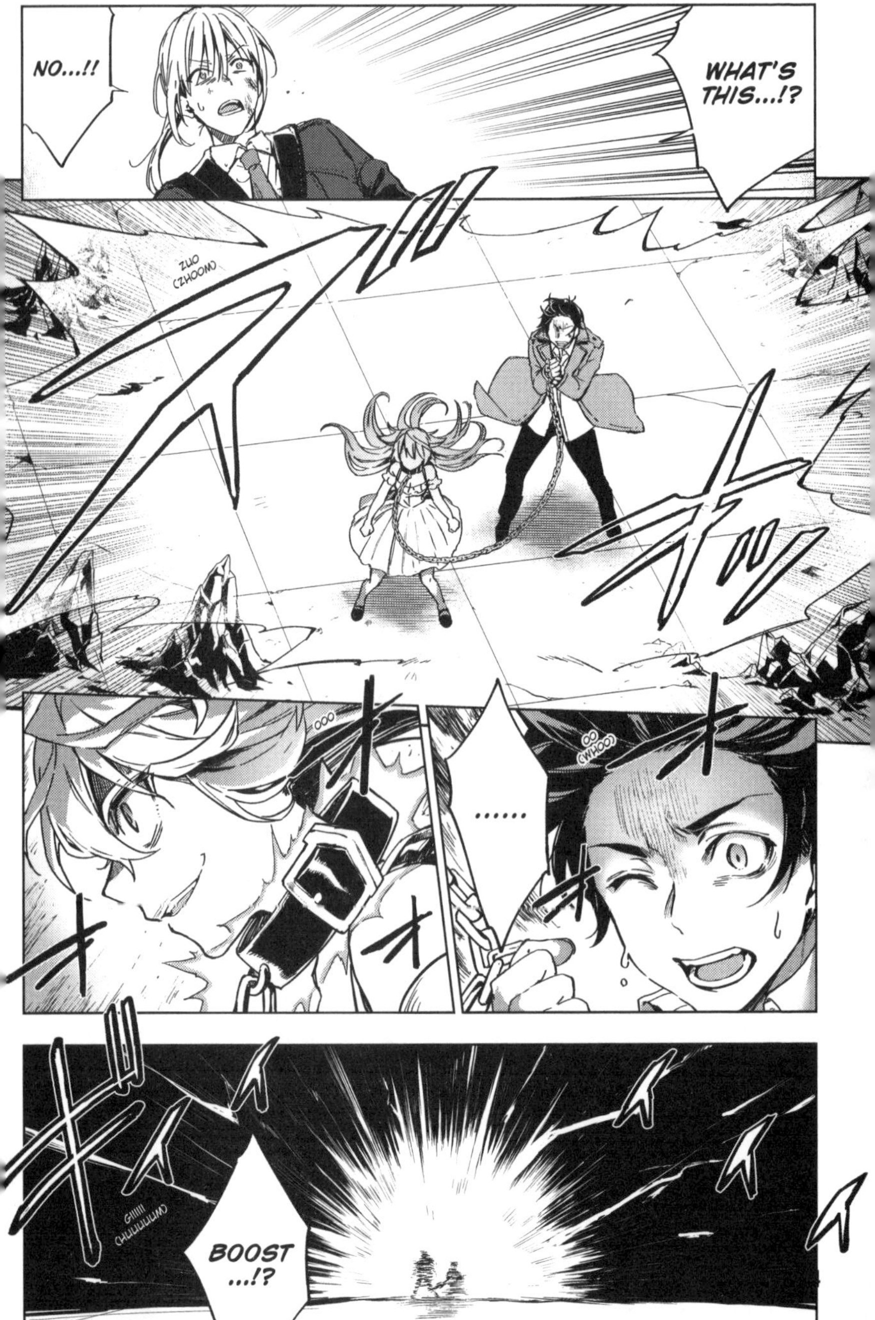
WHAT'S THIS...!?
NO...!!
ZUO (ZHOOM)
OO (WHOO)
......
OOO
GIIIII (WHHHHHM)
BOOST ...!?

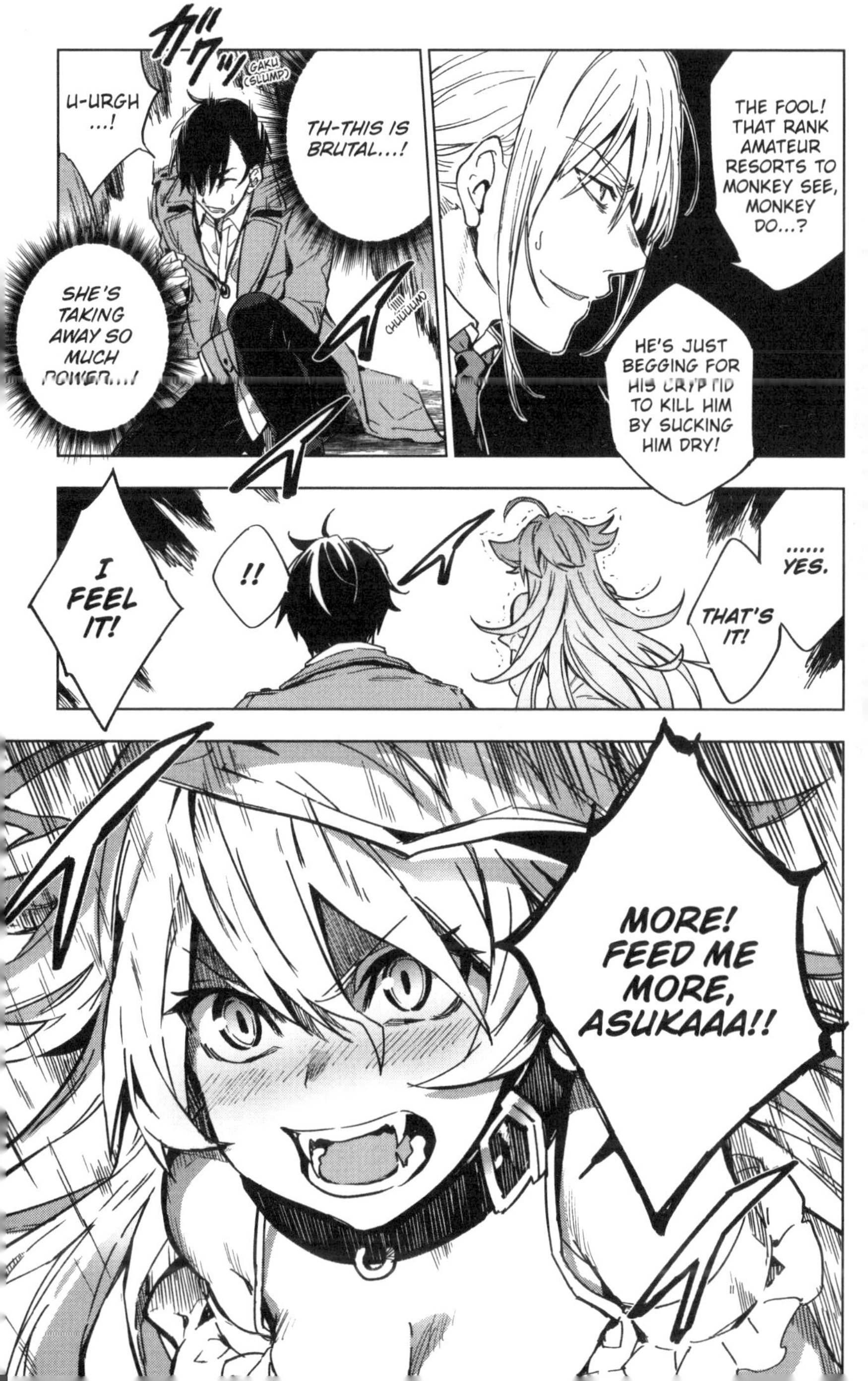
THE FOOL! THAT RANK AMATEUR RESORTS TO MONKEY SEE, MONKEY DO...?
HE'S JUST BEGGING FOR HIS CRYPTID TO KILL HIM BY SUCKING HIM DRY!
GAKU (SLUMP)
TH-THIS IS BRUTAL...!
U-URGH ...!
SHE'S TAKING AWAY SO MUCH POWER...!
......YES.
THAT'S IT!
!!
I FEEL IT!
MORE! FEED ME MORE, ASUKAAA!!

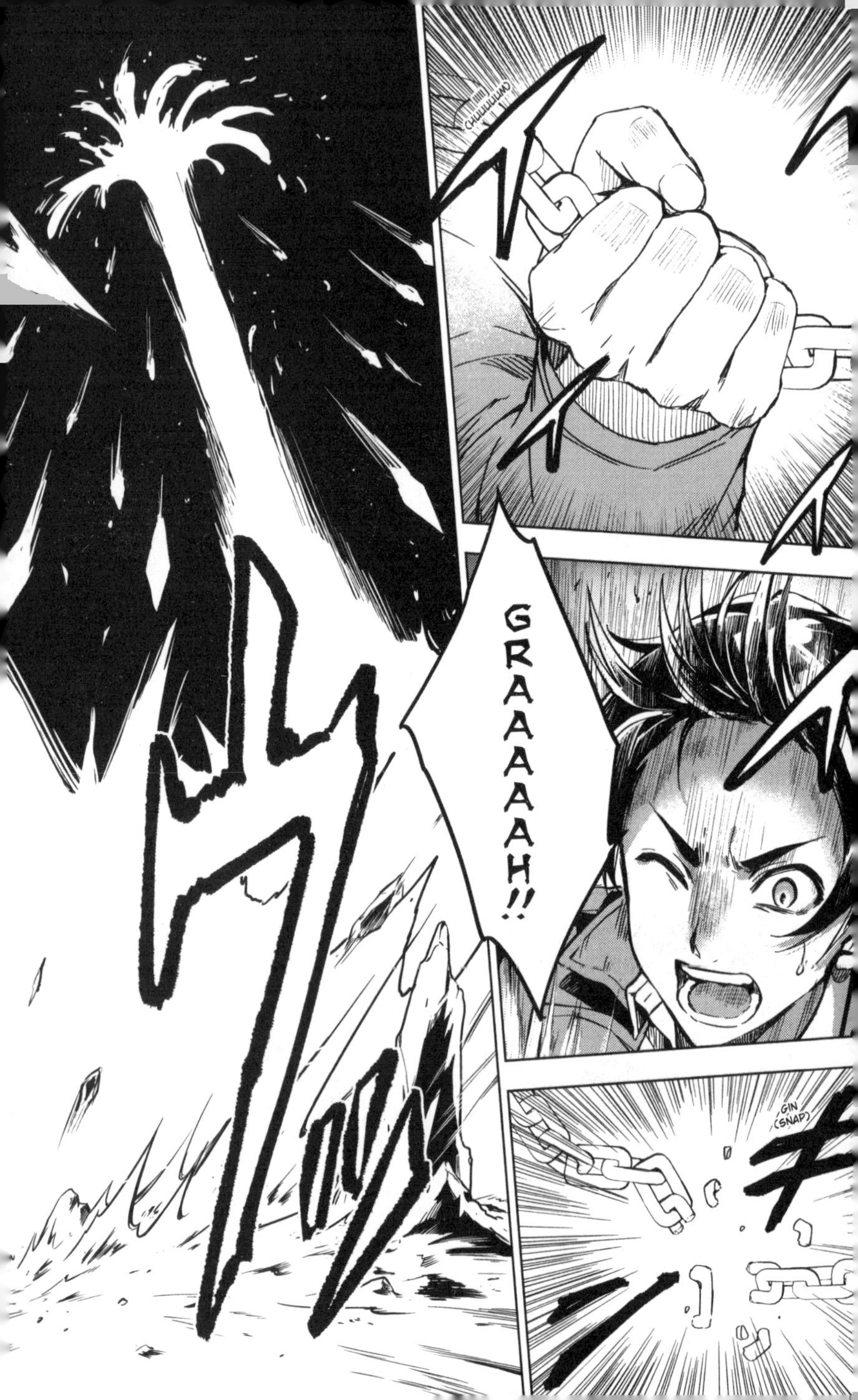
CHUUUUUM
GRAAAAAAH!!
GIN
(SNAP)

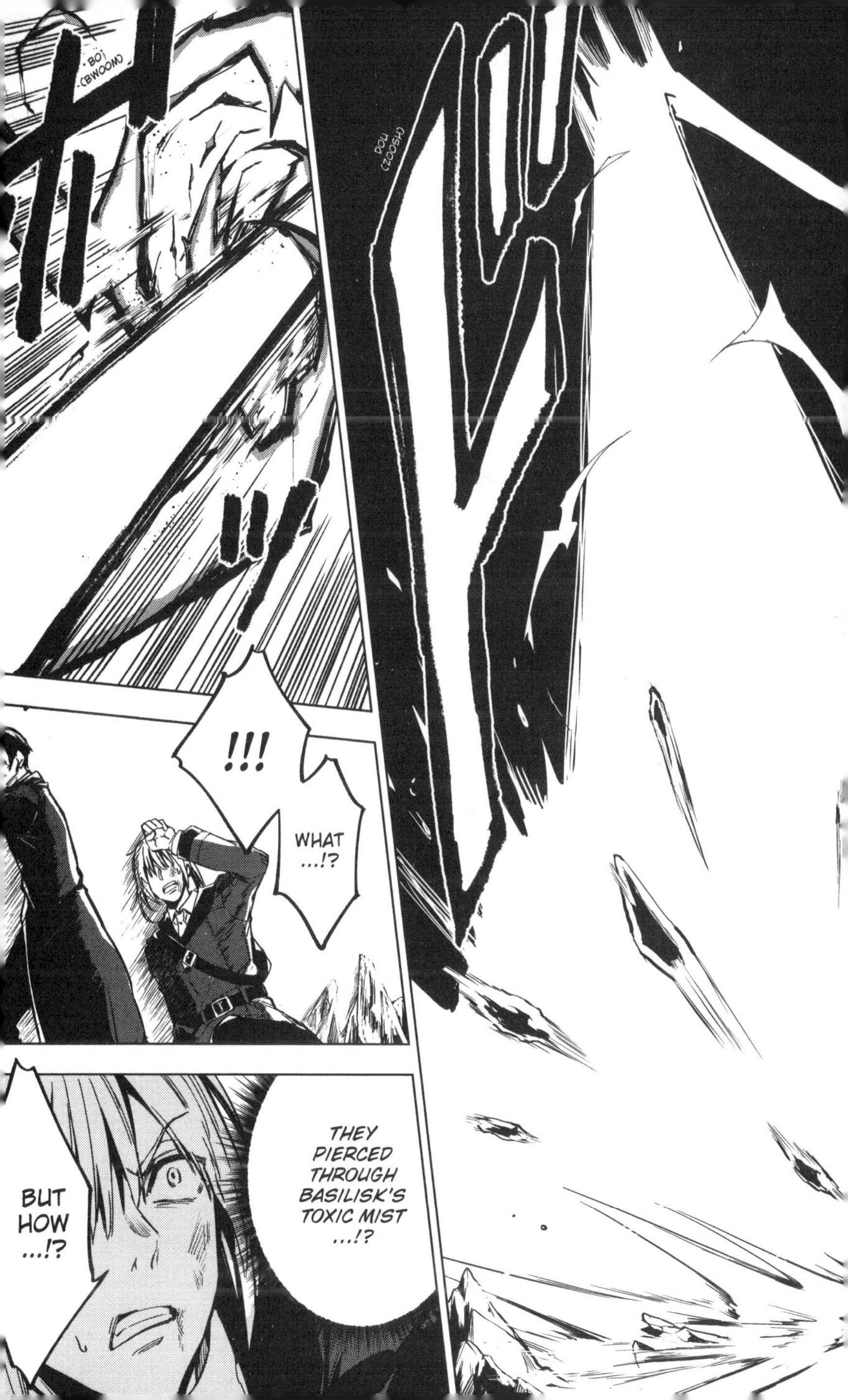
DOU (ZOOSH)
BO! (BWOOM)
!!!
WHAT ...!?
THEY PIERCED THROUGH BASILISK'S TOXIC MIST ...!?
BUT HOW ...!?

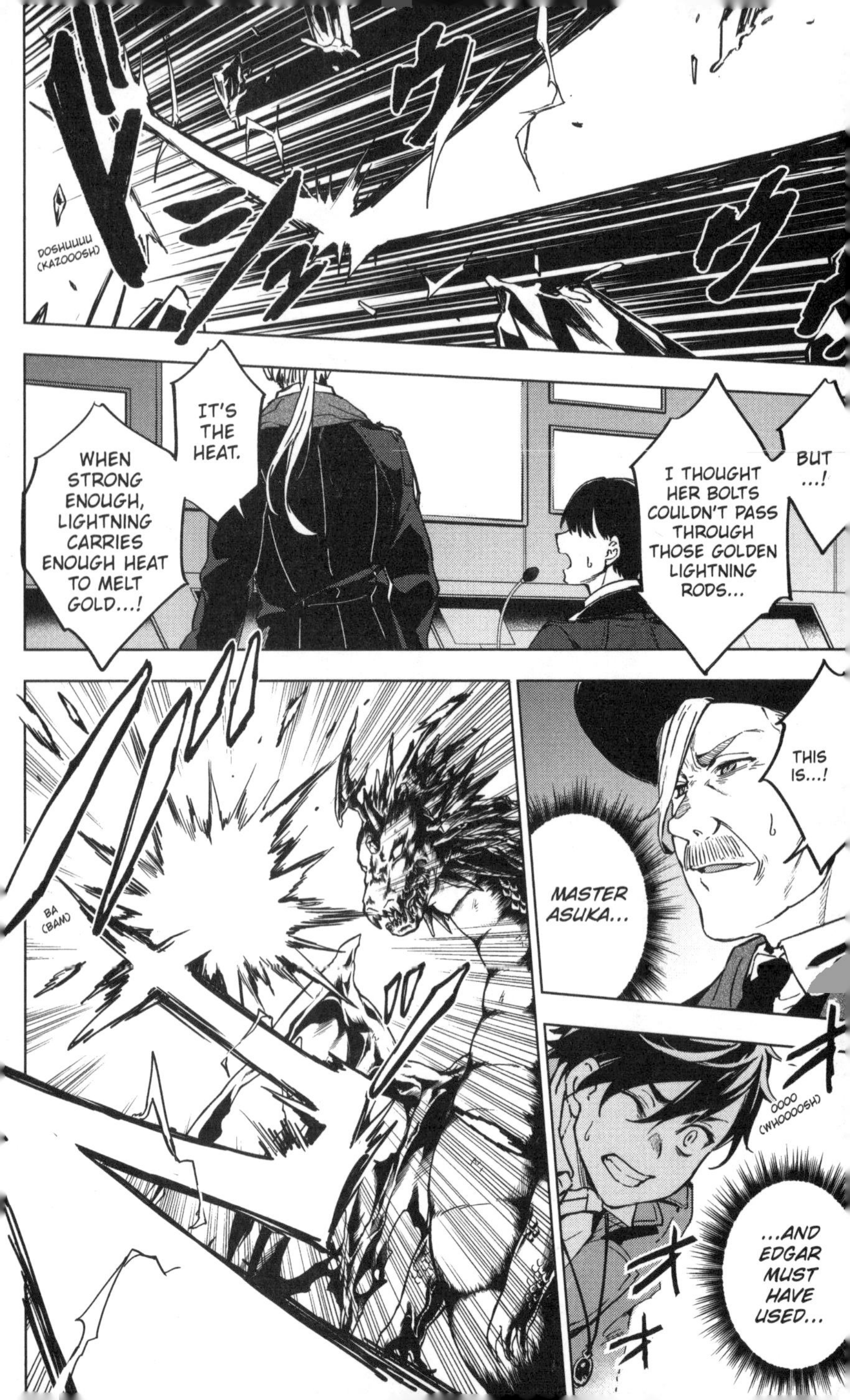
DOSHUUUU (KAZOOOSH)
BUT...!
I THOUGHT HER BOLTS COULDN'T PASS THROUGH THOSE GOLDEN LIGHTNING RODS...
IT'S THE HEAT.
WHEN STRONG ENOUGH, LIGHTNING CARRIES ENOUGH HEAT TO MELT GOLD...!
THIS IS...!
MASTER ASUKA...
OOOO (WHOOOOSH)
...AND EDGAR MUST HAVE USED...
BA (BAM)

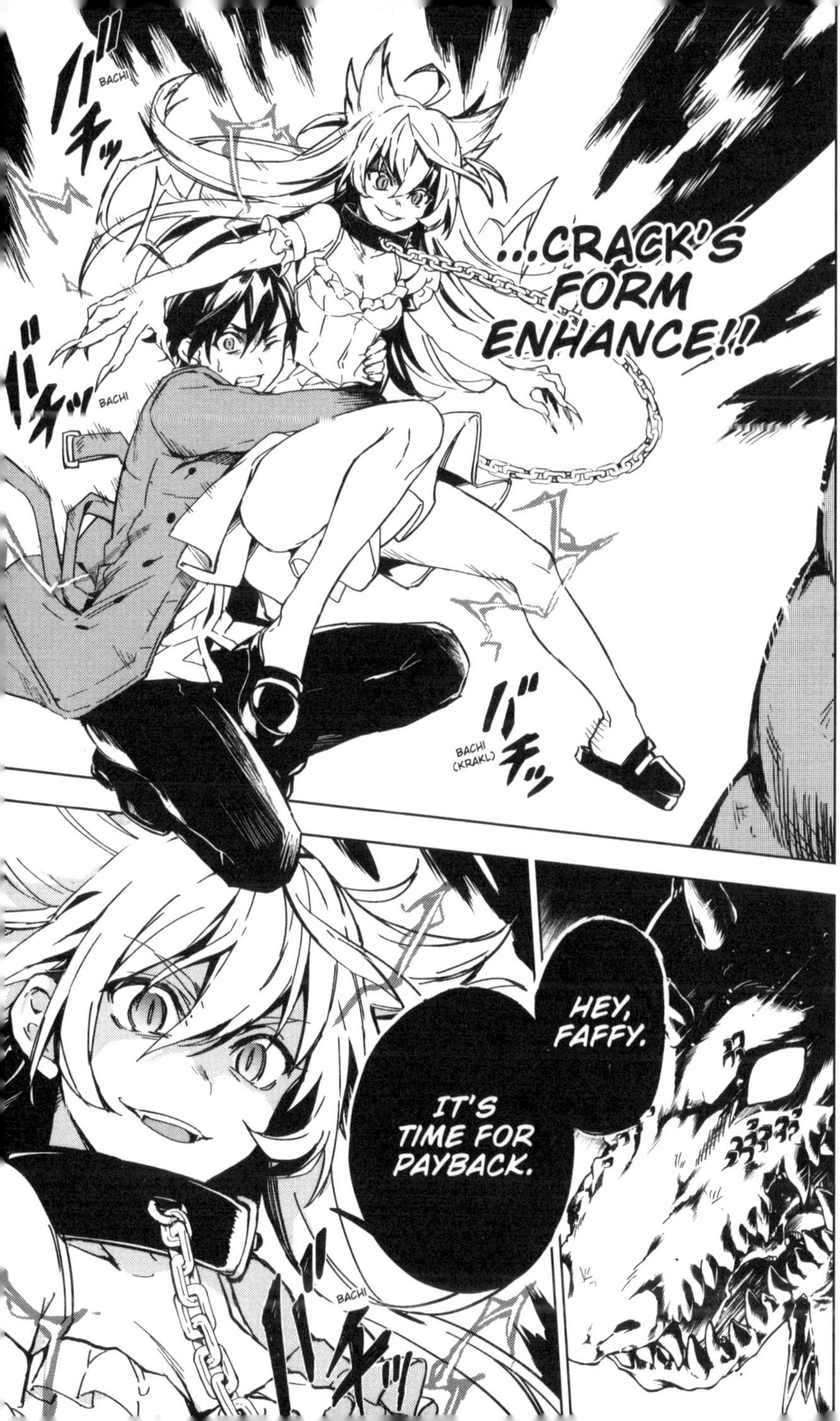
...CRACK'S FORM ENHANCE!!
バチッ
BACHI
バチッ
BACHI
バチッ
BACHI (KRAKL)
HEY, FAFFY.
IT'S TIME FOR PAYBACK.
バチッ
BACHI

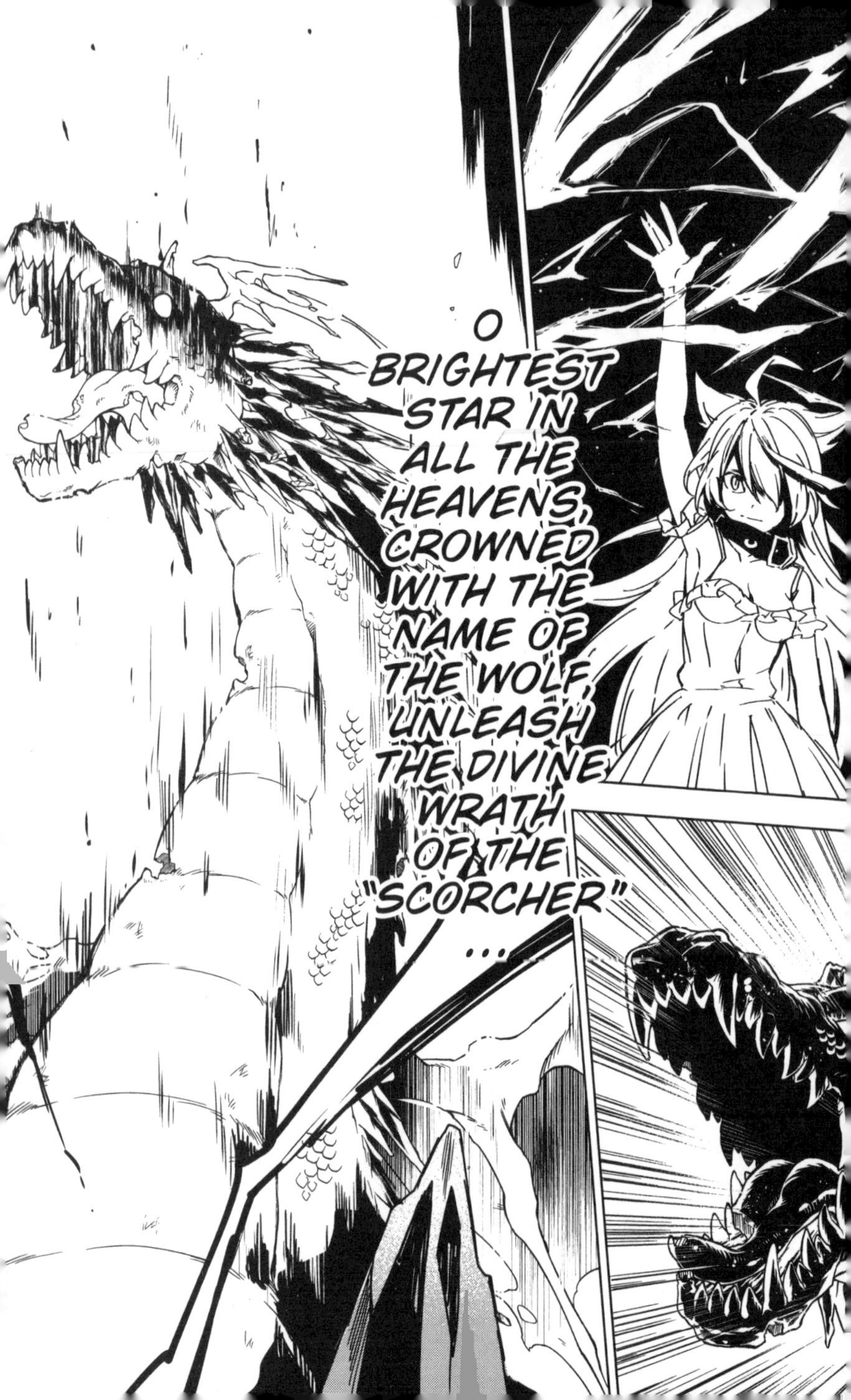
O BRIGHTEST STAR IN ALL THE HEAVENS, CROWNED WITH THE NAME OF THE WOLF, UNLEASH THE DIVINE WRATH OF THE "SCORCHER"...

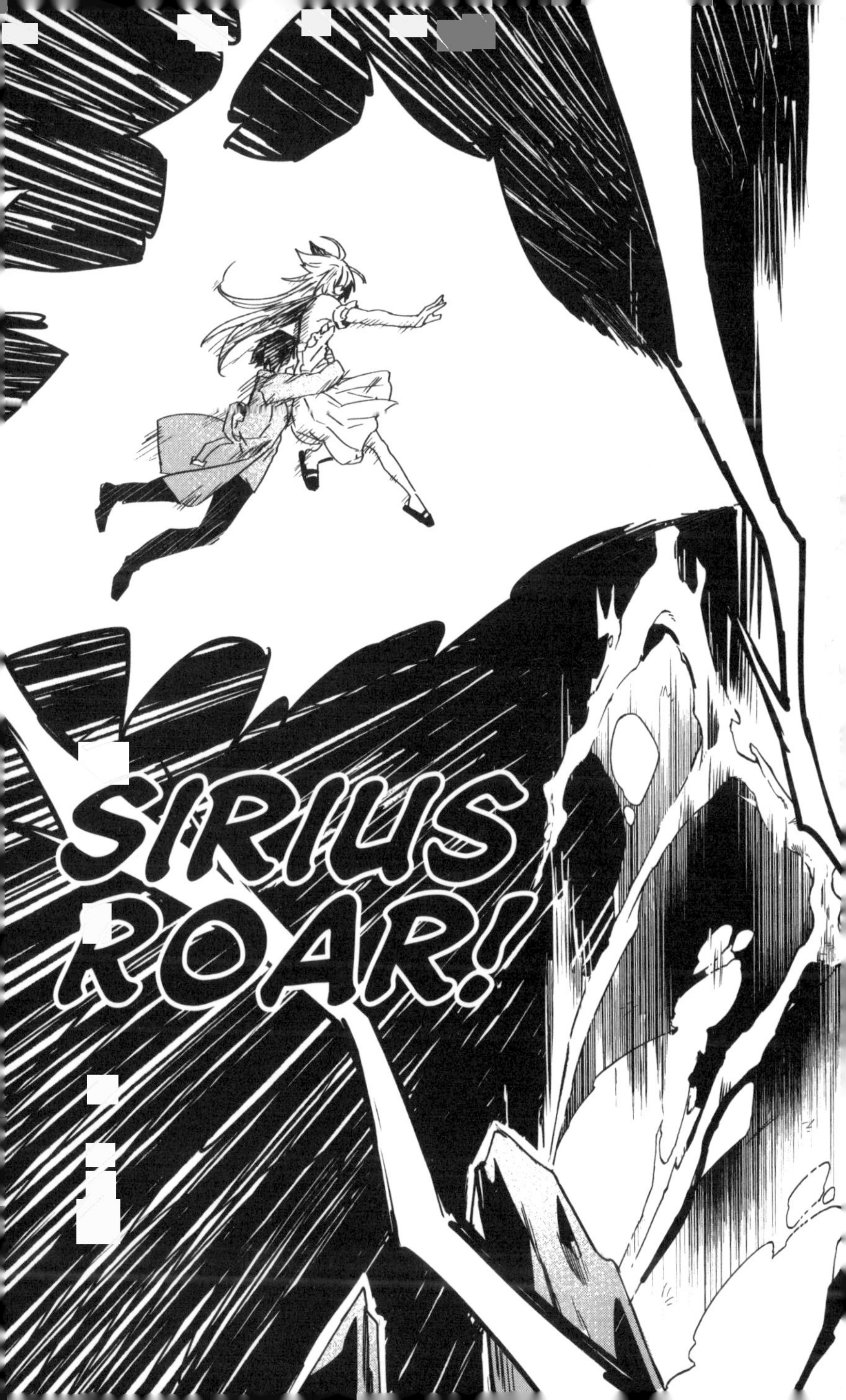
SIRIUS ROAR!

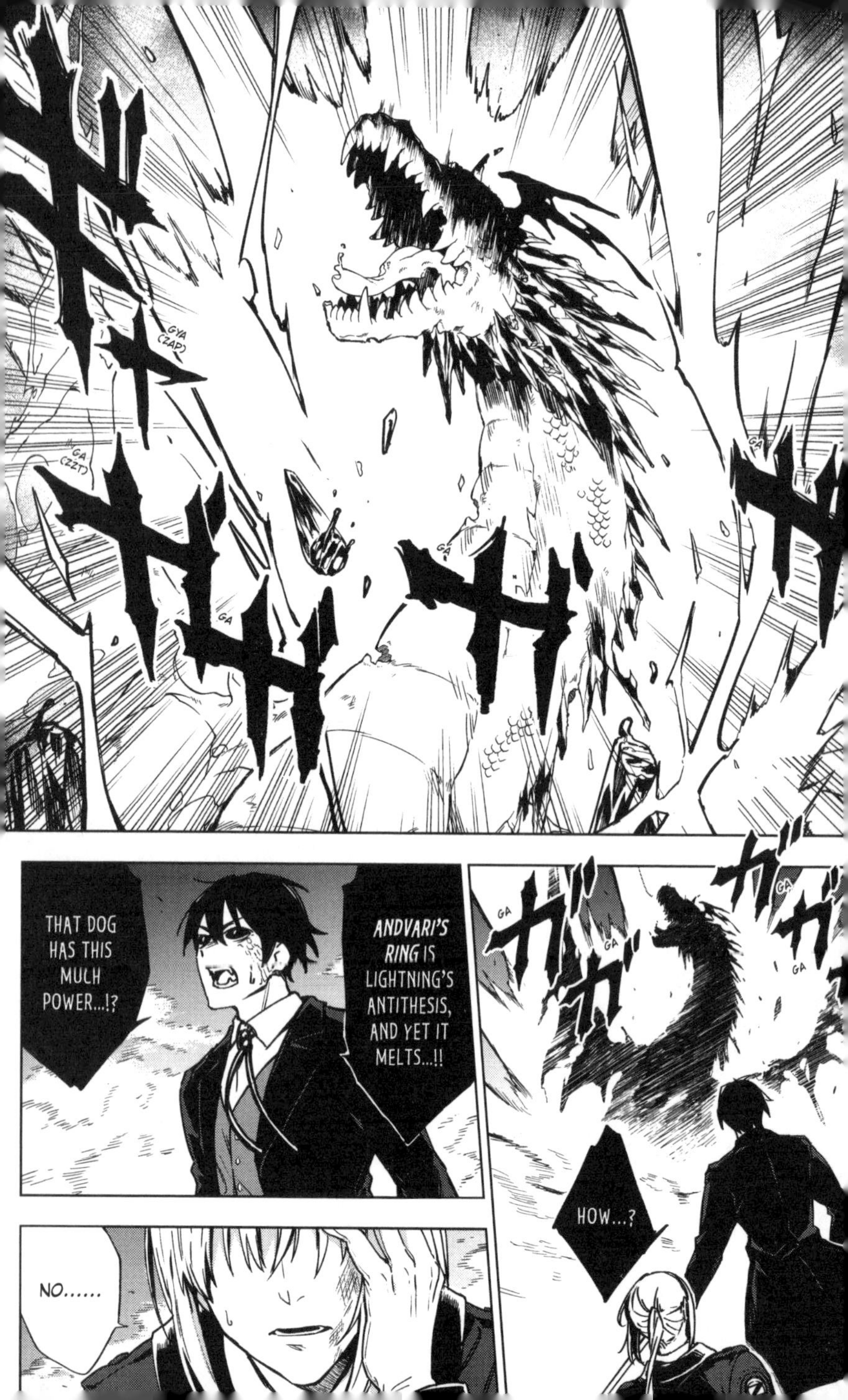
GA
GYA (ZAP)
GA
GA (ZZZT)
GA
GA
GA
GA
GA
GA
HOW...?
ANDVARI'S RING IS LIGHTNING'S ANTITHESIS, AND YET IT MELTS...!!
THAT DOG HAS THIS MUCH POWER...!?
NO......

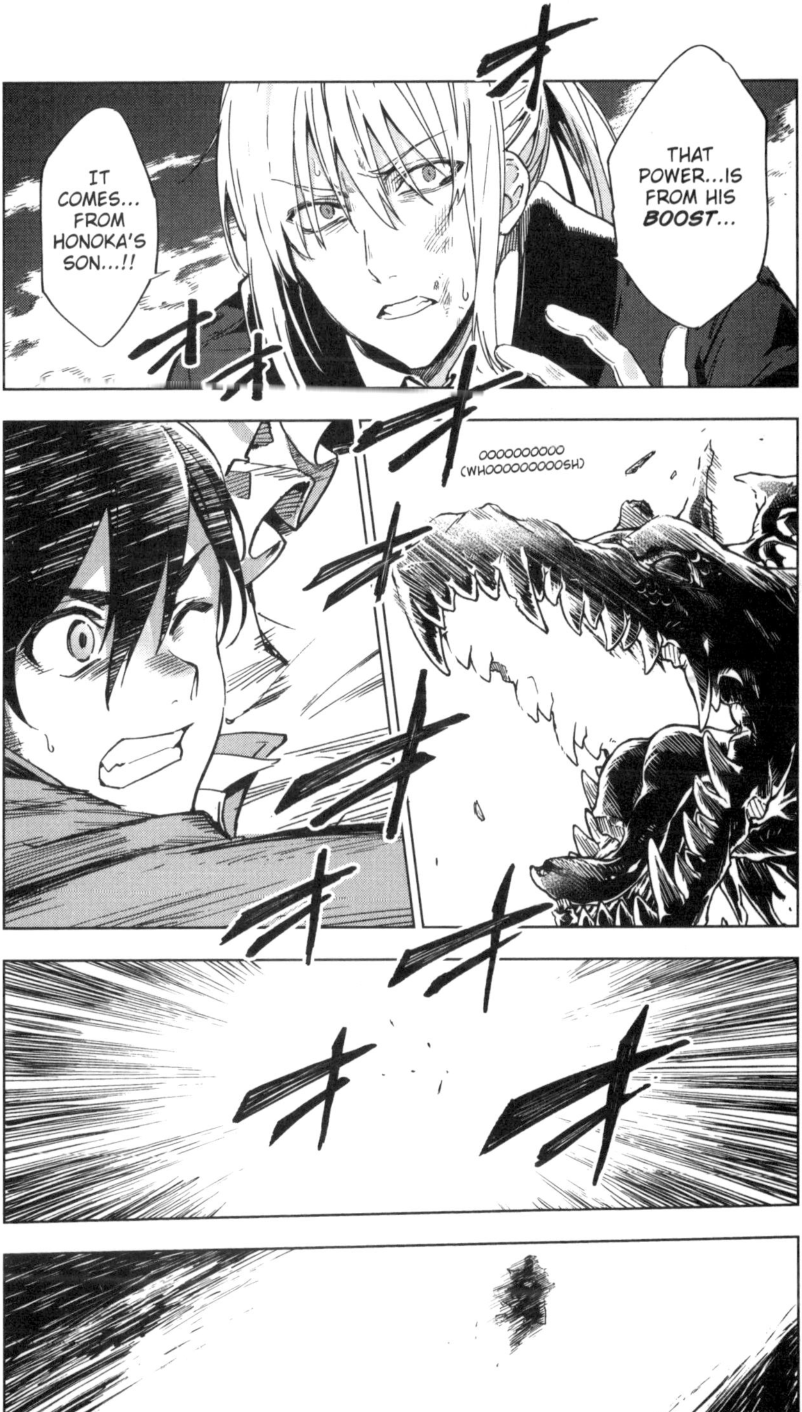
THAT POWER...IS FROM HIS *BOOST*...
IT COMES... FROM HONOKA'S SON...!!
OOOOOOOOOO
(WHOOOOOOOOOOSH)

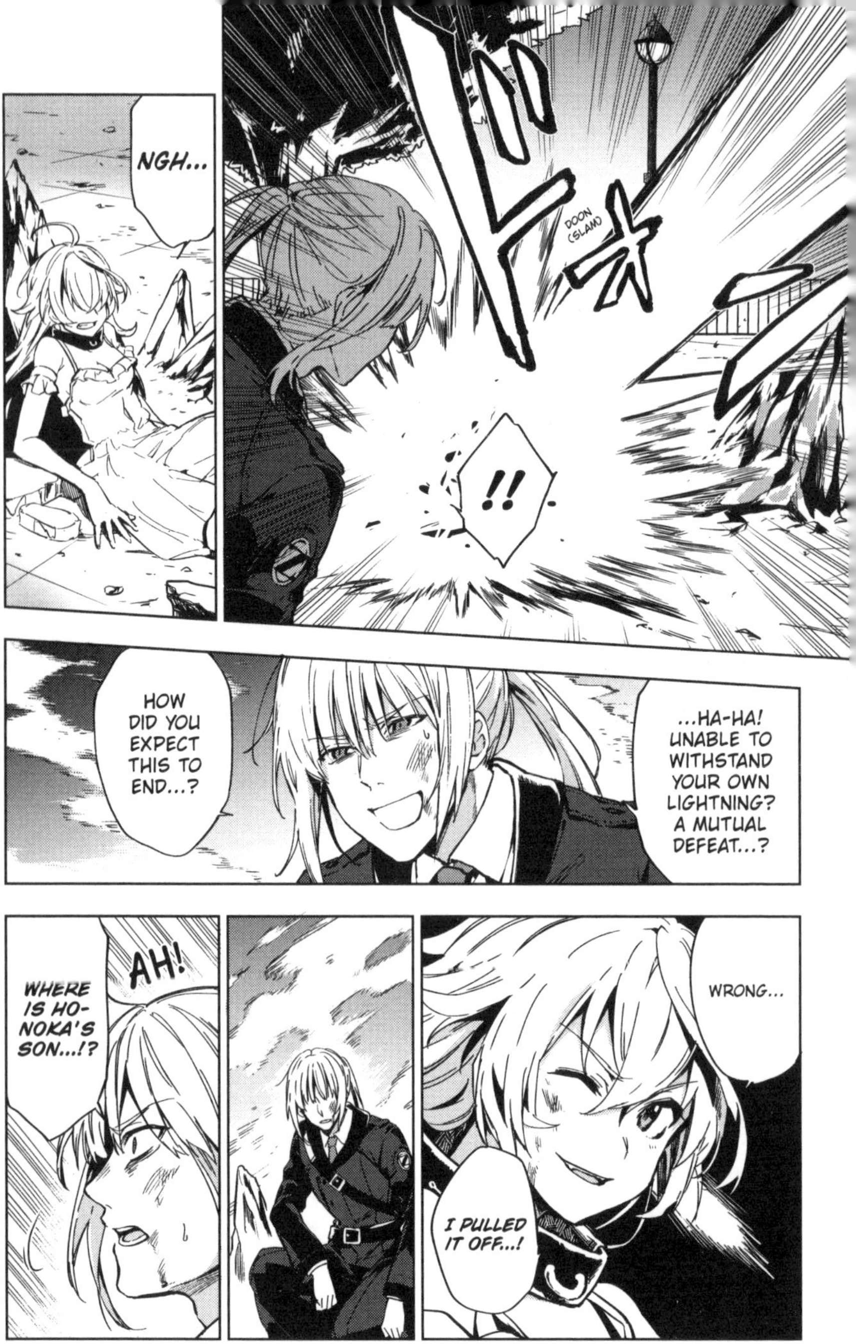
DOON (SLAM)
!!
NGH...
...HA-HA! UNABLE TO WITHSTAND YOUR OWN LIGHTNING? A MUTUAL DEFEAT...?
HOW DID YOU EXPECT THIS TO END...?
WRONG...
I PULLED IT OFF...!
AH!
WHERE IS HO-NOKA'S SON...!?

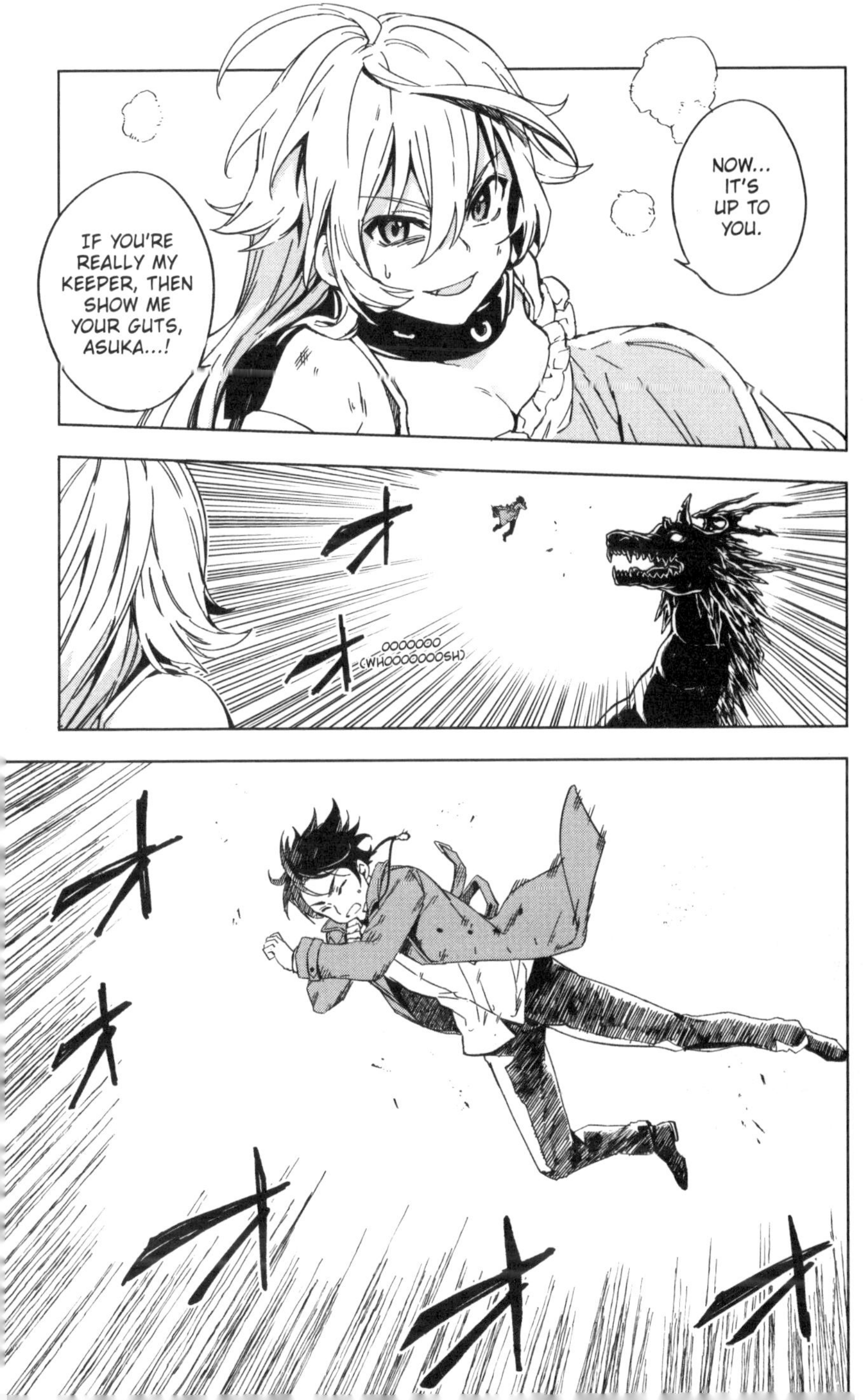
NOW... IT'S UP TO YOU.
IF YOU'RE REALLY MY KEEPER, THEN SHOW ME YOUR GUTS, ASUKA...!
OOOOOOO (WHOOOOOOOSH)

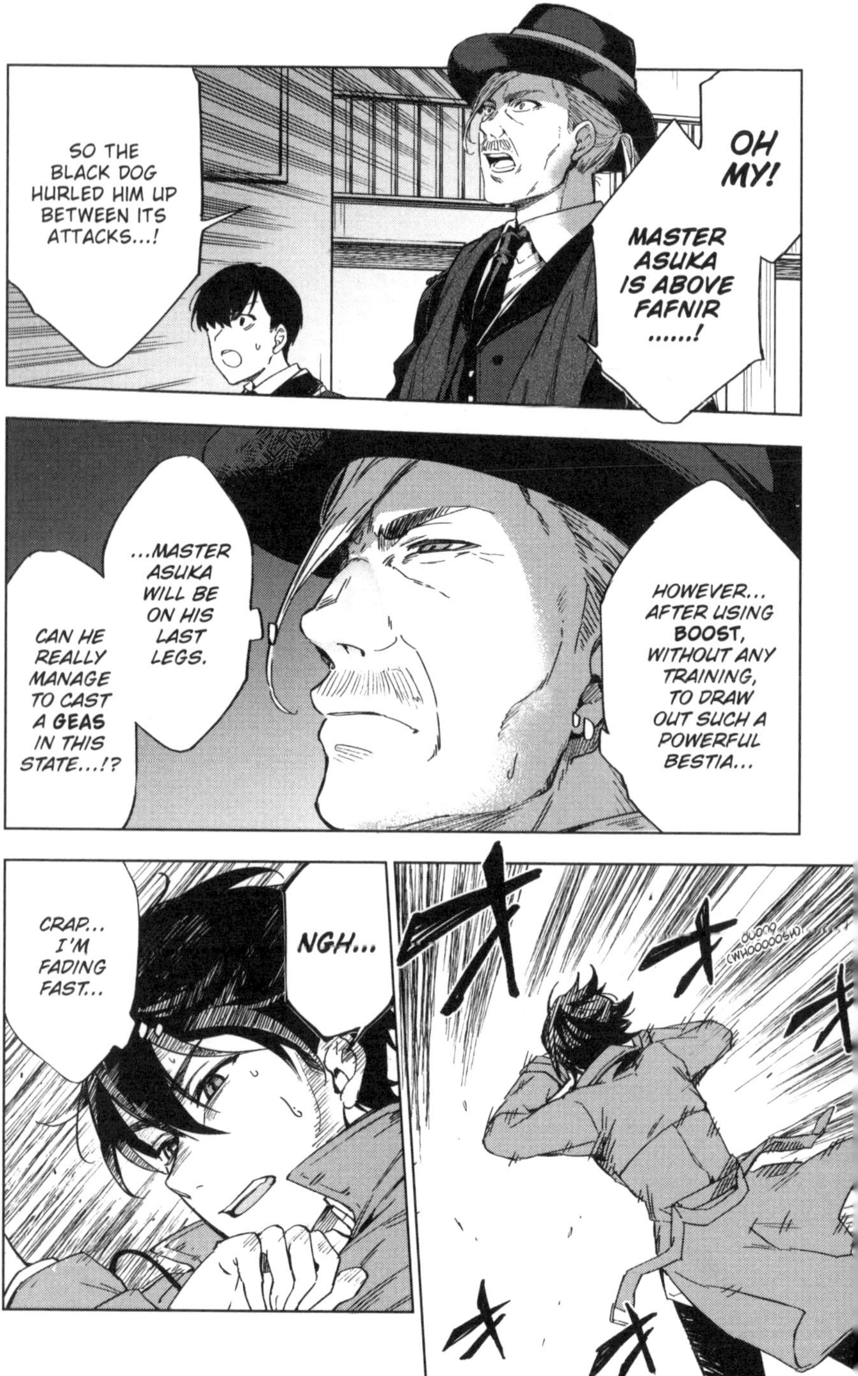
OH MY!
MASTER ASUKA IS ABOVE FAFNIR......!
SO THE BLACK DOG HURLED HIM UP BETWEEN ITS ATTACKS...!
HOWEVER... AFTER USING BOOST, WITHOUT ANY TRAINING, TO DRAW OUT SUCH A POWERFUL BESTIA...
...MASTER ASUKA WILL BE ON HIS LAST LEGS.
CAN HE REALLY MANAGE TO CAST A GEAS IN THIS STATE...!?
(WHOOOOOSH)
NGH...
CRAP... I'M FADING FAST...

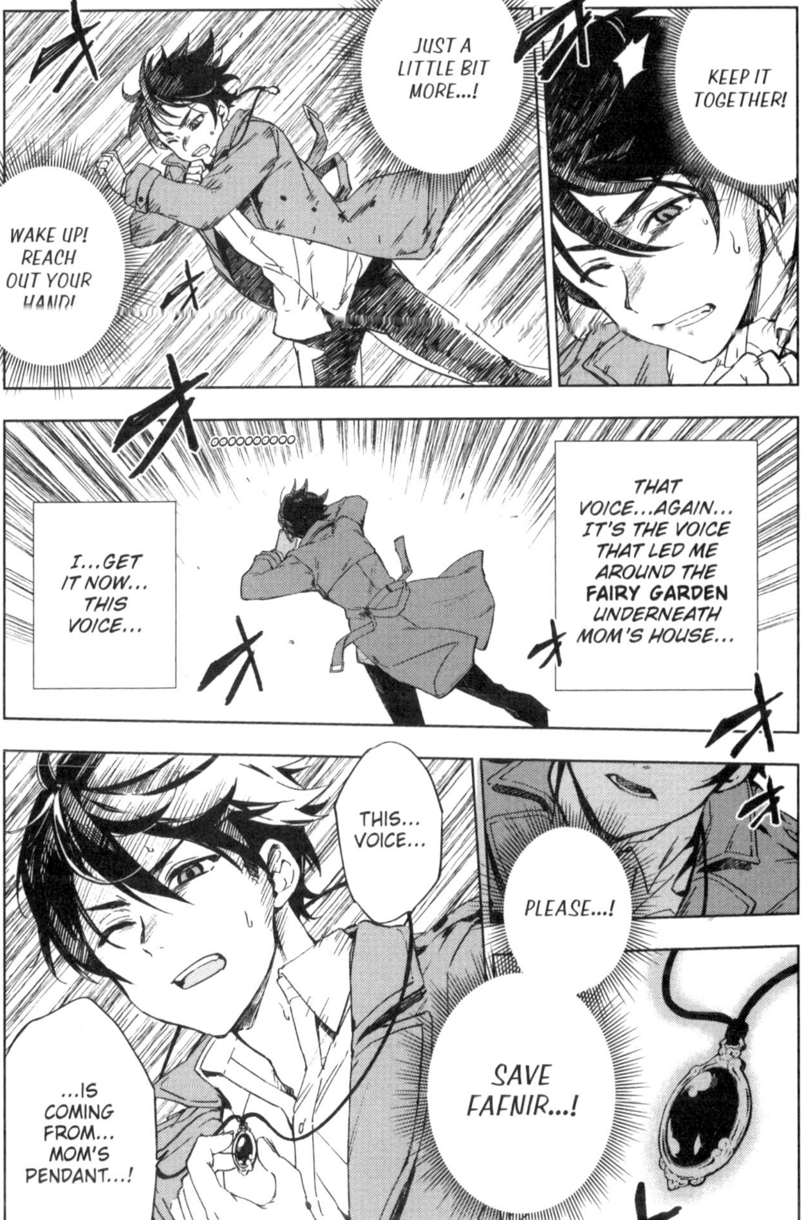
KEEP IT TOGETHER!
JUST A LITTLE BIT MORE...!
WAKE UP! REACH OUT YOUR HAND!
THAT VOICE...AGAIN... IT'S THE VOICE THAT LED ME AROUND THE **FAIRY GARDEN** UNDERNEATH MOM'S HOUSE...
OOOOOOOOOO
I...GET IT NOW... THIS VOICE...
PLEASE...!
SAVE FAFNIR...!
THIS... VOICE...
...IS COMING FROM... MOM'S PENDANT...!

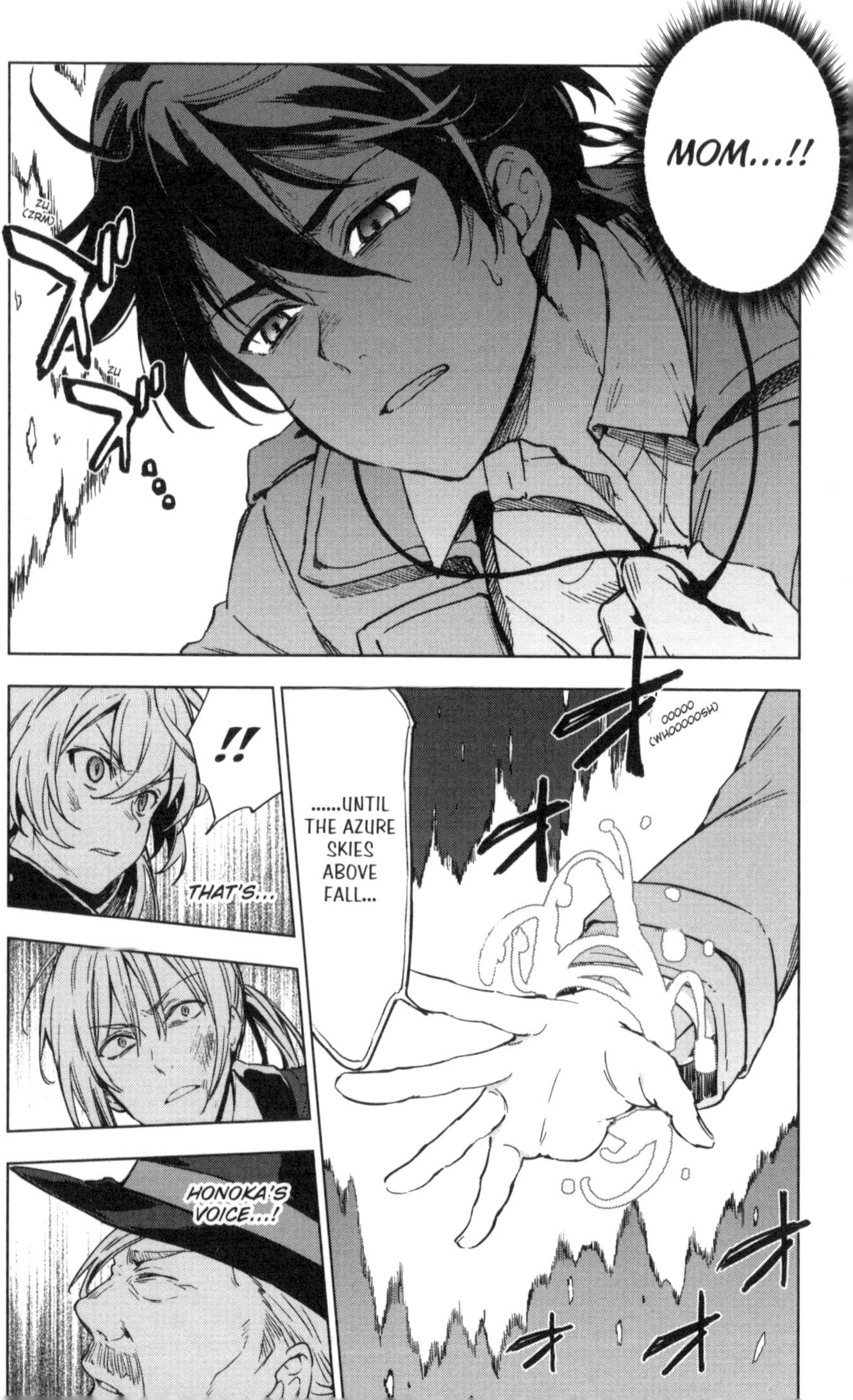
MOM...!!
ZU (ZRM)
ZU
OOOOO (WHOOOOOSH)
......UNTIL THE AZURE SKIES ABOVE FALL...
!!
THAT'S...
HONOKA'S VOICE...!

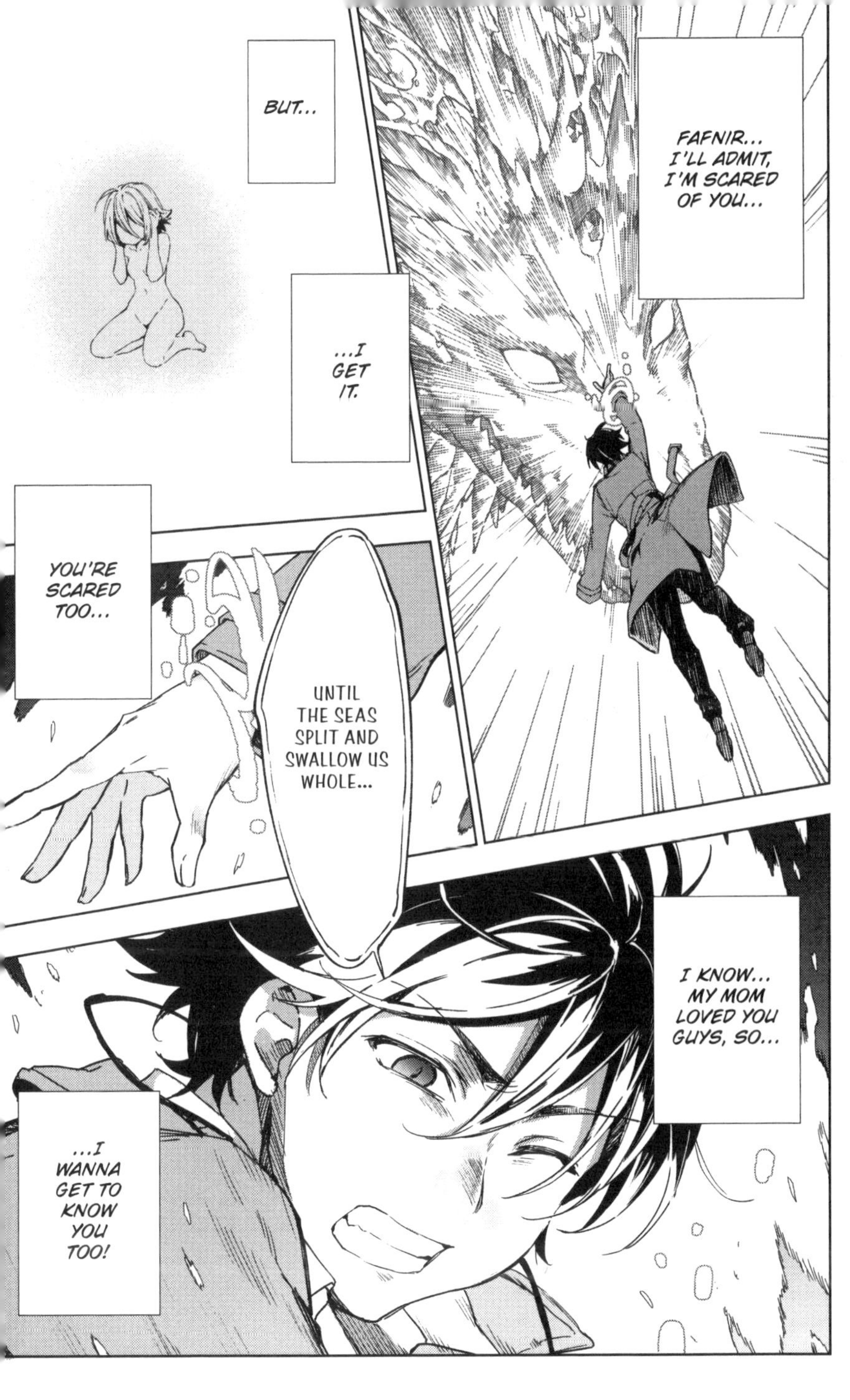
FAFNIR... I'LL ADMIT, I'M SCARED OF YOU...
BUT...
...I GET IT.
YOU'RE SCARED TOO...
UNTIL THE SEAS SPLIT AND SWALLOW US WHOLE...
I KNOW... MY MOM LOVED YOU GUYS, SO...
...I WANNA GET TO KNOW YOU TOO!

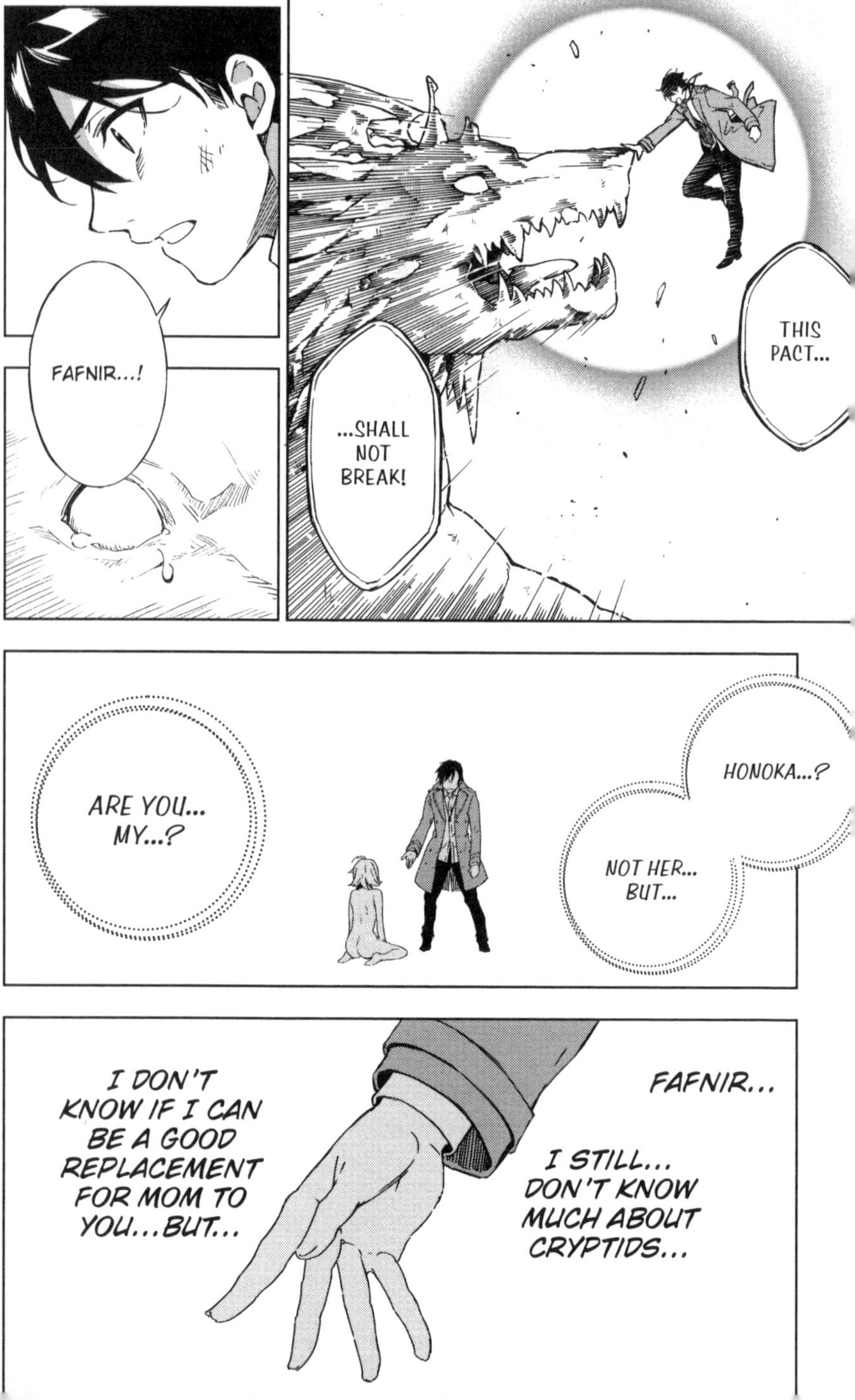
THIS PACT...
...SHALL NOT BREAK!
FAFNIR...!
HONOKA...?
NOT HER... BUT...
ARE YOU... MY...?
FAFNIR...
I STILL... DON'T KNOW MUCH ABOUT CRYPTIDS...
I DON'T KNOW IF I CAN BE A GOOD REPLACEMENT FOR MOM TO YOU...BUT...

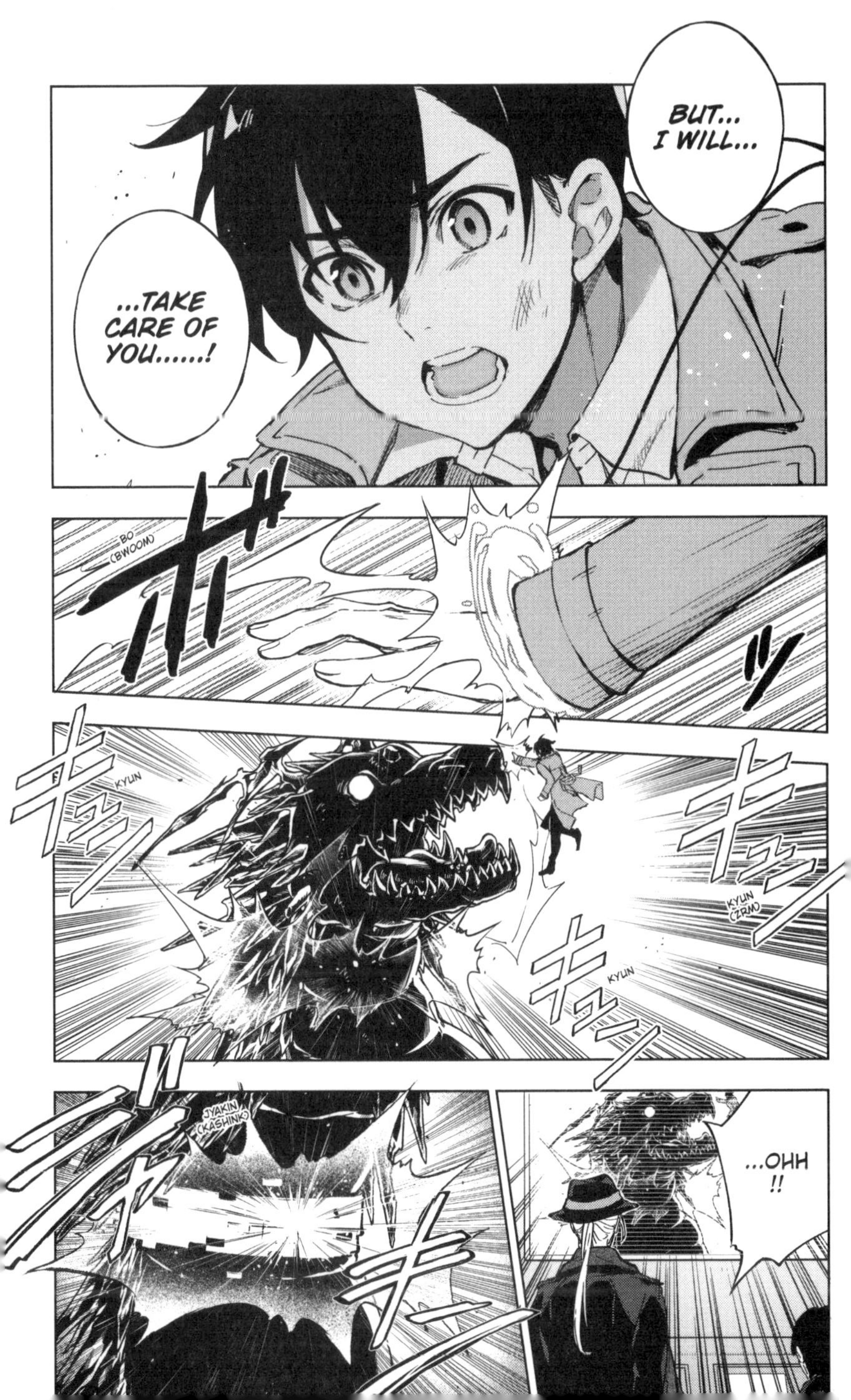
BUT... I WILL...
...TAKE CARE OF YOU......!
BO (BWOOM)
KYUN (ZRM)
KYUN
KYUN
...OHH !!
JYAKIN (KASHINK)

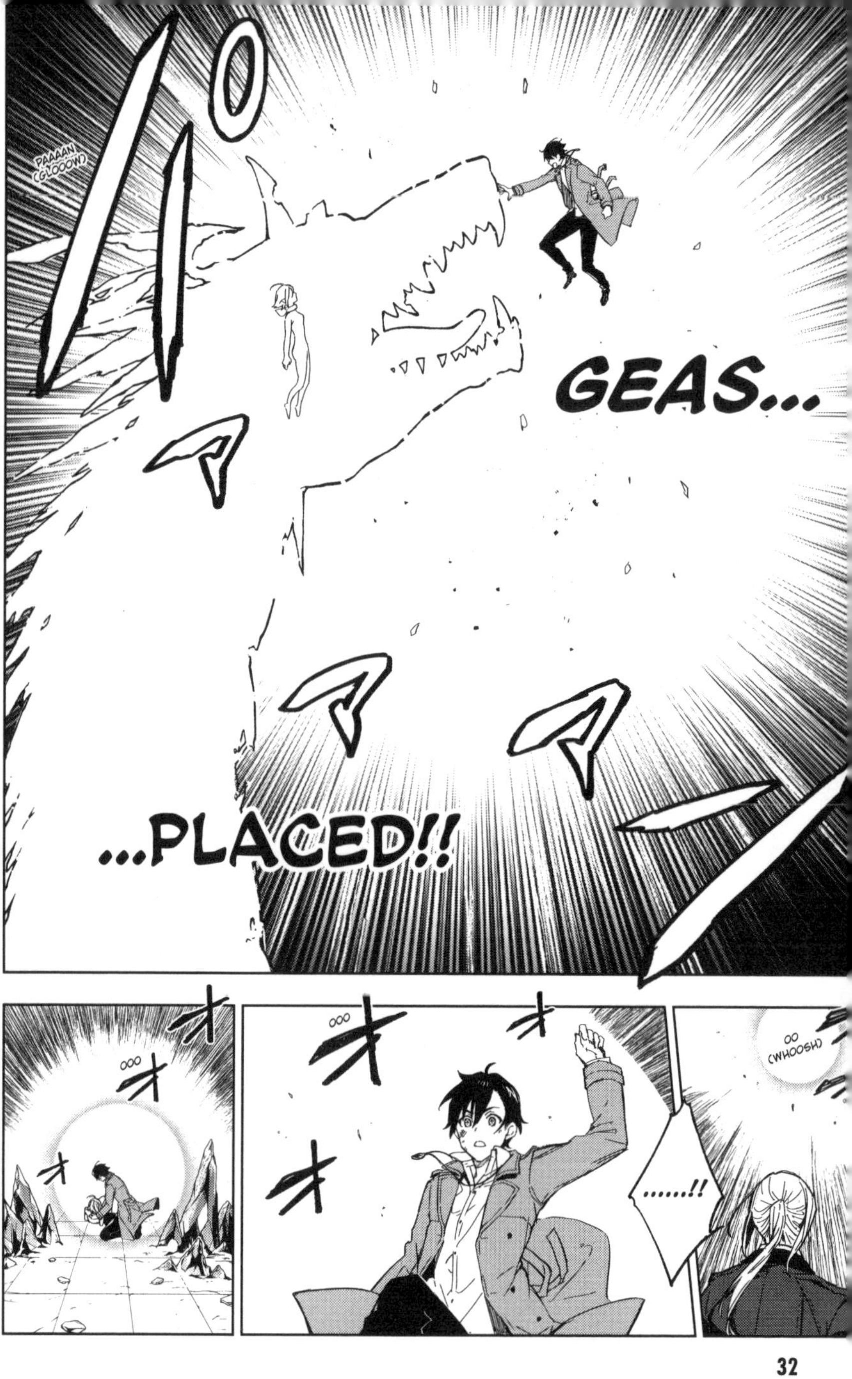
PAAAAN (GLOOOW)
GEAS...
...PLACED!!
OO (WHOOSH)
......!!
OOO
OOO

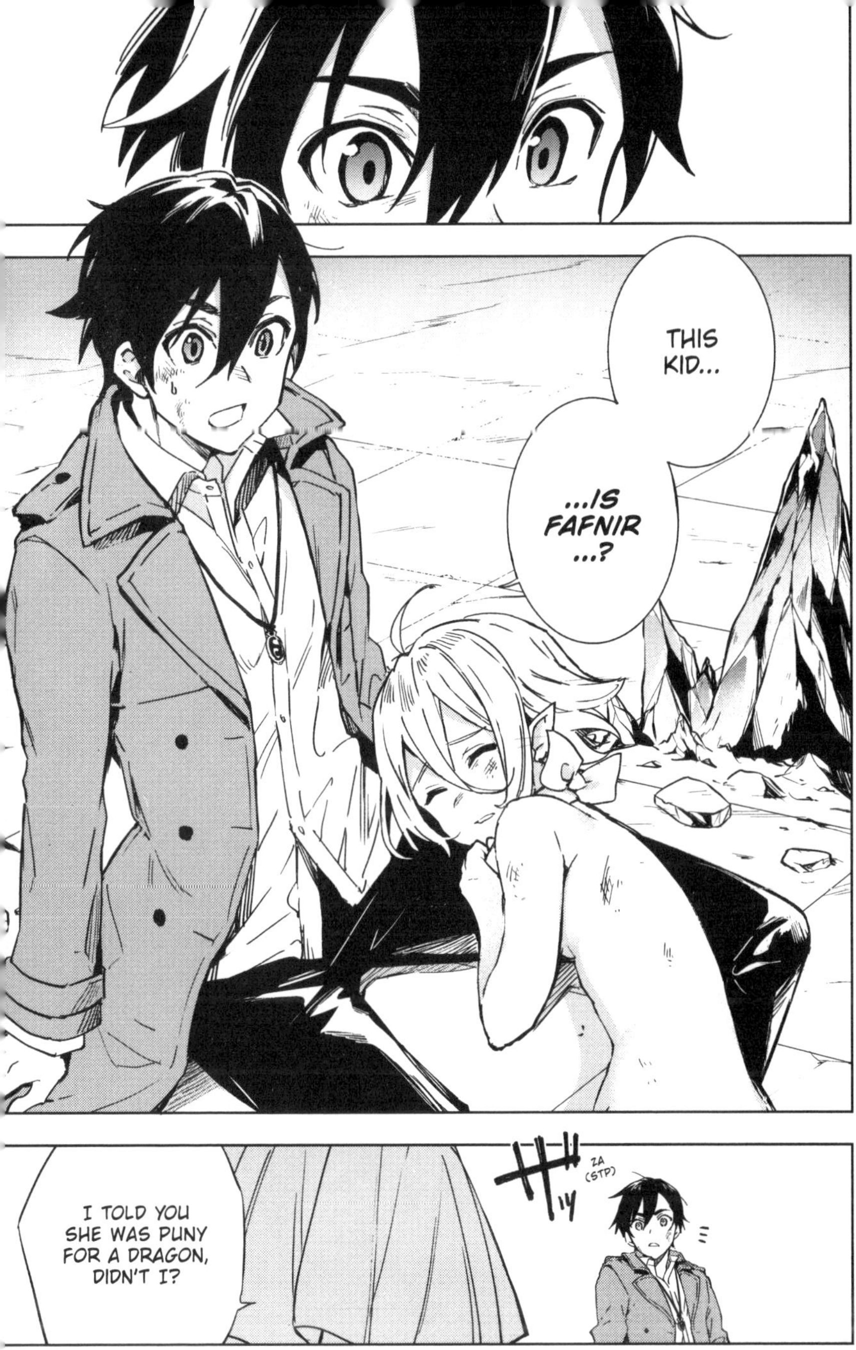
THIS KID...
...IS FAFNIR ...?
ZA (STP)
I TOLD YOU SHE WAS PUNY FOR A DRAGON, DIDN'T I?

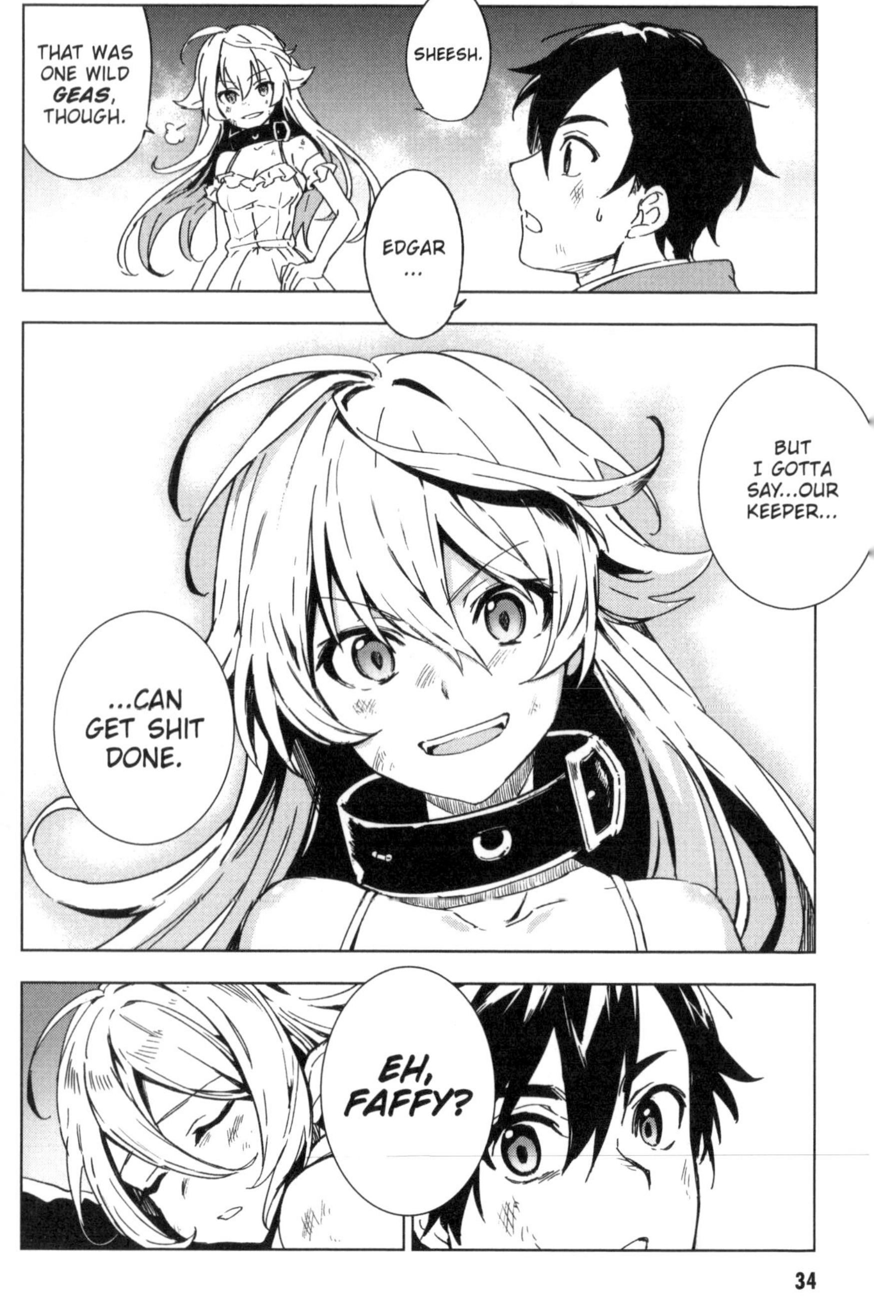
SHEESH.
EDGAR...
THAT WAS ONE WILD **GEAS**, THOUGH.
BUT I GOTTA SAY...OUR KEEPER...
...CAN GET SHIT DONE.
EH, FAFFY?

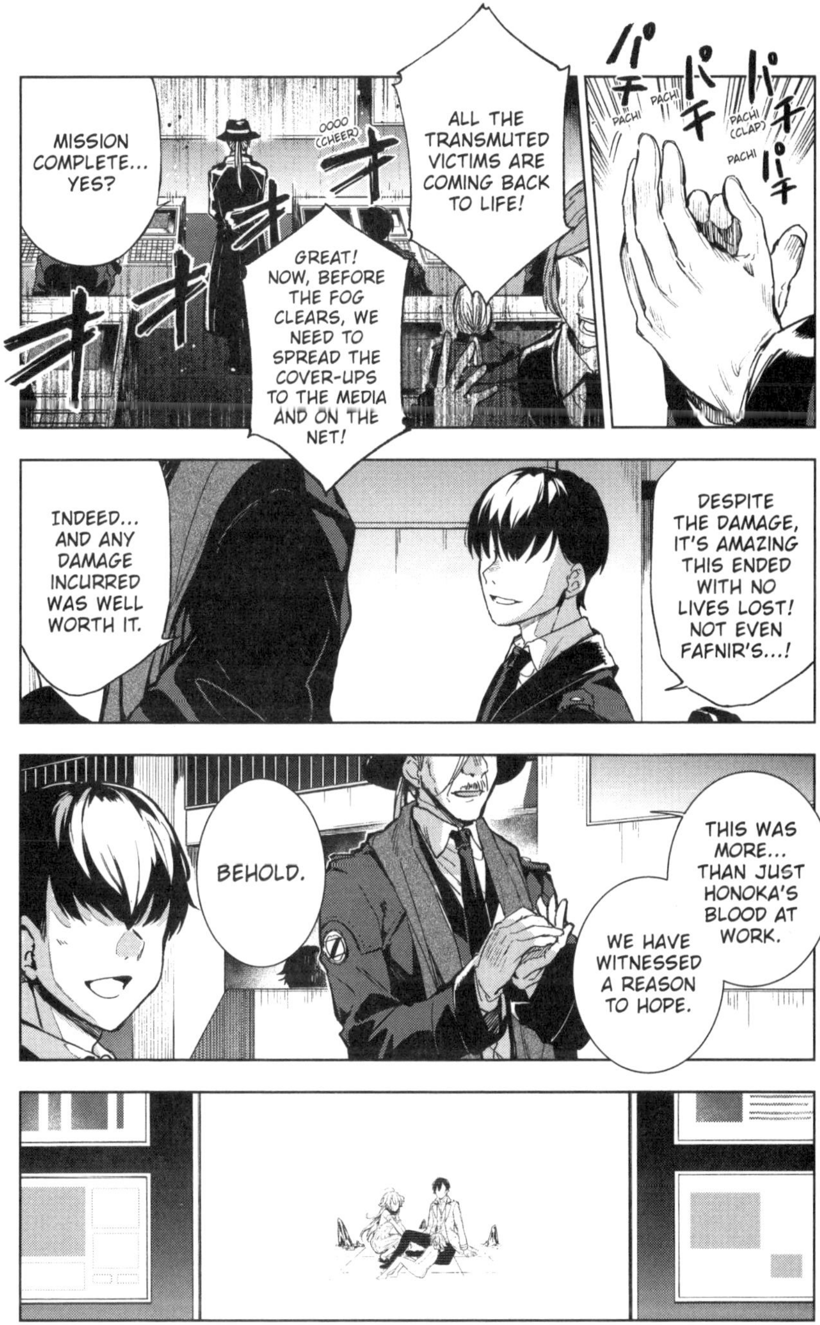
パチ
PACHI
パチ
PACHI
パチ
PACHI (CLAP)
パチ
PACHI
ALL THE TRANSMUTED VICTIMS ARE COMING BACK TO LIFE!
オオオオ
OOOO (CHEER)
MISSION COMPLETE... YES?
GREAT! NOW, BEFORE THE FOG CLEARS, WE NEED TO SPREAD THE COVER-UPS TO THE MEDIA AND ON THE NET!
DESPITE THE DAMAGE, IT'S AMAZING THIS ENDED WITH NO LIVES LOST! NOT EVEN FAFNIR'S...!
INDEED... AND ANY DAMAGE INCURRED WAS WELL WORTH IT.
THIS WAS MORE... THAN JUST HONOKA'S BLOOD AT WORK.
WE HAVE WITNESSED A REASON TO HOPE.
BEHOLD.

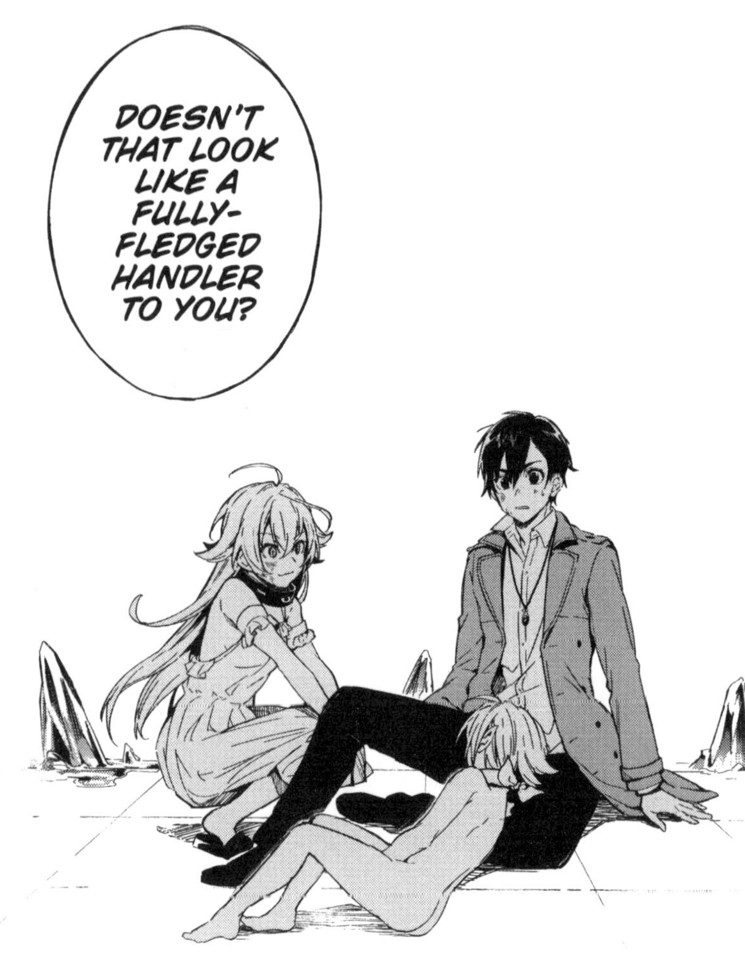
DOESN'T THAT LOOK LIKE A FULLY-FLEDGED HANDLER TO YOU?

Episode V

END

BESTIA

MAKOTO SANDA MIYAKOKASIWA ACO ARISAKA

BESTIA

MAKOTO SANDA MIYAKOKASIWA ACO ARISAKA

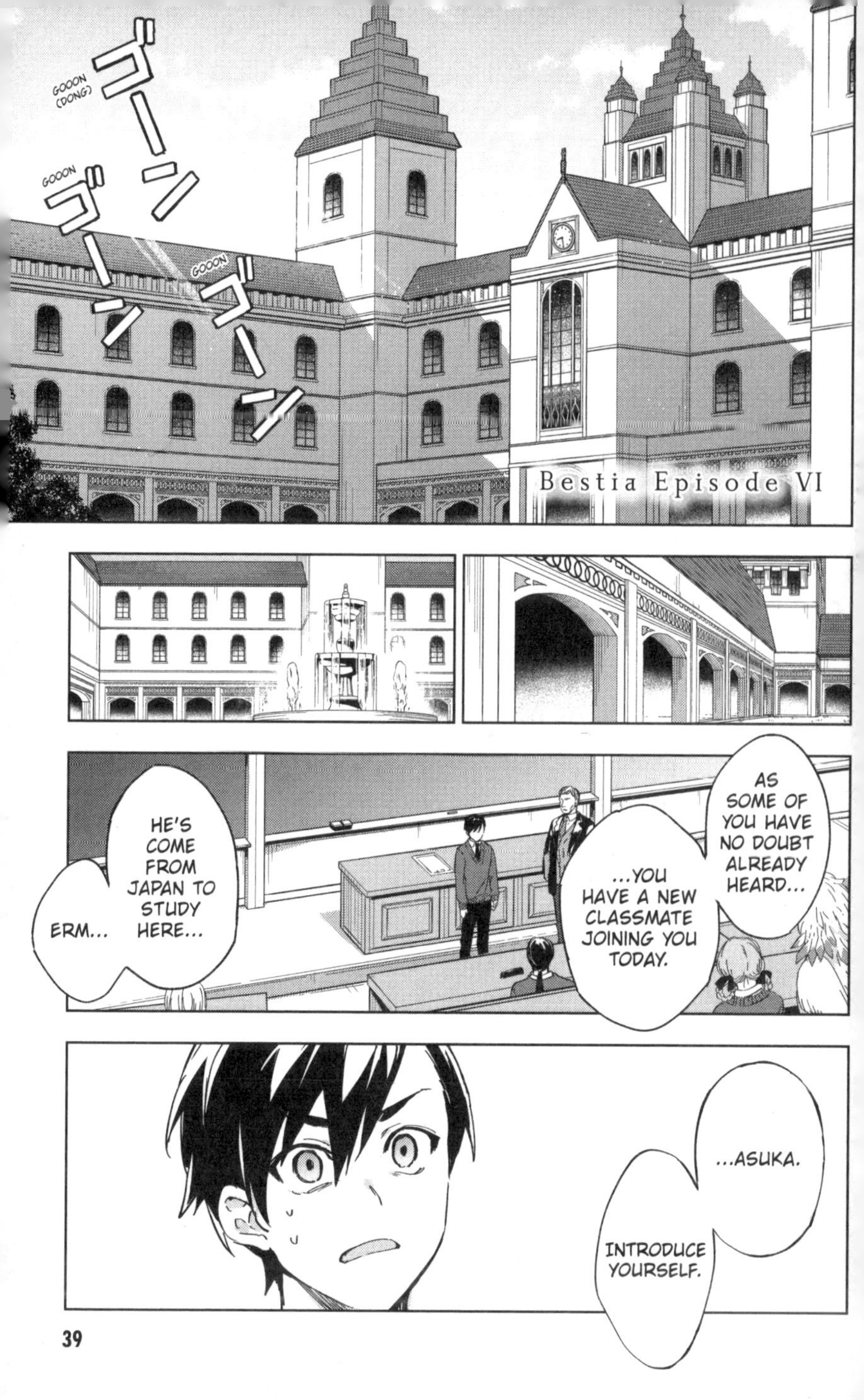
GOOON (DONG)
GOOON
GOOON
Bestia Episode VI
AS SOME OF YOU HAVE NO DOUBT ALREADY HEARD...
...YOU HAVE A NEW CLASSMATE JOINING YOU TODAY.
HE'S COME FROM JAPAN TO STUDY HERE...
ERM...
...ASUKA.
INTRODUCE YOURSELF.

A short break at school.

Episode VI

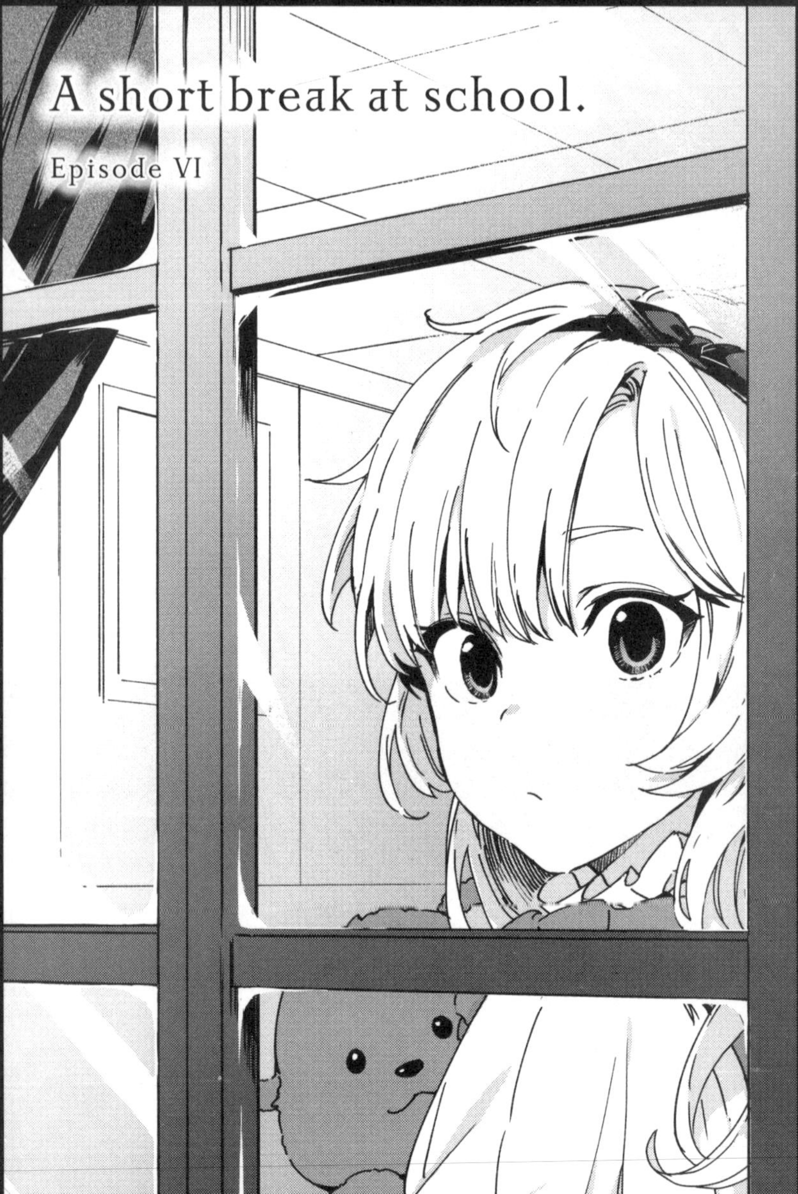

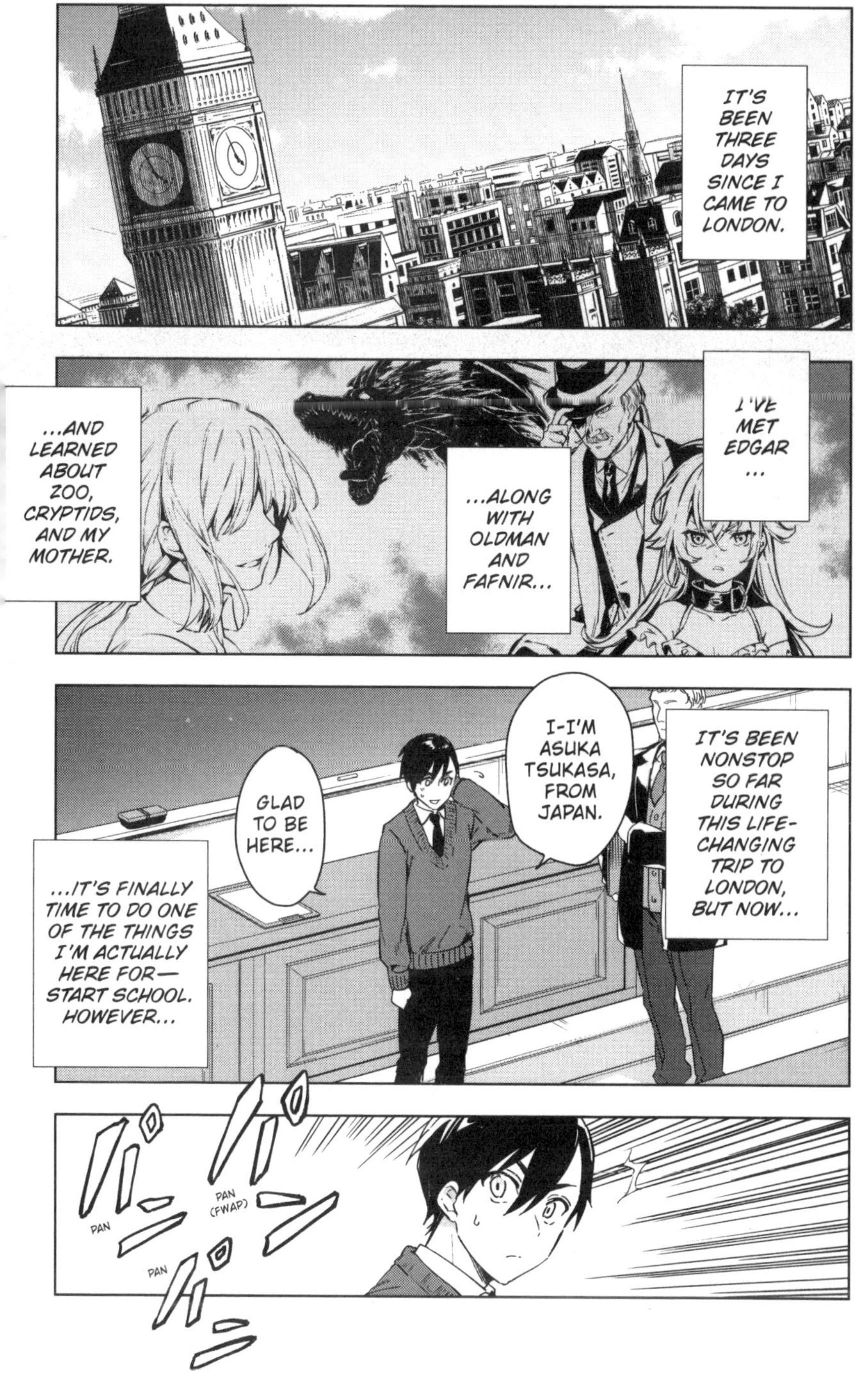
IT'S BEEN THREE DAYS SINCE I CAME TO LONDON.
I'VE MET EDGAR...
...ALONG WITH OLDMAN AND FAFNIR...
...AND LEARNED ABOUT ZOO, CRYPTIDS, AND MY MOTHER.
IT'S BEEN NONSTOP SO FAR DURING THIS LIFE-CHANGING TRIP TO LONDON, BUT NOW...
I-I'M ASUKA TSUKASA, FROM JAPAN.
GLAD TO BE HERE...
...IT'S FINALLY TIME TO DO ONE OF THE THINGS I'M ACTUALLY HERE FOR—START SCHOOL. HOWEVER...
PAN (FWAP)
PAN
PAN

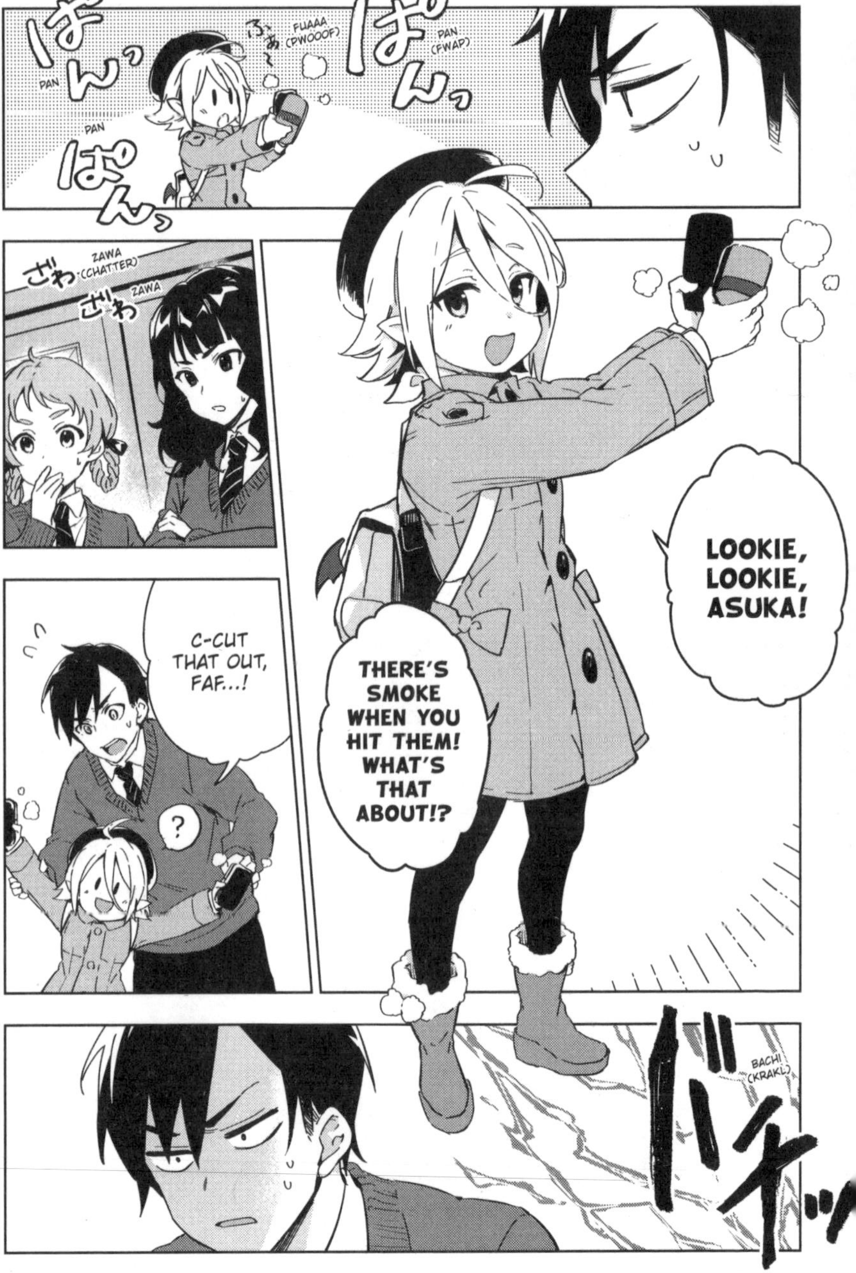
ぱんっ
PAN (FWAP)
ふぁ〜
FUAAA (PWOOOF)
ぱんっ
PAN
ぱんっ
PAN
LOOKIE, LOOKIE, ASUKA!
THERE'S SMOKE WHEN YOU HIT THEM! WHAT'S THAT ABOUT!?
ざわ
ZAWA (CHATTER)
ざわ
ZAWA
C-CUT THAT OUT, FAF...!
?
バチッ
BACHI (KRAKL)

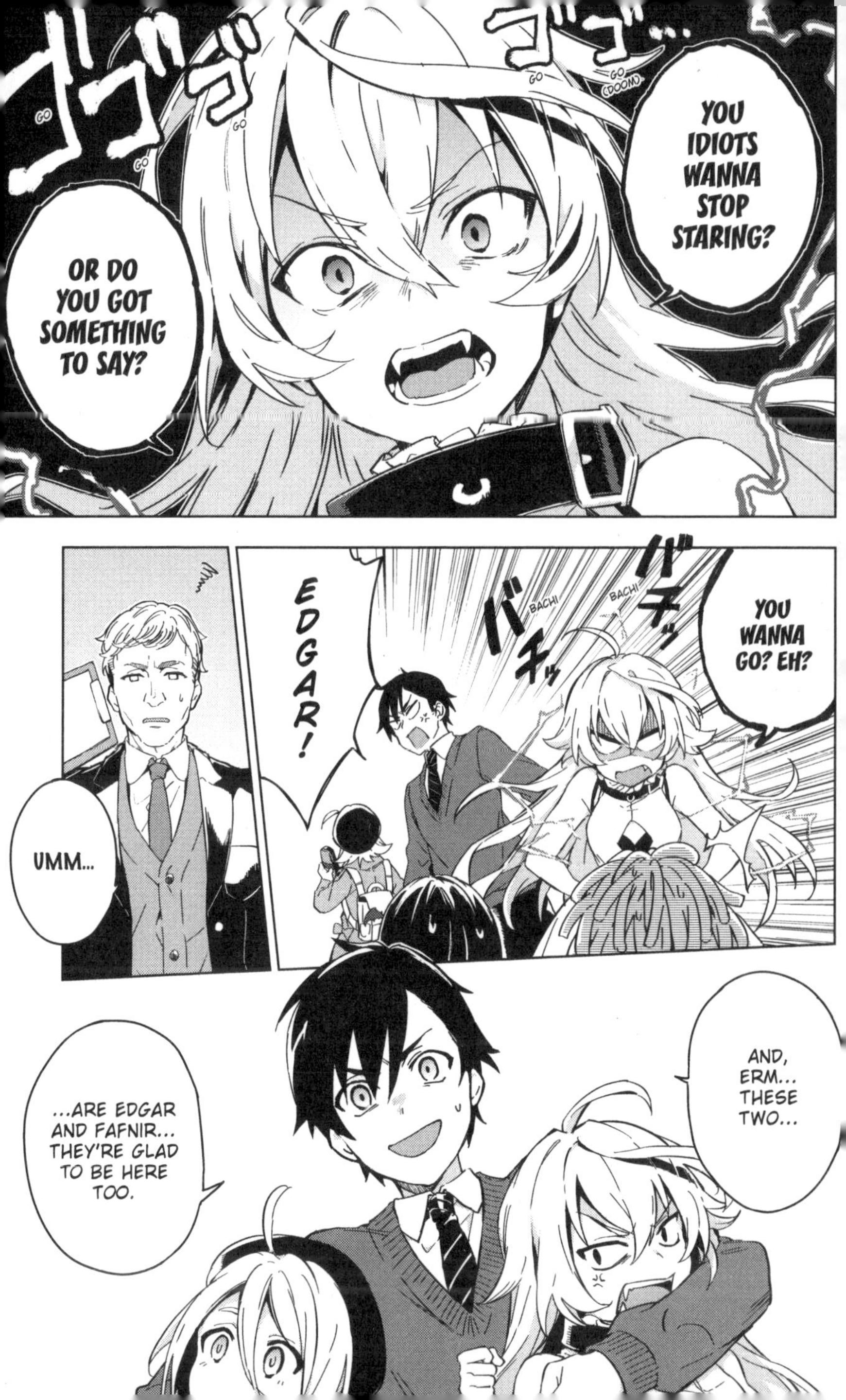
ゴゴ…
GO
GO
(DOOM)
YOU IDIOTS WANNA STOP STARING?
ゴゴゴ
GO
GO
GO
OR DO YOU GOT SOMETHING TO SAY?
YOU WANNA GO? EH?
バチッ
BACHI
バチッ
BACHI
EDGAR!
UMM...
AND, ERM... THESE TWO...
...ARE EDGAR AND FAFNIR... THEY'RE GLAD TO BE HERE TOO.

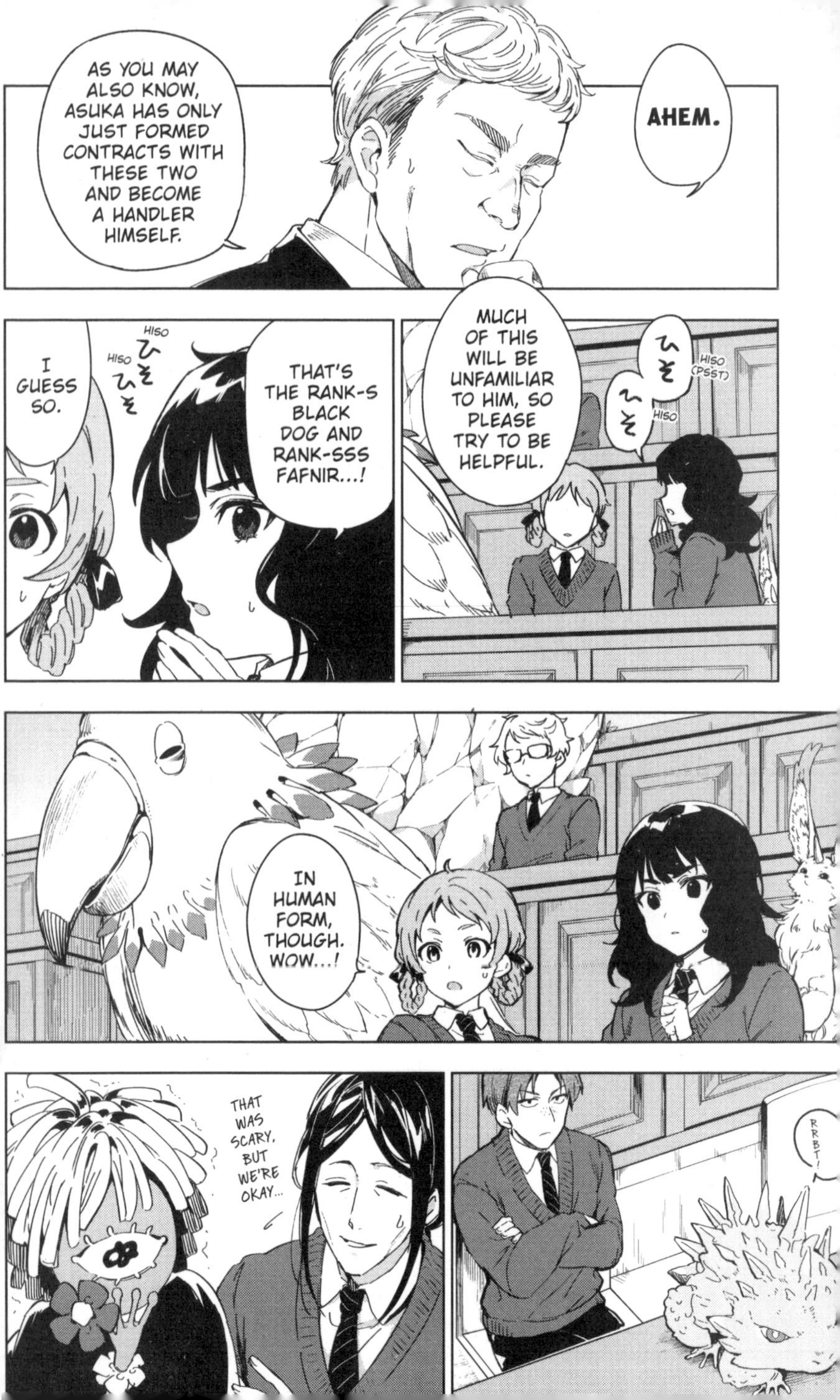
AHEM.
AS YOU MAY ALSO KNOW, ASUKA HAS ONLY JUST FORMED CONTRACTS WITH THESE TWO AND BECOME A HANDLER HIMSELF.
MUCH OF THIS WILL BE UNFAMILIAR TO HIM, SO PLEASE TRY TO BE HELPFUL.
ひそ HISO (PSST)
ひそ HISO
THAT'S THE RANK-S BLACK DOG AND RANK-SSS FAFNIR...!
ひそ HISO
ひそ HISO
I GUESS SO.
IN HUMAN FORM, THOUGH. WOW...!
RRBT!
THAT WAS SCARY, BUT WE'RE OKAY...

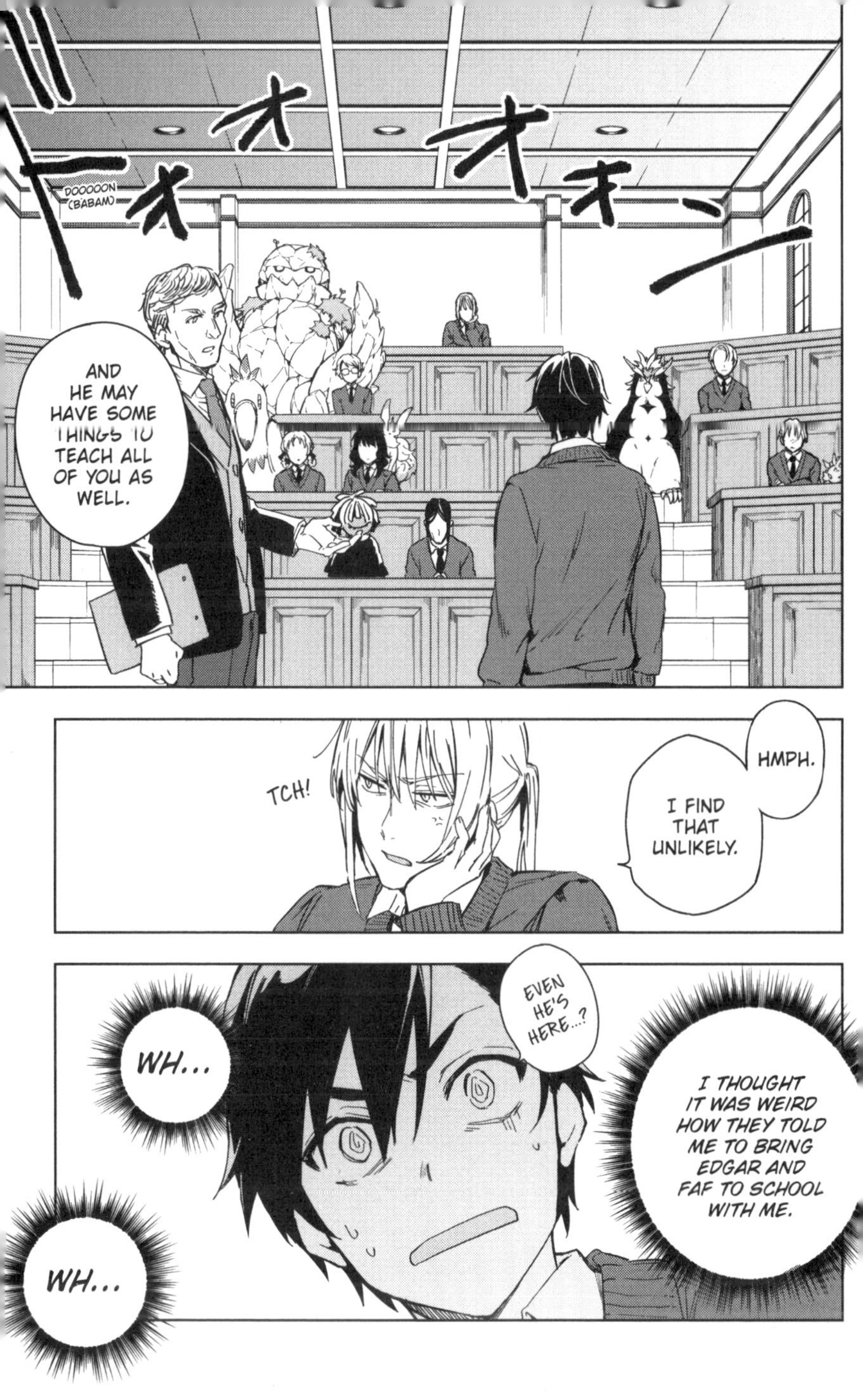
DOOOOON (BABAM)
AND HE MAY HAVE SOME THINGS TO TEACH ALL OF YOU AS WELL.
HMPH.
I FIND THAT UNLIKELY.
TCH!
EVEN HE'S HERE...?
I THOUGHT IT WAS WEIRD HOW THEY TOLD ME TO BRING EDGAR AND FAF TO SCHOOL WITH ME.
WH...
WH...

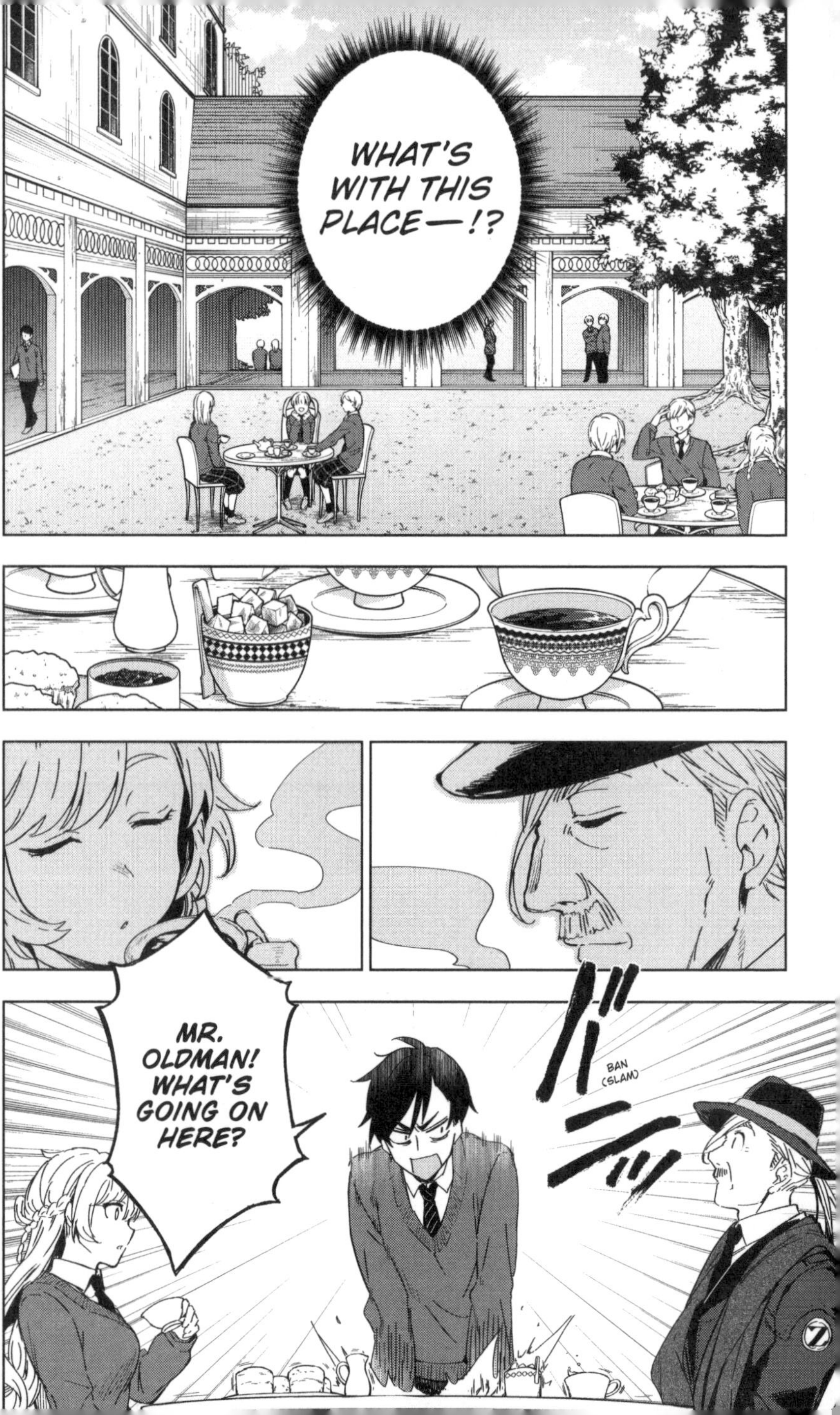
WHAT'S WITH THIS PLACE—!?
MR. OLDMAN! WHAT'S GOING ON HERE?
BAN (SLAM)

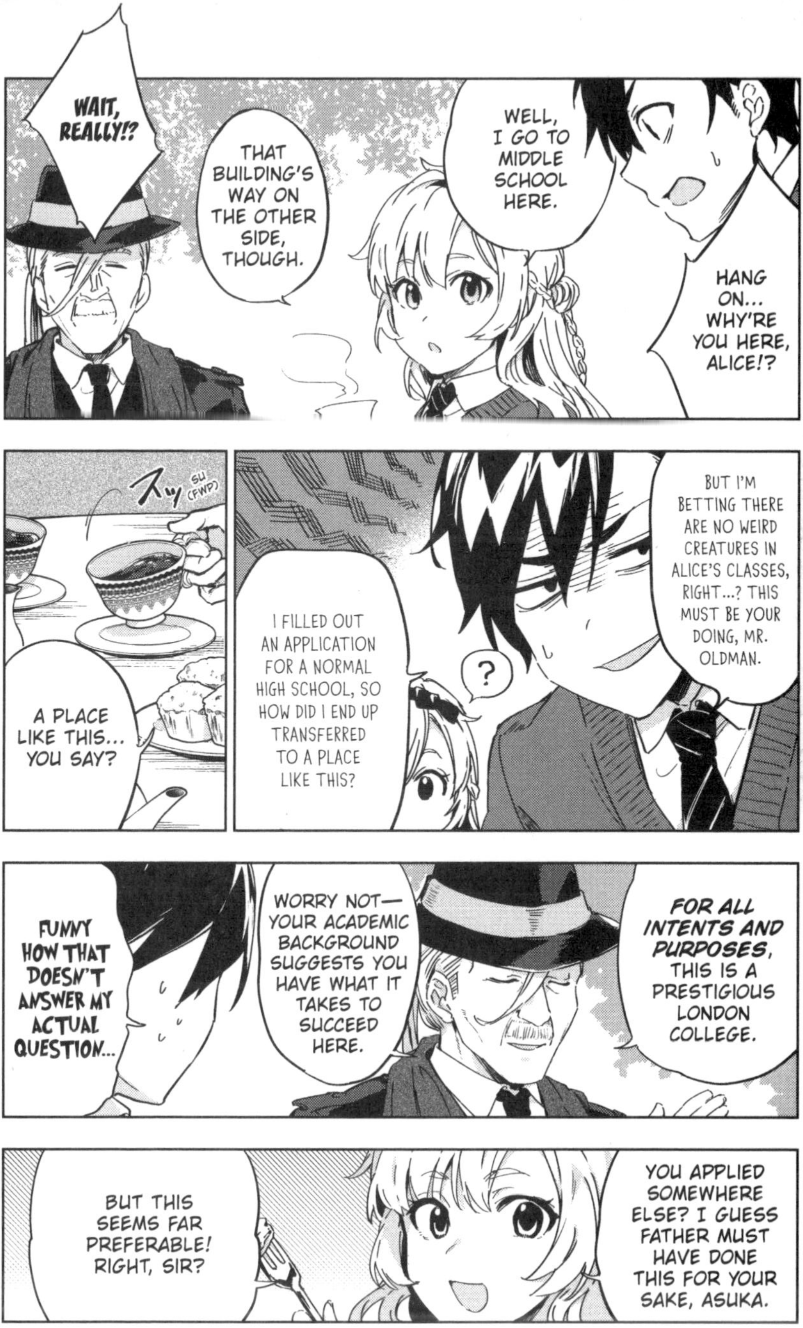
HANG ON... WHY'RE YOU HERE, ALICE!?
WELL, I GO TO MIDDLE SCHOOL HERE.
THAT BUILDING'S WAY ON THE OTHER SIDE, THOUGH.
WAIT, REALLY!?
BUT I'M BETTING THERE ARE NO WEIRD CREATURES IN ALICE'S CLASSES, RIGHT...? THIS MUST BE YOUR DOING, MR. OLDMAN.
I FILLED OUT AN APPLICATION FOR A NORMAL HIGH SCHOOL, SO HOW DID I END UP TRANSFERRED TO A PLACE LIKE THIS?
?
スッ
SU (FWP)
A PLACE LIKE THIS... YOU SAY?
FOR ALL INTENTS AND PURPOSES, THIS IS A PRESTIGIOUS LONDON COLLEGE.
WORRY NOT—YOUR ACADEMIC BACKGROUND SUGGESTS YOU HAVE WHAT IT TAKES TO SUCCEED HERE.
FUNNY HOW THAT DOESN'T ANSWER MY ACTUAL QUESTION...
YOU APPLIED SOMEWHERE ELSE? I GUESS FATHER MUST HAVE DONE THIS FOR YOUR SAKE, ASUKA.
BUT THIS SEEMS FAR PREFERABLE! RIGHT, SIR?

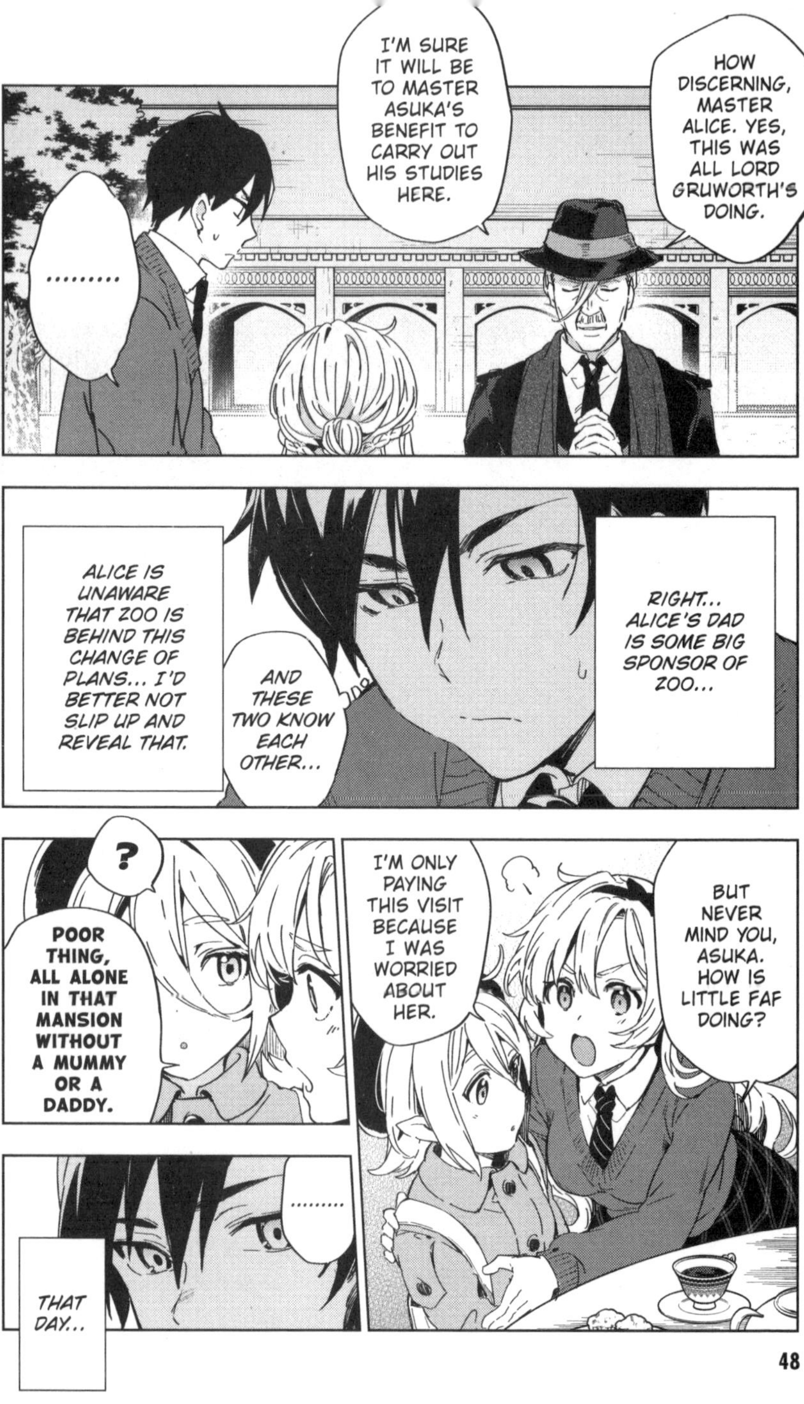
I'M SURE IT WILL BE TO MASTER ASUKA'S BENEFIT TO CARRY OUT HIS STUDIES HERE.
HOW DISCERNING, MASTER ALICE. YES, THIS WAS ALL LORD GRUWORTH'S DOING.
....
RIGHT... ALICE'S DAD IS SOME BIG SPONSOR OF ZOO...
AND THESE TWO KNOW EACH OTHER...
ALICE IS UNAWARE THAT ZOO IS BEHIND THIS CHANGE OF PLANS... I'D BETTER NOT SLIP UP AND REVEAL THAT.
BUT NEVER MIND YOU, ASUKA. HOW IS LITTLE FAF DOING?
I'M ONLY PAYING THIS VISIT BECAUSE I WAS WORRIED ABOUT HER.
?
POOR THING, ALL ALONE IN THAT MANSION WITHOUT A MUMMY OR A DADDY.
....
THAT DAY...

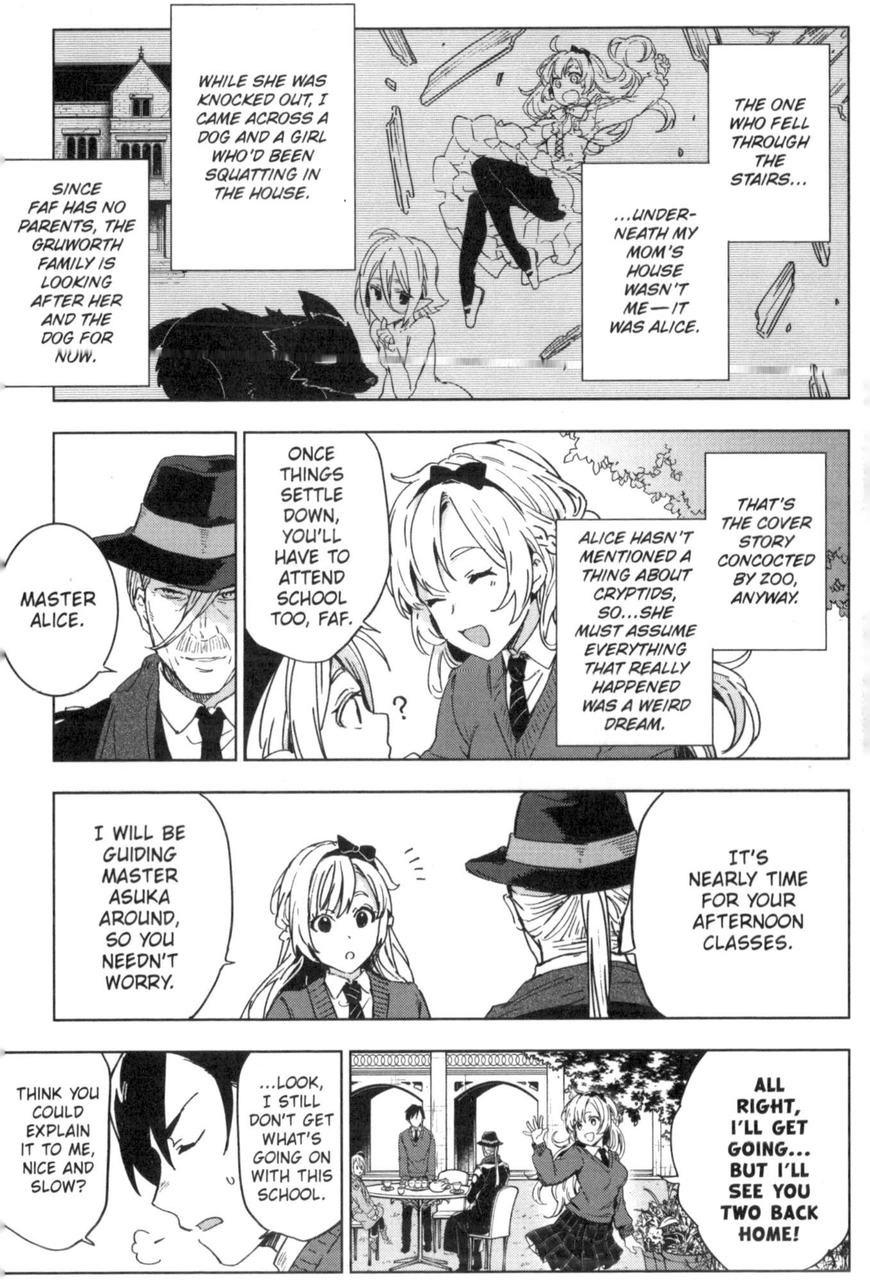
THE ONE WHO FELL THROUGH THE STAIRS...
...UNDERNEATH MY MOM'S HOUSE WASN'T ME—IT WAS ALICE.
WHILE SHE WAS KNOCKED OUT, I CAME ACROSS A DOG AND A GIRL WHO'D BEEN SQUATTING IN THE HOUSE.
SINCE FAF HAS NO PARENTS, THE GRUWORTH FAMILY IS LOOKING AFTER HER AND THE DOG FOR NOW.
THAT'S THE COVER STORY CONCOCTED BY ZOO, ANYWAY.
ALICE HASN'T MENTIONED A THING ABOUT CRYPTIDS, SO...SHE MUST ASSUME EVERYTHING THAT REALLY HAPPENED WAS A WEIRD DREAM.
ONCE THINGS SETTLE DOWN, YOU'LL HAVE TO ATTEND SCHOOL TOO, FAF.
?
MASTER ALICE.
IT'S NEARLY TIME FOR YOUR AFTERNOON CLASSES.
I WILL BE GUIDING MASTER ASUKA AROUND, SO YOU NEEDN'T WORRY.
ALL RIGHT, I'LL GET GOING... BUT I'LL SEE YOU TWO BACK HOME!
...LOOK, I STILL DON'T GET WHAT'S GOING ON WITH THIS SCHOOL.
THINK YOU COULD EXPLAIN IT TO ME, NICE AND SLOW?

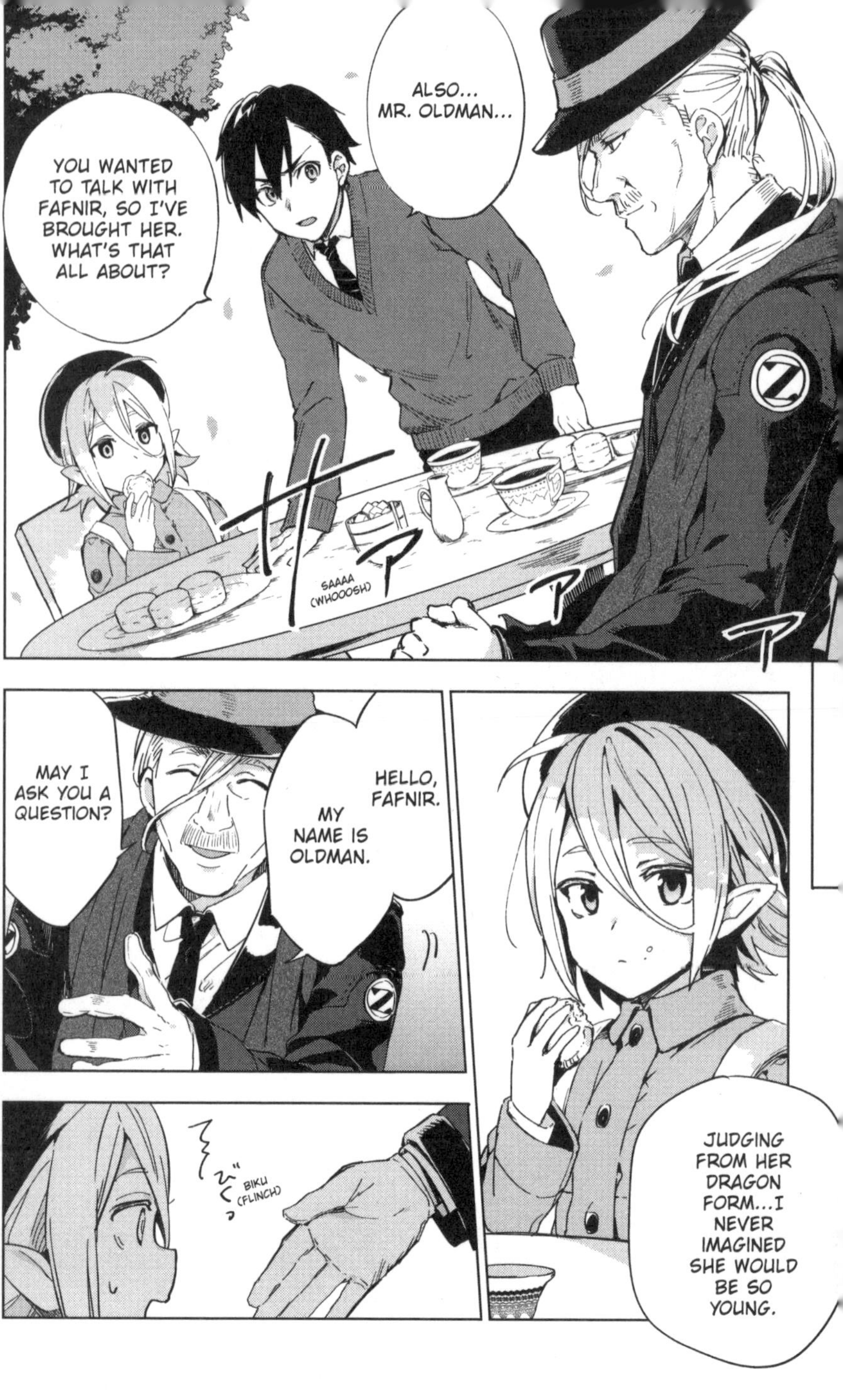
ALSO... MR. OLDMAN...
YOU WANTED TO TALK WITH FAFNIR, SO I'VE BROUGHT HER. WHAT'S THAT ALL ABOUT?
SAAAA (WHOOOSH)
JUDGING FROM HER DRAGON FORM...I NEVER IMAGINED SHE WOULD BE SO YOUNG.
HELLO, FAFNIR.
MY NAME IS OLDMAN.
MAY I ASK YOU A QUESTION?
BIKU (FLINCH)

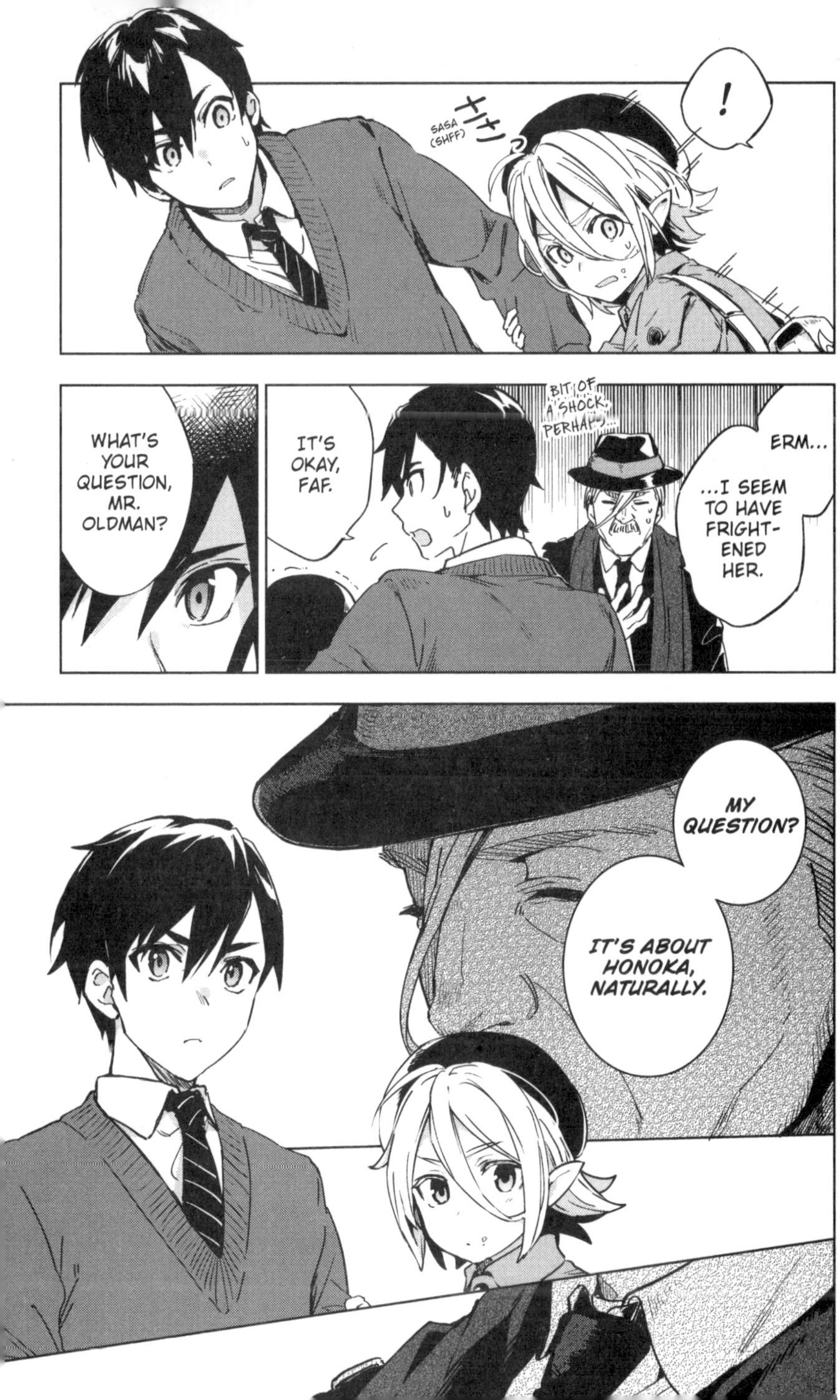
!
ササ
SASA (SHFF)
ERM...
...I SEEM TO HAVE FRIGHTENED HER.
BIT OF A SHOCK, PERHAPS...
IT'S OKAY, FAF.
WHAT'S YOUR QUESTION, MR. OLDMAN?
MY QUESTION?
IT'S ABOUT HONOKA, NATURALLY.

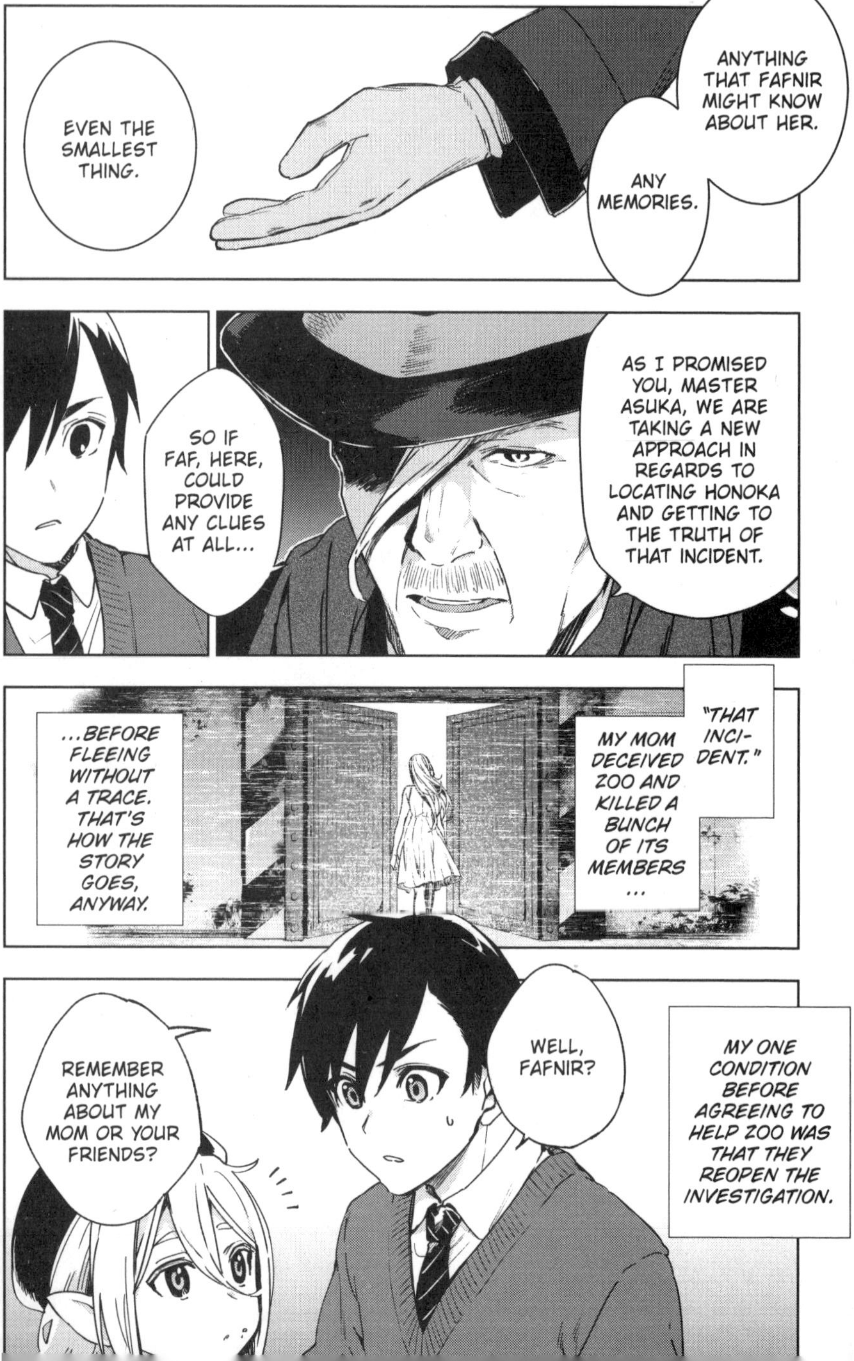
ANYTHING THAT FAFNIR MIGHT KNOW ABOUT HER.
ANY MEMORIES.
EVEN THE SMALLEST THING.
AS I PROMISED YOU, MASTER ASUKA, WE ARE TAKING A NEW APPROACH IN REGARDS TO LOCATING HONOKA AND GETTING TO THE TRUTH OF THAT INCIDENT.
SO IF FAF, HERE, COULD PROVIDE ANY CLUES AT ALL...
"THAT INCI-DENT."
MY MOM DECEIVED ZOO AND KILLED A BUNCH OF ITS MEMBERS...
...BEFORE FLEEING WITHOUT A TRACE. THAT'S HOW THE STORY GOES, ANYWAY.
MY ONE CONDITION BEFORE AGREEING TO HELP ZOO WAS THAT THEY REOPEN THE INVESTIGATION.
WELL, FAFNIR?
REMEMBER ANYTHING ABOUT MY MOM OR YOUR FRIENDS?

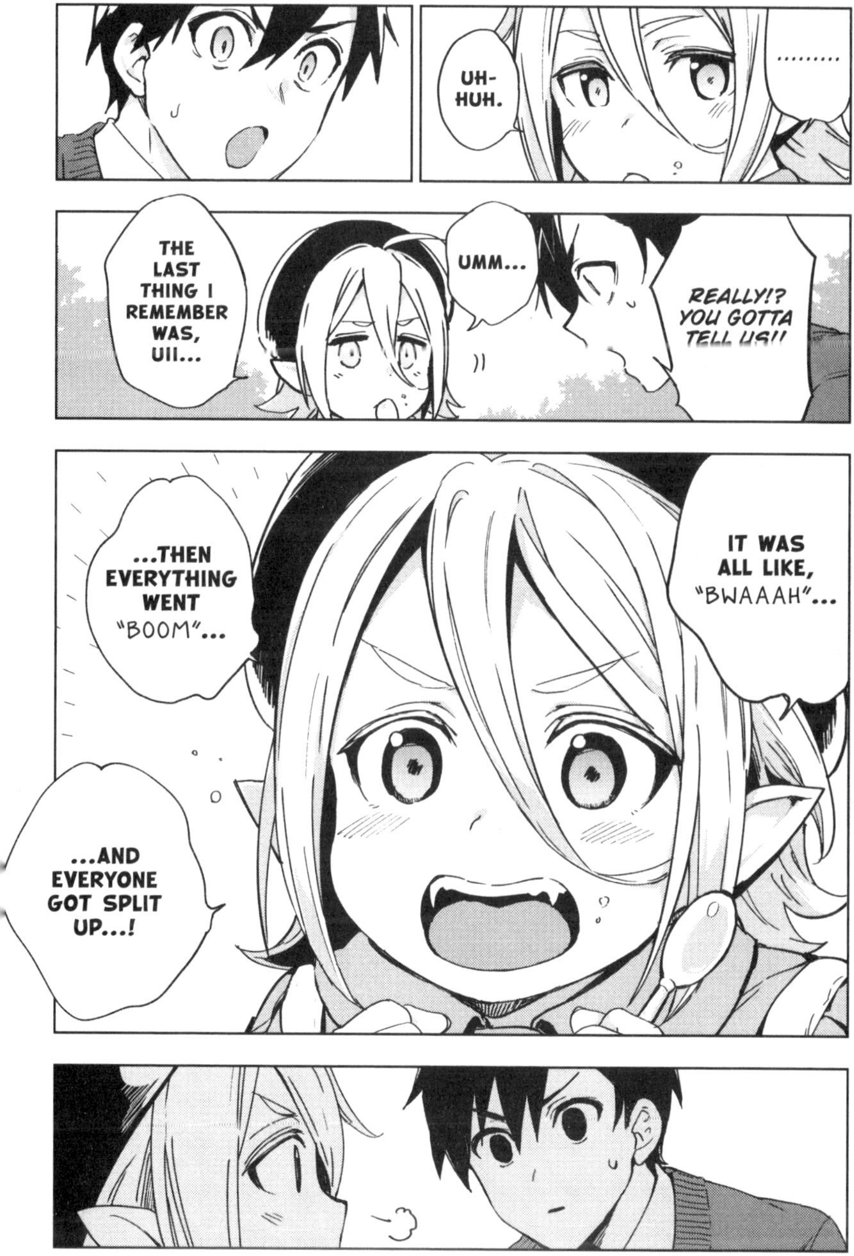
....
UH-HUH.
REALLY!? YOU GOTTA TELL US!!
UMM...
THE LAST THING I REMEMBER WAS, UII...
IT WAS ALL LIKE, "BWAAAH"...
...THEN EVERYTHING WENT "BOOM"...
...AND EVERYONE GOT SPLIT UP...!

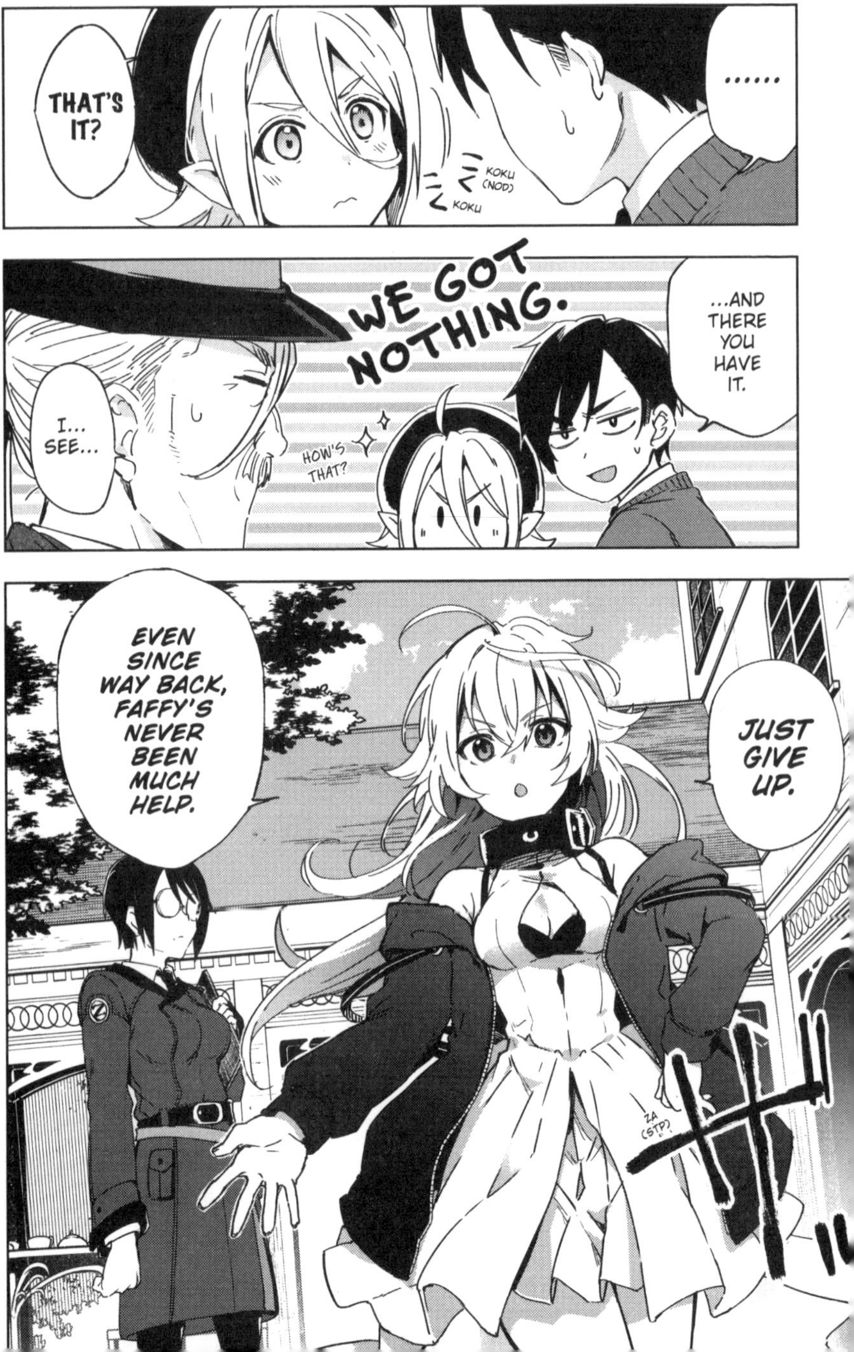
......
THAT'S IT?
KOKU (NOD)
KOKU
...AND THERE YOU HAVE IT.
WE GOT NOTHING.
HOW'S THAT?
I... SEE...
JUST GIVE UP.
EVEN SINCE WAY BACK, FAFFY'S NEVER BEEN MUCH HELP.
ZA (STP)

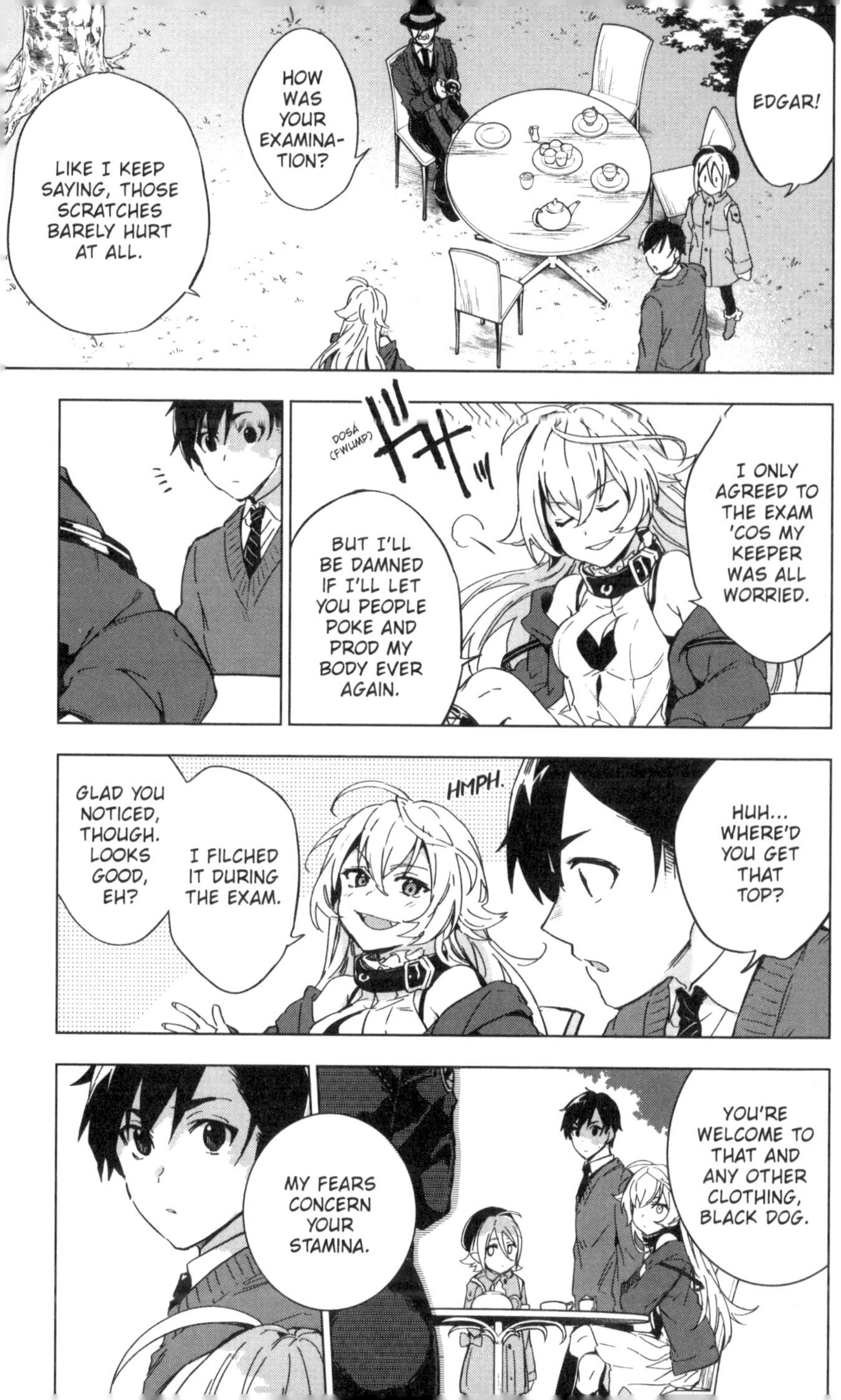
EDGAR!
HOW WAS YOUR EXAMINATION?
LIKE I KEEP SAYING, THOSE SCRATCHES BARELY HURT AT ALL.
I ONLY AGREED TO THE EXAM 'COS MY KEEPER WAS ALL WORRIED.
DOSA (FWUMP)
BUT I'LL BE DAMNED IF I'LL LET YOU PEOPLE POKE AND PROD MY BODY EVER AGAIN.
HUH... WHERE'D YOU GET THAT TOP?
HMPH.
I FILCHED IT DURING THE EXAM.
GLAD YOU NOTICED, THOUGH. LOOKS GOOD, EH?
YOU'RE WELCOME TO THAT AND ANY OTHER CLOTHING, BLACK DOG.
MY FEARS CONCERN YOUR STAMINA.

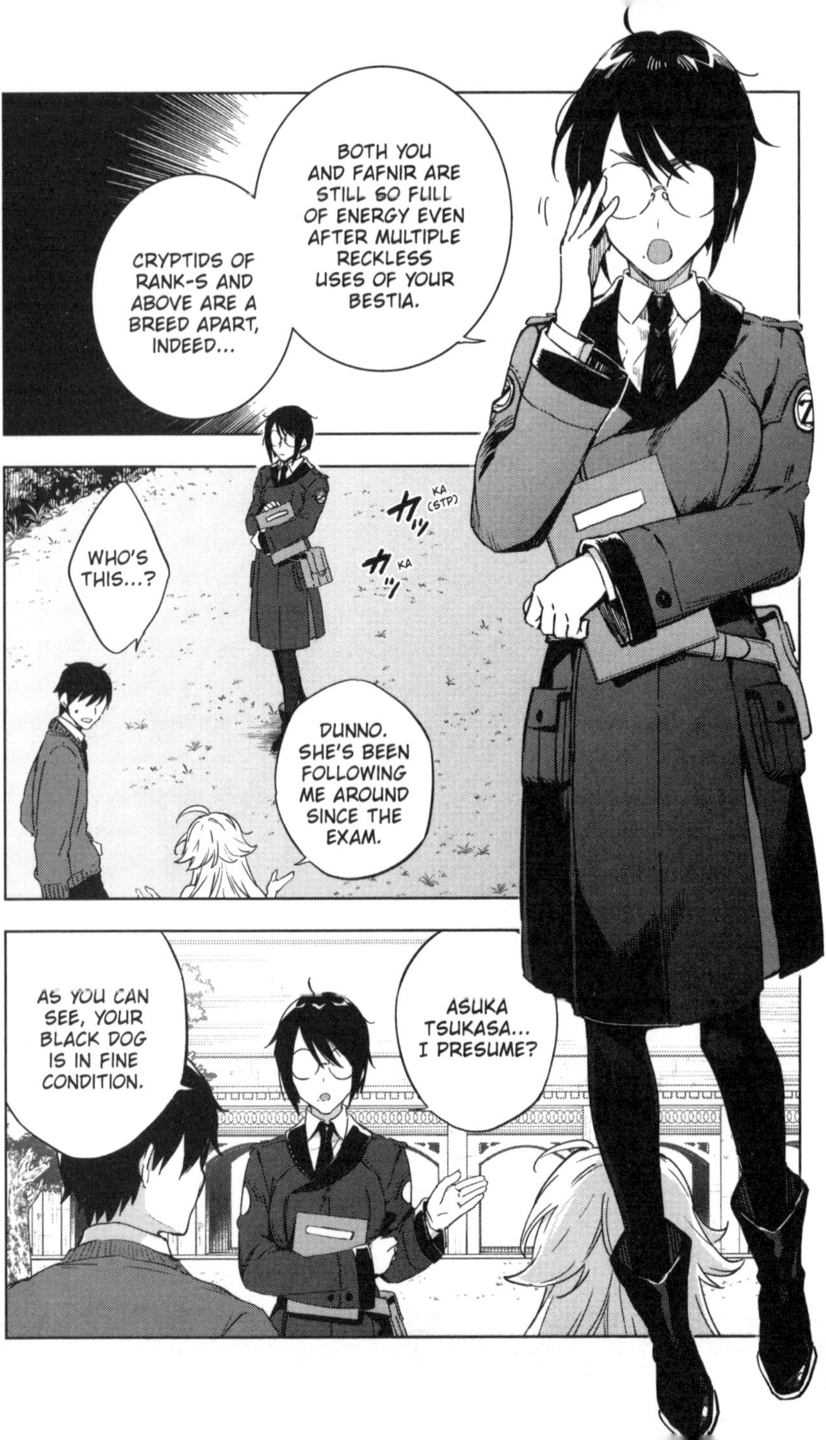
BOTH YOU AND FAFNIR ARE STILL SO FULL OF ENERGY EVEN AFTER MULTIPLE RECKLESS USES OF YOUR BESTIA.
CRYPTIDS OF RANK-S AND ABOVE ARE A BREED APART, INDEED...
カッ KA (STP)
カッ KA
WHO'S THIS...?
DUNNO. SHE'S BEEN FOLLOWING ME AROUND SINCE THE EXAM.
ASUKA TSUKASA... I PRESUME?
AS YOU CAN SEE, YOUR BLACK DOG IS IN FINE CONDITION.

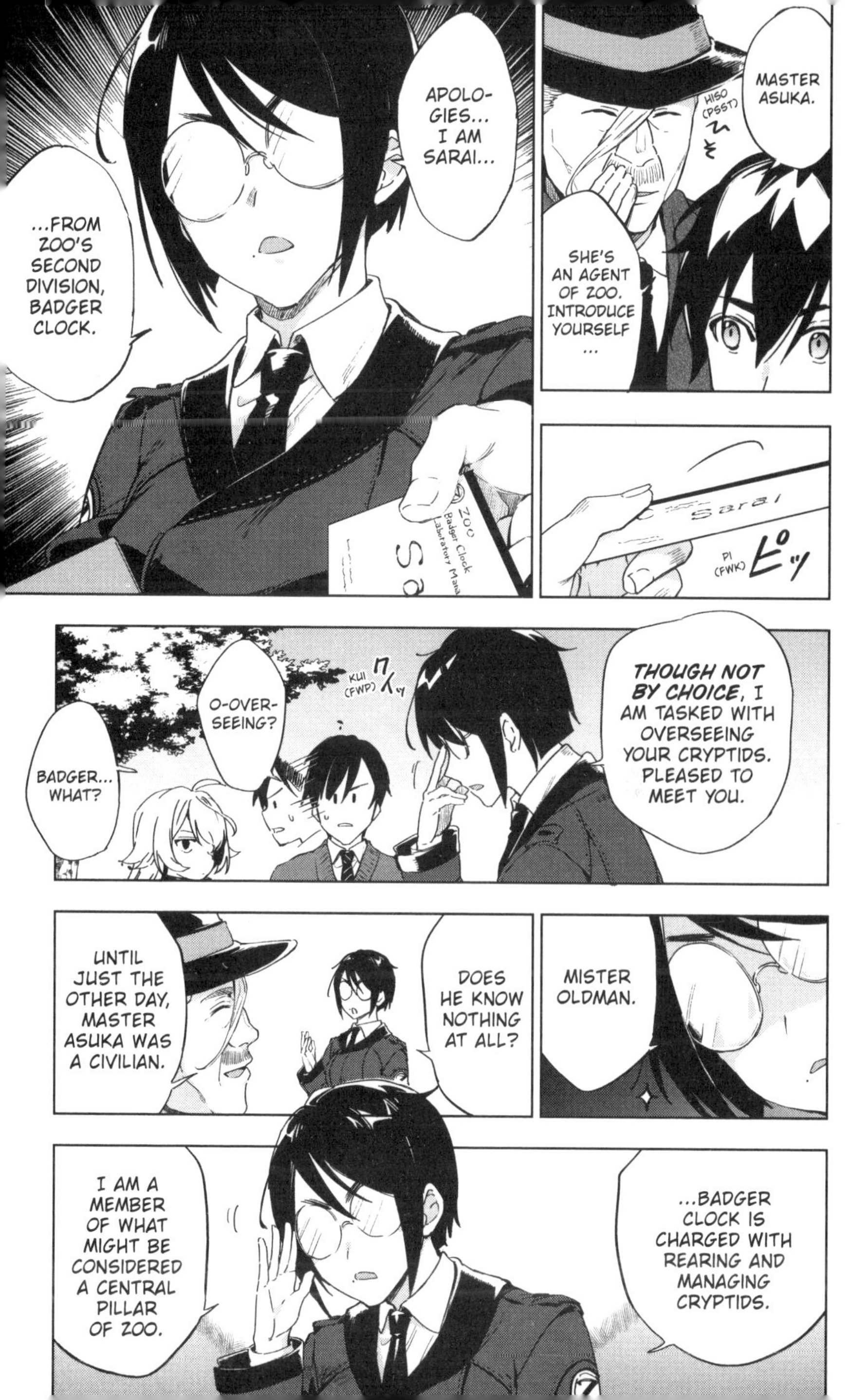
MASTER ASUKA.
HISO (PSST)
SHE'S AN AGENT OF ZOO. INTRODUCE YOURSELF ...
Sarai
PI (FWK)
APOLOGIES... I AM SARAI...
...FROM ZOO'S SECOND DIVISION, BADGER CLOCK.
ZOO
Badger Clock
THOUGH NOT BY CHOICE, I AM TASKED WITH OVERSEEING YOUR CRYPTIDS. PLEASED TO MEET YOU.
KUI (FWP)
O-OVERSEEING?
BADGER... WHAT?
MISTER OLDMAN.
DOES HE KNOW NOTHING AT ALL?
UNTIL JUST THE OTHER DAY, MASTER ASUKA WAS A CIVILIAN.
...BADGER CLOCK IS CHARGED WITH REARING AND MANAGING CRYPTIDS.
I AM A MEMBER OF WHAT MIGHT BE CONSIDERED A CENTRAL PILLAR OF ZOO.

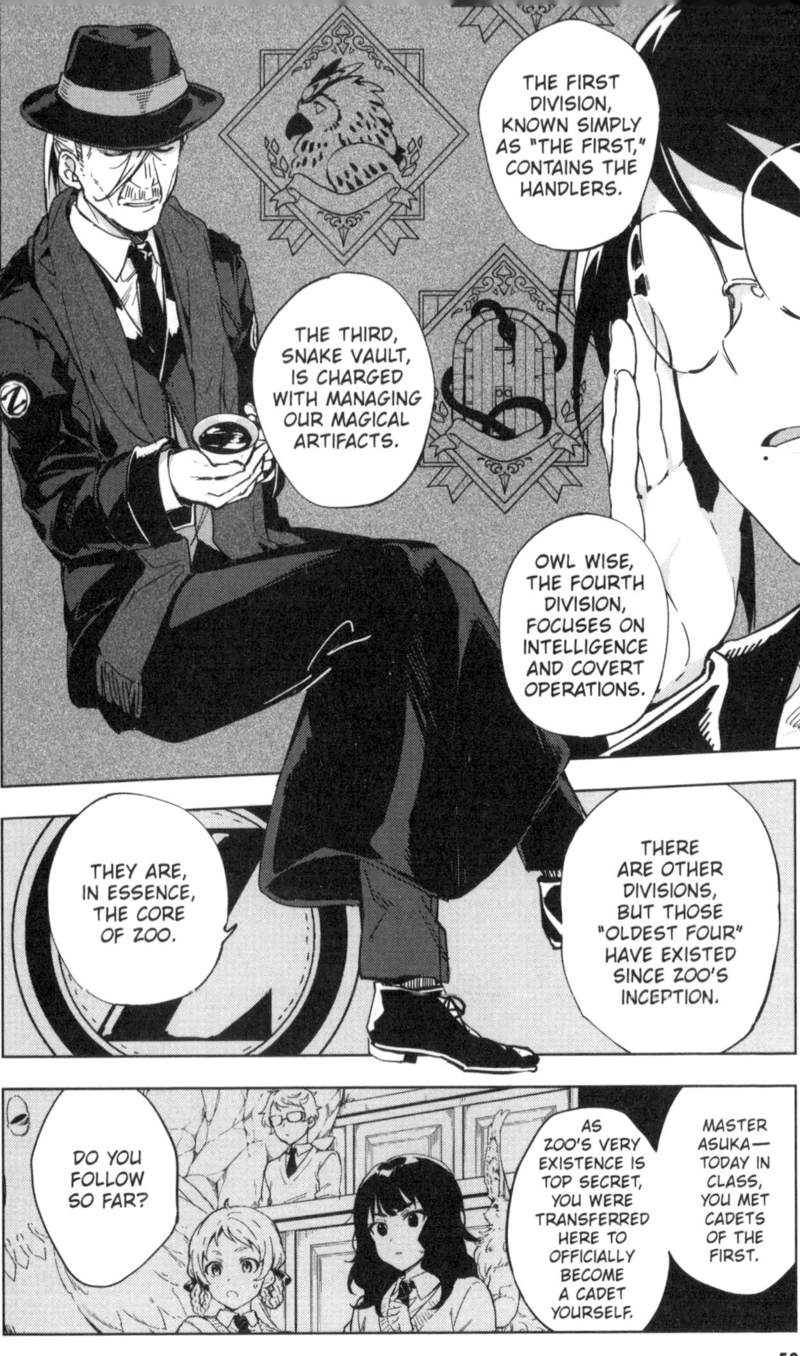
THE FIRST DIVISION, KNOWN SIMPLY AS "THE FIRST," CONTAINS THE HANDLERS.
THE THIRD, SNAKE VAULT, IS CHARGED WITH MANAGING OUR MAGICAL ARTIFACTS.
OWL WISE, THE FOURTH DIVISION, FOCUSES ON INTELLIGENCE AND COVERT OPERATIONS.
THERE ARE OTHER DIVISIONS, BUT THOSE "OLDEST FOUR" HAVE EXISTED SINCE ZOO'S INCEPTION.
THEY ARE, IN ESSENCE, THE CORE OF ZOO.
MASTER ASUKA— TODAY IN CLASS, YOU MET CADETS OF THE FIRST.
AS ZOO'S VERY EXISTENCE IS TOP SECRET, YOU WERE TRANSFERRED HERE TO OFFICIALLY BECOME A CADET YOURSELF.
DO YOU FOLLOW SO FAR?

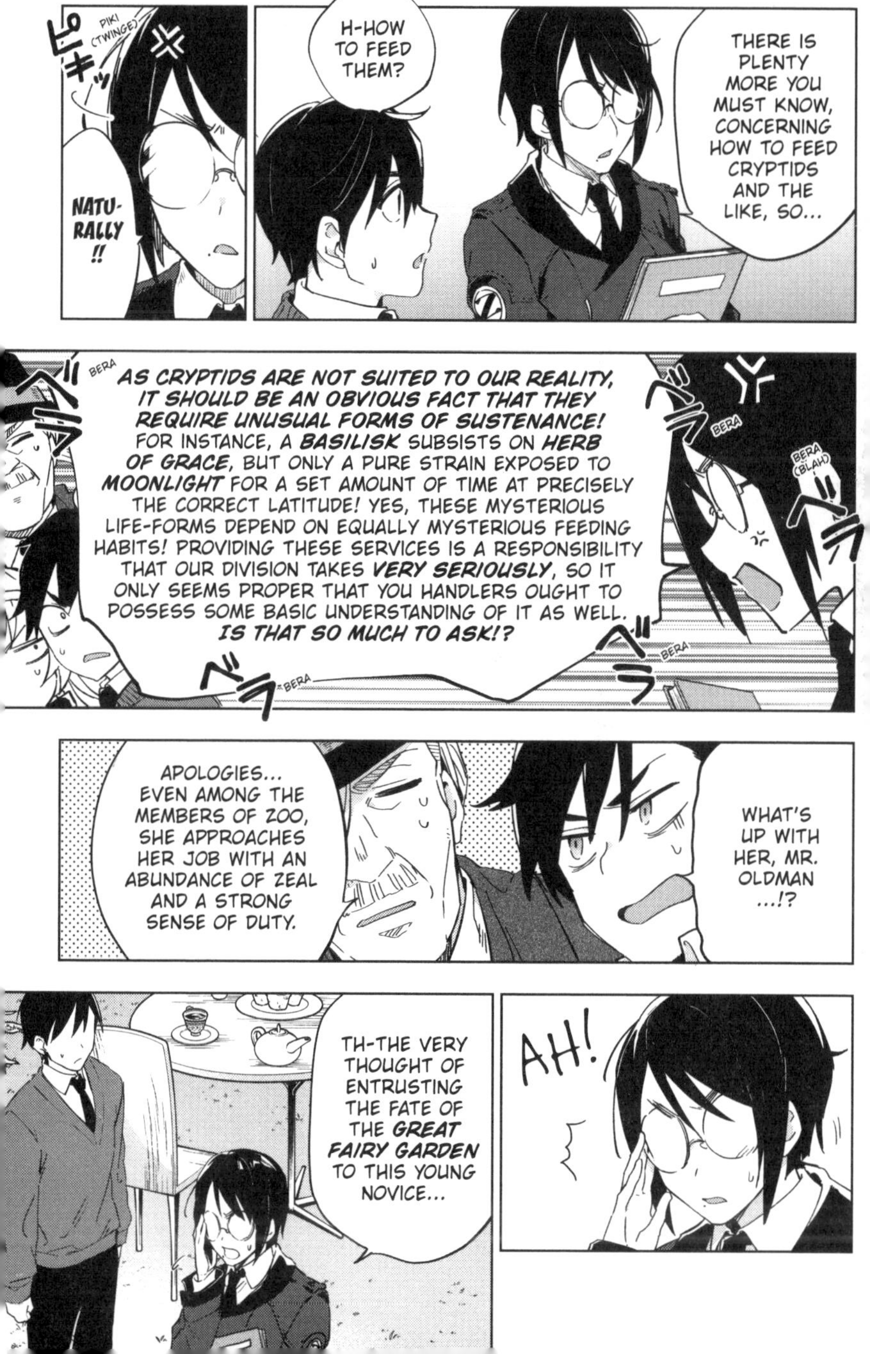

THERE IS PLENTY MORE YOU MUST KNOW, CONCERNING HOW TO FEED CRYPTIDS AND THE LIKE, SO...
H-HOW TO FEED THEM?
PIKI (TWINGE)
NATU-RALLY!!
BERA
BERA
BERA (BLAH)
AS CRYPTIDS ARE NOT SUITED TO OUR REALITY, IT SHOULD BE AN OBVIOUS FACT THAT THEY REQUIRE UNUSUAL FORMS OF SUSTENANCE! FOR INSTANCE, A BASILISK SUBSISTS ON HERB OF GRACE, BUT ONLY A PURE STRAIN EXPOSED TO MOONLIGHT FOR A SET AMOUNT OF TIME AT PRECISELY THE CORRECT LATITUDE! YES, THESE MYSTERIOUS LIFE-FORMS DEPEND ON EQUALLY MYSTERIOUS FEEDING HABITS! PROVIDING THESE SERVICES IS A RESPONSIBILITY THAT OUR DIVISION TAKES VERY SERIOUSLY, SO IT ONLY SEEMS PROPER THAT YOU HANDLERS OUGHT TO POSSESS SOME BASIC UNDERSTANDING OF IT AS WELL. IS THAT SO MUCH TO ASK!?
BERA
BERA
WHAT'S UP WITH HER, MR. OLDMAN...!?
APOLOGIES... EVEN AMONG THE MEMBERS OF ZOO, SHE APPROACHES HER JOB WITH AN ABUNDANCE OF ZEAL AND A STRONG SENSE OF DUTY.
AH!
TH-THE VERY THOUGHT OF ENTRUSTING THE FATE OF THE GREAT FAIRY GARDEN TO THIS YOUNG NOVICE...

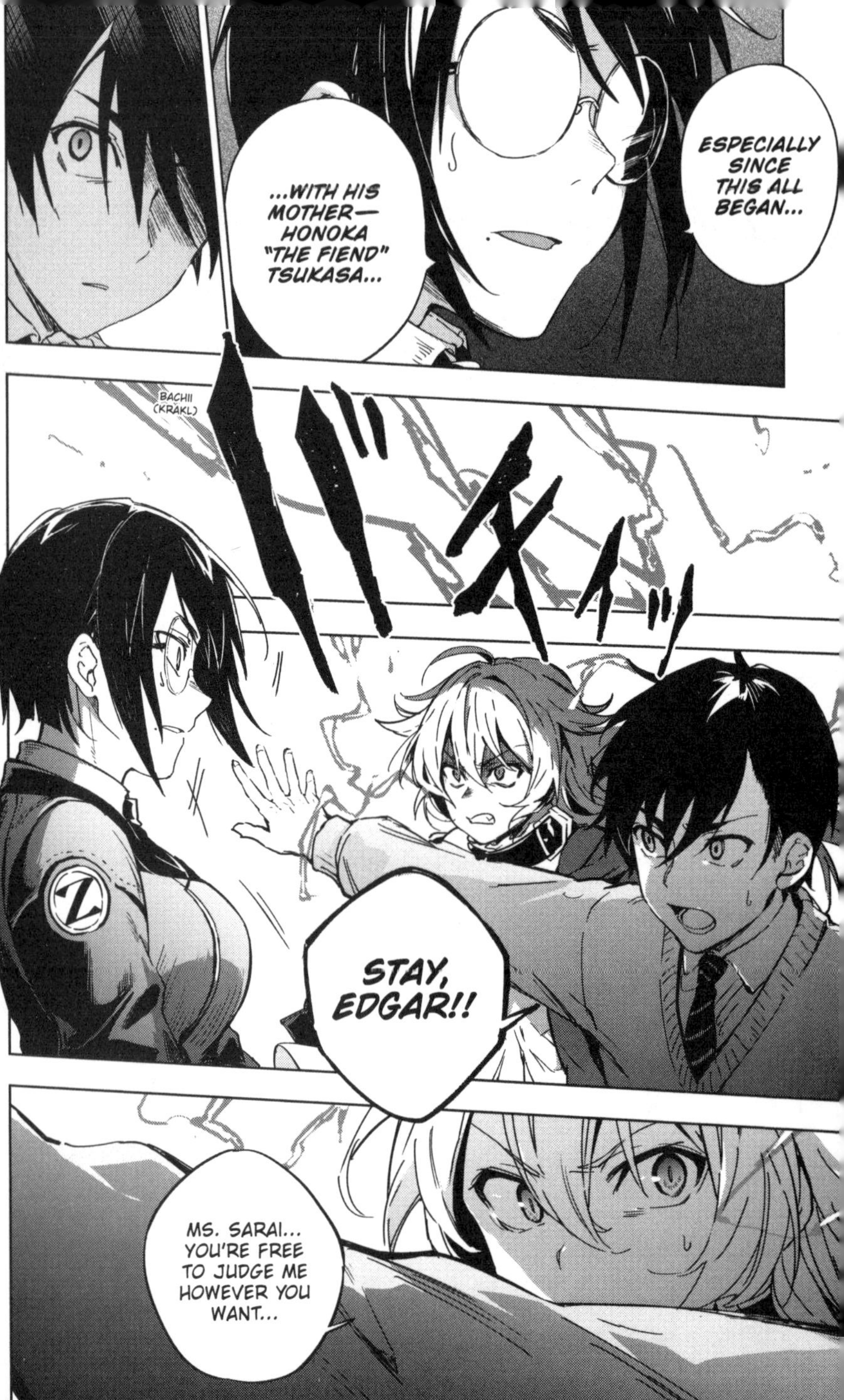
ESPECIALLY SINCE THIS ALL BEGAN...
...WITH HIS MOTHER—HONOKA "THE FIEND" TSUKASA...
BACHII (KRÄKL)
STAY, EDGAR!!
MS. SARAI... YOU'RE FREE TO JUDGE ME HOWEVER YOU WANT...

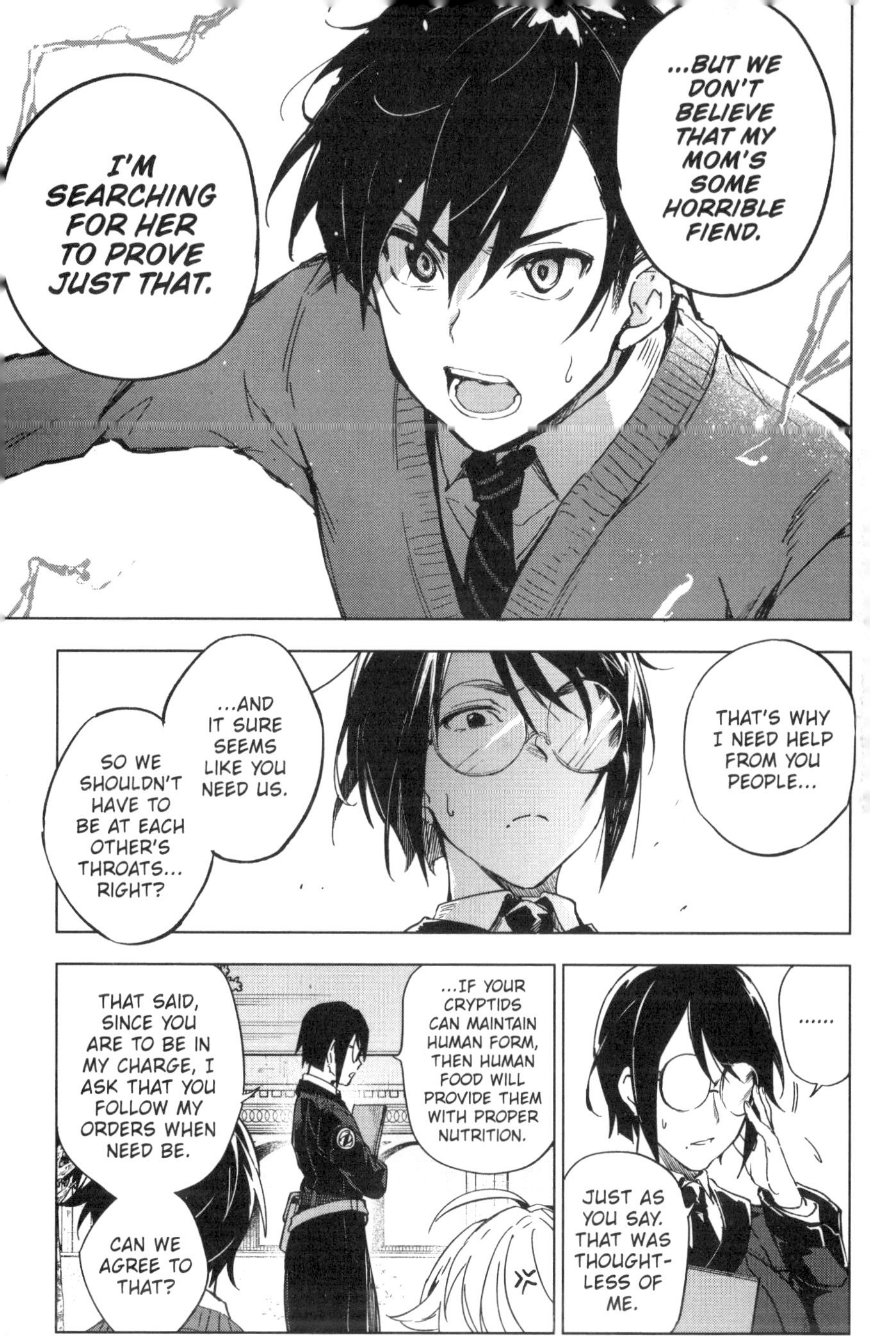
...BUT WE DON'T BELIEVE THAT MY MOM'S SOME HORRIBLE FIEND.
I'M SEARCHING FOR HER TO PROVE JUST THAT.
THAT'S WHY I NEED HELP FROM YOU PEOPLE...
...AND IT SURE SEEMS LIKE YOU NEED US.
SO WE SHOULDN'T HAVE TO BE AT EACH OTHER'S THROATS... RIGHT?
......
JUST AS YOU SAY. THAT WAS THOUGHTLESS OF ME.
...IF YOUR CRYPTIDS CAN MAINTAIN HUMAN FORM, THEN HUMAN FOOD WILL PROVIDE THEM WITH PROPER NUTRITION.
THAT SAID, SINCE YOU ARE TO BE IN MY CHARGE, I ASK THAT YOU FOLLOW MY ORDERS WHEN NEED BE.
CAN WE AGREE TO THAT?

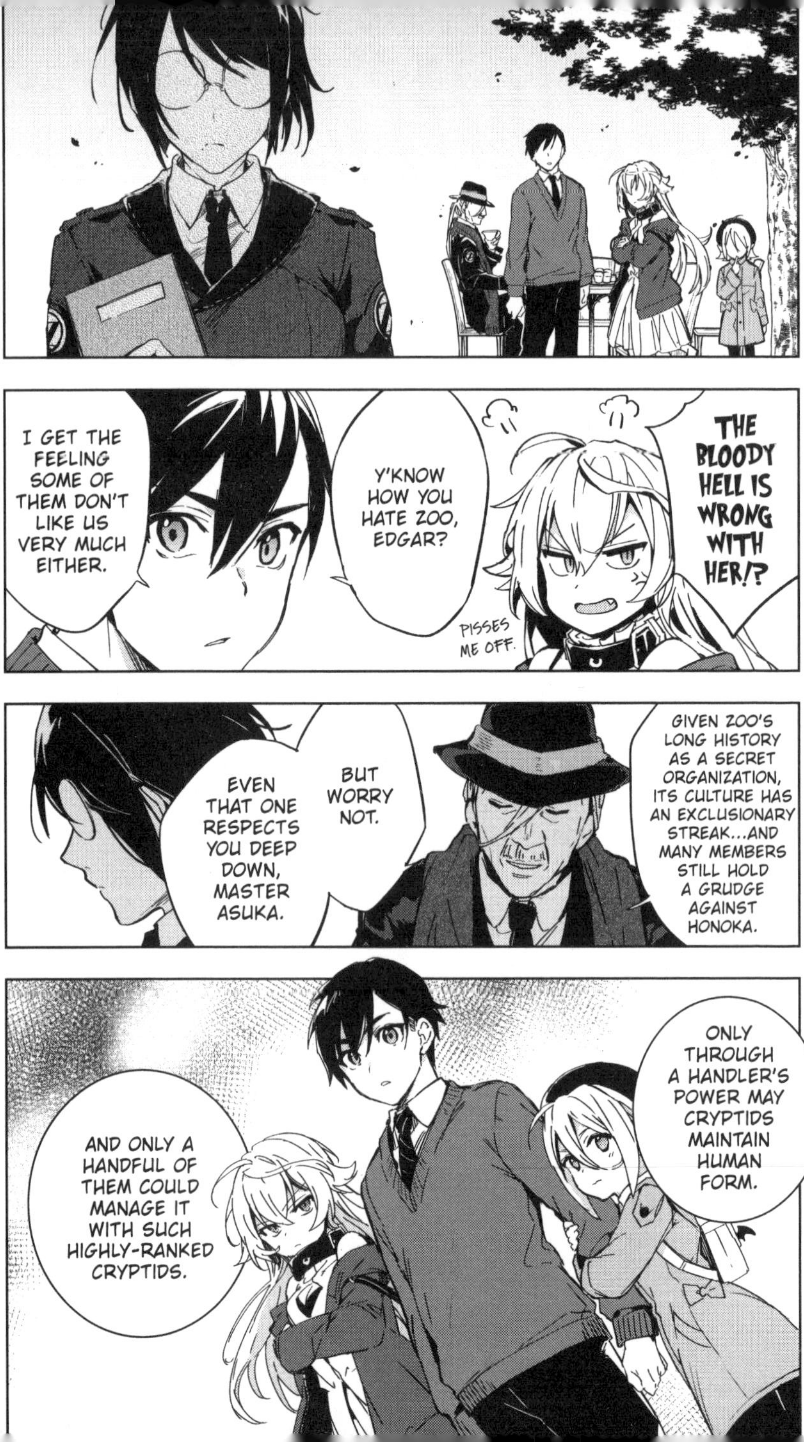
THE BLOODY HELL IS WRONG WITH HER!?
PISSES ME OFF.
Y'KNOW HOW YOU HATE ZOO, EDGAR?
I GET THE FEELING SOME OF THEM DON'T LIKE US VERY MUCH EITHER.
GIVEN ZOO'S LONG HISTORY AS A SECRET ORGANIZATION, ITS CULTURE HAS AN EXCLUSIONARY STREAK...AND MANY MEMBERS STILL HOLD A GRUDGE AGAINST HONOKA.
BUT WORRY NOT.
EVEN THAT ONE RESPECTS YOU DEEP DOWN, MASTER ASUKA.
ONLY THROUGH A HANDLER'S POWER MAY CRYPTIDS MAINTAIN HUMAN FORM.
AND ONLY A HANDFUL OF THEM COULD MANAGE IT WITH SUCH HIGHLY-RANKED CRYPTIDS.

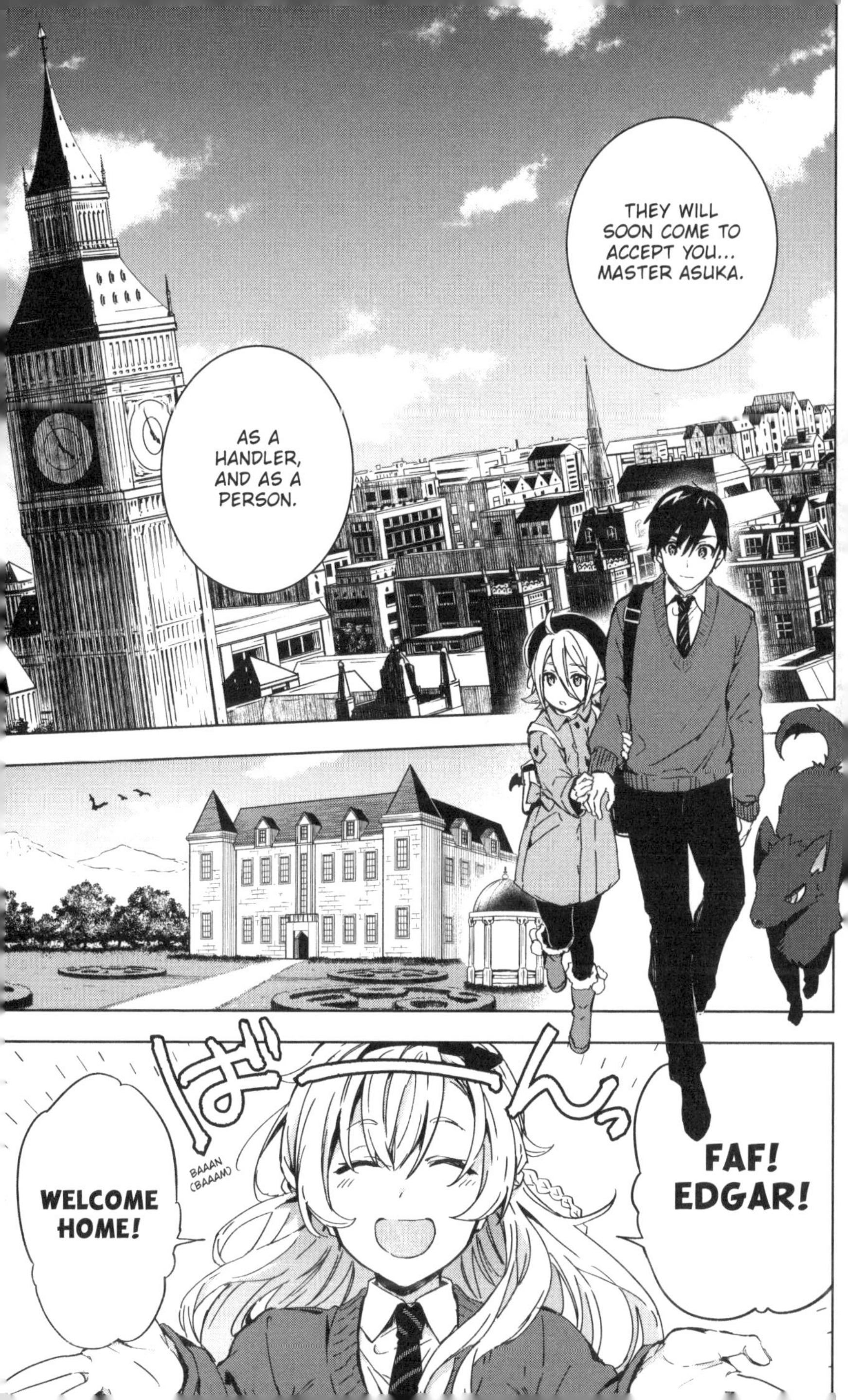
THEY WILL SOON COME TO ACCEPT YOU... MASTER ASUKA.
AS A HANDLER, AND AS A PERSON.
FAF! EDGAR!
BAAAN (BAAAM)
WELCOME HOME!

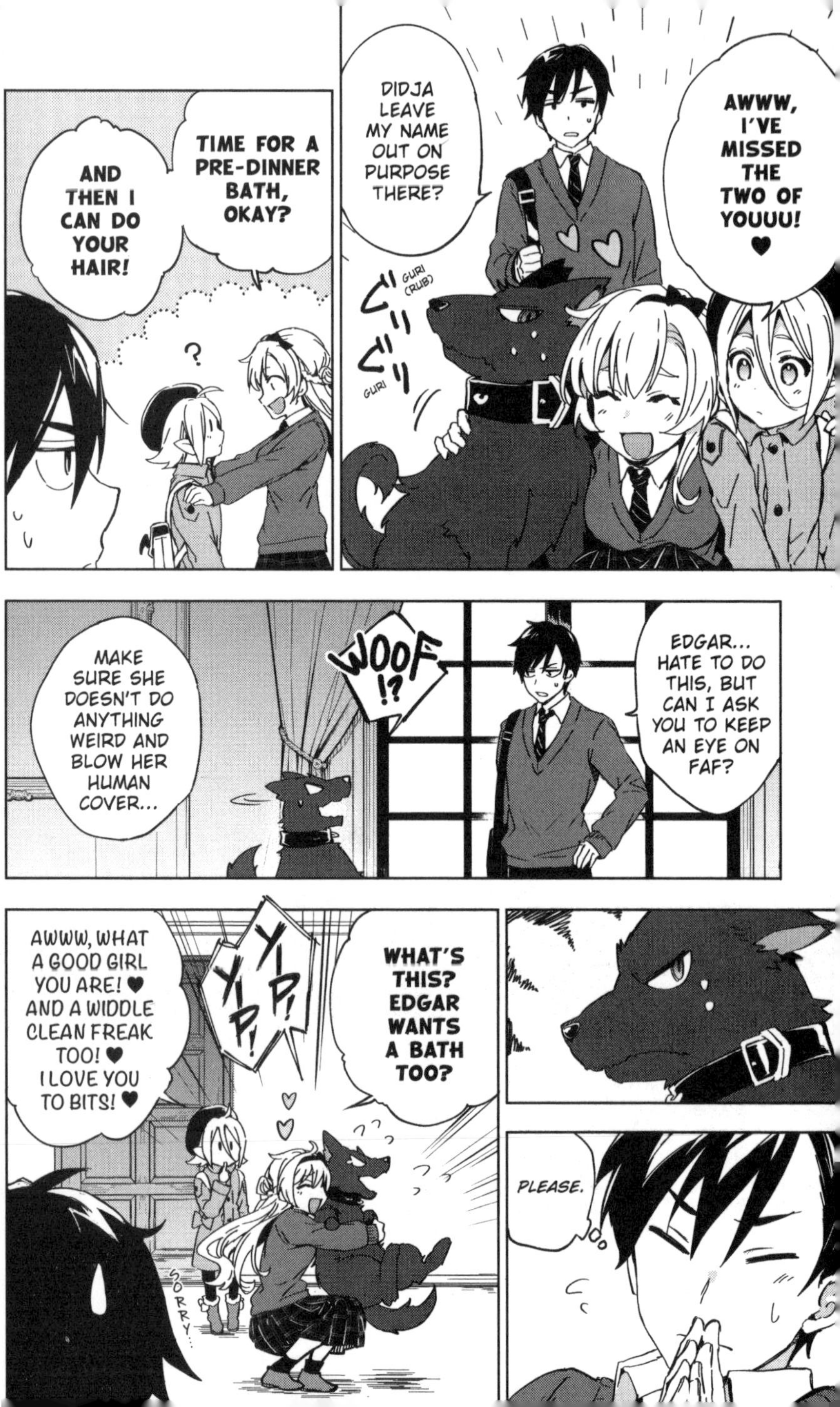
AWWW, I'VE MISSED THE TWO OF YOUUU! ♥
DIDJA LEAVE MY NAME OUT ON PURPOSE THERE?
GURI (RUB)
GURI
TIME FOR A PRE-DINNER BATH, OKAY?
AND THEN I CAN DO YOUR HAIR!
?
EDGAR... HATE TO DO THIS, BUT CAN I ASK YOU TO KEEP AN EYE ON FAF?
WOOF!?
MAKE SURE SHE DOESN'T DO ANYTHING WEIRD AND BLOW HER HUMAN COVER...
PLEASE.
WHAT'S THIS? EDGAR WANTS A BATH TOO?
YIP! YIP!
AWWW, WHAT A GOOD GIRL YOU ARE! ♥ AND A WIDDLE CLEAN FREAK TOO! ♥ I LOVE YOU TO BITS! ♥
SORRY...

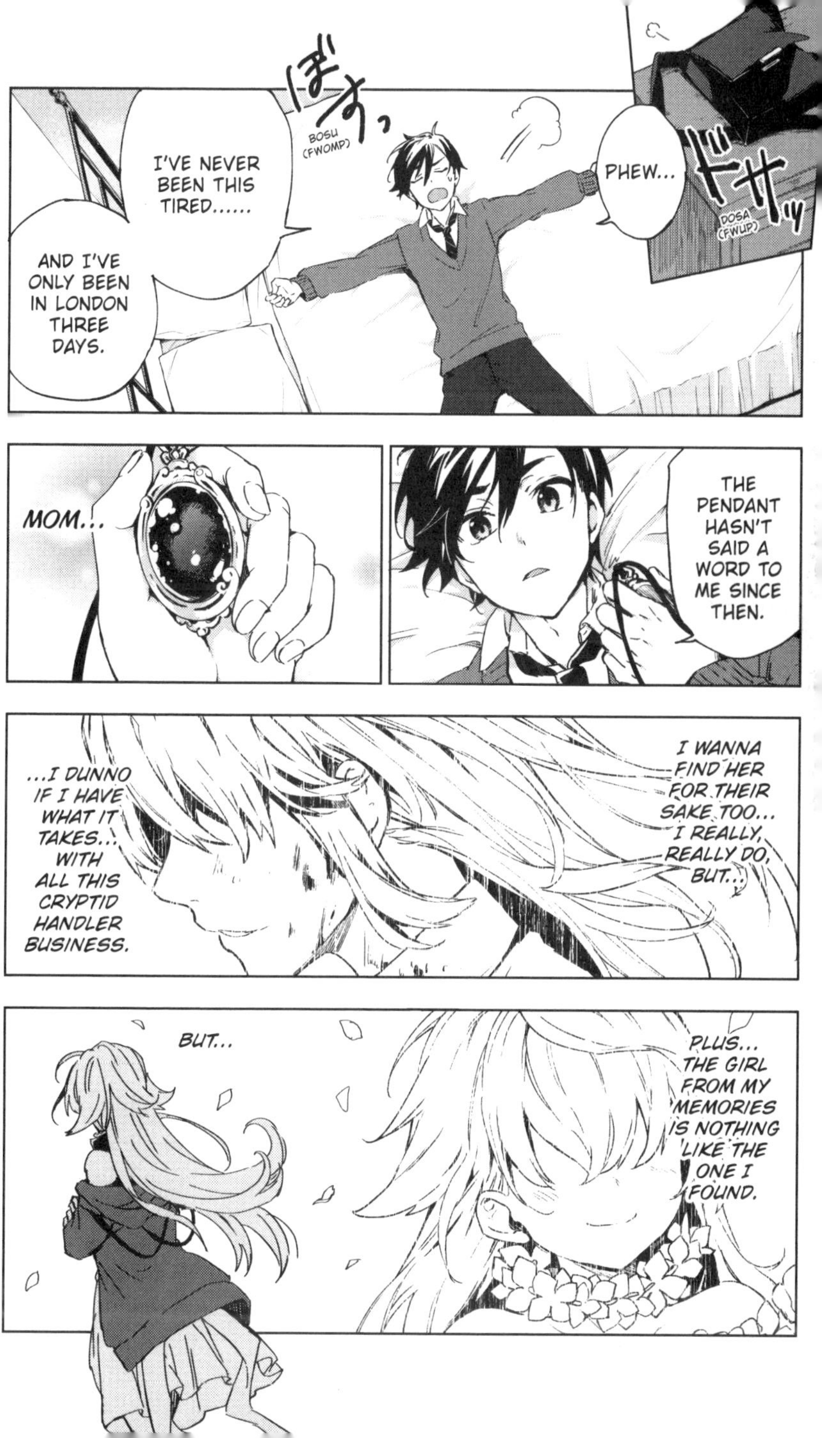
ドサッ
DOSA (FWUP)
PHEW...
ぼすっ
BOSU (FWOMP)
I'VE NEVER BEEN THIS TIRED......
AND I'VE ONLY BEEN IN LONDON THREE DAYS.
THE PENDANT HASN'T SAID A WORD TO ME SINCE THEN.
MOM...
I WANNA FIND HER FOR THEIR SAKE TOO... I REALLY, REALLY DO, BUT...
...I DUNNO IF I HAVE WHAT IT TAKES... WITH ALL THIS CRYPTID HANDLER BUSINESS.
PLUS... THE GIRL FROM MY MEMORIES IS NOTHING LIKE THE ONE I FOUND.
BUT...

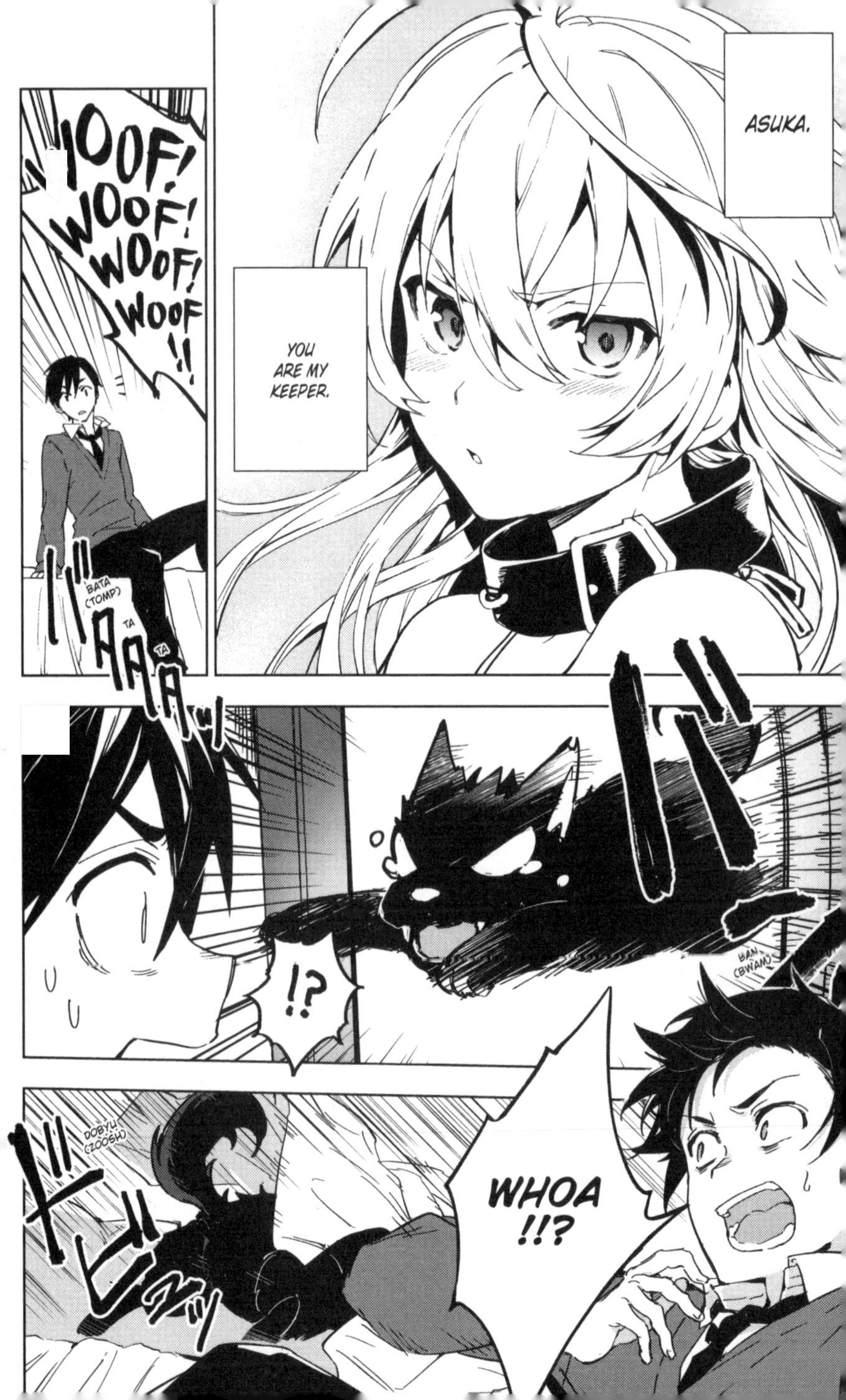
ASUKA.
YOU ARE MY KEEPER.
WOOF! WOOF! WOOF! WOOF!!!
BATA (TOMP)
TA
TA
BAN (BWAM)
!?
WHOA!!?
DOBYU (ZOOSH)

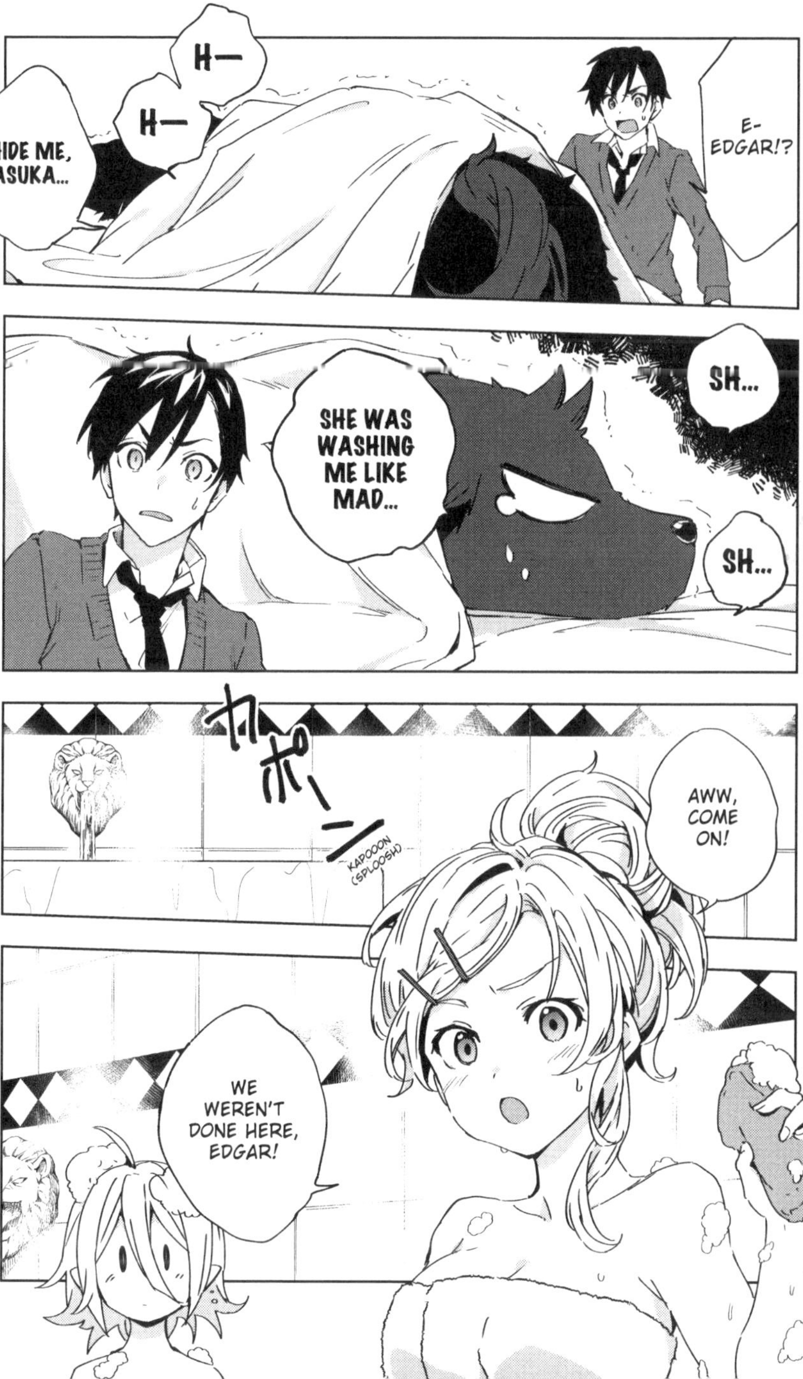
E-EDGAR!?
H—
H—
HIDE ME, ASUKA...
SH...
SH...
SHE WAS WASHING ME LIKE MAD...
カポーン
KAPOOON (SPLOOSH)
AWW, COME ON!
WE WEREN'T DONE HERE, EDGAR!

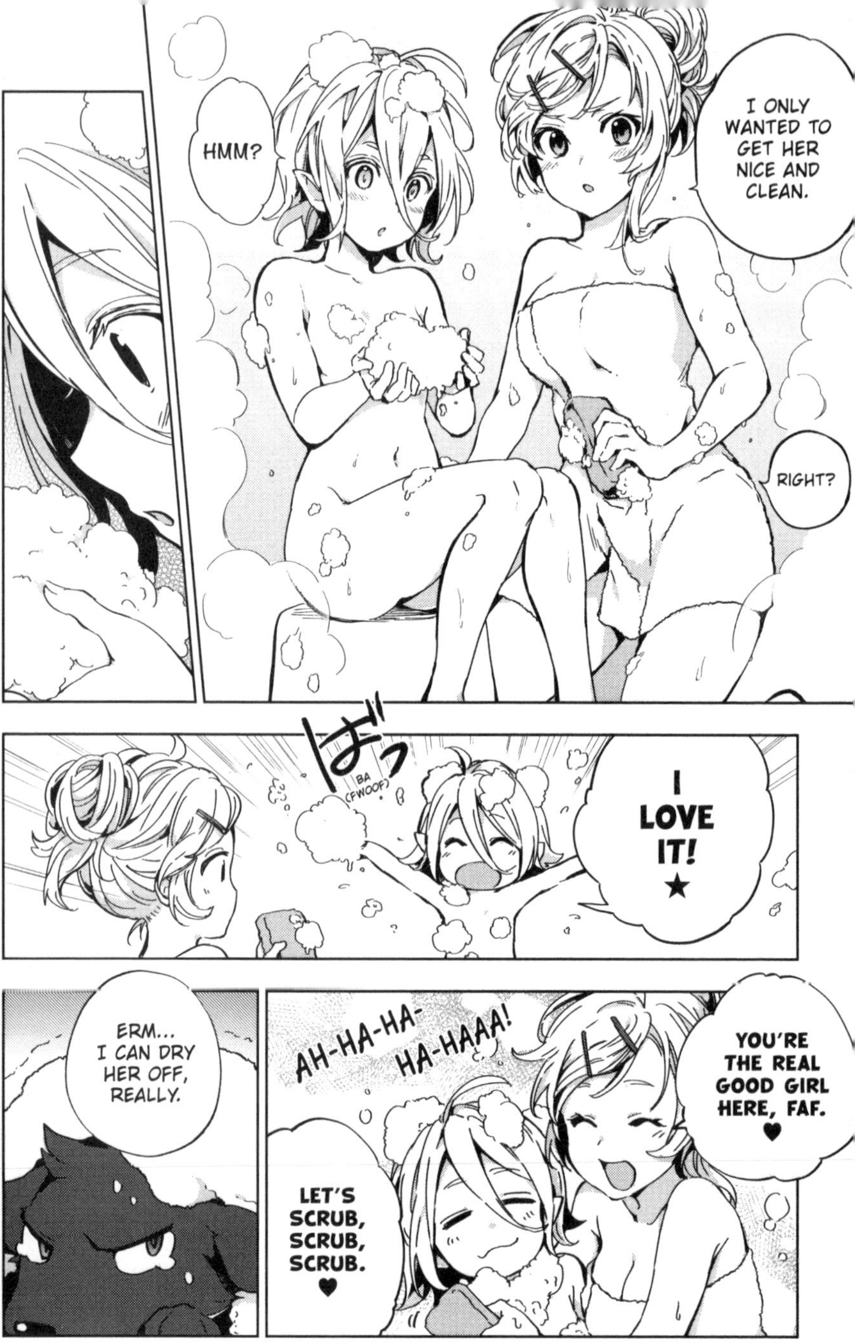
I ONLY WANTED TO GET HER NICE AND CLEAN.
HMM?
RIGHT?
ばっ
BA (FWOOF)
I LOVE IT! ★
YOU'RE THE REAL GOOD GIRL HERE, FAF. ♥
AH-HA-HA-HA-HAAA!
LET'S SCRUB, SCRUB, SCRUB. ♥
ERM... I CAN DRY HER OFF, REALLY.

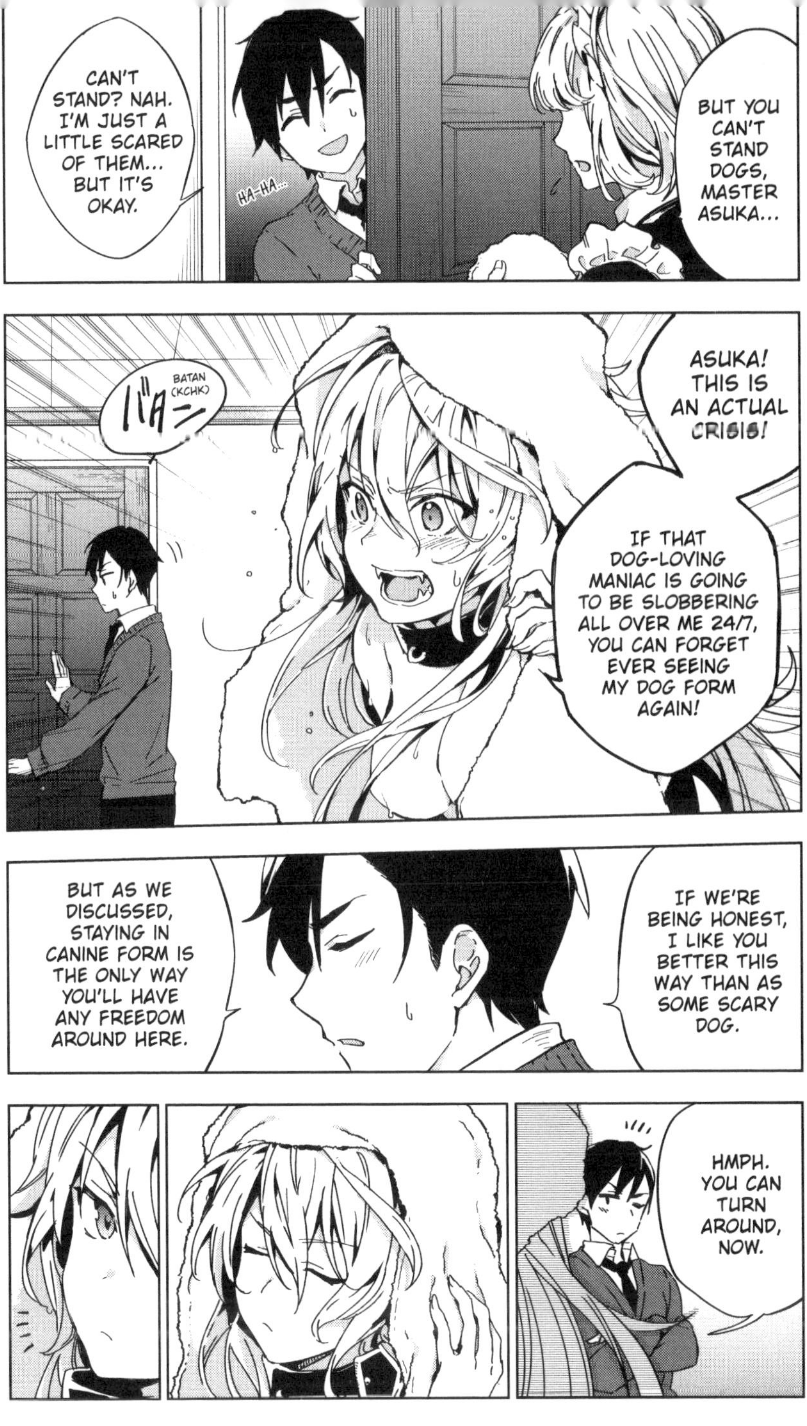
BUT YOU CAN'T STAND DOGS, MASTER ASUKA...
HA-HA...
CAN'T STAND? NAH. I'M JUST A LITTLE SCARED OF THEM... BUT IT'S OKAY.
ASUKA! THIS IS AN ACTUAL CRISIS!
IF THAT DOG-LOVING MANIAC IS GOING TO BE SLOBBERING ALL OVER ME 24/7, YOU CAN FORGET EVER SEEING MY DOG FORM AGAIN!
バタン
BATAN (KCHK)
IF WE'RE BEING HONEST, I LIKE YOU BETTER THIS WAY THAN AS SOME SCARY DOG.
BUT AS WE DISCUSSED, STAYING IN CANINE FORM IS THE ONLY WAY YOU'LL HAVE ANY FREEDOM AROUND HERE.
HMPH. YOU CAN TURN AROUND, NOW.

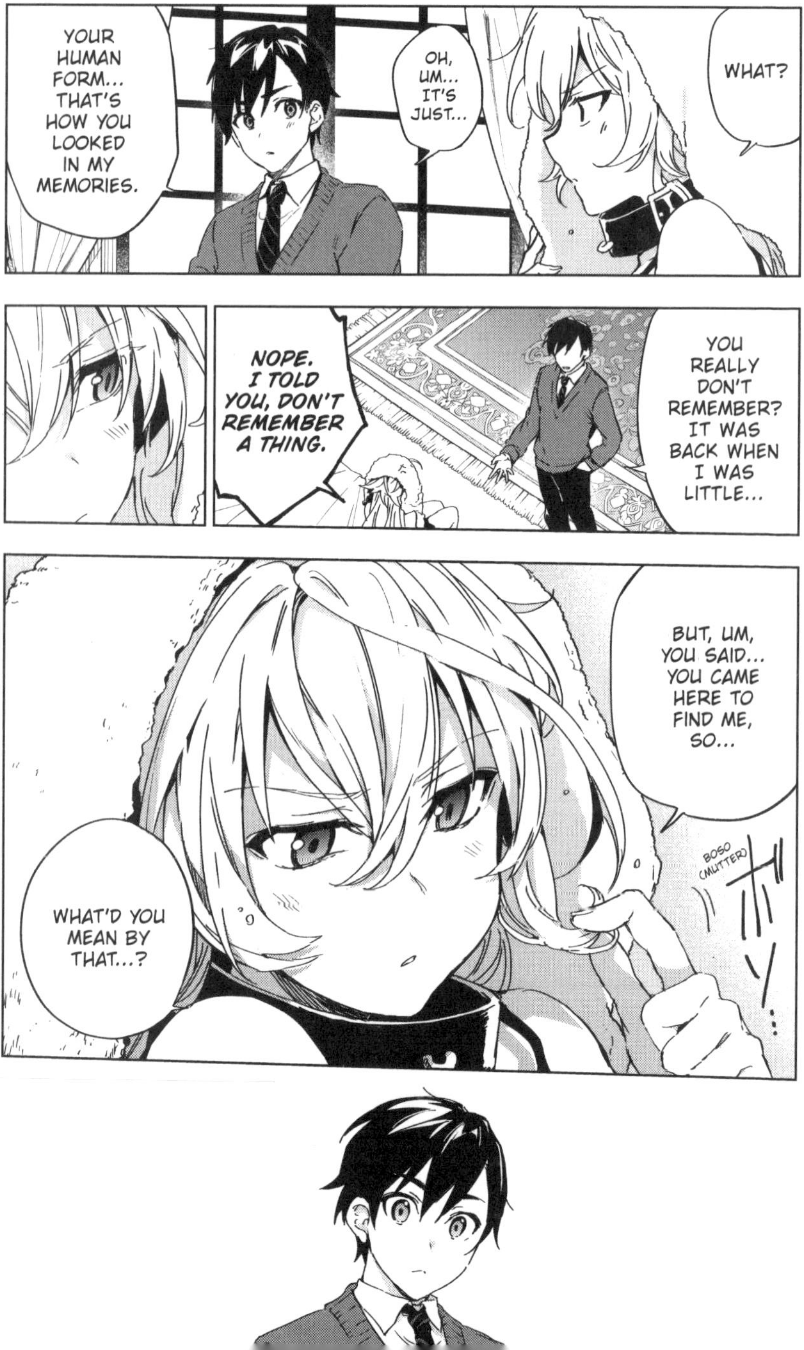
WHAT?
OH, UM... IT'S JUST...
YOUR HUMAN FORM... THAT'S HOW YOU LOOKED IN MY MEMORIES.
YOU REALLY DON'T REMEMBER? IT WAS BACK WHEN I WAS LITTLE...
NOPE. I TOLD YOU, DON'T REMEMBER A THING.
BUT, UM, YOU SAID... YOU CAME HERE TO FIND ME, SO...
BOSO (MUTTER)
WHAT'D YOU MEAN BY THAT...?

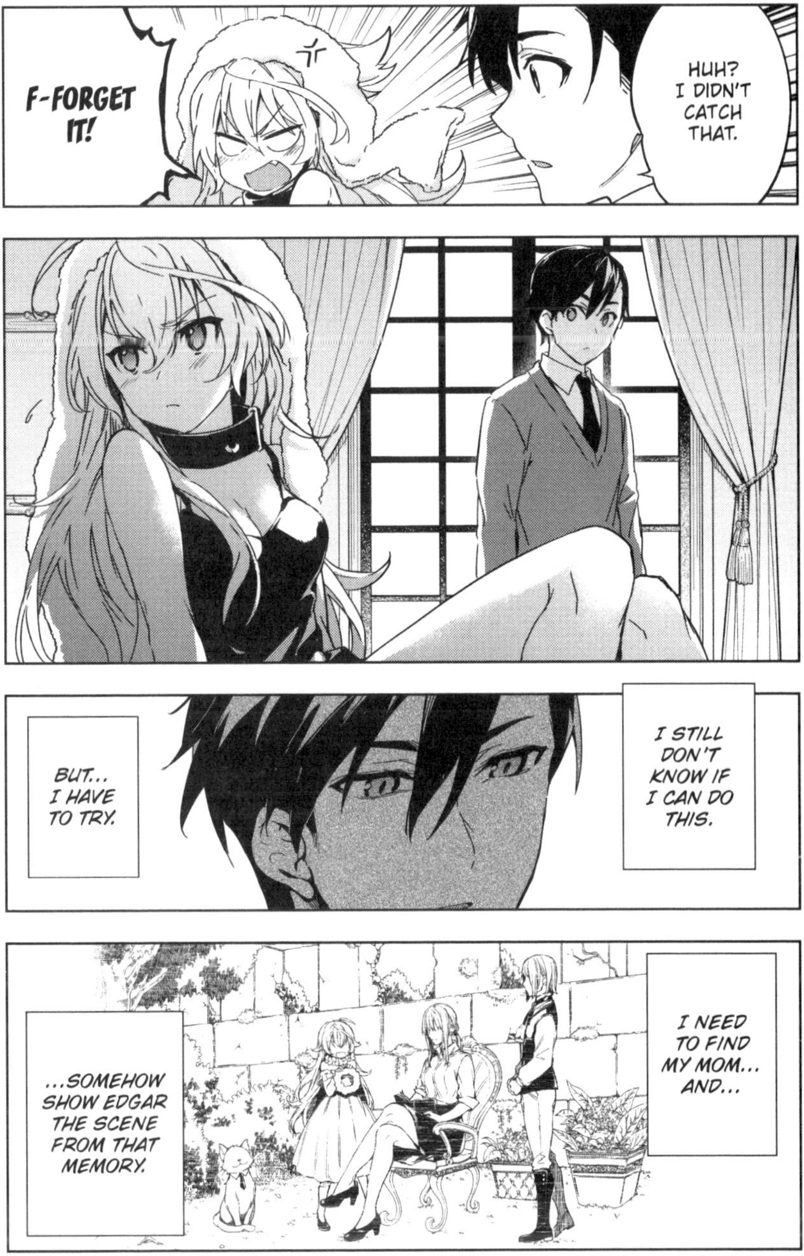
HUH? I DIDN'T CATCH THAT.
F-FORGET IT!
I STILL DON'T KNOW IF I CAN DO THIS.
BUT... I HAVE TO TRY.
I NEED TO FIND MY MOM... AND...
...SOMEHOW SHOW EDGAR THE SCENE FROM THAT MEMORY.

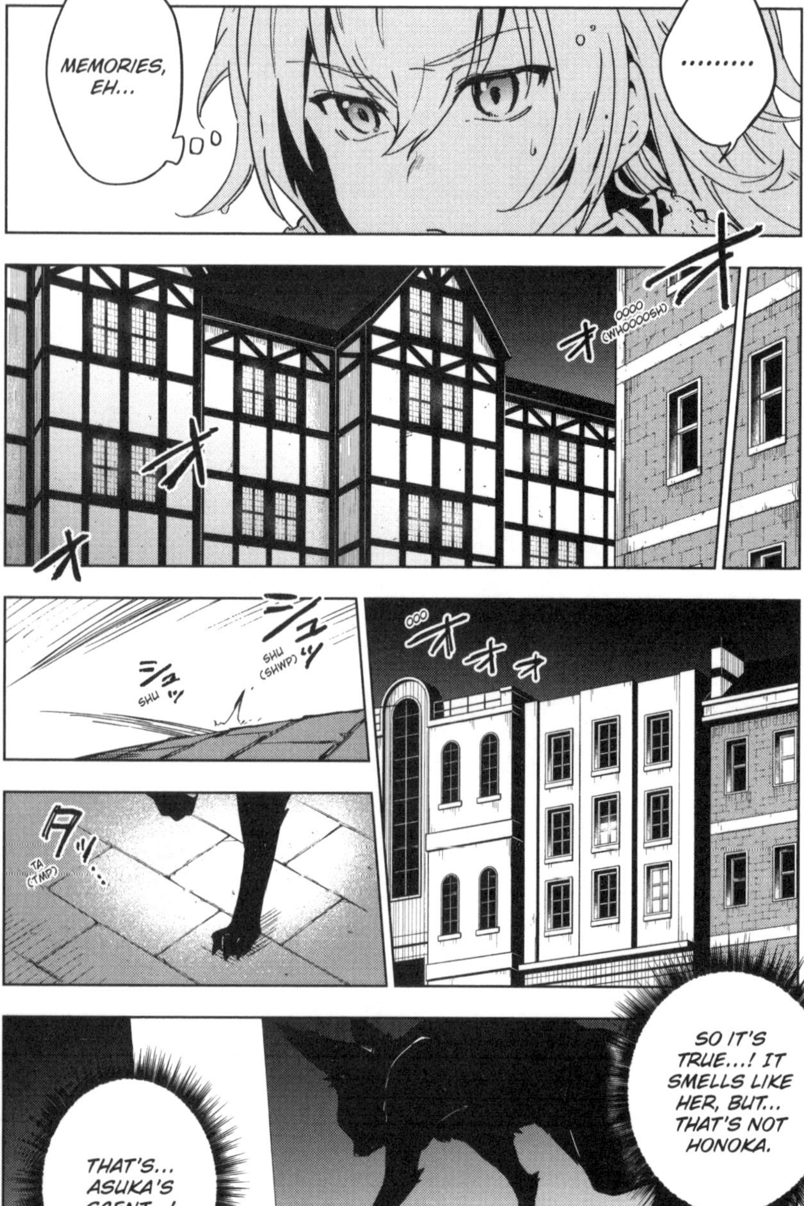
....
MEMORIES, EH...
OOOO (WHOOOOSH)
OOO
SHU (SHWP)
SHU
TA (TMP)
SO IT'S TRUE...! IT SMELLS LIKE HER, BUT... THAT'S NOT HONOKA.
THAT'S... ASUKA'S SCENT...!

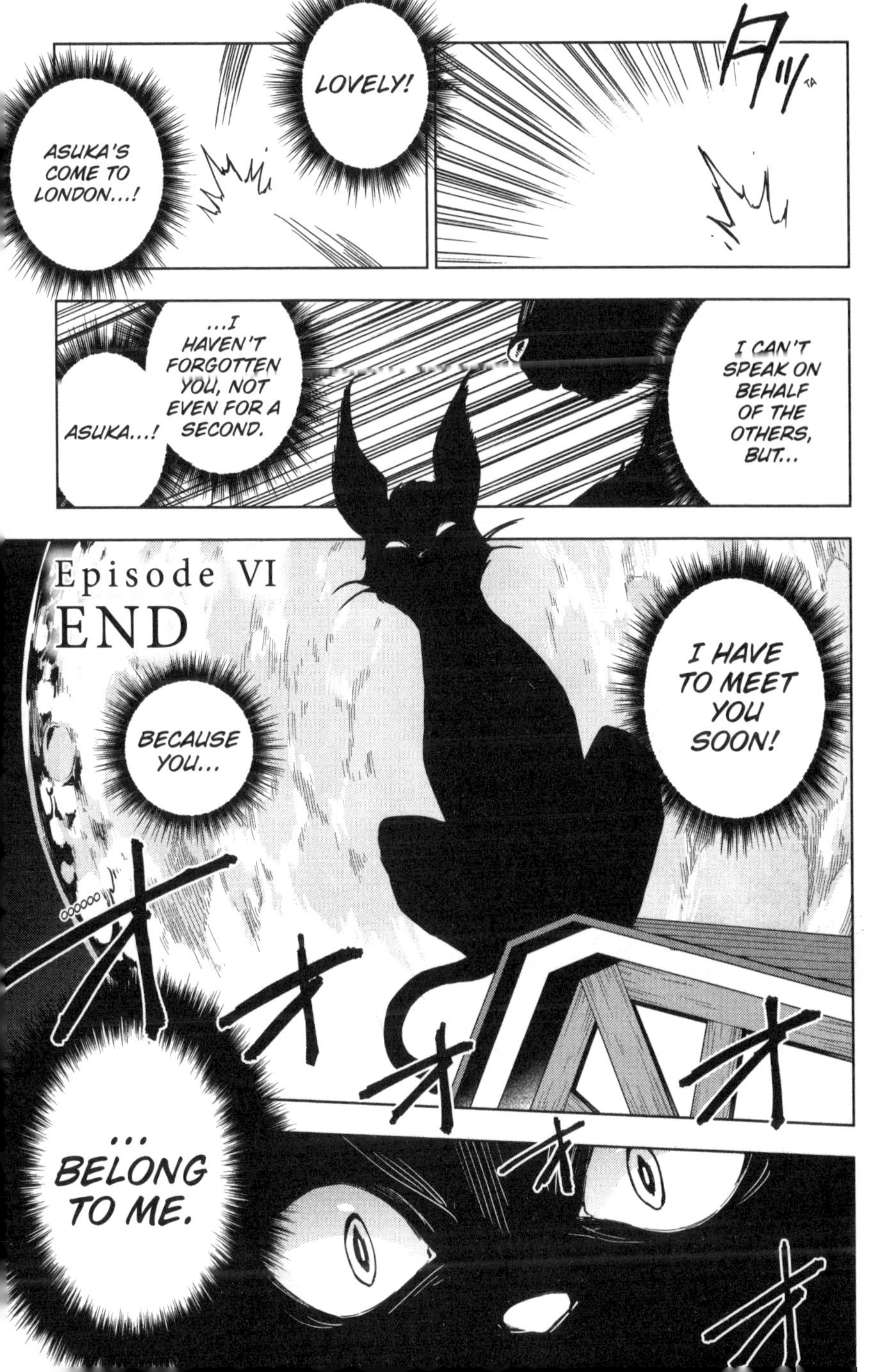
TA
LOVELY!
ASUKA'S COME TO LONDON...!
I CAN'T SPEAK ON BEHALF OF THE OTHERS, BUT...
...I HAVEN'T FORGOTTEN YOU, NOT EVEN FOR A SECOND.
ASUKA...!
I HAVE TO MEET YOU SOON!
Episode VI
END
BECAUSE YOU...
OOOOOO
...BELONG TO ME.

Bestia

MAKOTO SANDA MIYAKOKASIWA ACO ARISAKA

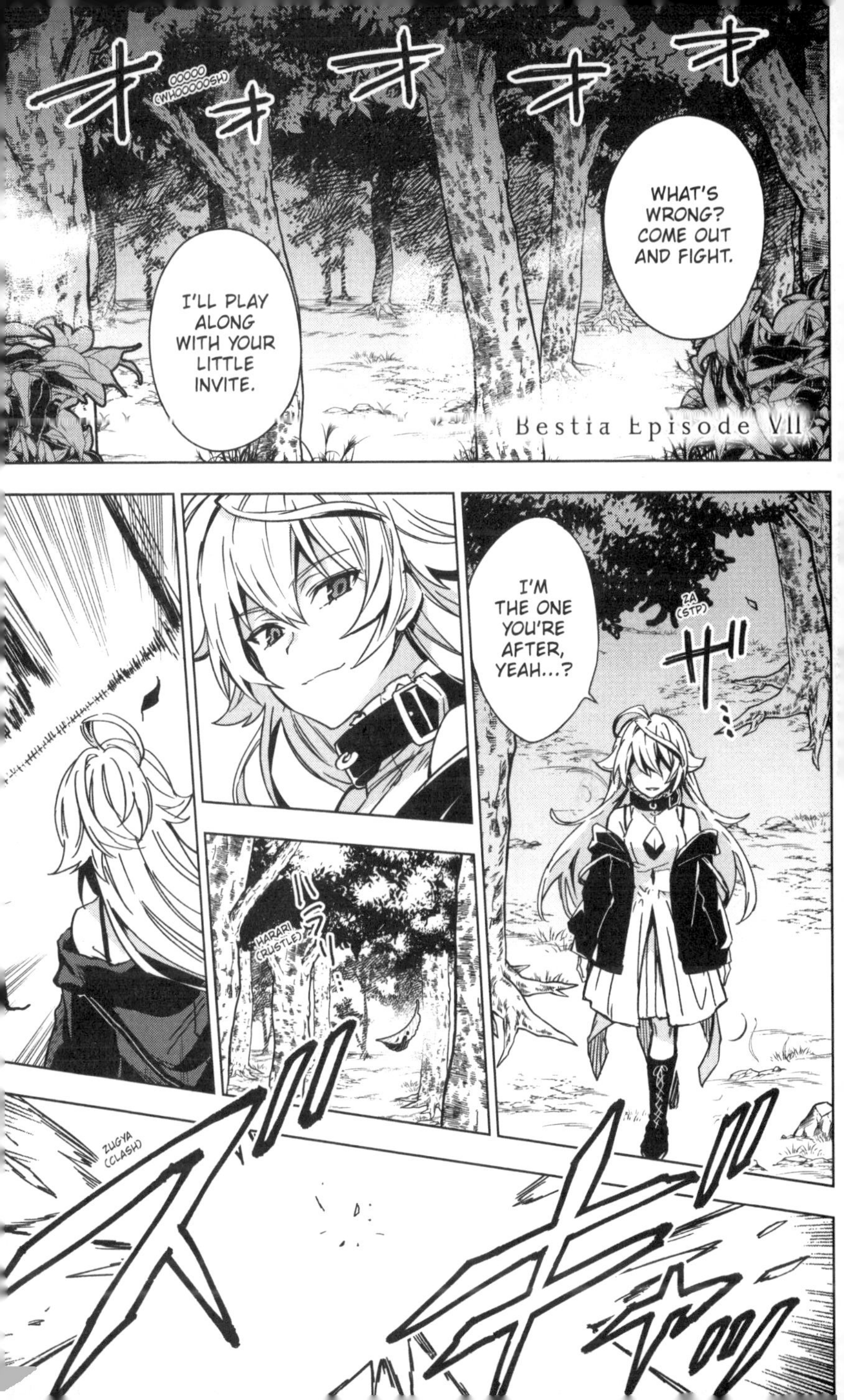
OOOOO (WHOOOOOSH)
WHAT'S WRONG? COME OUT AND FIGHT.
I'LL PLAY ALONG WITH YOUR LITTLE INVITE.
Bestia Episode VII
ZA (STP)
I'M THE ONE YOU'RE AFTER, YEAH...?
HARARI (RUSTLE)
ZUGYA (CLASH)

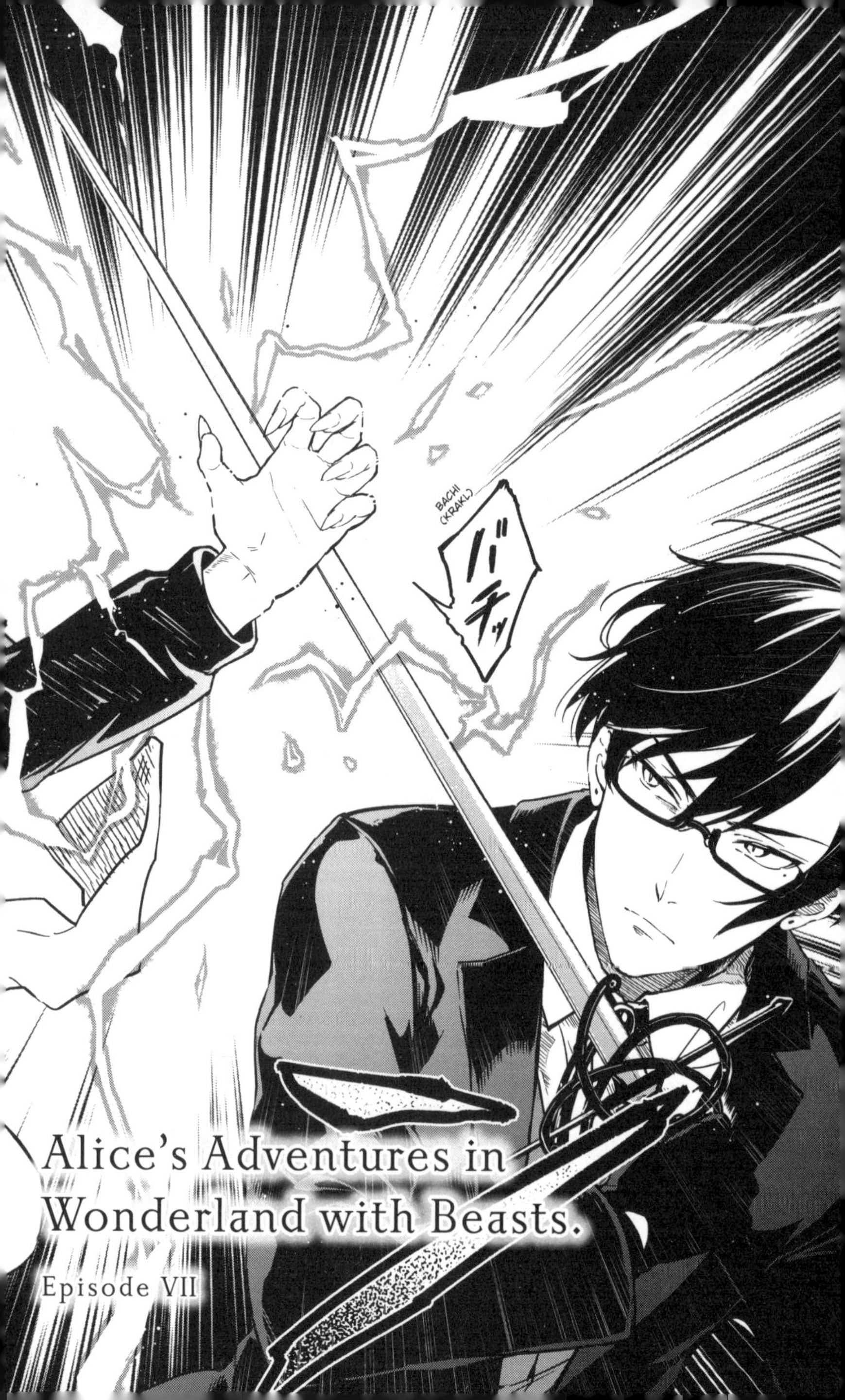
バチッ
BACHI (KRAKL)

Alice's Adventures in Wonderland with Beasts.

Episode VII

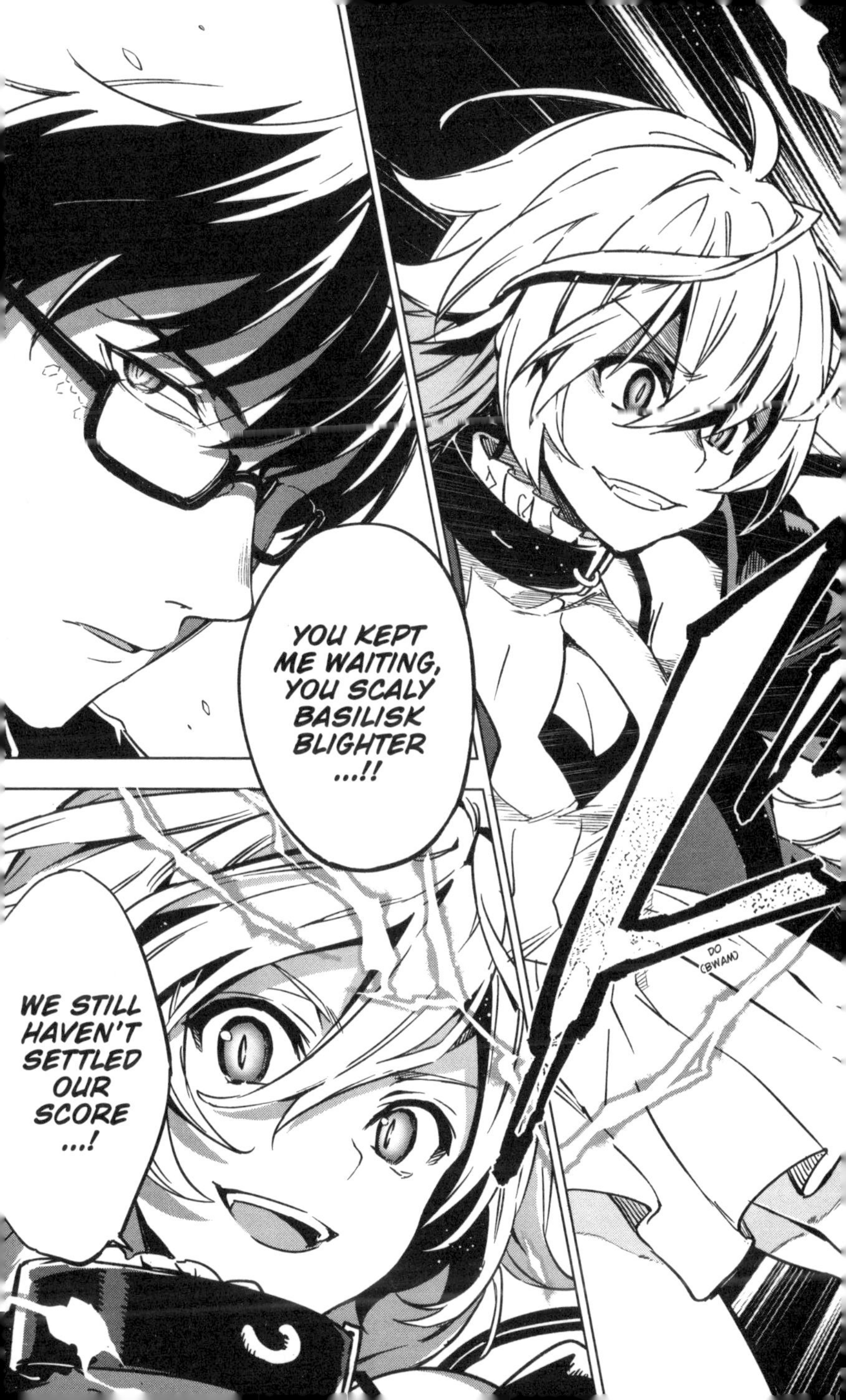
YOU KEPT ME WAITING, YOU SCALY BASILISK BLIGHTER ...!!
DO (BWAM)
WE STILL HAVEN'T SETTLED OUR SCORE ...!

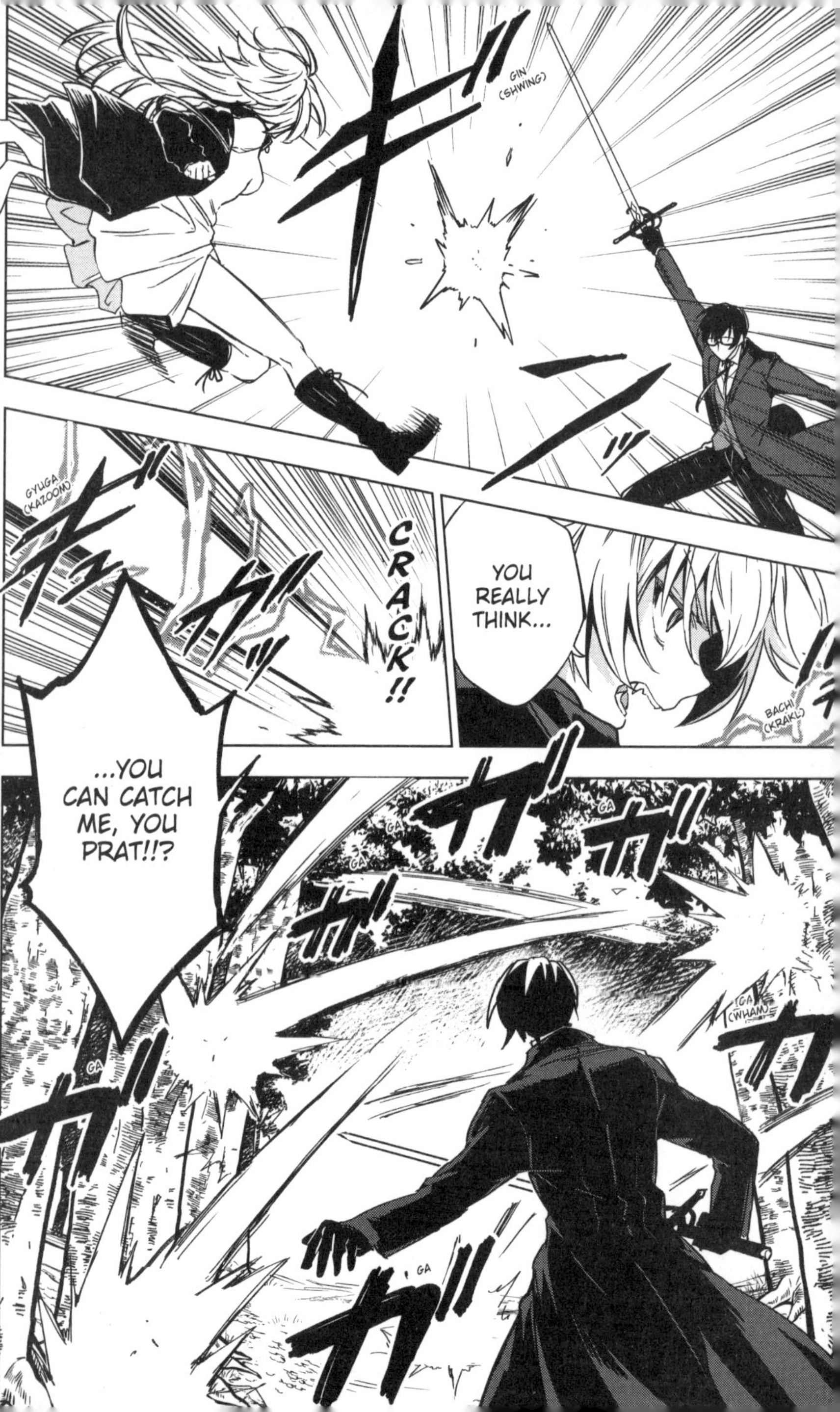
GIN (SHWING)
YOU REALLY THINK...
BACHI (KRAKL)
GYUGA (KAZOOM)
CRACK!!
...YOU CAN CATCH ME, YOU PRAT!!?
GA
GA
GA
GA (WHAM)
GA
GA

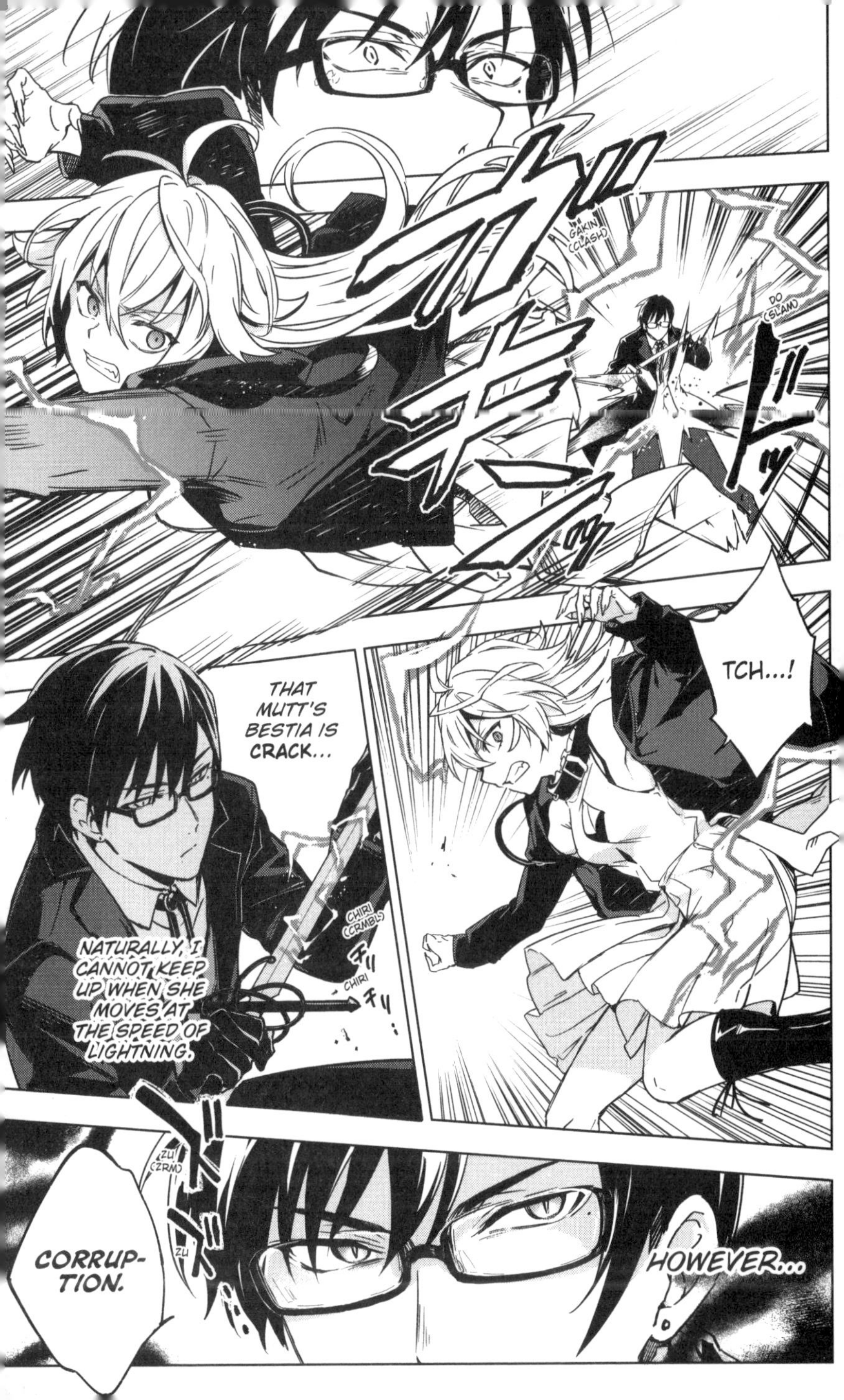
GAKIN (CLASH)
DO (SLAM)
TCH...!
THAT MUTT'S BESTIA IS CRACK...
CHIRI (CRMBL)
CHIRI
NATURALLY, I CANNOT KEEP UP WHEN SHE MOVES AT THE SPEED OF LIGHTNING.
HOWEVER...
ZU (ZRM)
ZU
CORRUP-TION.

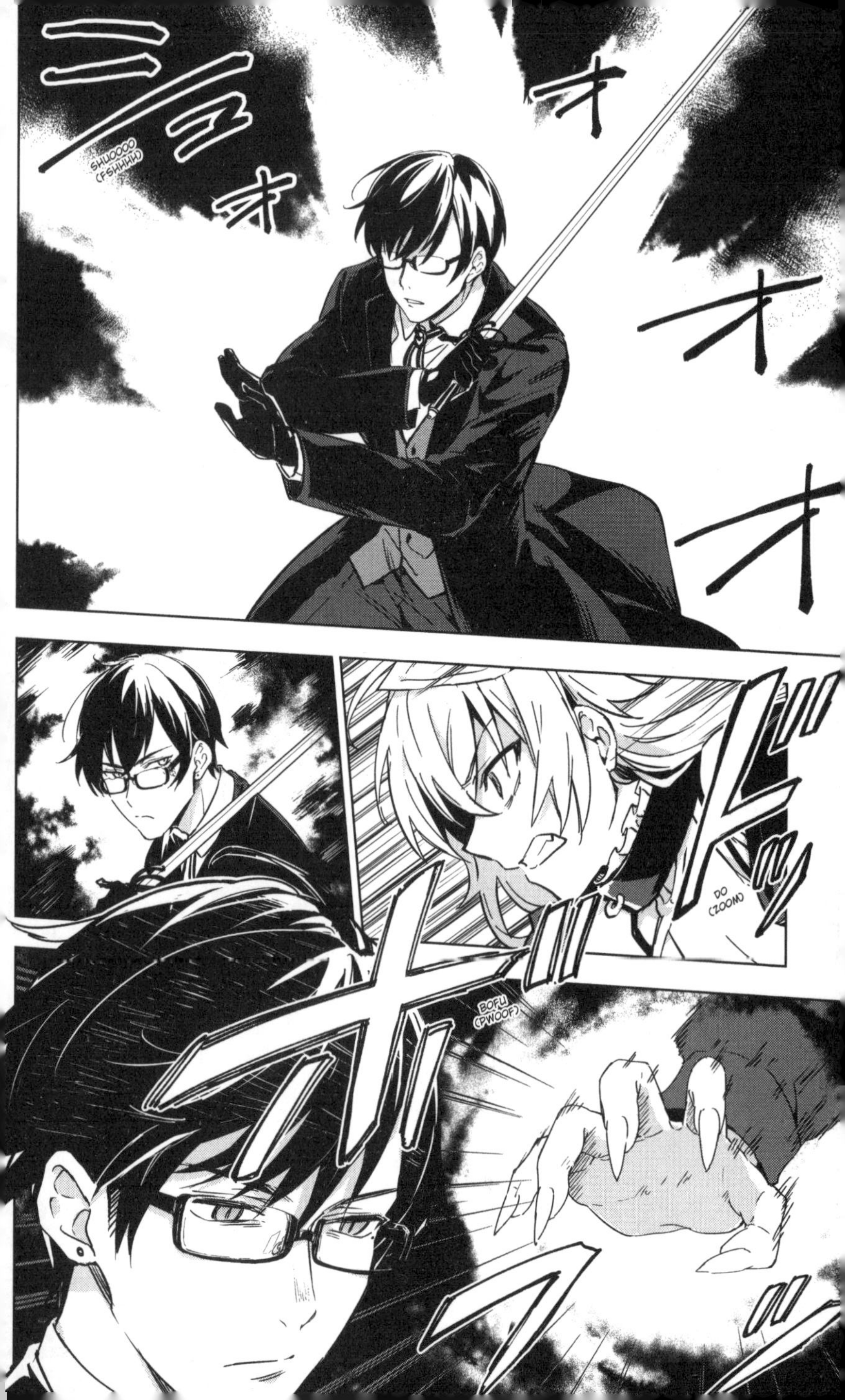
SHUOOOO (FSHHHH)
DO (ZOOM)
BOFU (PWOOF)

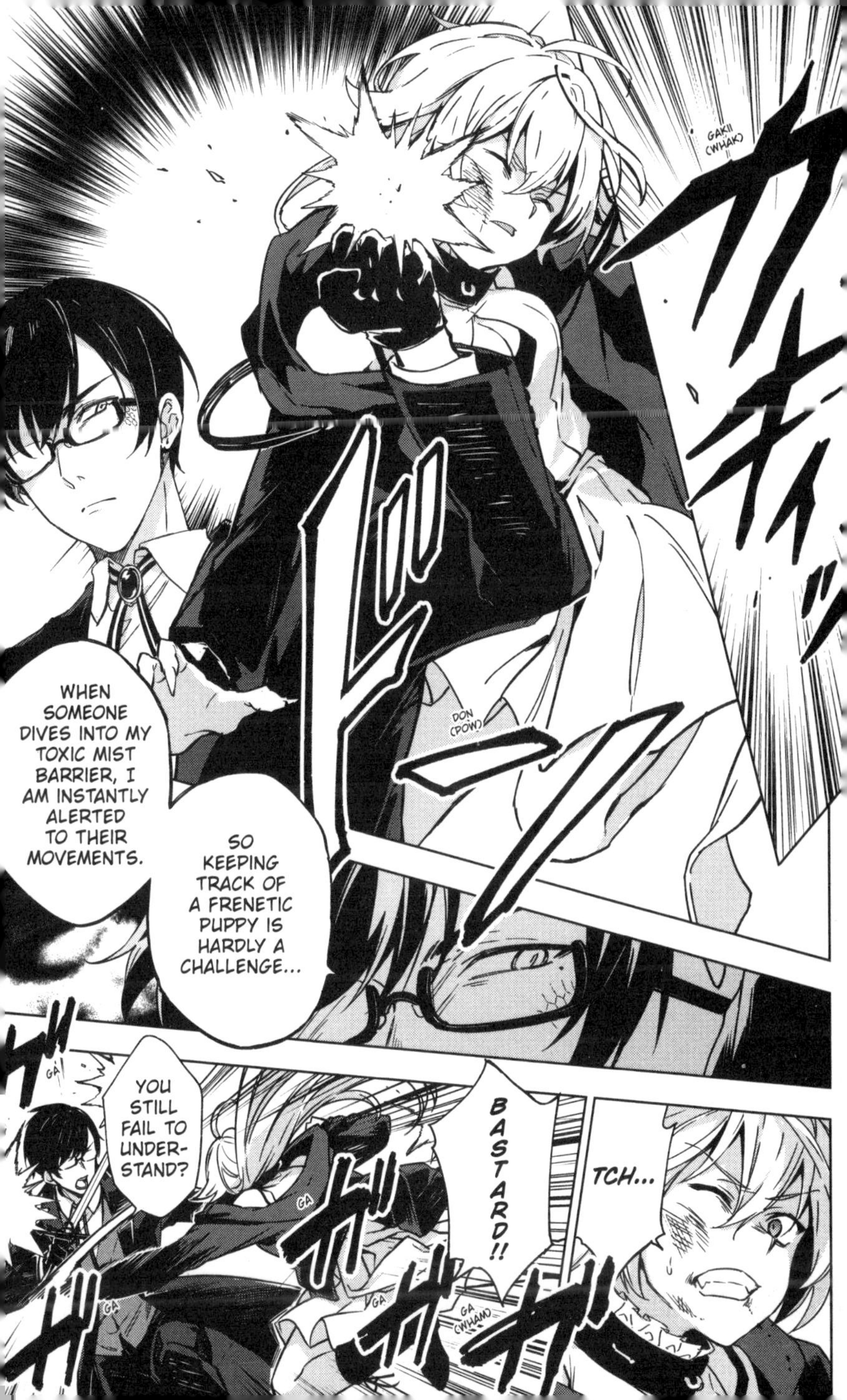
GAKII (WHAK)
DON (POW)
WHEN SOMEONE DIVES INTO MY TOXIC MIST BARRIER, I AM INSTANTLY ALERTED TO THEIR MOVEMENTS.
SO KEEPING TRACK OF A FRENETIC PUPPY IS HARDLY A CHALLENGE...
TCH...
BASTARD!!
YOU STILL FAIL TO UNDER-STAND?
GA
GA
GA
GA
GA (WHAM)

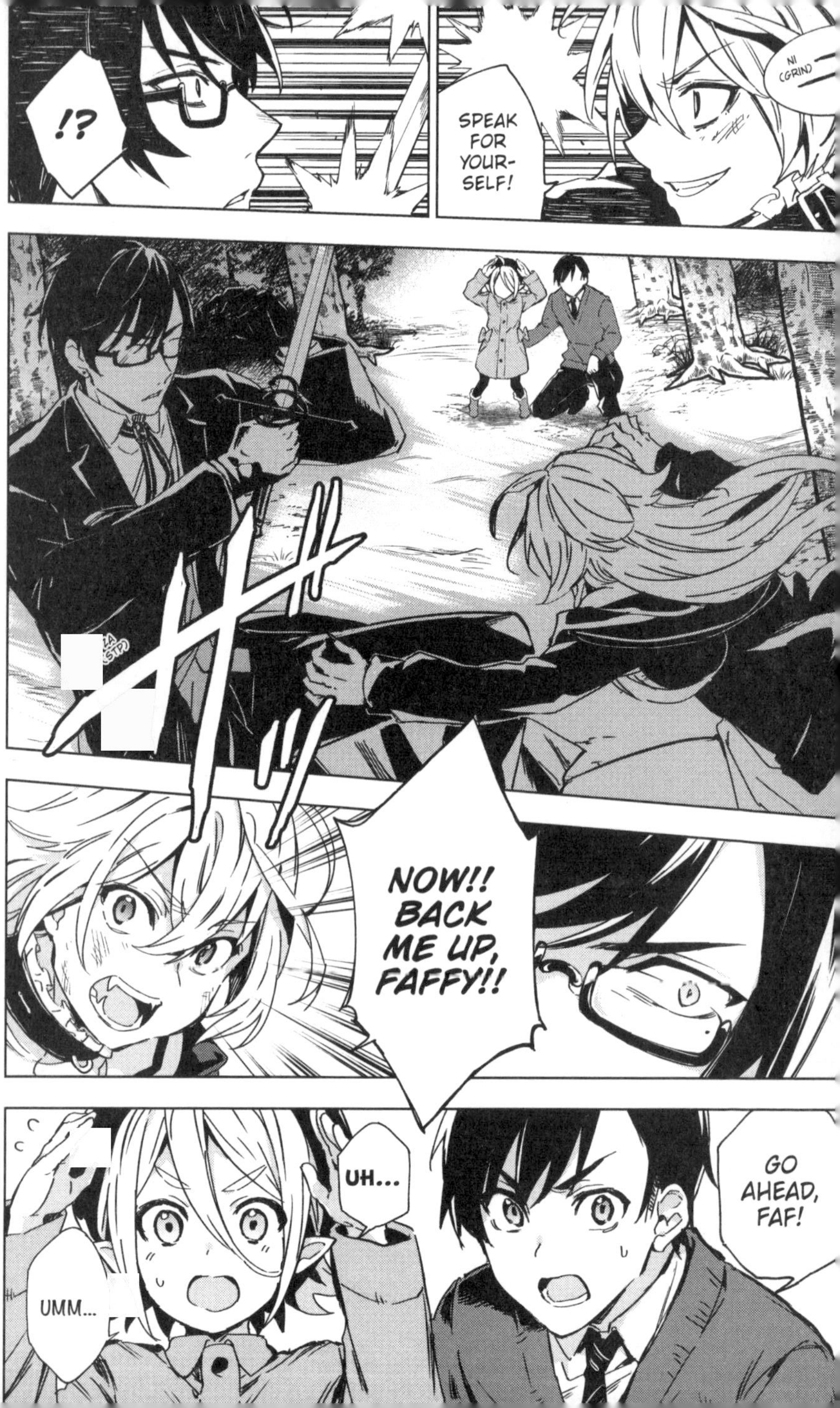
NI (GRIND)
SPEAK FOR YOUR-SELF!
!?
ZA (STP)
NOW!! BACK ME UP, FAFFY!!
GO AHEAD, FAF!
UH...
UMM...

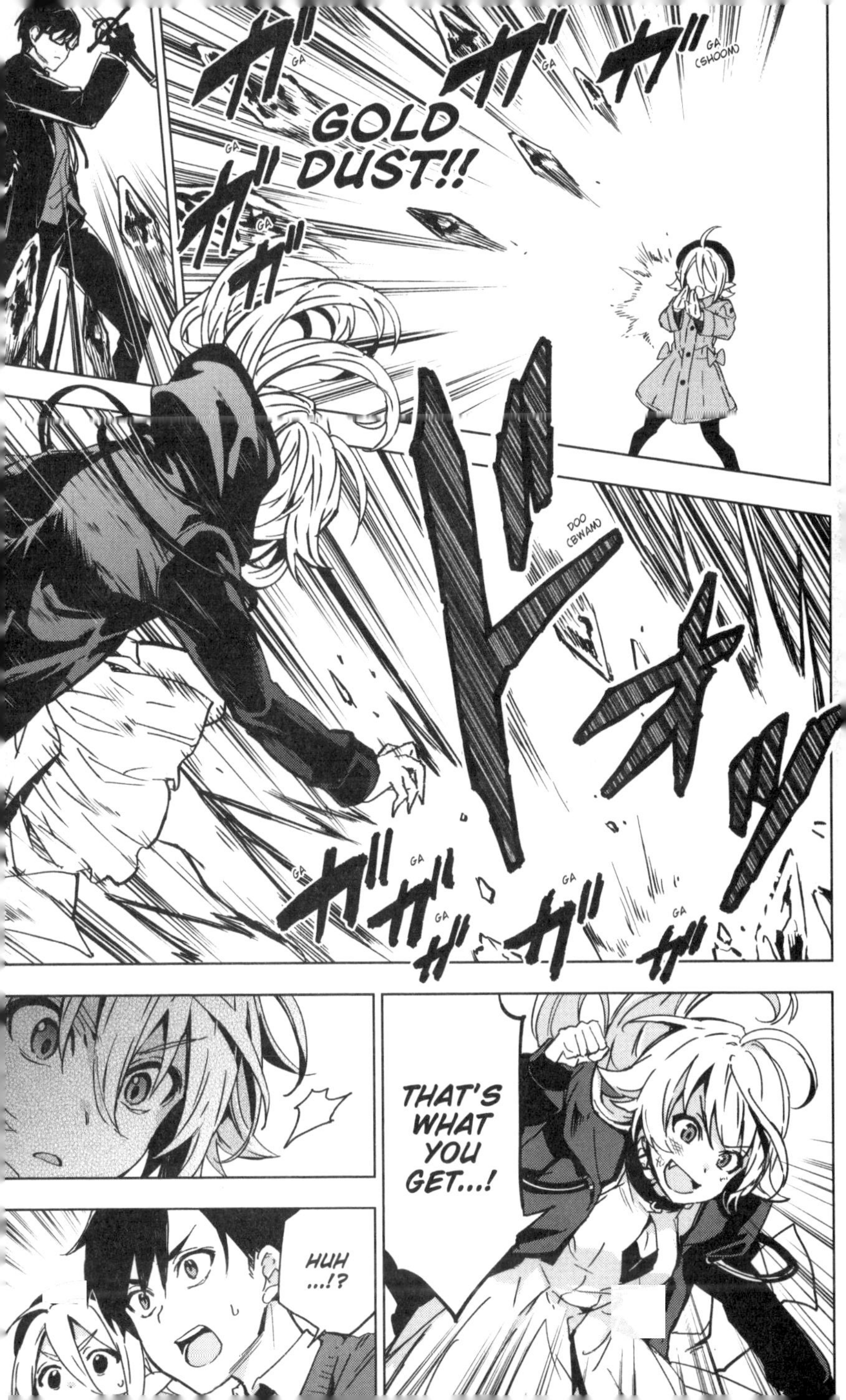
GA (SHOOM)
GA
GA
GOLD DUST!!
GA
GA
DOO (BWAM)
GA
GA
GA
GA
GA
GA
THAT'S WHAT YOU GET...!
HUH ...!?

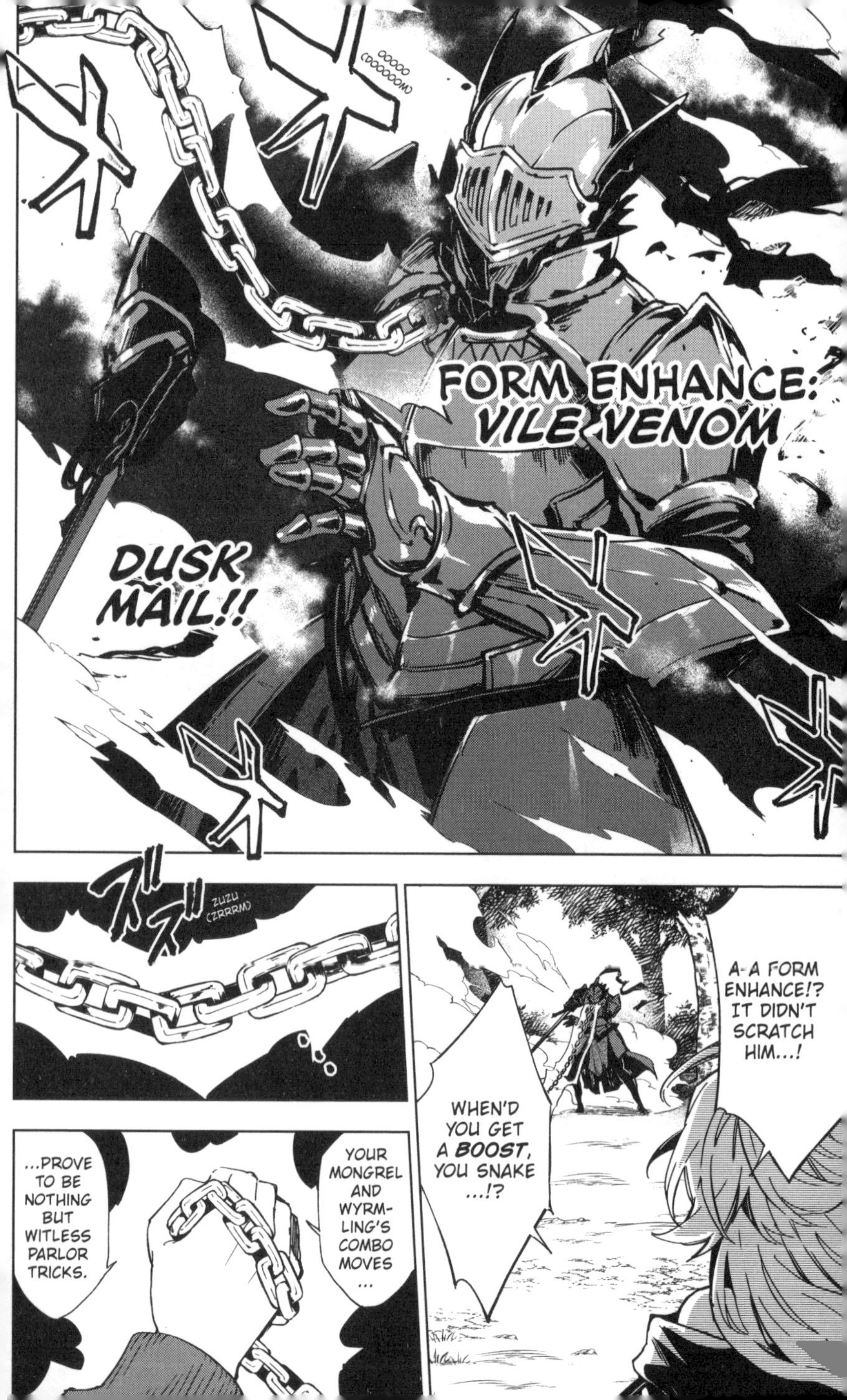
OOOOO (DOOOOOOM)
FORM ENHANCE: *VILE VENOM*
DUSK MAIL!!
A-A FORM ENHANCE!? IT DIDN'T SCRATCH HIM...!
WHEN'D YOU GET A *BOOST*, YOU SNAKE ...!?
ZUZU (ZRRRM)
YOUR MONGREL AND WYRM-LING'S COMBO MOVES ...
...PROVE TO BE NOTHING BUT WITLESS PARLOR TRICKS.

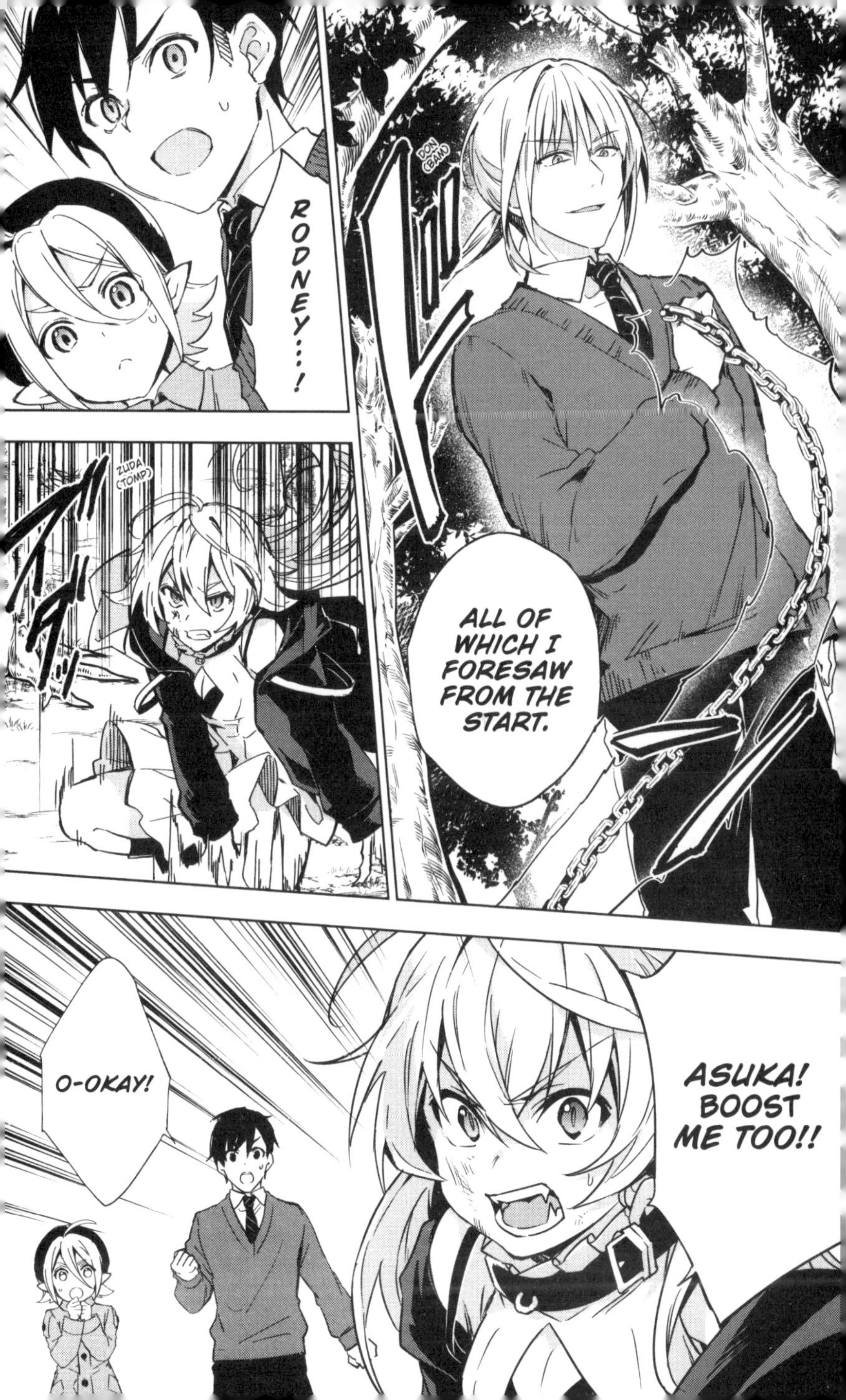
DON (BAM)
ALL OF WHICH I FORESAW FROM THE START.
RODNEY...!
ZUDA (TOMP)
ASUKA! BOOST ME TOO!!
O-OKAY!

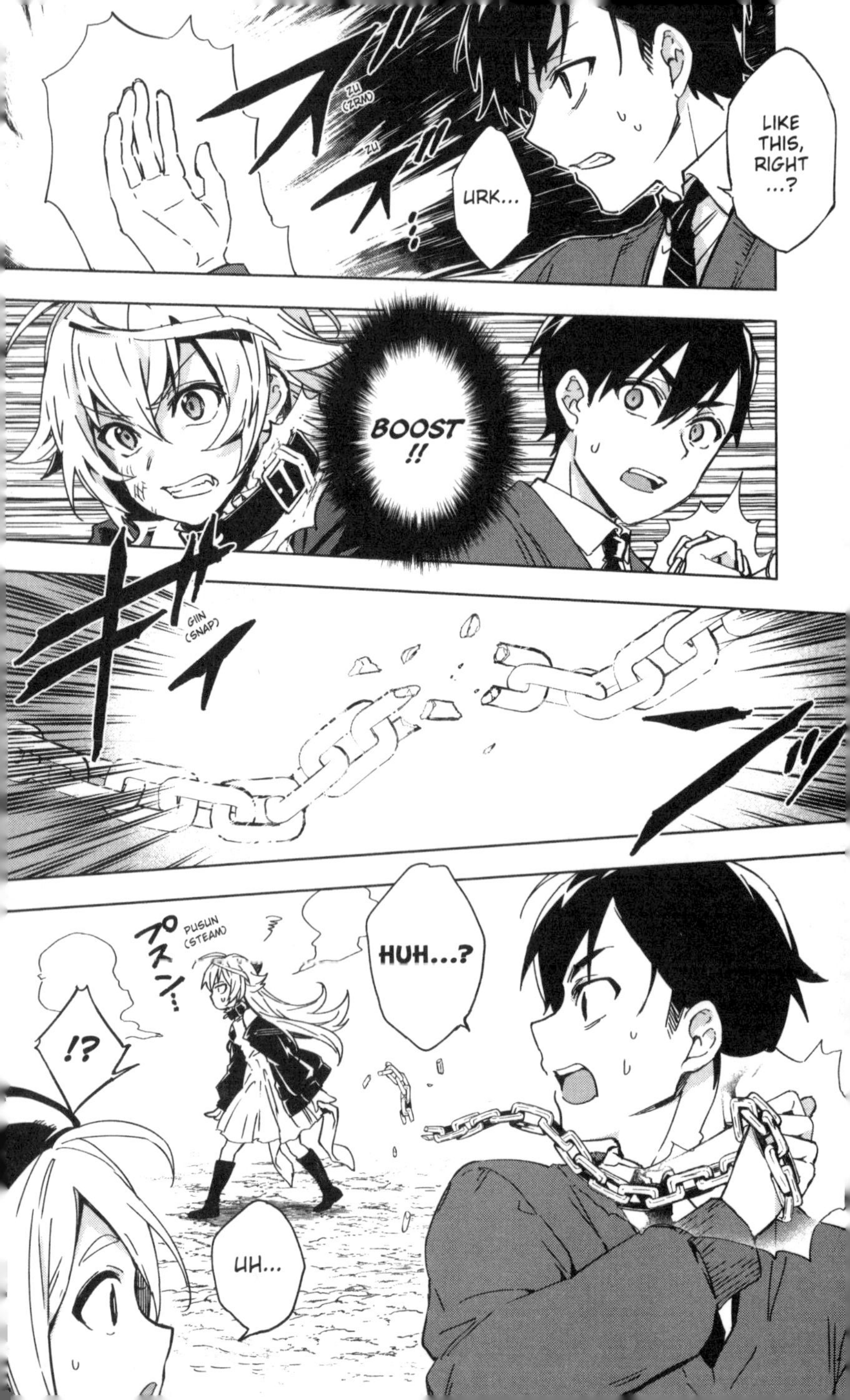
LIKE THIS, RIGHT ...?
URK...
ZU (ZRM)
ZU
BOOST !!
GIIN (SNAP)
HUH...?
PUSUN (STEAM)
!?
UH...

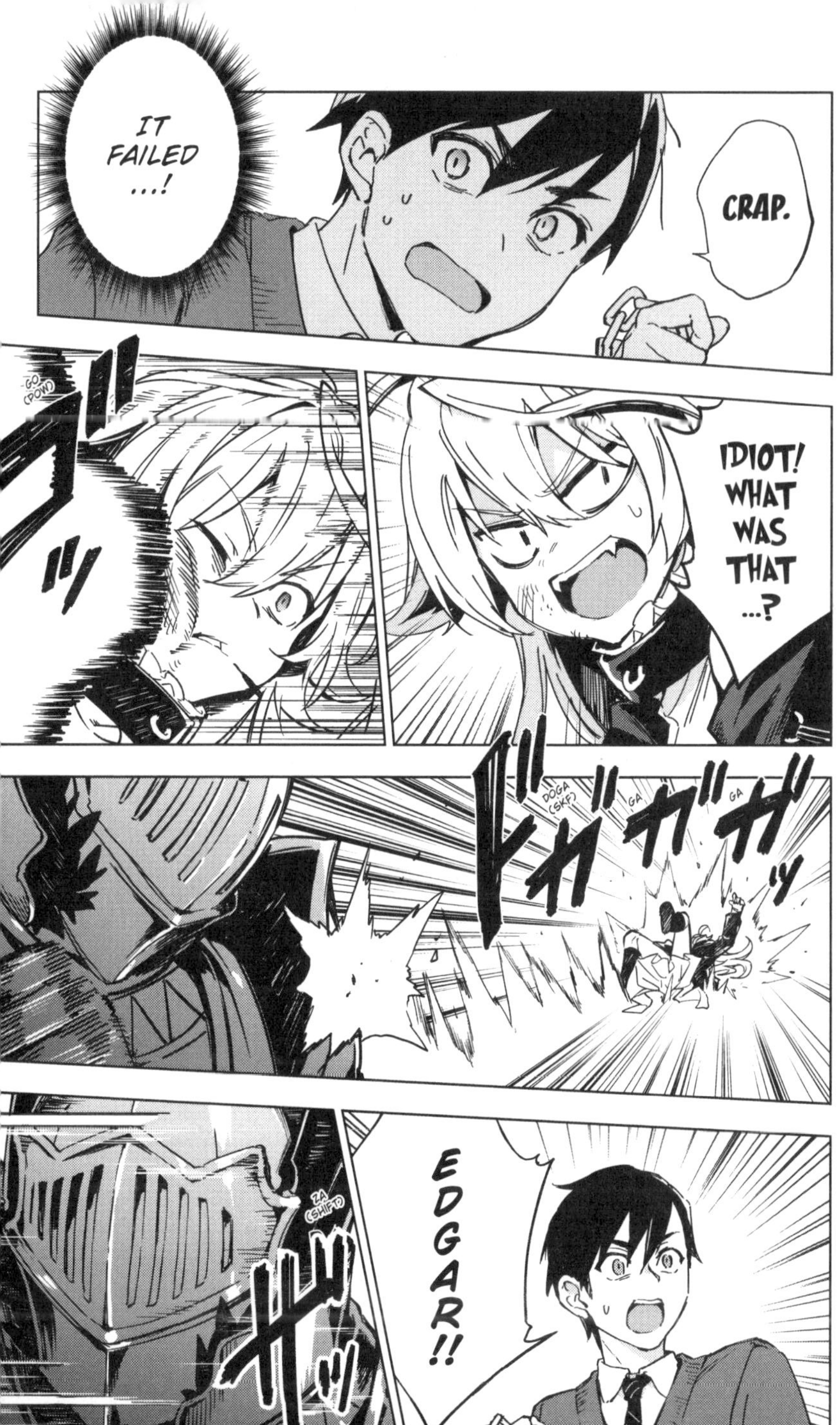
CRAP.
IT FAILED ...!
IDIOT! WHAT WAS THAT ...?
GO (POW)
DOGA (SKF)
GA
GA
EDGAR!!
ZA (SHIFT)

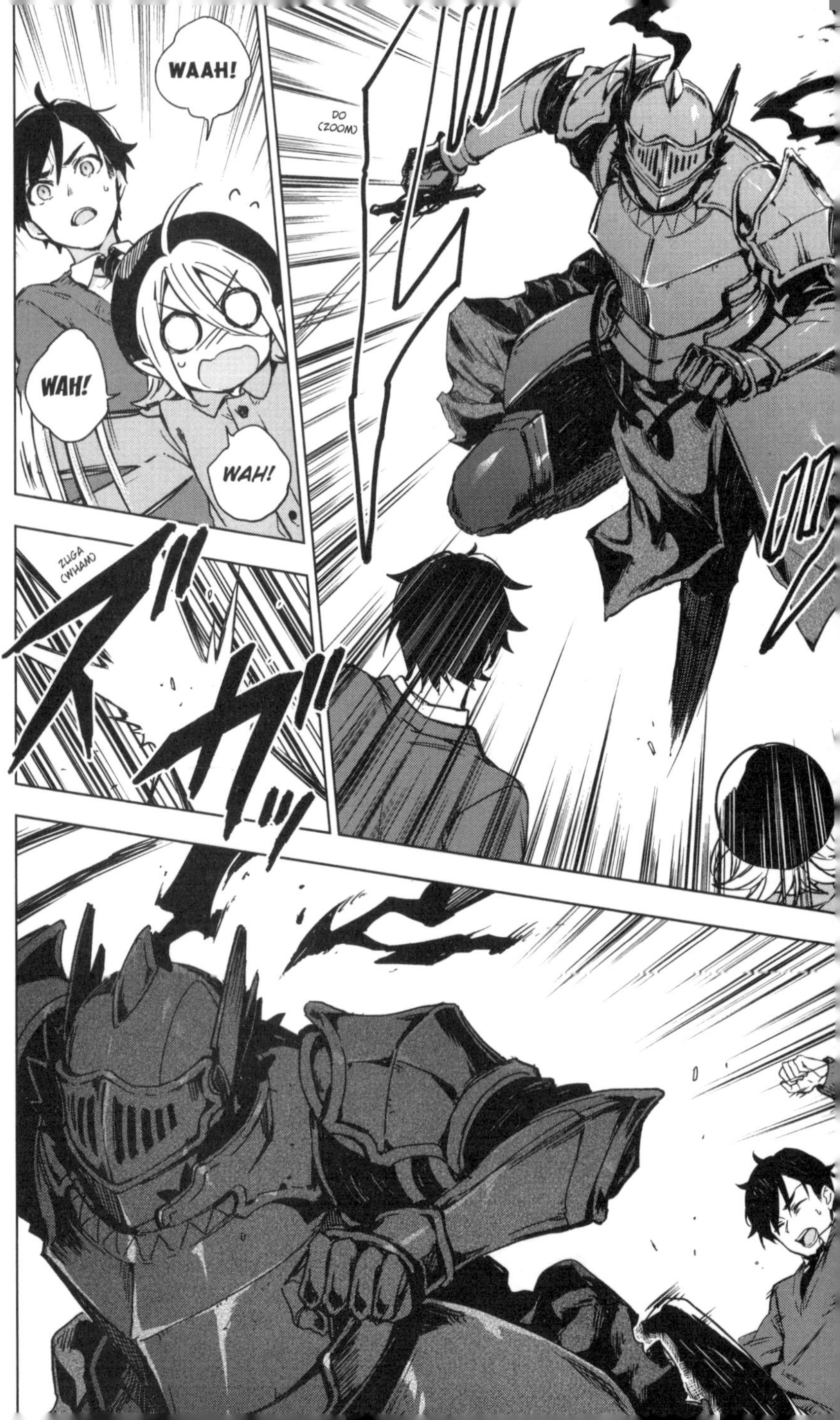
DO
(ZOOM)
WAAH!
WAH!
WAH!
ZUGA
(WHAM)

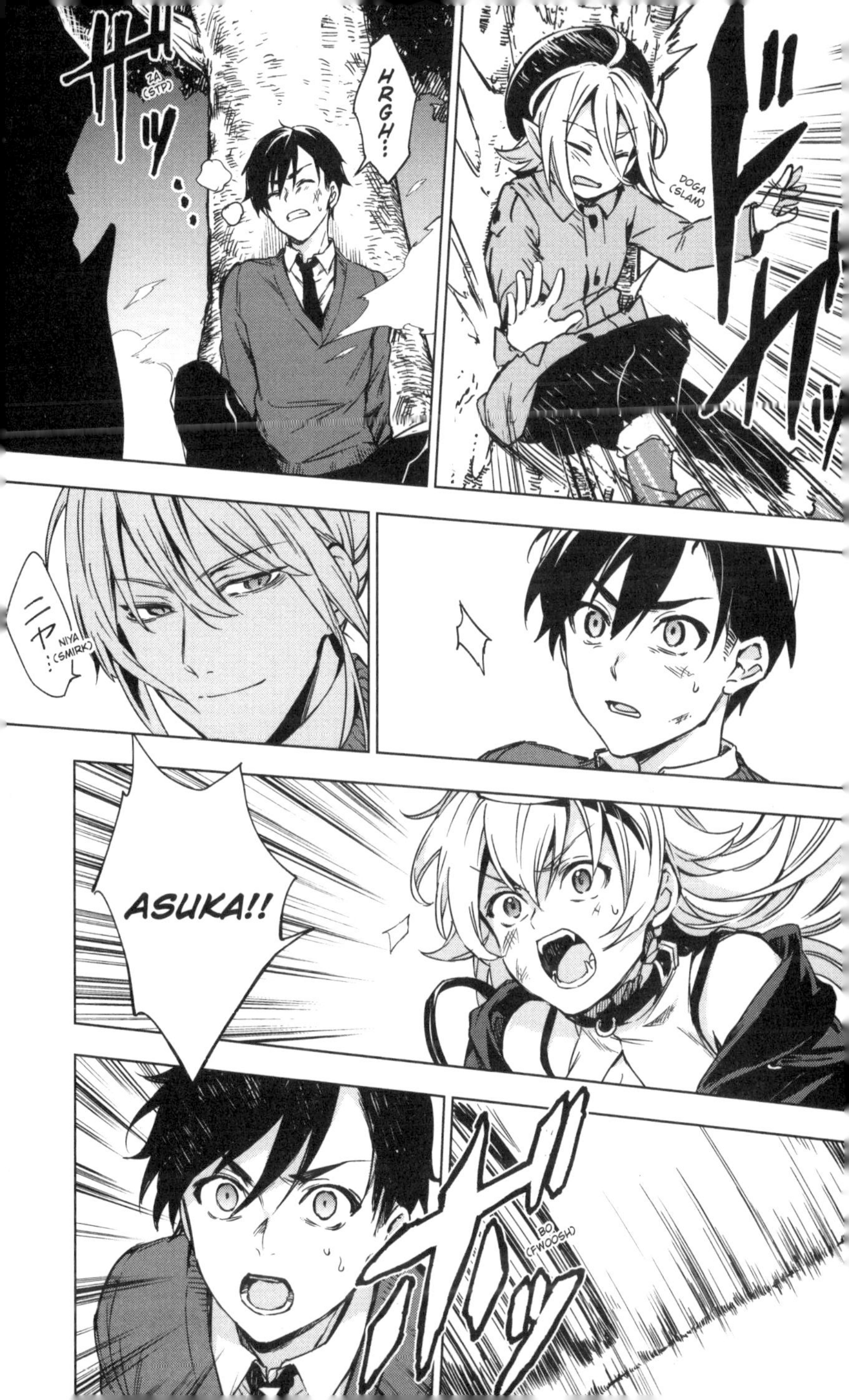
ドガッ
DOGA (SLAM)
HRGH...
ザッ
ZA (STP)
ニヤ…
NIYA (SMIRK)
ASUKA!!
ボッ
BO (FWOOSH)

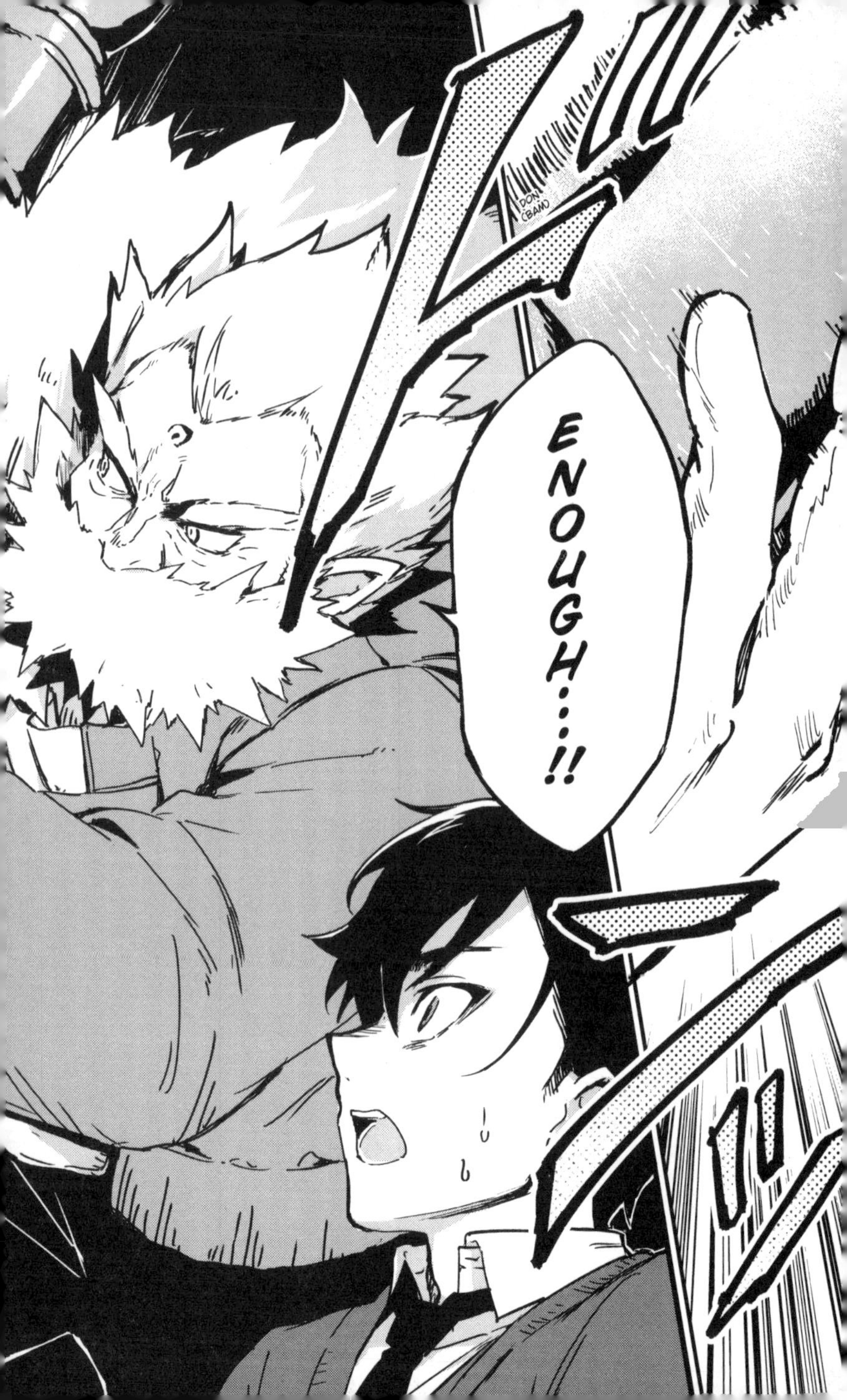
DON (BAM)
ENOUGH...!!

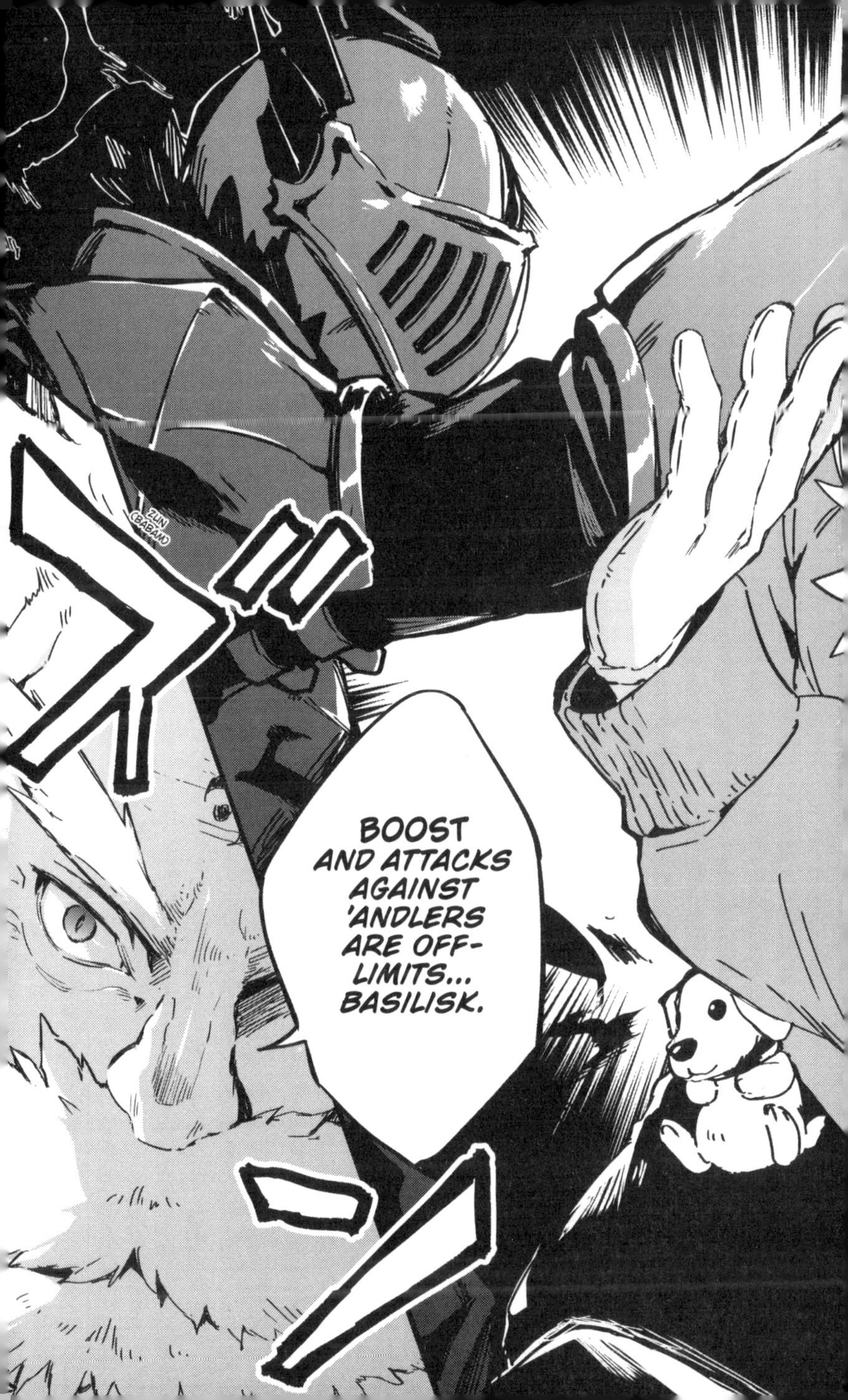
ZUN (BABAM)
BOOST AND ATTACKS AGAINST 'ANDLERS ARE OFF-LIMITS... BASILISK.

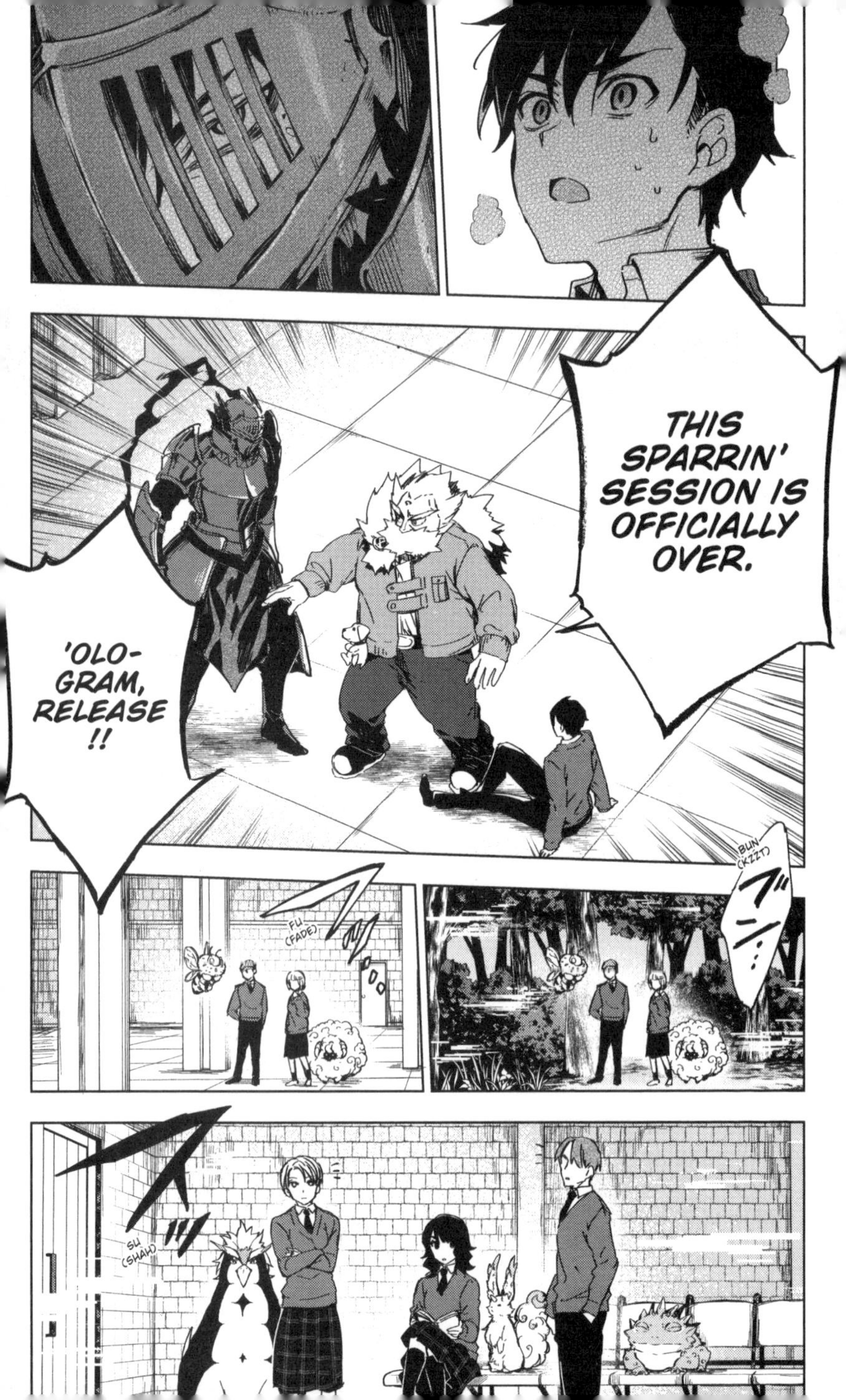
THIS SPARRIN' SESSION IS OFFICIALLY OVER.
'OLO-GRAM, RELEASE!!
BUN (KZZT)
FU (FADE)
SU (SHAH)

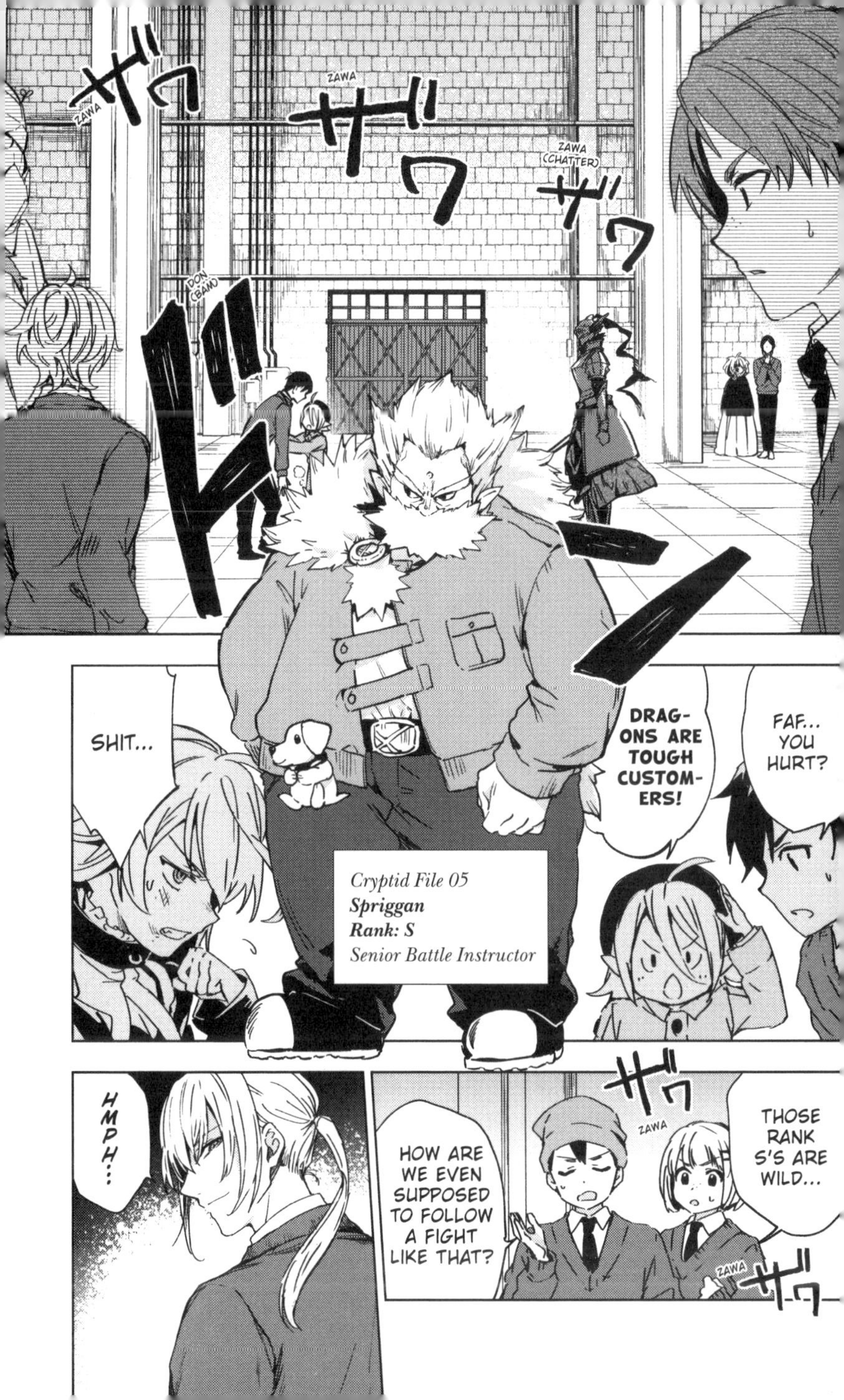
ZAWA
ZAWA
ZAWA (CHATTER)
DON (BAM)
FAF... YOU HURT?
DRAGONS ARE TOUGH CUSTOMERS!
SHIT...
Cryptid File 05
Spriggan
Rank: S
Senior Battle Instructor
ZAWA
THOSE RANK S'S ARE WILD...
HOW ARE WE EVEN SUPPOSED TO FOLLOW A FIGHT LIKE THAT?
ZAWA
HMPH...

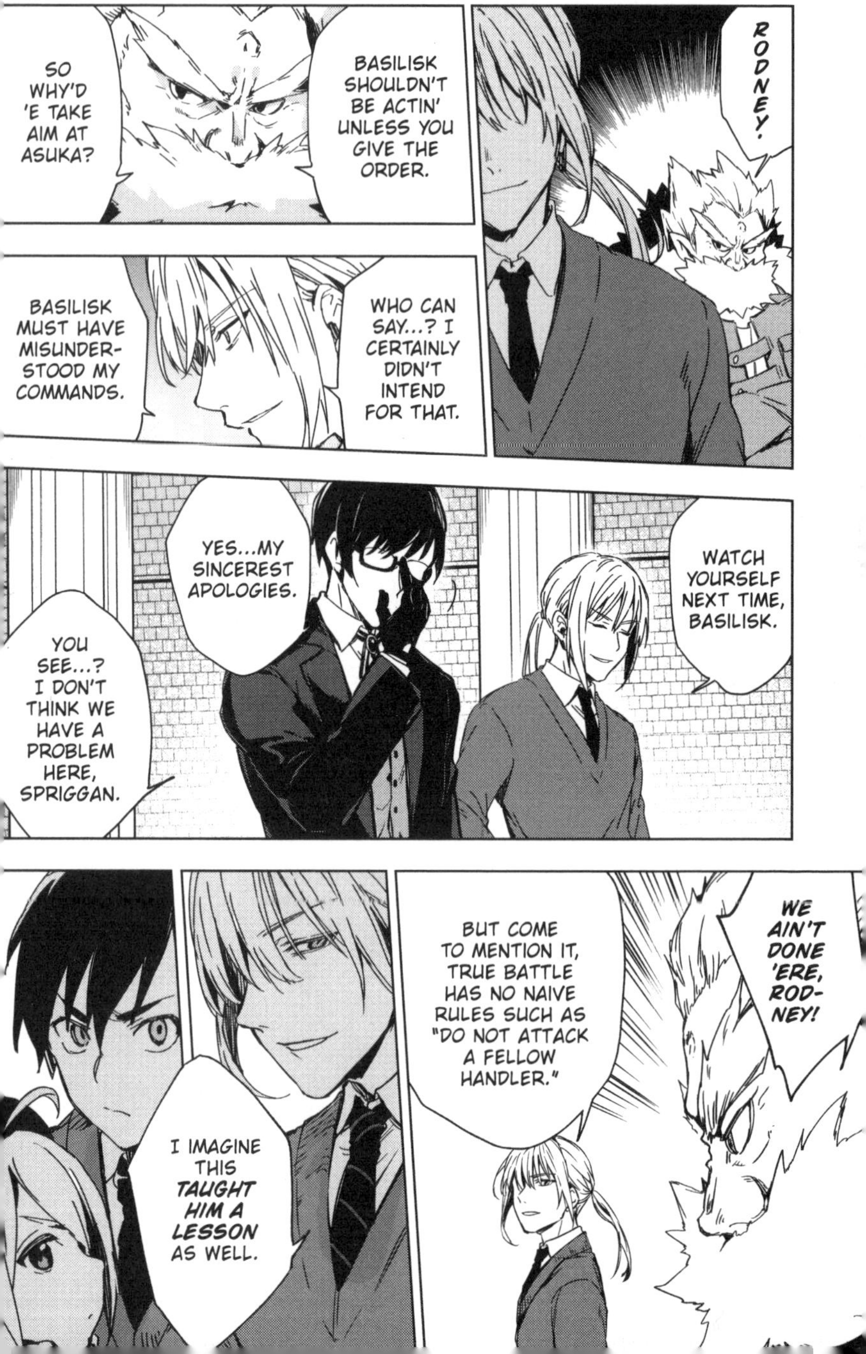
RODNEY.
BASILISK SHOULDN'T BE ACTIN' UNLESS YOU GIVE THE ORDER.
SO WHY'D 'E TAKE AIM AT ASUKA?
WHO CAN SAY...? I CERTAINLY DIDN'T INTEND FOR THAT.
BASILISK MUST HAVE MISUNDERSTOOD MY COMMANDS.
WATCH YOURSELF NEXT TIME, BASILISK.
YES...MY SINCEREST APOLOGIES.
YOU SEE...? I DON'T THINK WE HAVE A PROBLEM HERE, SPRIGGAN.
WE AIN'T DONE 'ERE, RODNEY!
BUT COME TO MENTION IT, TRUE BATTLE HAS NO NAIVE RULES SUCH AS "DO NOT ATTACK A FELLOW HANDLER."
I IMAGINE THIS *TAUGHT HIM A LESSON* AS WELL.

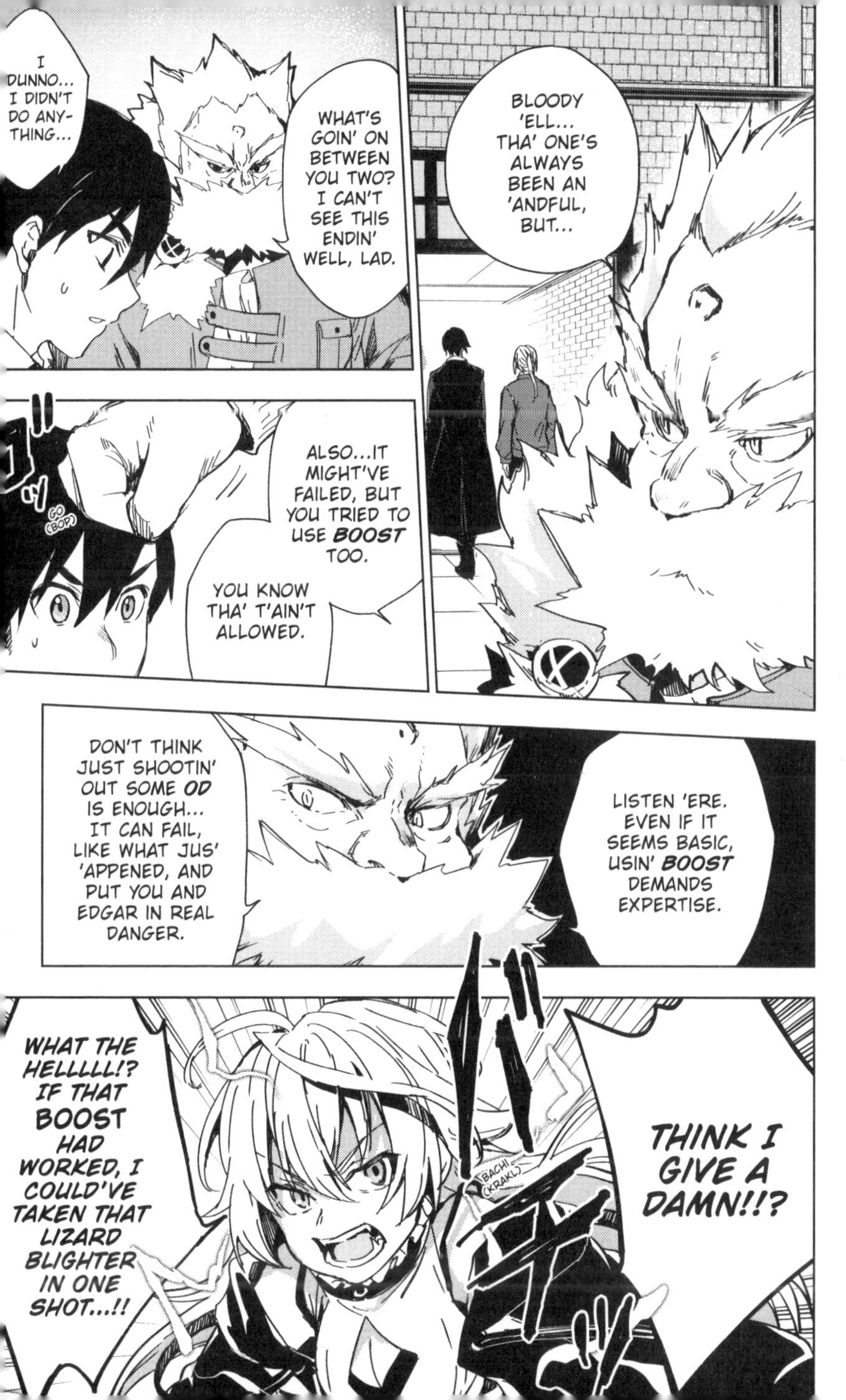
BLOODY 'ELL... THA' ONE'S ALWAYS BEEN AN 'ANDFUL, BUT...
WHAT'S GOIN' ON BETWEEN YOU TWO? I CAN'T SEE THIS ENDIN' WELL, LAD.
I DUNNO... I DIDN'T DO ANY-THING...
ALSO...IT MIGHT'VE FAILED, BUT YOU TRIED TO USE BOOST TOO.
GO (BOP)
YOU KNOW THA' T'AIN'T ALLOWED.
LISTEN 'ERE. EVEN IF IT SEEMS BASIC, USIN' BOOST DEMANDS EXPERTISE.
DON'T THINK JUST SHOOTIN' OUT SOME OD IS ENOUGH... IT CAN FAIL, LIKE WHAT JUS' 'APPENED, AND PUT YOU AND EDGAR IN REAL DANGER.
WHAT THE HELLLLL!? IF THAT BOOST HAD WORKED, I COULD'VE TAKEN THAT LIZARD BLIGHTER IN ONE SHOT...!!
BACHI (KRAKL)
THINK I GIVE A DAMN!!?

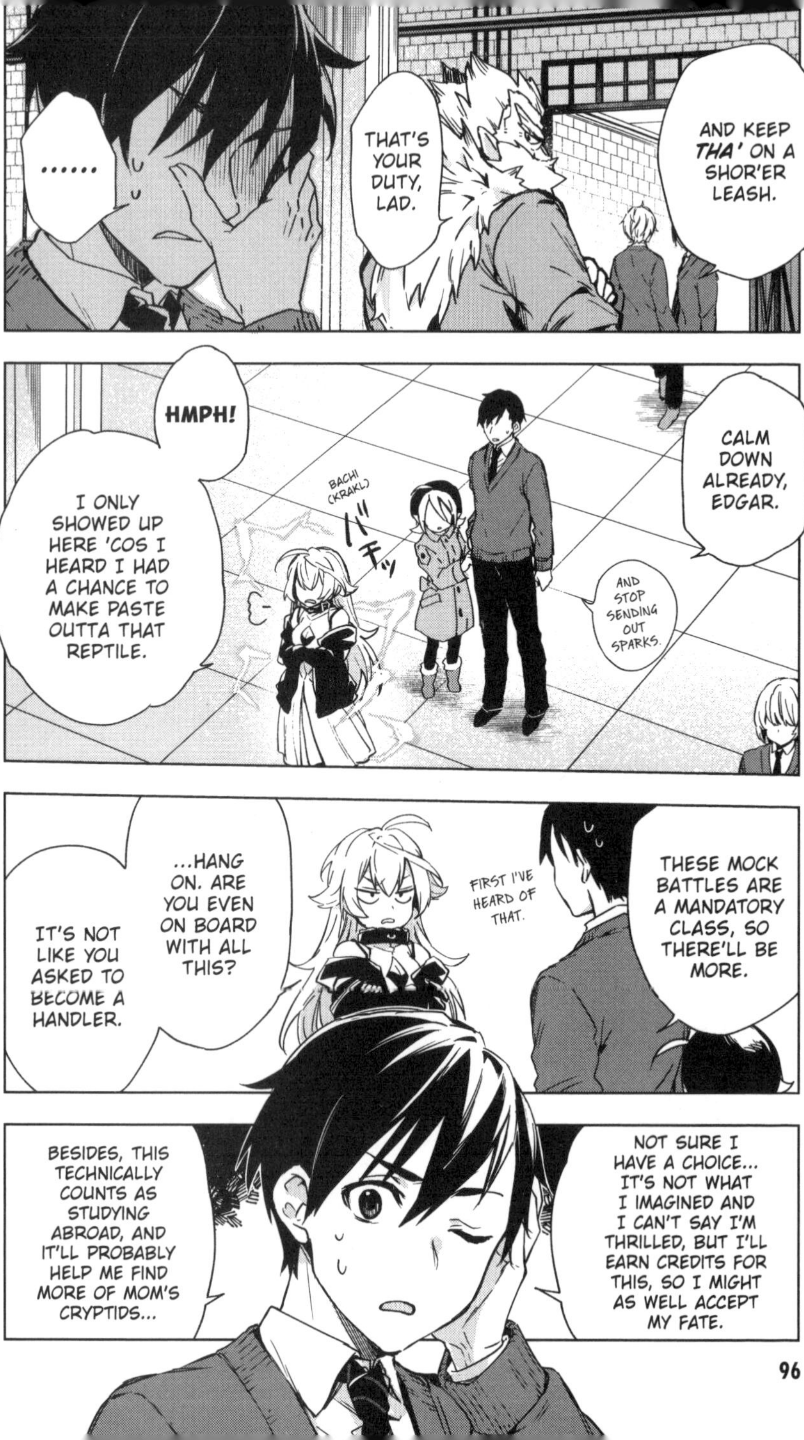
AND KEEP *THA'* ON A SHOR'ER LEASH.
THAT'S YOUR DUTY, LAD.
......
CALM DOWN ALREADY, EDGAR.
AND STOP SENDING OUT SPARKS.
BACHI (KRAKL)
HMPH!
I ONLY SHOWED UP HERE 'COS I HEARD I HAD A CHANCE TO MAKE PASTE OUTTA THAT REPTILE.
THESE MOCK BATTLES ARE A MANDATORY CLASS, SO THERE'LL BE MORE.
FIRST I'VE HEARD OF THAT.
...HANG ON. ARE YOU EVEN ON BOARD WITH ALL THIS?
IT'S NOT LIKE YOU ASKED TO BECOME A HANDLER.
NOT SURE I HAVE A CHOICE... IT'S NOT WHAT I IMAGINED AND I CAN'T SAY I'M THRILLED, BUT I'LL EARN CREDITS FOR THIS, SO I MIGHT AS WELL ACCEPT MY FATE.
BESIDES, THIS TECHNICALLY COUNTS AS STUDYING ABROAD, AND IT'LL PROBABLY HELP ME FIND MORE OF MOM'S CRYPTIDS...

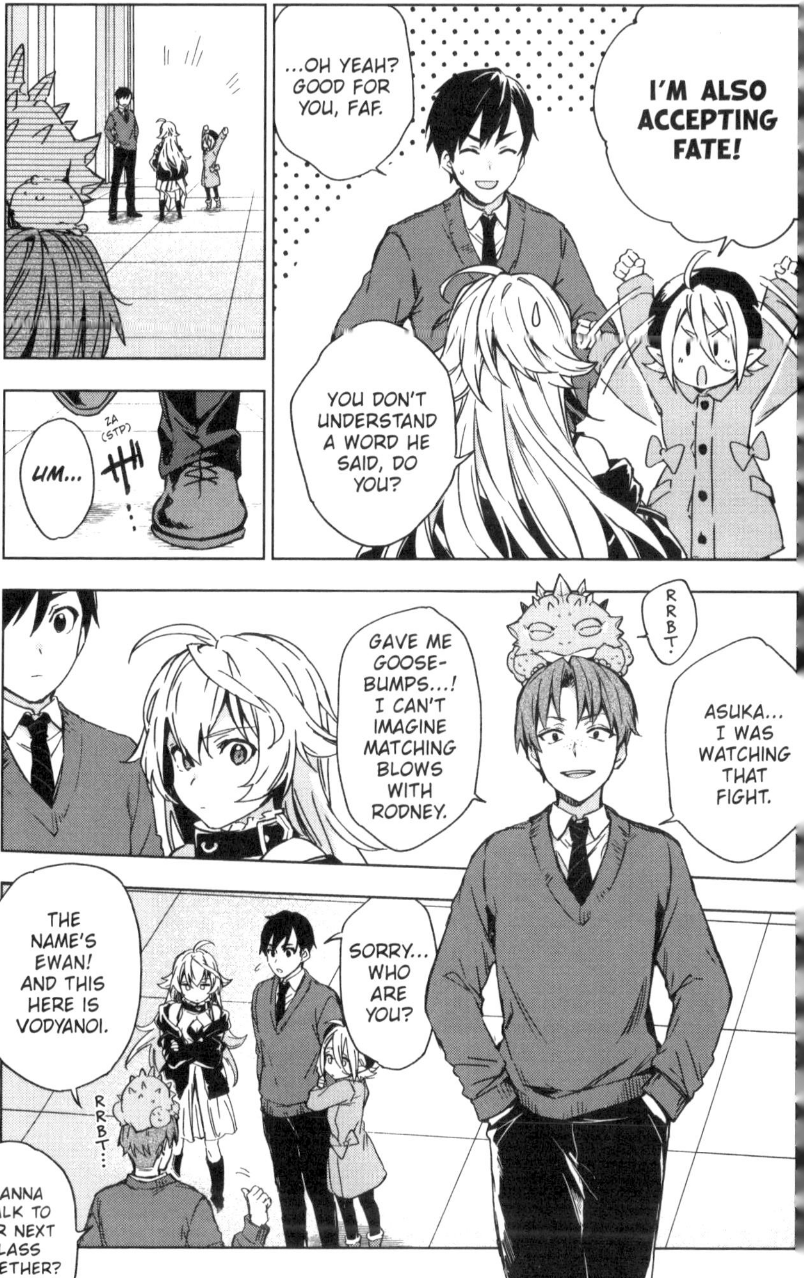
I'M ALSO ACCEPTING FATE!
...OH YEAH? GOOD FOR YOU, FAF.
YOU DON'T UNDERSTAND A WORD HE SAID, DO YOU?
ZA (STP)
UM...
RRBT.
ASUKA... I WAS WATCHING THAT FIGHT.
GAVE ME GOOSE-BUMPS...! I CAN'T IMAGINE MATCHING BLOWS WITH RODNEY.
SORRY... WHO ARE YOU?
THE NAME'S EWAN! AND THIS HERE IS VODYANOI.
RRBT...
WANNA WALK TO OUR NEXT CLASS TOGETHER?

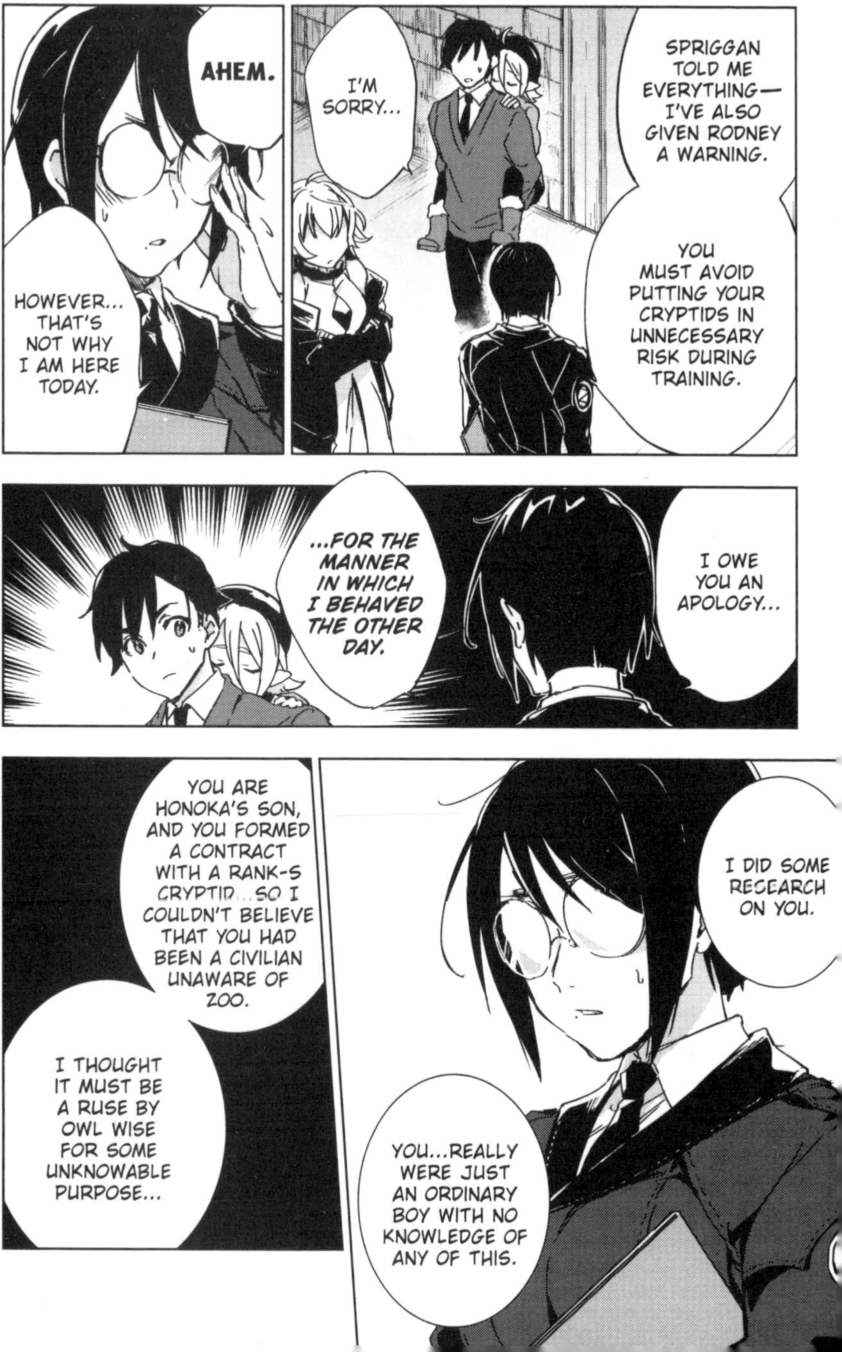

SPRIGGAN TOLD ME EVERYTHING—I'VE ALSO GIVEN RODNEY A WARNING.
YOU MUST AVOID PUTTING YOUR CRYPTIDS IN UNNECESSARY RISK DURING TRAINING.
I'M SORRY...
AHEM.
HOWEVER... THAT'S NOT WHY I AM HERE TODAY.
I OWE YOU AN APOLOGY...
...FOR THE MANNER IN WHICH I BEHAVED THE OTHER DAY.
I DID SOME RESEARCH ON YOU.
YOU...REALLY WERE JUST AN ORDINARY BOY WITH NO KNOWLEDGE OF ANY OF THIS.
YOU ARE HONOKA'S SON, AND YOU FORMED A CONTRACT WITH A RANK-S CRYPTID...SO I COULDN'T BELIEVE THAT YOU HAD BEEN A CIVILIAN UNAWARE OF ZOO.
I THOUGHT IT MUST BE A RUSE BY OWL WISE FOR SOME UNKNOWABLE PURPOSE...

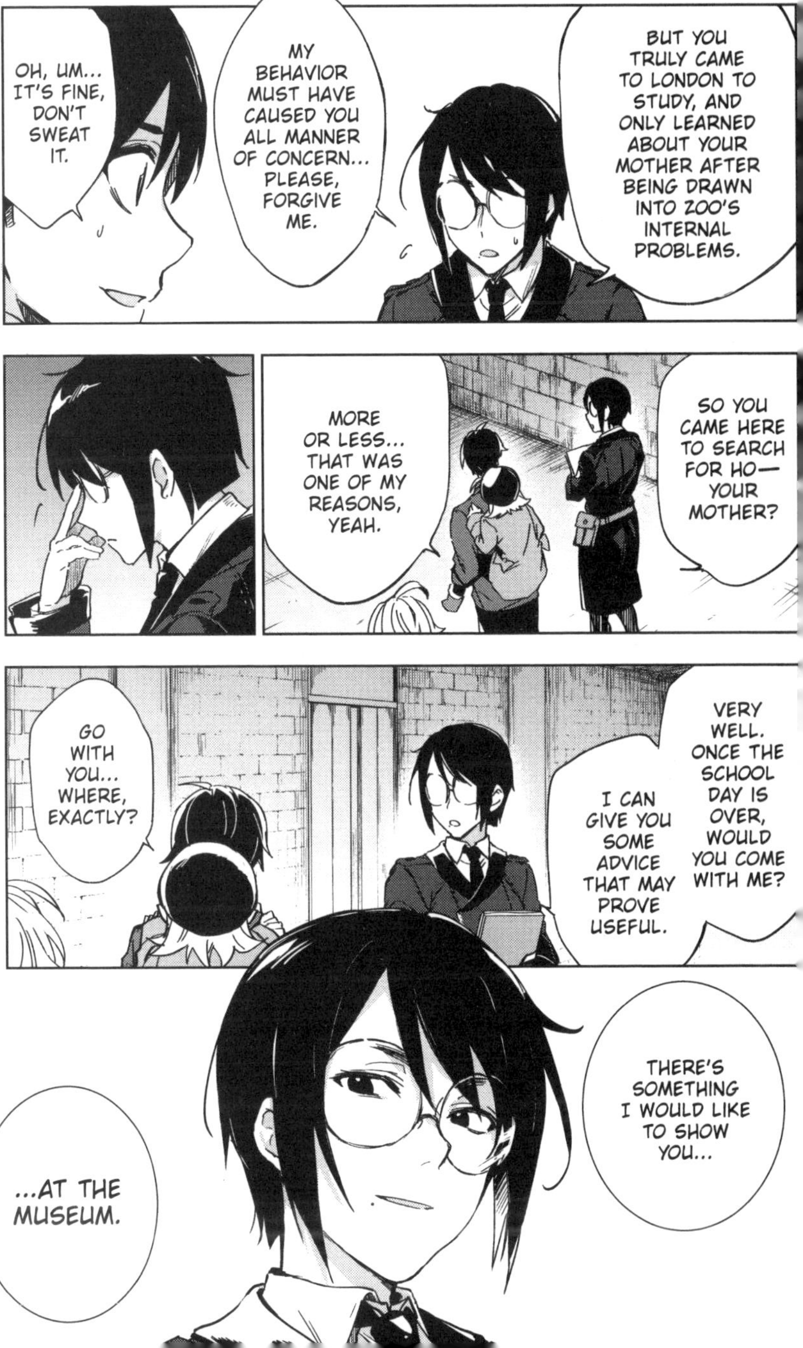
BUT YOU TRULY CAME TO LONDON TO STUDY, AND ONLY LEARNED ABOUT YOUR MOTHER AFTER BEING DRAWN INTO ZOO'S INTERNAL PROBLEMS.
MY BEHAVIOR MUST HAVE CAUSED YOU ALL MANNER OF CONCERN... PLEASE, FORGIVE ME.
OH, UM... IT'S FINE, DON'T SWEAT IT.
SO YOU CAME HERE TO SEARCH FOR HO— YOUR MOTHER?
MORE OR LESS... THAT WAS ONE OF MY REASONS, YEAH.
VERY WELL. ONCE THE SCHOOL DAY IS OVER, WOULD YOU COME WITH ME?
I CAN GIVE YOU SOME ADVICE THAT MAY PROVE USEFUL.
GO WITH YOU... WHERE, EXACTLY?
THERE'S SOMETHING I WOULD LIKE TO SHOW YOU...
...AT THE MUSEUM.

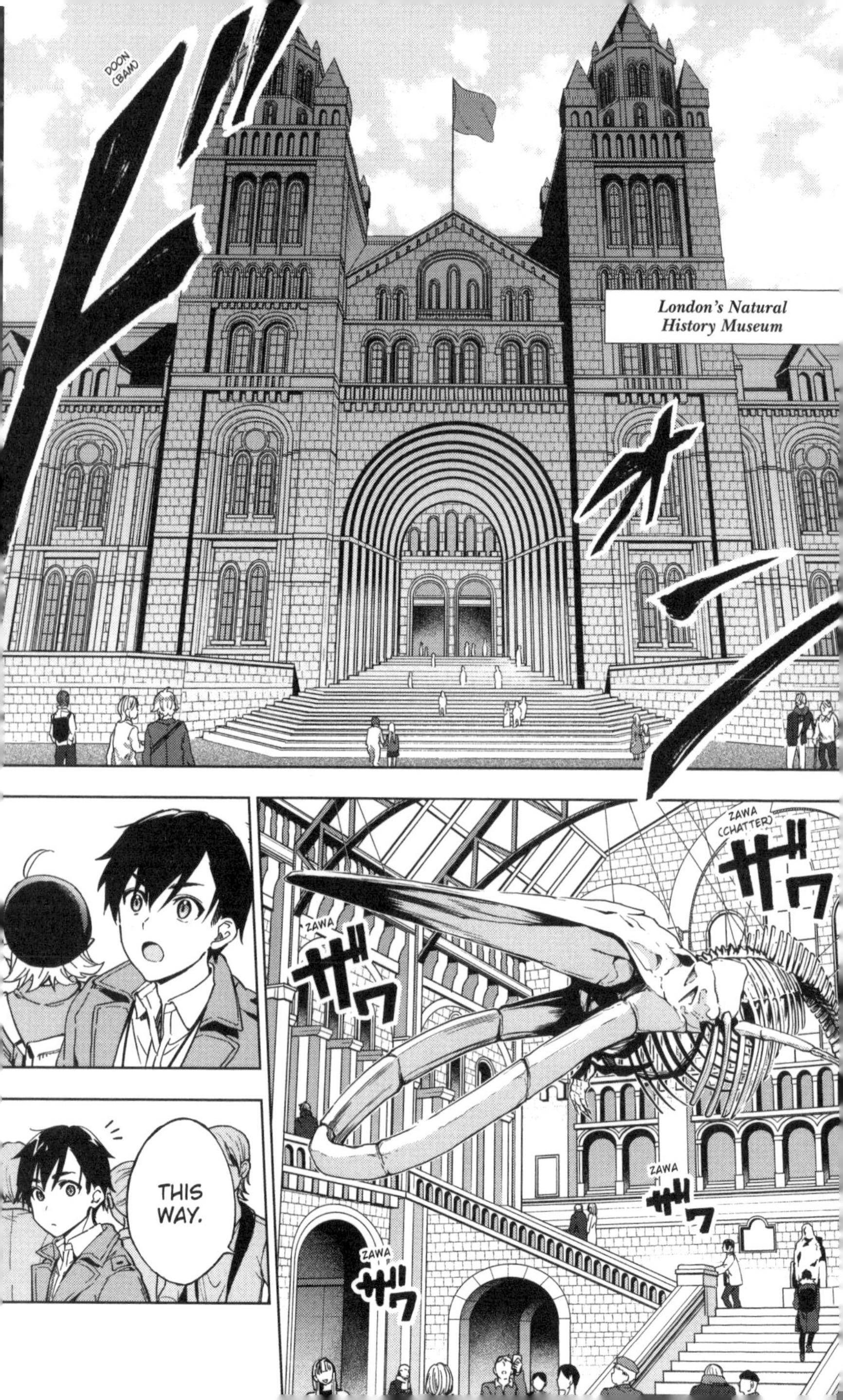
London's Natural History Museum
DOON (BAM)
ZAWA (CHATTER)
ZAWA
ZAWA
ZAWA
THIS WAY.

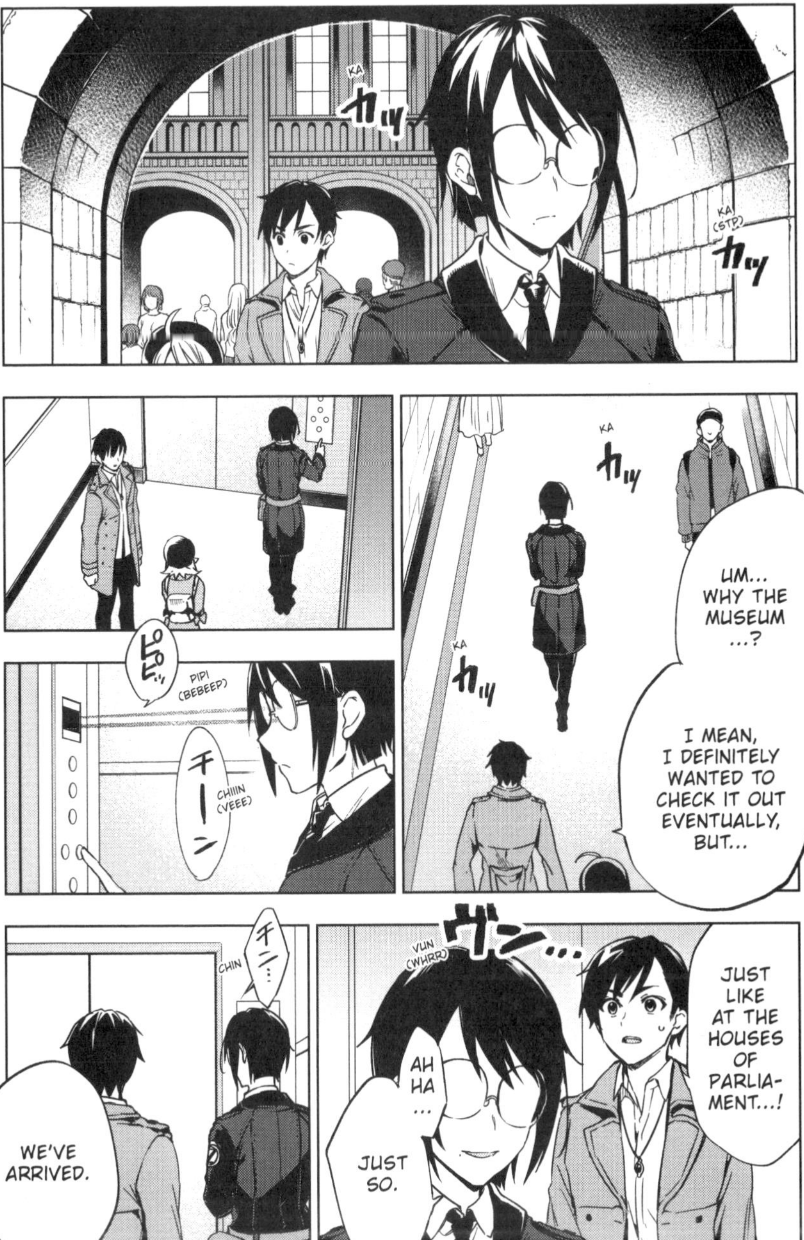
KA
カッ
KA (STP)
カッ
KA
カッ
UM... WHY THE MUSEUM ...?
I MEAN, I DEFINITELY WANTED TO CHECK IT OUT EVENTUALLY, BUT...
KA
カッ
ピポピッ
PIPI (BEBEEP)
チーン
CHIIIN (VEEE)
ヴン…
VUN (WHRR)
JUST LIKE AT THE HOUSES OF PARLIA-MENT...!
AH HA ...
JUST SO.
チン…
CHIN
WE'VE ARRIVED.

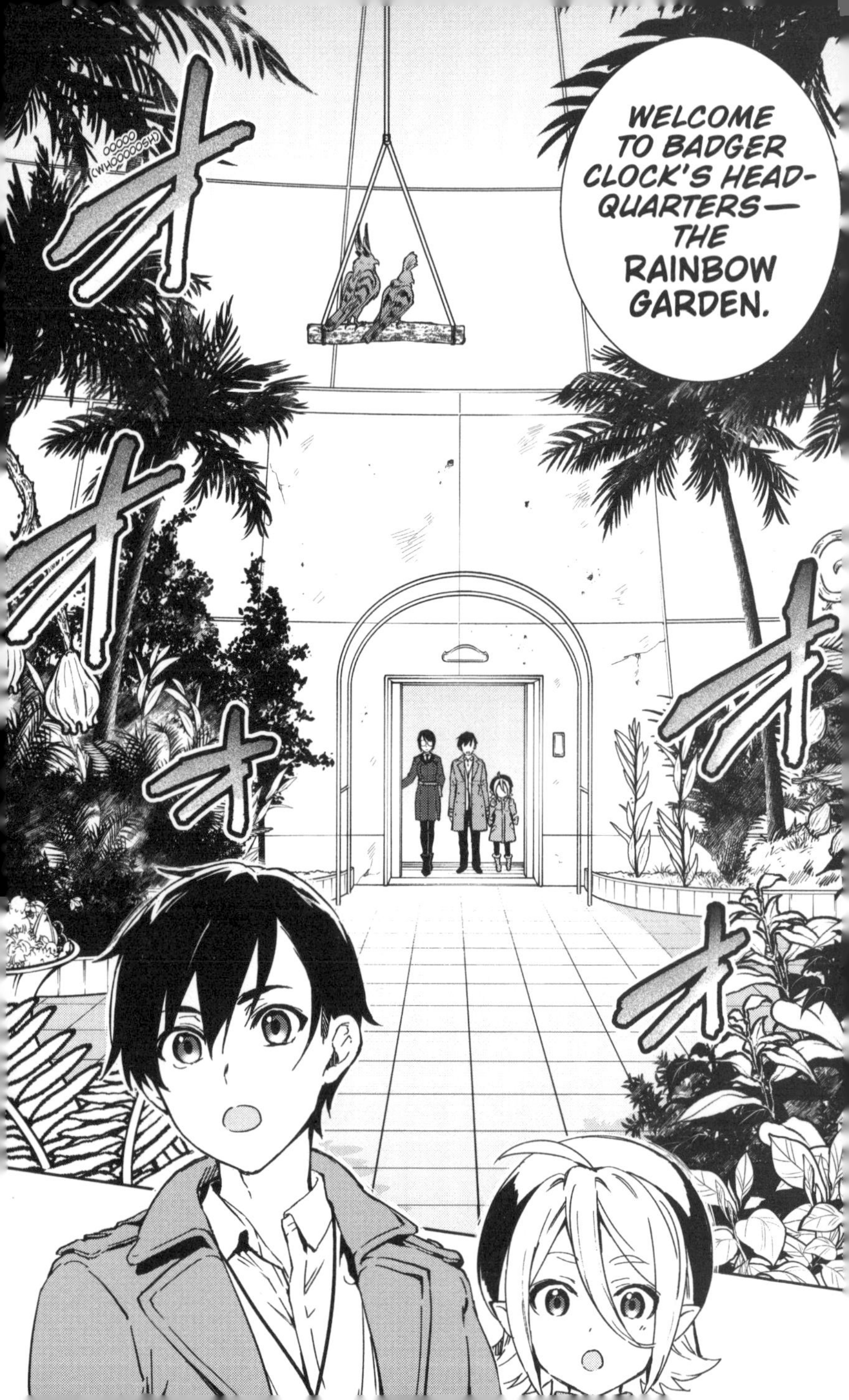
WELCOME TO BADGER CLOCK'S HEAD-QUARTERS—THE RAINBOW GARDEN.
(WHOOOOOOSH OOOOO)

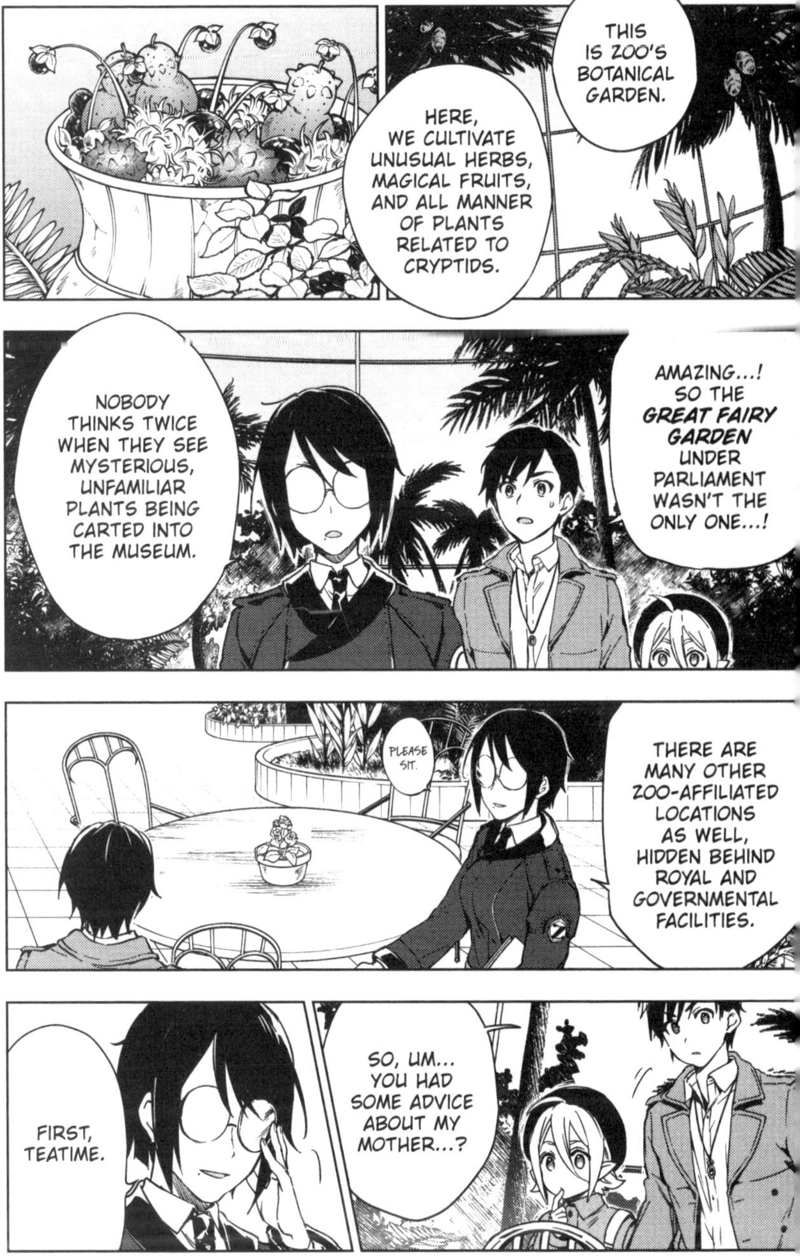
THIS IS ZOO'S BOTANICAL GARDEN.
HERE, WE CULTIVATE UNUSUAL HERBS, MAGICAL FRUITS, AND ALL MANNER OF PLANTS RELATED TO CRYPTIDS.
AMAZING...! SO THE GREAT FAIRY GARDEN UNDER PARLIAMENT WASN'T THE ONLY ONE...!
NOBODY THINKS TWICE WHEN THEY SEE MYSTERIOUS, UNFAMILIAR PLANTS BEING CARTED INTO THE MUSEUM.
THERE ARE MANY OTHER ZOO-AFFILIATED LOCATIONS AS WELL, HIDDEN BEHIND ROYAL AND GOVERNMENTAL FACILITIES.
PLEASE SIT.
SO, UM... YOU HAD SOME ADVICE ABOUT MY MOTHER...?
FIRST, TEATIME.

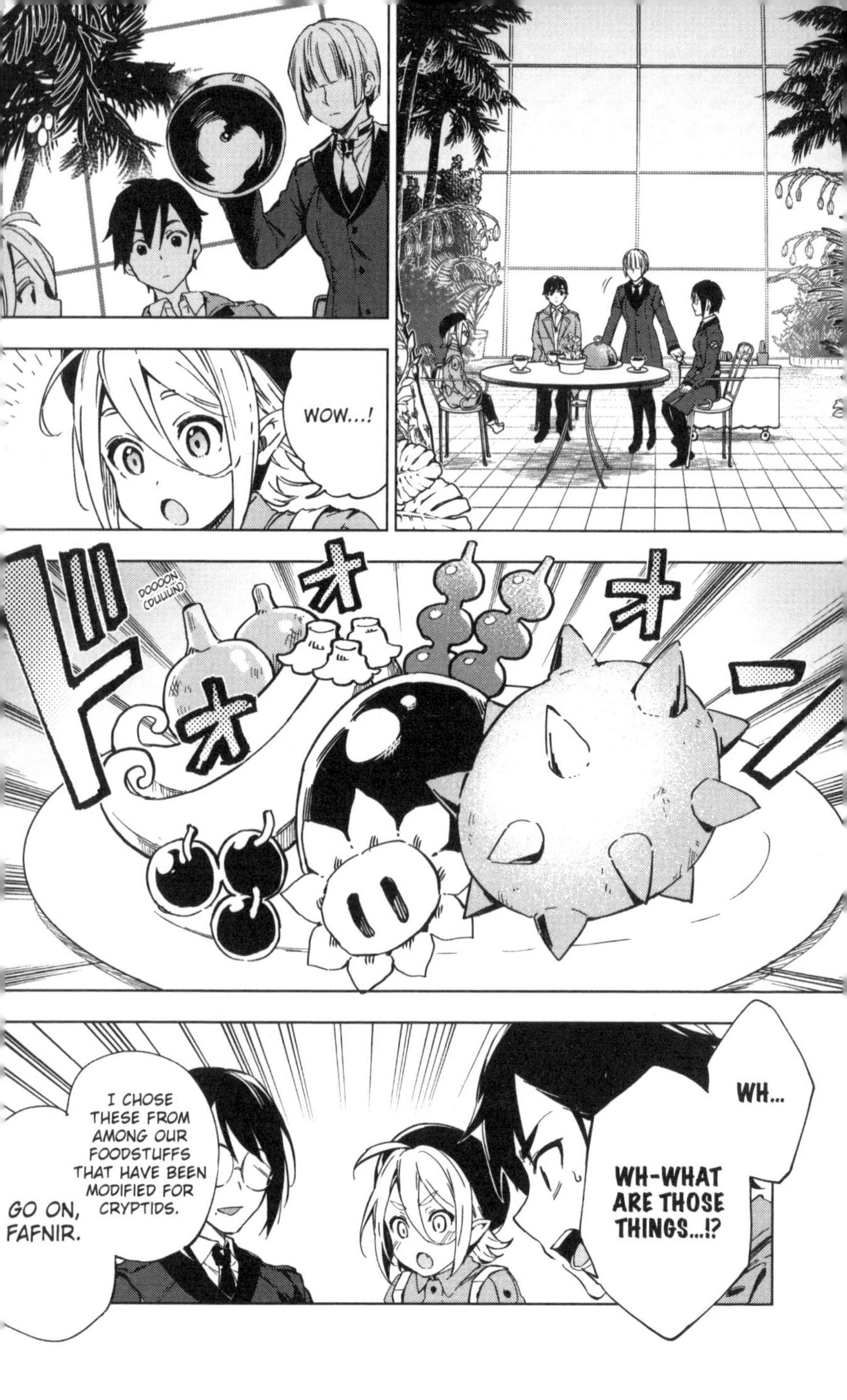
WOW...!
ドオオオーン
DOOOON (DUUUN)
WH...
WH-WHAT ARE THOSE THINGS...!?
I CHOSE THESE FROM AMONG OUR FOODSTUFFS THAT HAVE BEEN MODIFIED FOR CRYPTIDS.
GO ON, FAFNIR.

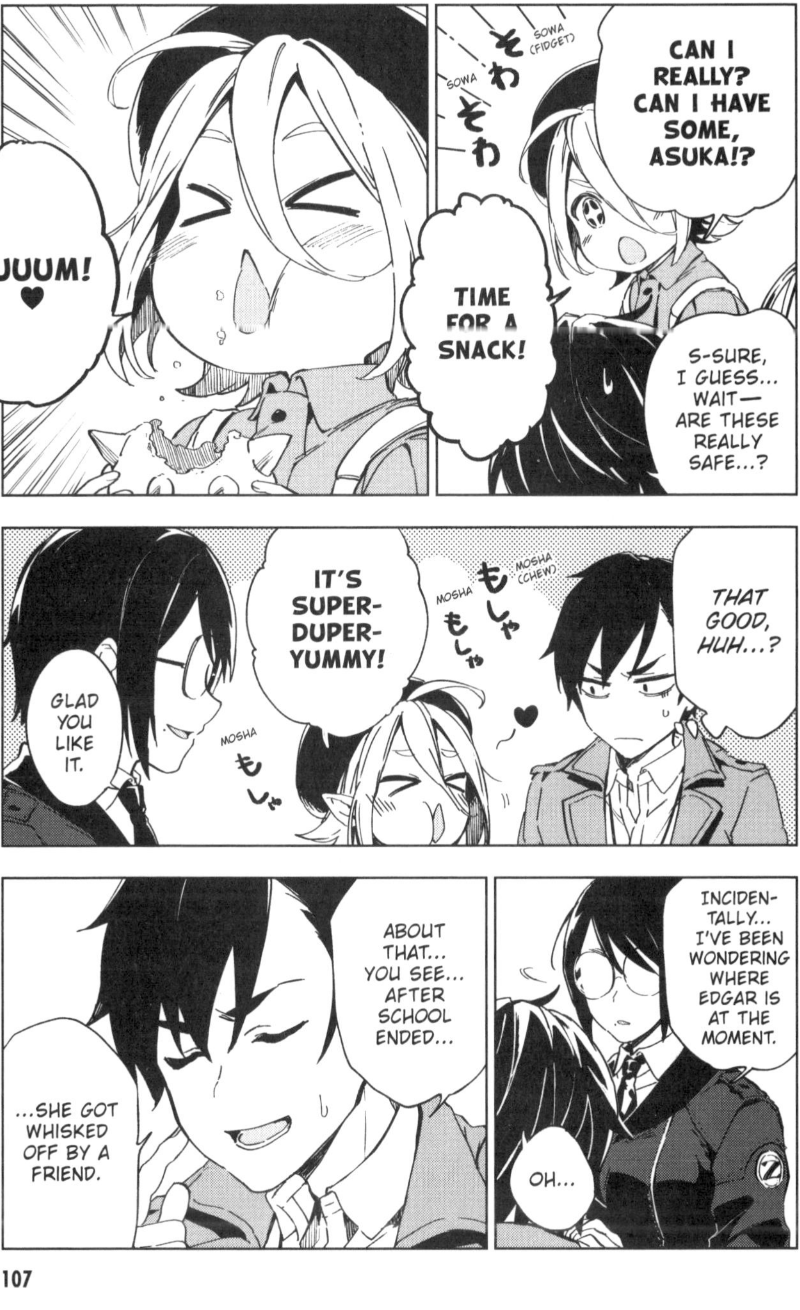

CAN I REALLY? CAN I HAVE SOME, ASUKA!?
そわ SOWA (FIDGET)
そわ SOWA
S-SURE, I GUESS... WAIT—ARE THESE REALLY SAFE...?
TIME FOR A SNACK!
YUUUM! ♥
THAT GOOD, HUH...?
もしゃ MOSHA (CHEW)
もしゃ MOSHA
IT'S SUPER-DUPER-YUMMY!
もしゃ MOSHA
GLAD YOU LIKE IT.
INCIDENTALLY... I'VE BEEN WONDERING WHERE EDGAR IS AT THE MOMENT.
OH...
ABOUT THAT... YOU SEE... AFTER SCHOOL ENDED...
...SHE GOT WHISKED OFF BY A FRIEND.

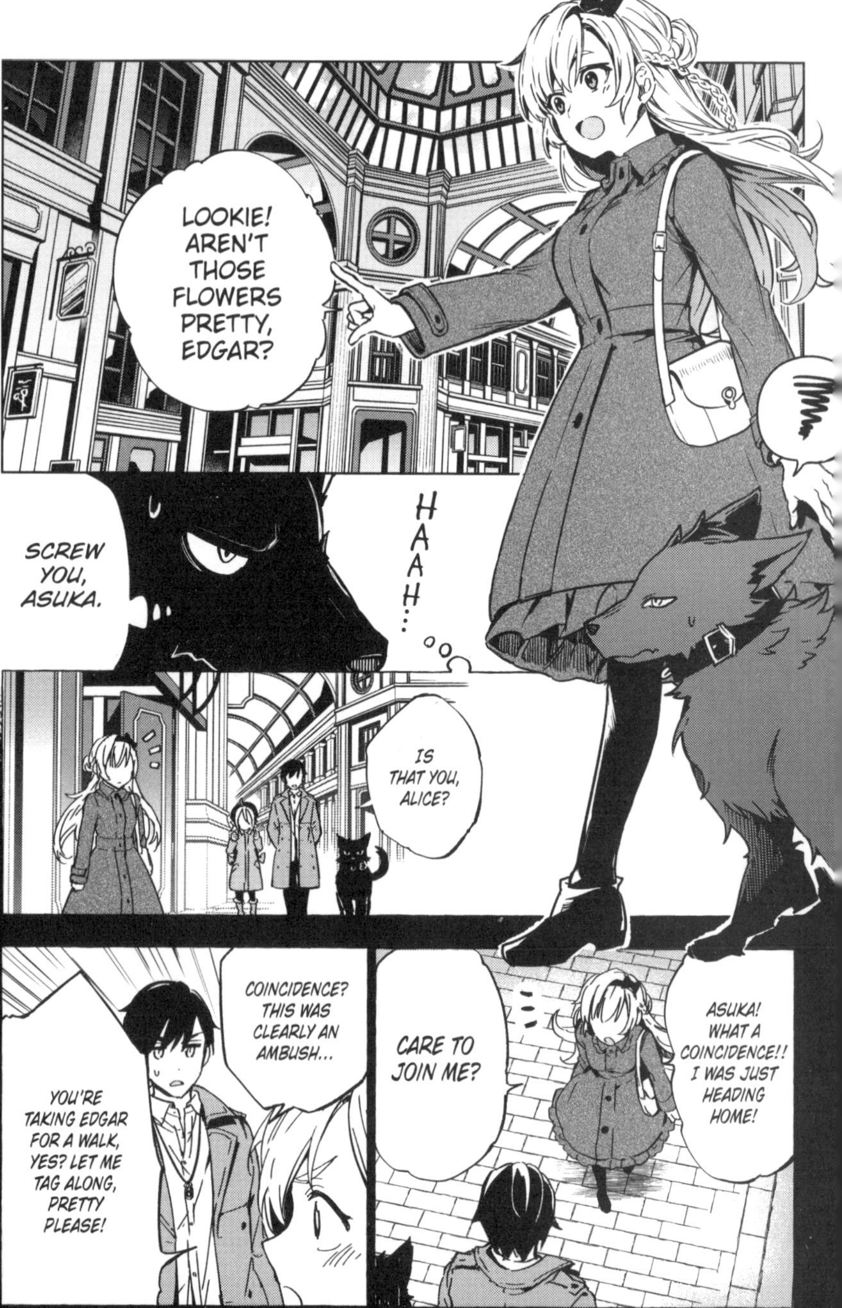
LOOKIE! AREN'T THOSE FLOWERS PRETTY, EDGAR?
HAAAH...
SCREW YOU, ASUKA.
IS THAT YOU, ALICE?
ASUKA! WHAT A COINCIDENCE!! I WAS JUST HEADING HOME!
CARE TO JOIN ME?
COINCIDENCE? THIS WAS CLEARLY AN AMBUSH...
YOU'RE TAKING EDGAR FOR A WALK, YES? LET ME TAG ALONG, PRETTY PLEASE!

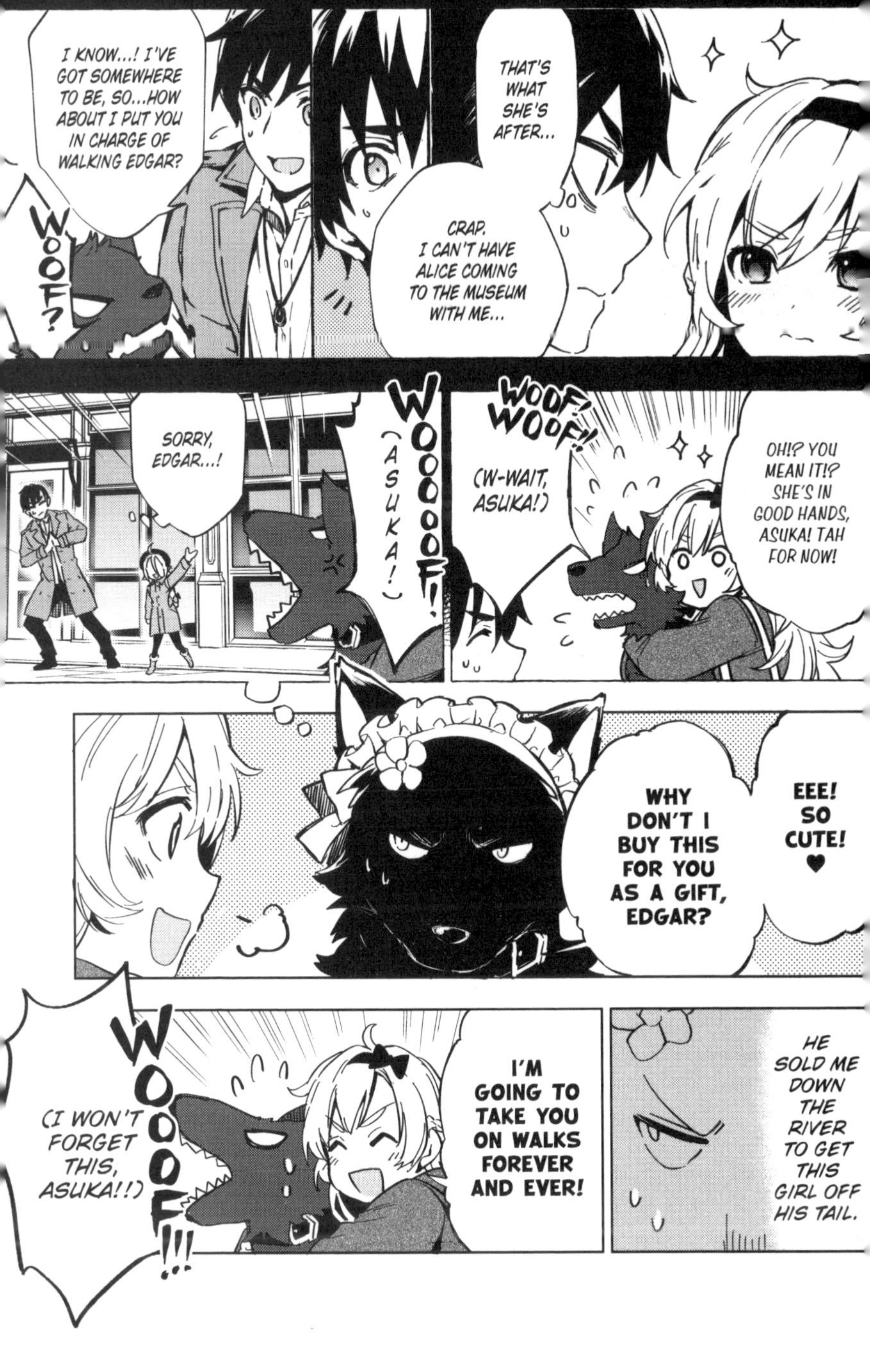

THAT'S WHAT SHE'S AFTER...
CRAP. I CAN'T HAVE ALICE COMING TO THE MUSEUM WITH ME...
I KNOW...! I'VE GOT SOMEWHERE TO BE, SO...HOW ABOUT I PUT YOU IN CHARGE OF WALKING EDGAR?
WOOF?
OH!? YOU MEAN IT!? SHE'S IN GOOD HANDS, ASUKA! TAH FOR NOW!
WOOF! WOOF!!
(W-WAIT, ASUKA!)
WOOOOOOF!
(ASUKA!)
SORRY, EDGAR...!
EEE! SO CUTE! ♥
WHY DON'T I BUY THIS FOR YOU AS A GIFT, EDGAR?
HE SOLD ME DOWN THE RIVER TO GET THIS GIRL OFF HIS TAIL.
I'M GOING TO TAKE YOU ON WALKS FOREVER AND EVER!
WOOOOF!!!
(I WON'T FORGET THIS, ASUKA!!)

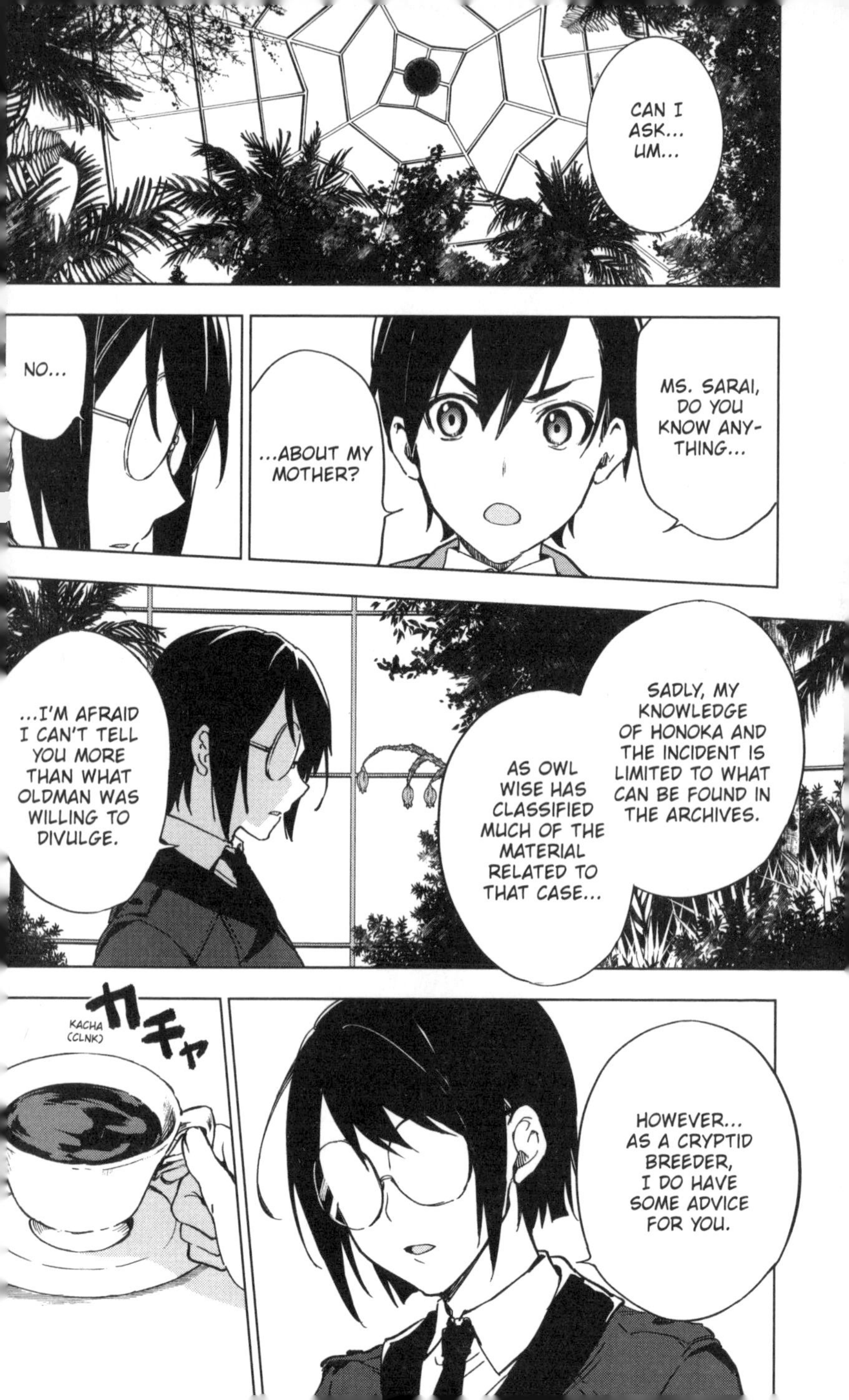
CAN I ASK... UM...
MS. SARAI, DO YOU KNOW ANY-THING...
...ABOUT MY MOTHER?
NO...
SADLY, MY KNOWLEDGE OF HONOKA AND THE INCIDENT IS LIMITED TO WHAT CAN BE FOUND IN THE ARCHIVES.
AS OWL WISE HAS CLASSIFIED MUCH OF THE MATERIAL RELATED TO THAT CASE...
...I'M AFRAID I CAN'T TELL YOU MORE THAN WHAT OLDMAN WAS WILLING TO DIVULGE.
HOWEVER... AS A CRYPTID BREEDER, I DO HAVE SOME ADVICE FOR YOU.
カチャ
KACHA (CLNK)

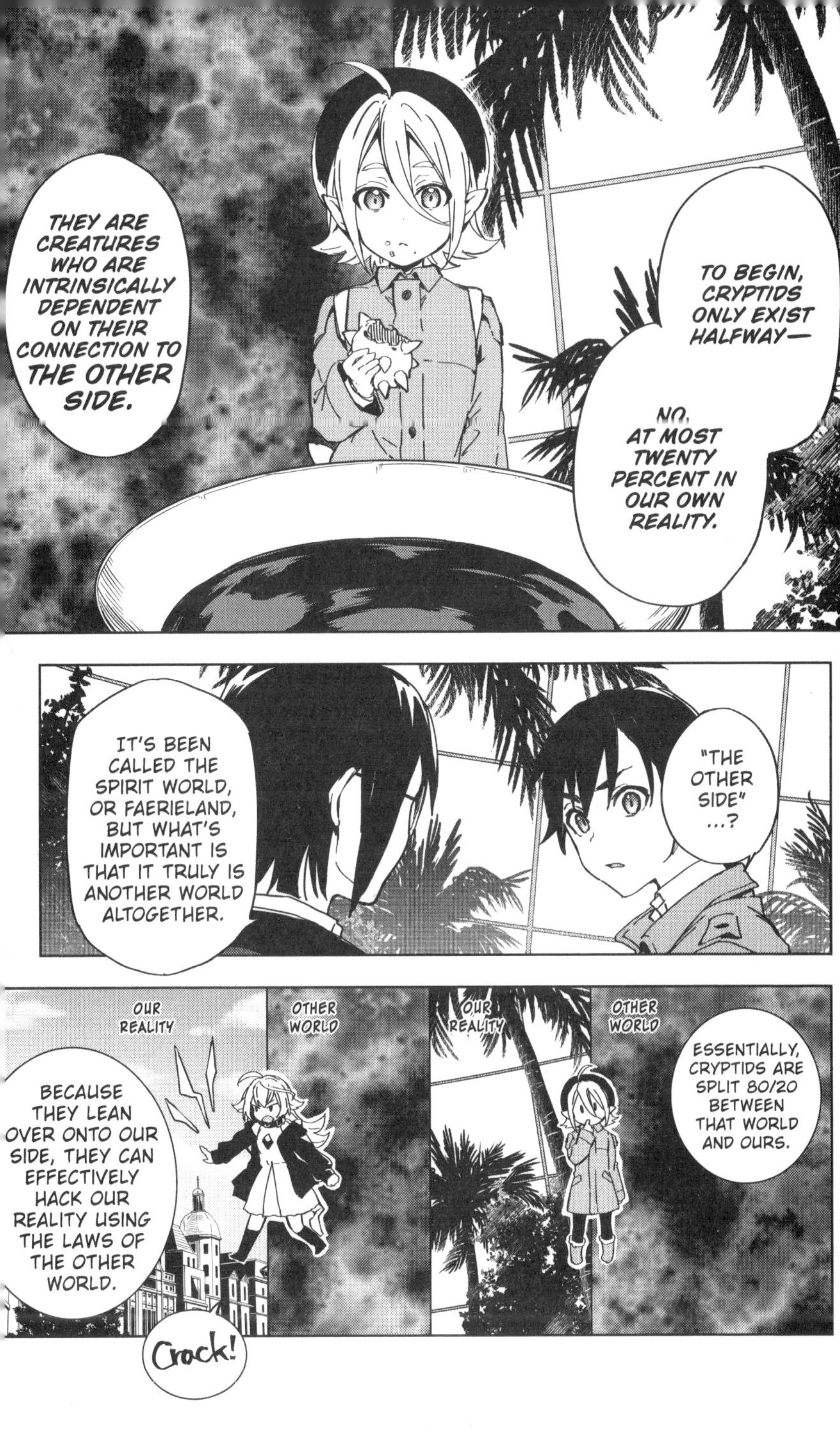
TO BEGIN, CRYPTIDS ONLY EXIST HALFWAY—
NO, AT MOST TWENTY PERCENT IN OUR OWN REALITY.
THEY ARE CREATURES WHO ARE INTRINSICALLY DEPENDENT ON THEIR CONNECTION TO THE OTHER SIDE.
"THE OTHER SIDE" ...?
IT'S BEEN CALLED THE SPIRIT WORLD, OR FAERIELAND, BUT WHAT'S IMPORTANT IS THAT IT TRULY IS ANOTHER WORLD ALTOGETHER.
OTHER WORLD
OUR REALITY
ESSENTIALLY, CRYPTIDS ARE SPLIT 80/20 BETWEEN THAT WORLD AND OURS.
OTHER WORLD
OUR REALITY
BECAUSE THEY LEAN OVER ONTO OUR SIDE, THEY CAN EFFECTIVELY HACK OUR REALITY USING THE LAWS OF THE OTHER WORLD.
Crack!

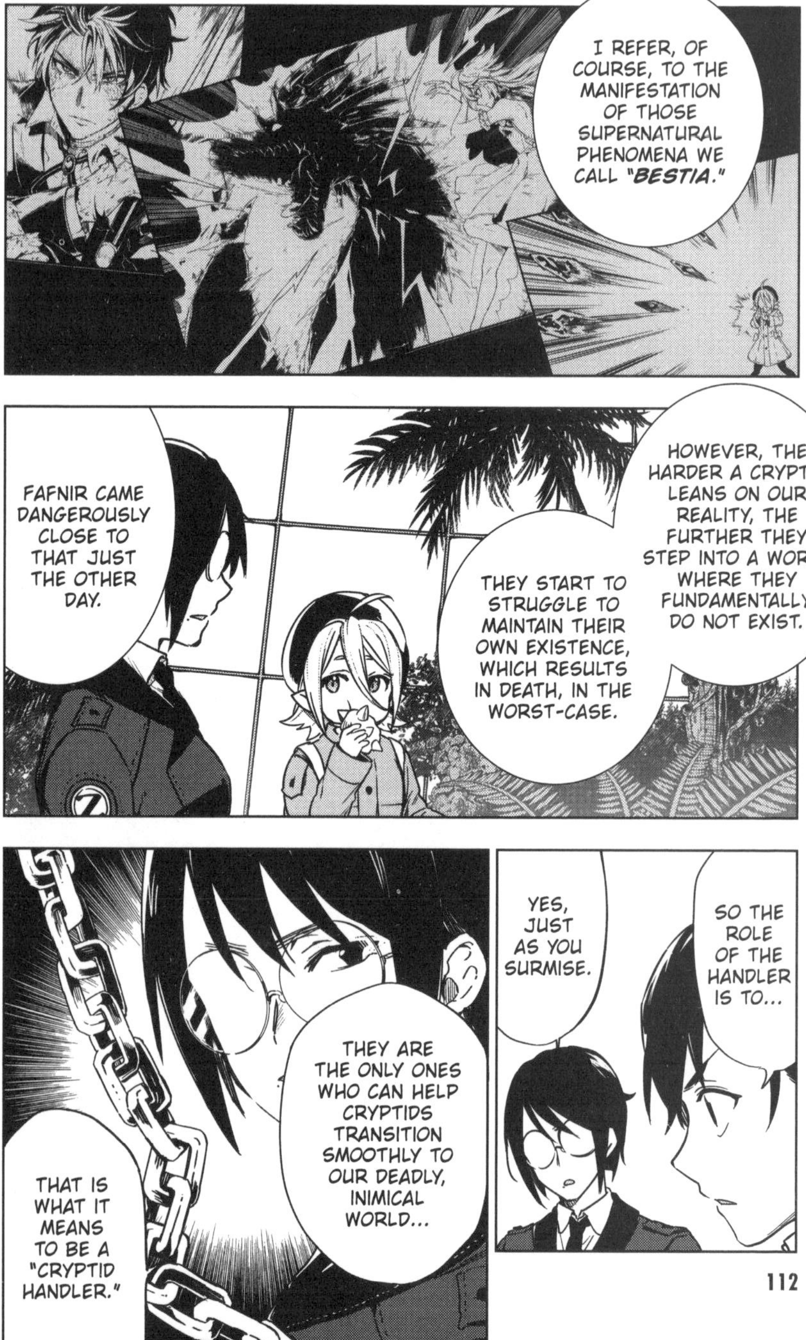
I REFER, OF COURSE, TO THE MANIFESTATION OF THOSE SUPERNATURAL PHENOMENA WE CALL "*BESTIA*."
HOWEVER, THE HARDER A CRYPTID LEANS ON OUR REALITY, THE FURTHER THEY STEP INTO A WORLD WHERE THEY FUNDAMENTALLY DO NOT EXIST.
THEY START TO STRUGGLE TO MAINTAIN THEIR OWN EXISTENCE, WHICH RESULTS IN DEATH, IN THE WORST-CASE.
FAFNIR CAME DANGEROUSLY CLOSE TO THAT JUST THE OTHER DAY.
SO THE ROLE OF THE HANDLER IS TO...
YES, JUST AS YOU SURMISE.
THEY ARE THE ONLY ONES WHO CAN HELP CRYPTIDS TRANSITION SMOOTHLY TO OUR DEADLY, INIMICAL WORLD...
THAT IS WHAT IT MEANS TO BE A "CRYPTID HANDLER."

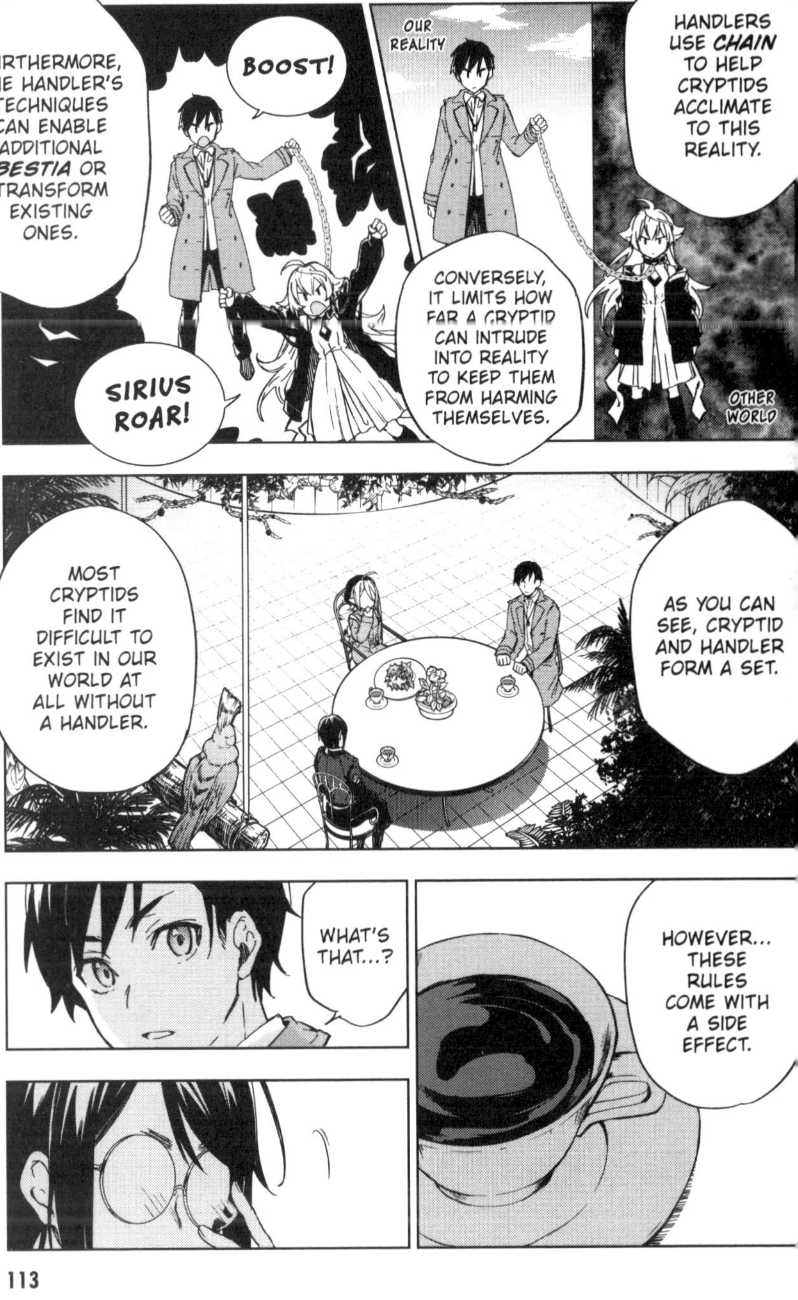
HANDLERS USE CHAIN TO HELP CRYPTIDS ACCLIMATE TO THIS REALITY.
OUR REALITY
CONVERSELY, IT LIMITS HOW FAR A CRYPTID CAN INTRUDE INTO REALITY TO KEEP THEM FROM HARMING THEMSELVES.
OTHER WORLD
BOOST!
FURTHERMORE, THE HANDLER'S TECHNIQUES CAN ENABLE ADDITIONAL BESTIA OR TRANSFORM EXISTING ONES.
SIRIUS ROAR!
AS YOU CAN SEE, CRYPTID AND HANDLER FORM A SET.
MOST CRYPTIDS FIND IT DIFFICULT TO EXIST IN OUR WORLD AT ALL WITHOUT A HANDLER.
HOWEVER... THESE RULES COME WITH A SIDE EFFECT.
WHAT'S THAT...?

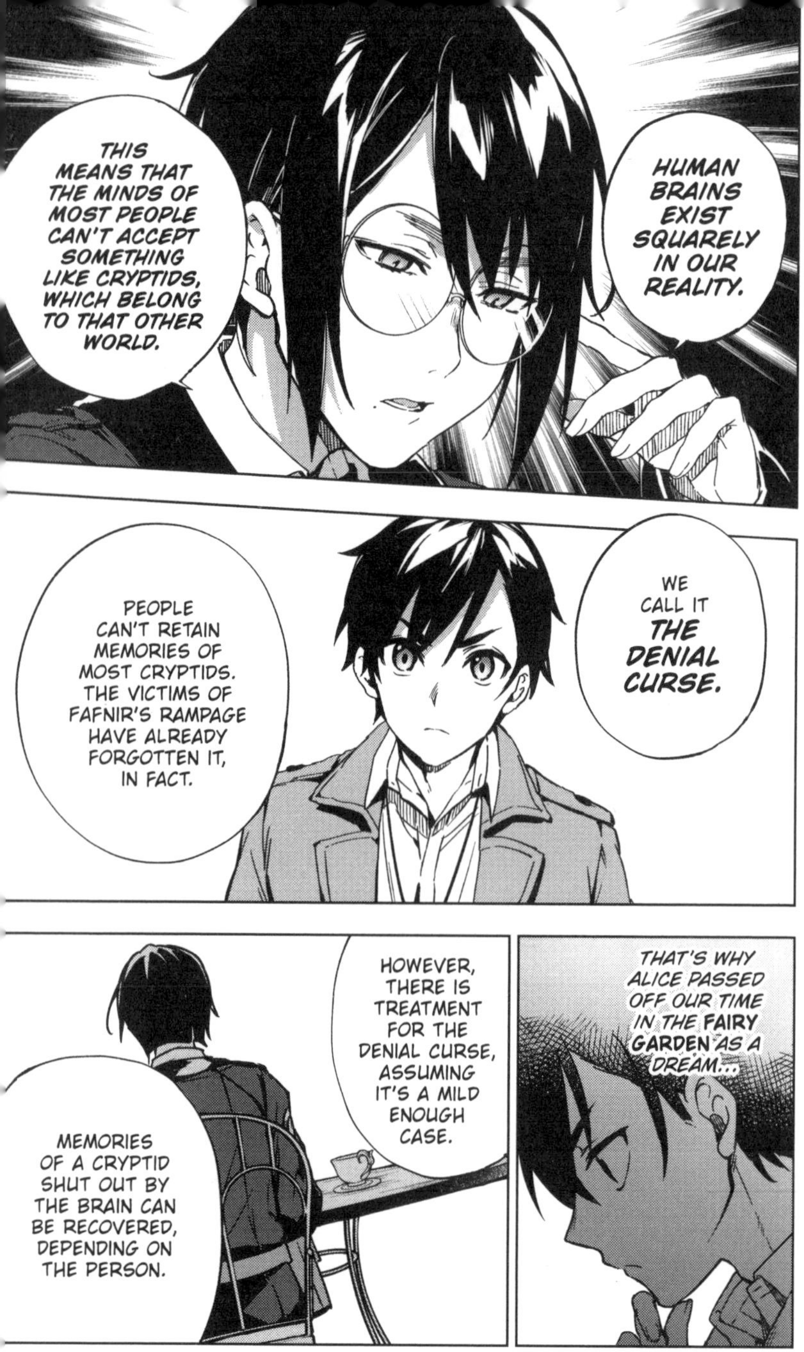
HUMAN BRAINS EXIST SQUARELY IN OUR REALITY.
THIS MEANS THAT THE MINDS OF MOST PEOPLE CAN'T ACCEPT SOMETHING LIKE CRYPTIDS, WHICH BELONG TO THAT OTHER WORLD.
WE CALL IT THE DENIAL CURSE.
PEOPLE CAN'T RETAIN MEMORIES OF MOST CRYPTIDS. THE VICTIMS OF FAFNIR'S RAMPAGE HAVE ALREADY FORGOTTEN IT, IN FACT.
THAT'S WHY ALICE PASSED OFF OUR TIME IN THE FAIRY GARDEN AS A DREAM...
HOWEVER, THERE IS TREATMENT FOR THE DENIAL CURSE, ASSUMING IT'S A MILD ENOUGH CASE.
MEMORIES OF A CRYPTID SHUT OUT BY THE BRAIN CAN BE RECOVERED, DEPENDING ON THE PERSON.

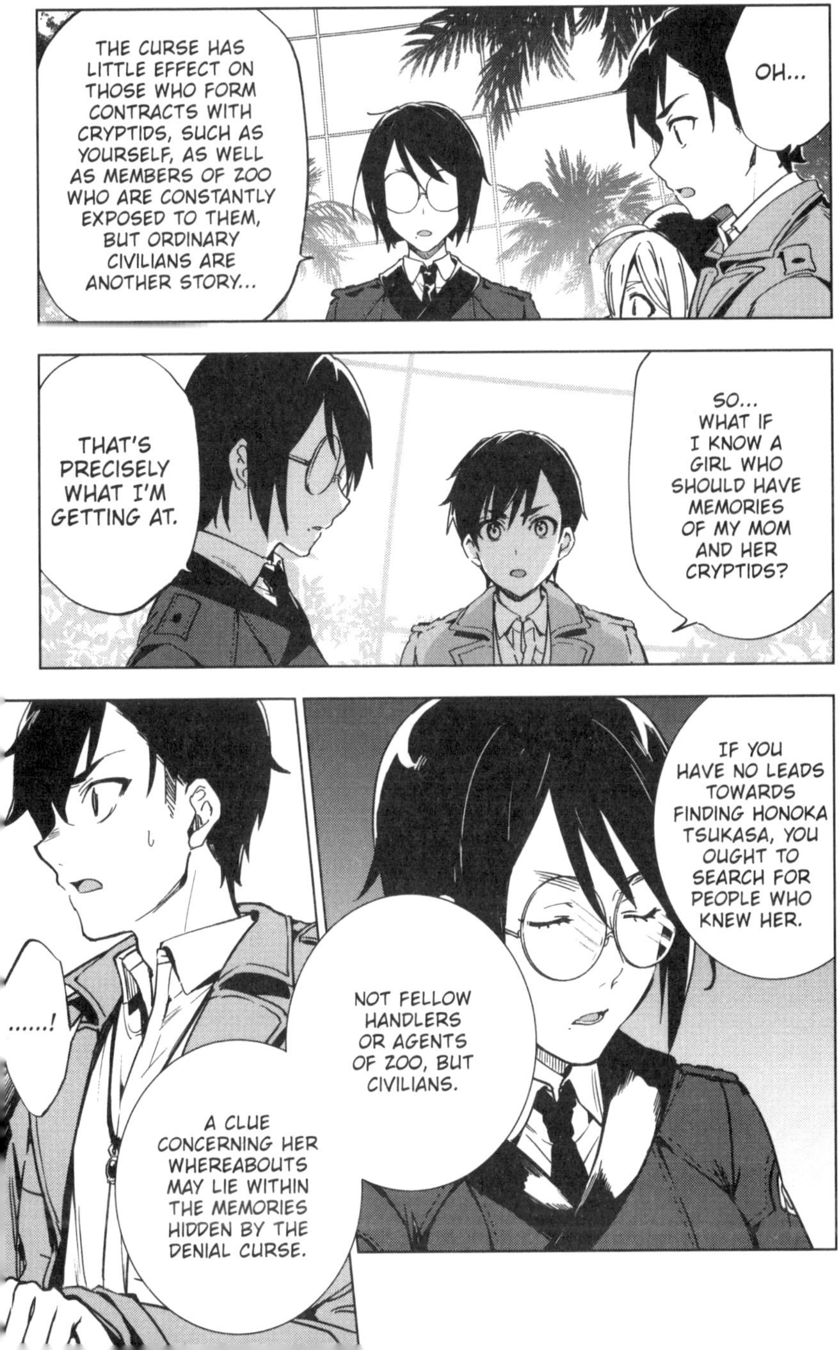
OH...
THE CURSE HAS LITTLE EFFECT ON THOSE WHO FORM CONTRACTS WITH CRYPTIDS, SUCH AS YOURSELF, AS WELL AS MEMBERS OF ZOO WHO ARE CONSTANTLY EXPOSED TO THEM, BUT ORDINARY CIVILIANS ARE ANOTHER STORY...
SO... WHAT IF I KNOW A GIRL WHO SHOULD HAVE MEMORIES OF MY MOM AND HER CRYPTIDS?
THAT'S PRECISELY WHAT I'M GETTING AT.
IF YOU HAVE NO LEADS TOWARDS FINDING HONOKA TSUKASA, YOU OUGHT TO SEARCH FOR PEOPLE WHO KNEW HER.
NOT FELLOW HANDLERS OR AGENTS OF ZOO, BUT CIVILIANS.
A CLUE CONCERNING HER WHEREABOUTS MAY LIE WITHIN THE MEMORIES HIDDEN BY THE DENIAL CURSE.
......!

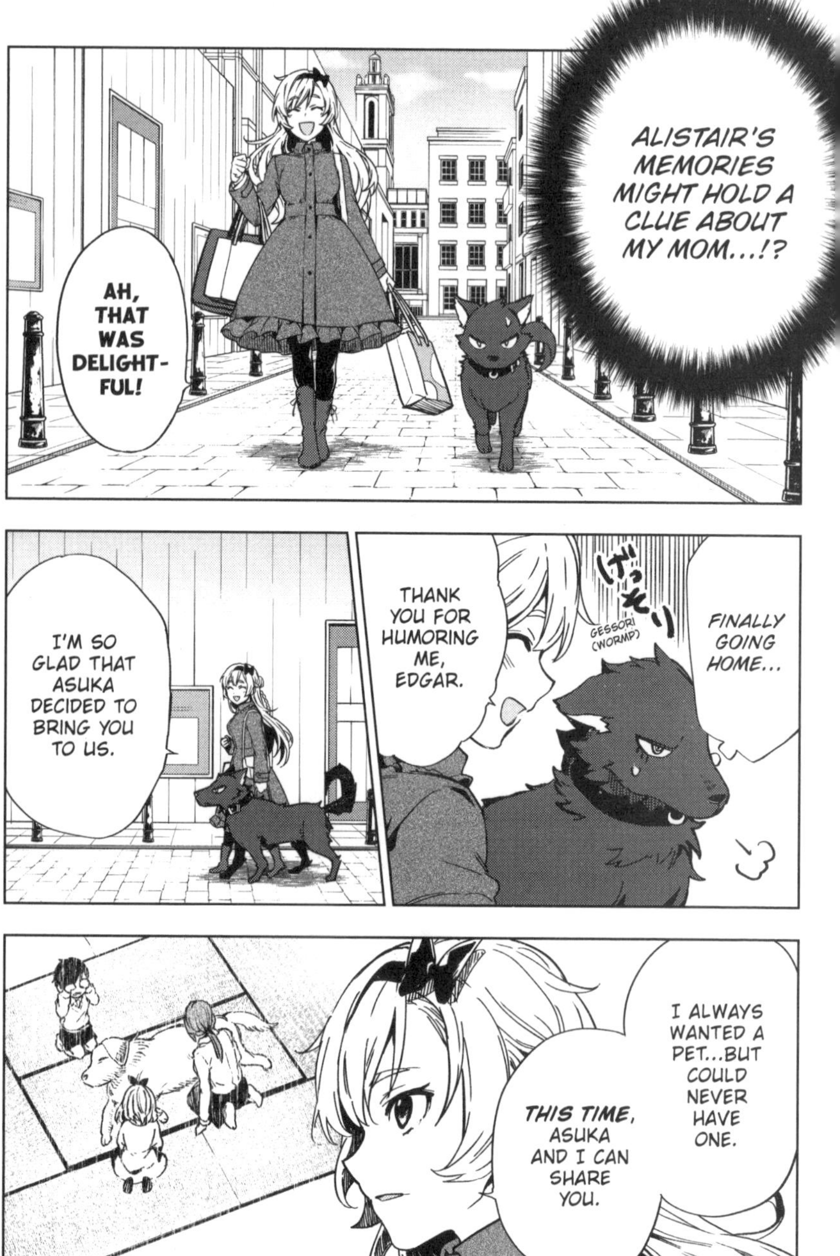
ALISTAIR'S MEMORIES MIGHT HOLD A CLUE ABOUT MY MOM...!?
AH, THAT WAS DELIGHT-FUL!
FINALLY GOING HOME...
げっそり
GESSORI (WORMP)
THANK YOU FOR HUMORING ME, EDGAR.
I'M SO GLAD THAT ASUKA DECIDED TO BRING YOU TO US.
I ALWAYS WANTED A PET...BUT COULD NEVER HAVE ONE.
THIS TIME, ASUKA AND I CAN SHARE YOU.

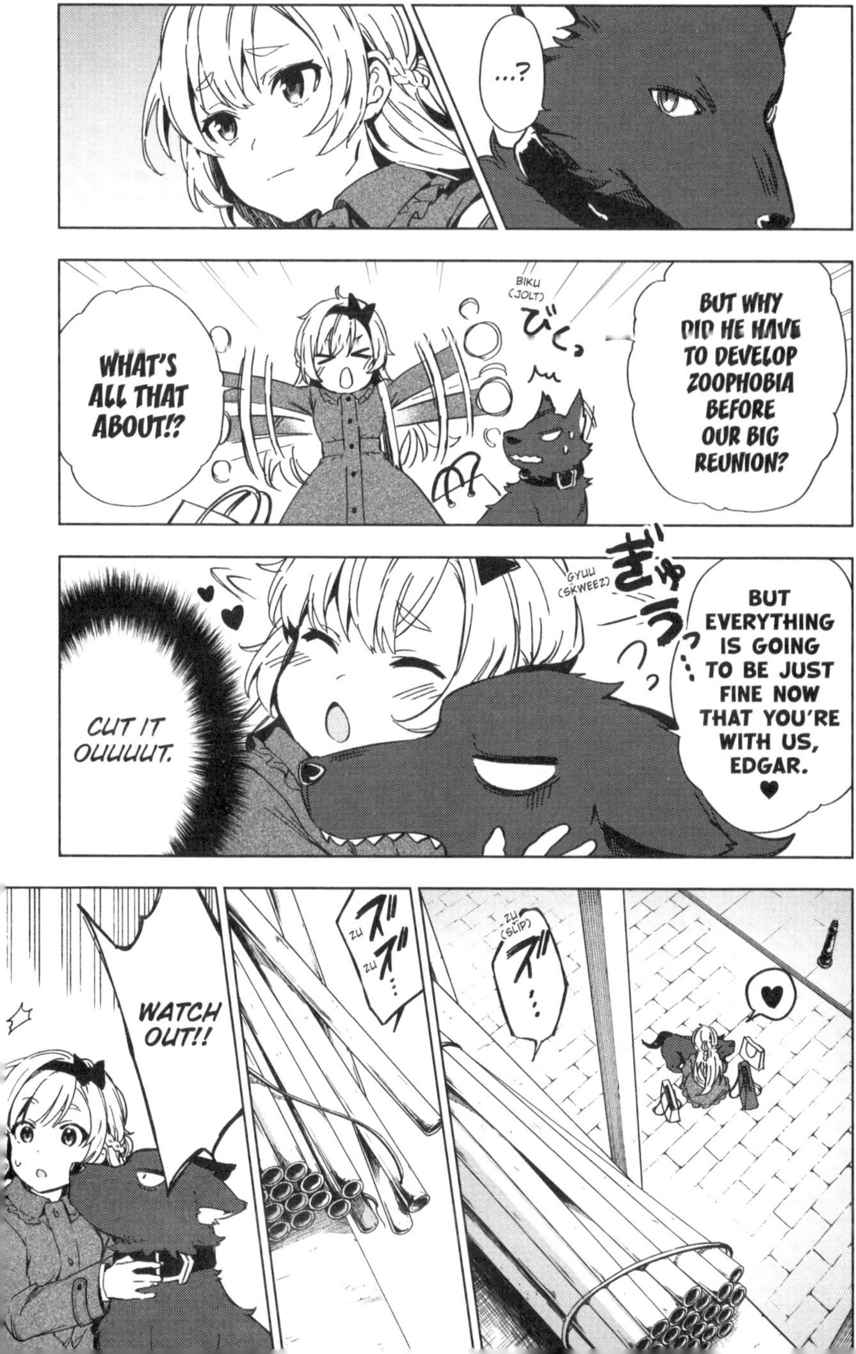
...?
BUT WHY DID HE HAVE TO DEVELOP ZOOPHOBIA BEFORE OUR BIG REUNION?
BIKU (JOLT)
びくっ
WHAT'S ALL THAT ABOUT!?
BUT EVERYTHING IS GOING TO BE JUST FINE NOW THAT YOU'RE WITH US, EDGAR. ♥
GYUU (SKWEEZ)
ぎゅうっ
CUT IT OUUUUT.
♥
ZU (SLIP)
ズ…
ZU ZU
ズズ…
WATCH OUT!!

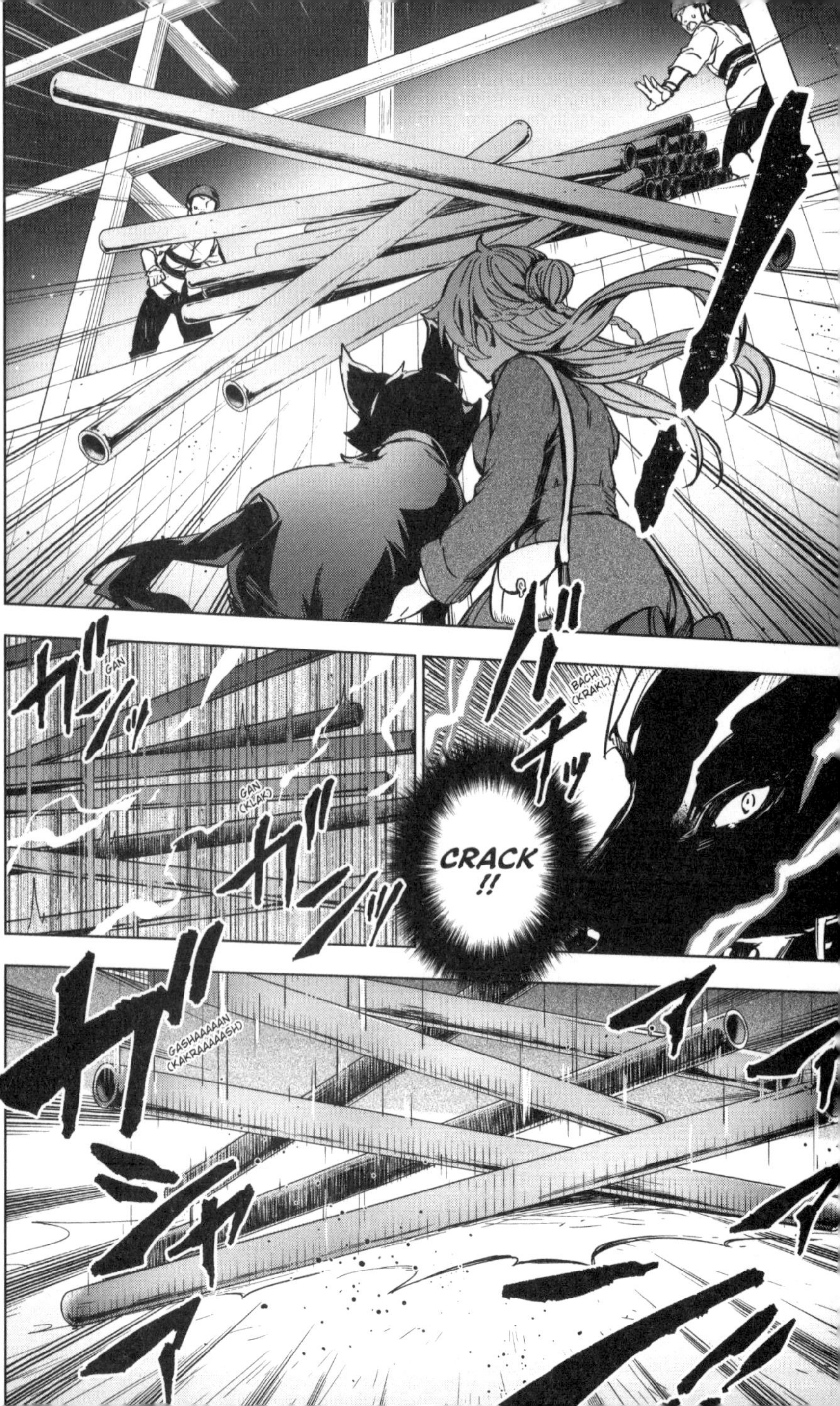
BACHI (KRAKL)
CRACK !!
GAN
GAN (KLAK)
GASHAAAAAN (KAKRAAAAASH)

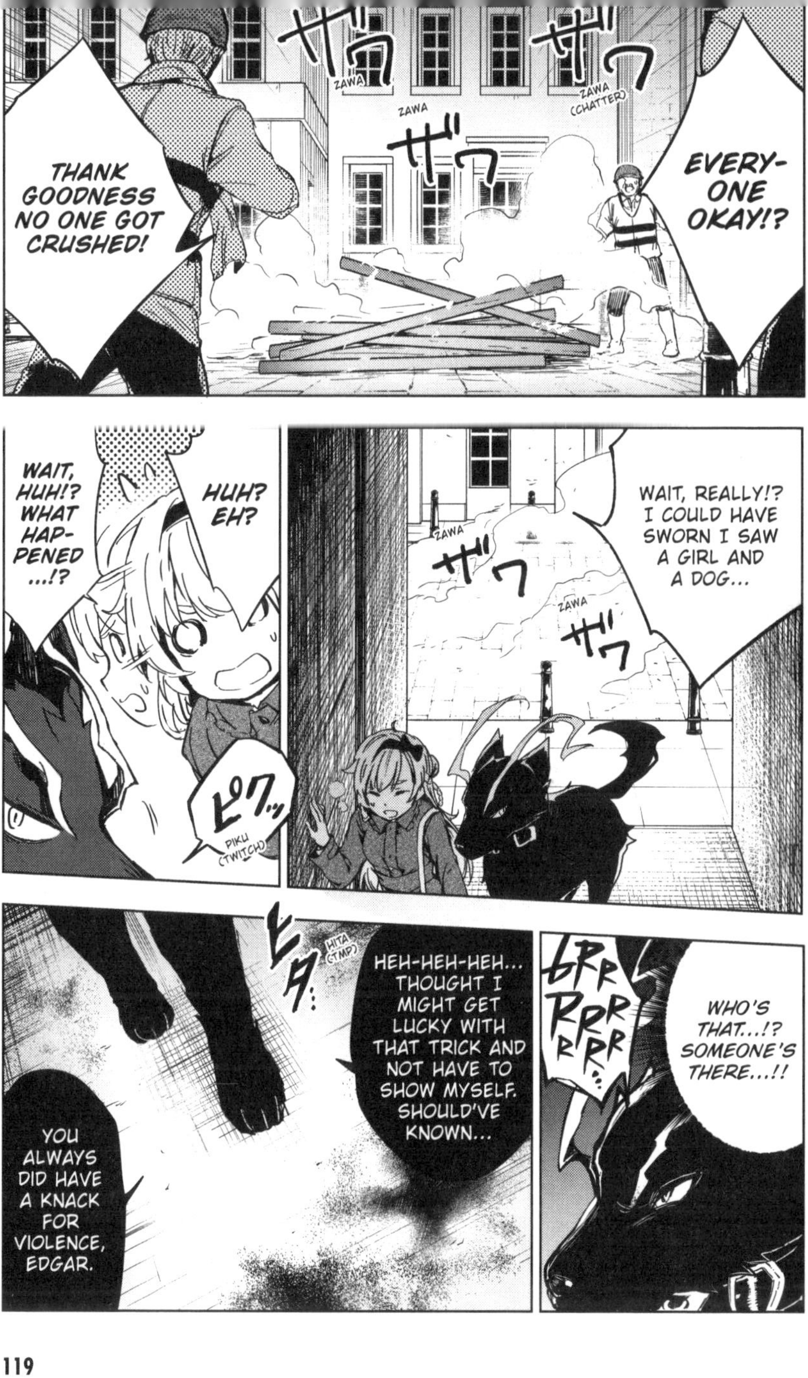
EVERY-ONE OKAY!?
ザワ
ZAWA (CHATTER)
ザワ
ZAWA
ザワ
ZAWA
THANK GOODNESS NO ONE GOT CRUSHED!
WAIT, REALLY!? I COULD HAVE SWORN I SAW A GIRL AND A DOG...
ザワ
ZAWA
ザワ
ZAWA
HUH? EH?
WAIT, HUH!? WHAT HAP-PENED ...!?
ピクッ
PIKU (TWITCH)
WHO'S THAT...!? SOMEONE'S THERE...!!
GRRRRRRRRR...
ヒタ
HITA (STMP)
HEH-HEH-HEH... THOUGHT I MIGHT GET LUCKY WITH THAT TRICK AND NOT HAVE TO SHOW MYSELF. SHOULD'VE KNOWN...
YOU ALWAYS DID HAVE A KNACK FOR VIOLENCE, EDGAR.

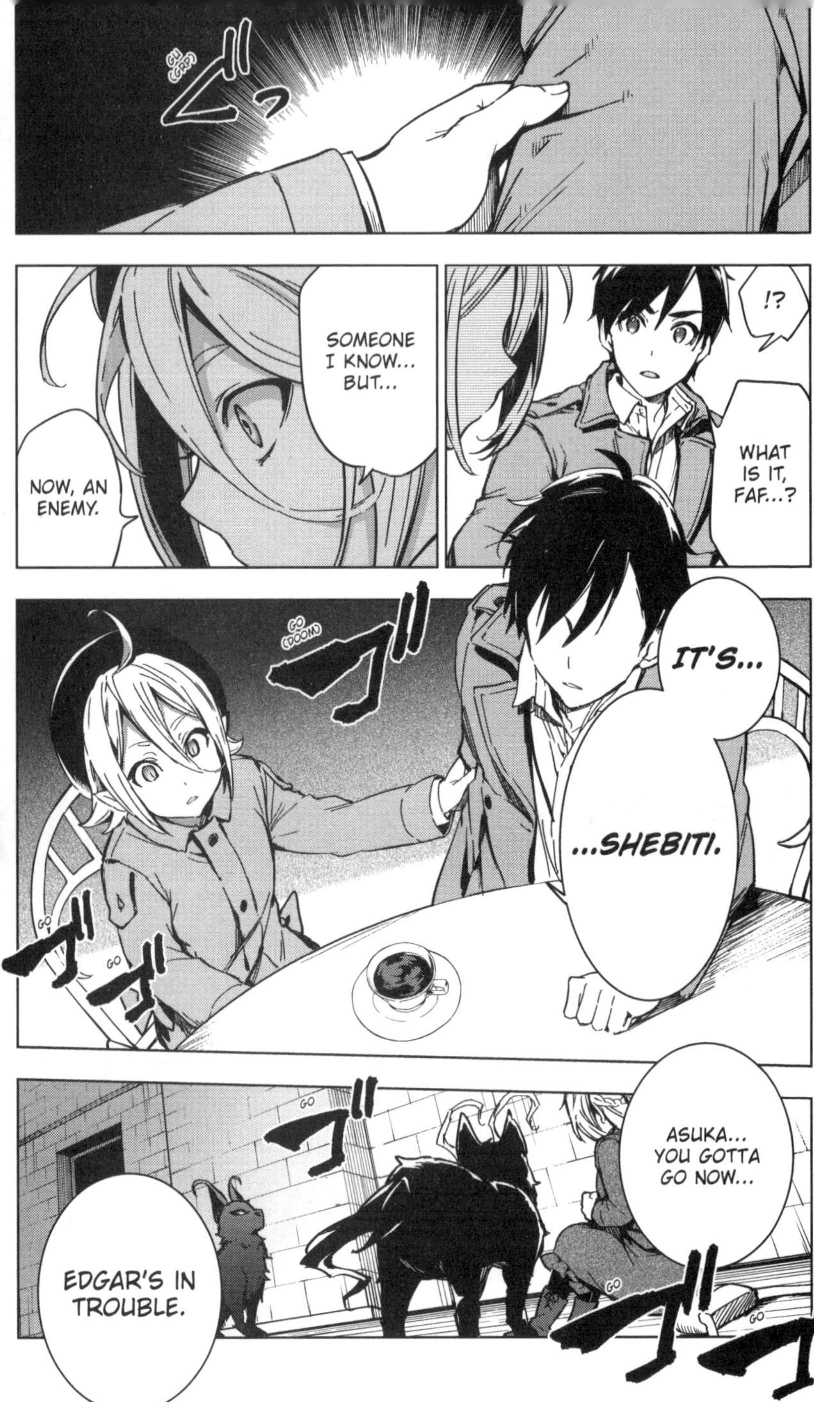
GU (GRIP)
!?
WHAT IS IT, FAF...?
SOMEONE I KNOW... BUT...
NOW, AN ENEMY.
GO (DOOM)
IT'S...
...SHEBITI.
GO
GO
GO
ASUKA... YOU GOTTA GO NOW...
EDGAR'S IN TROUBLE.
GO
GO

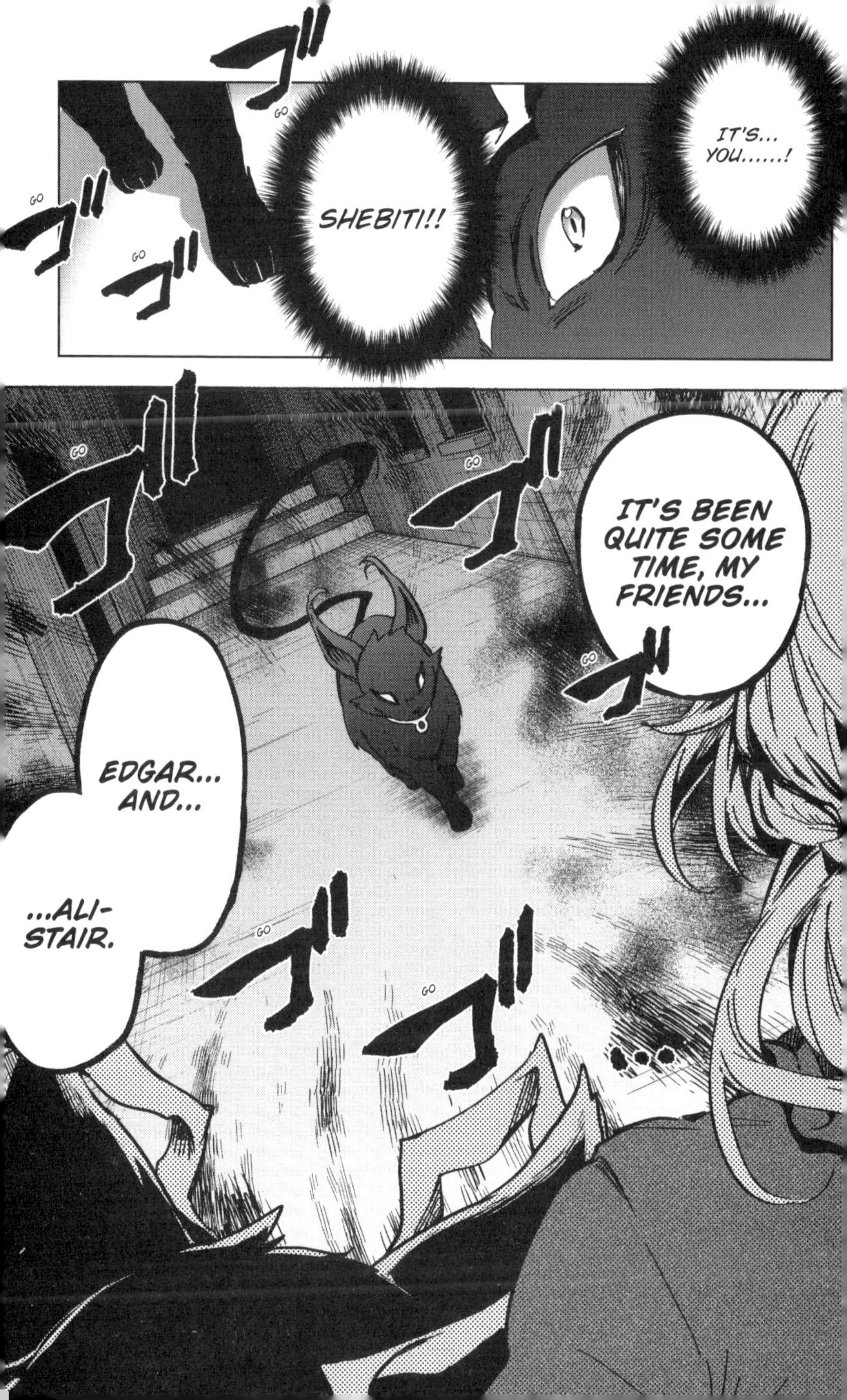
GO
GO
GO
IT'S... YOU......!
SHEBITI!!
GO
GO
IT'S BEEN QUITE SOME TIME, MY FRIENDS...
GO
GO
EDGAR... AND...
...
GO
GO
...ALI-STAIR.

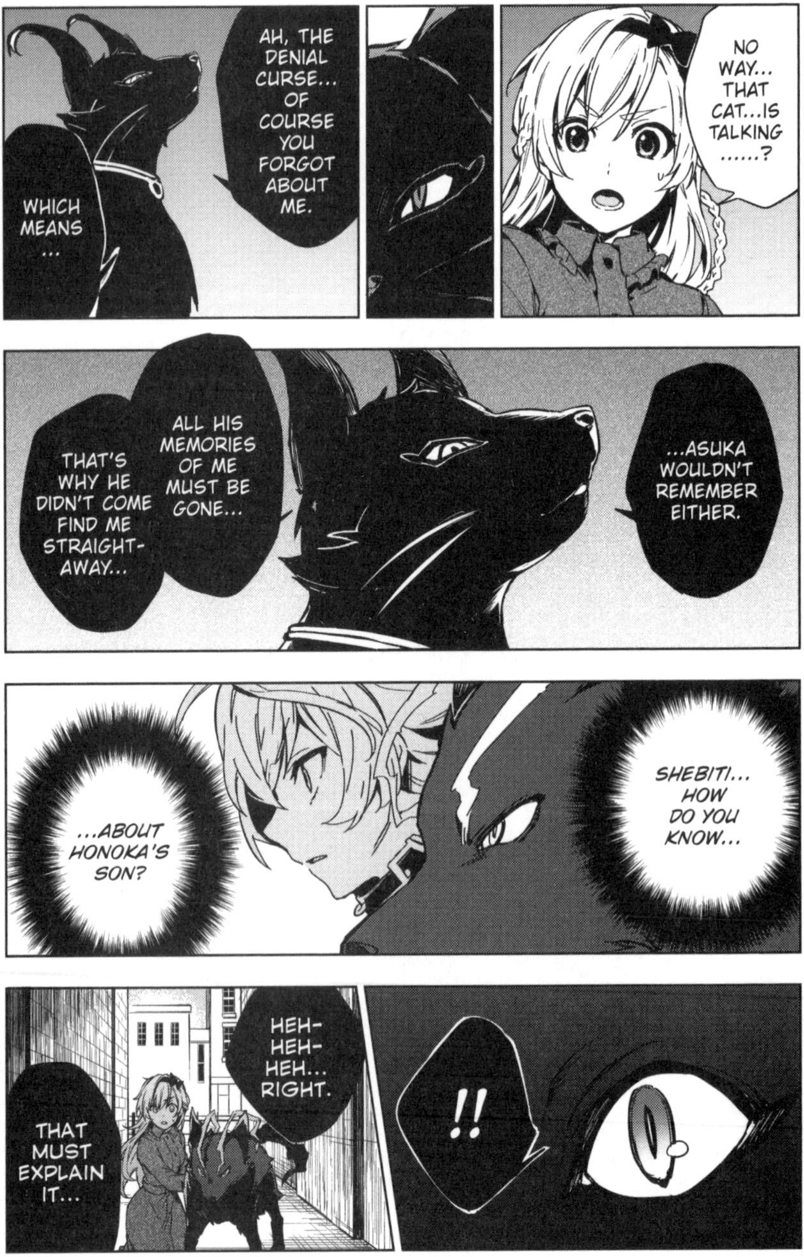
NO WAY... THAT CAT...IS TALKING ......?
AH, THE DENIAL CURSE... OF COURSE YOU FORGOT ABOUT ME.
WHICH MEANS ...
...ASUKA WOULDN'T REMEMBER EITHER.
ALL HIS MEMORIES OF ME MUST BE GONE...
THAT'S WHY HE DIDN'T COME FIND ME STRAIGHT-AWAY...
SHEBITI... HOW DO YOU KNOW...
...ABOUT HONOKA'S SON?
!!
HEH-HEH-HEH... RIGHT.
THAT MUST EXPLAIN IT...

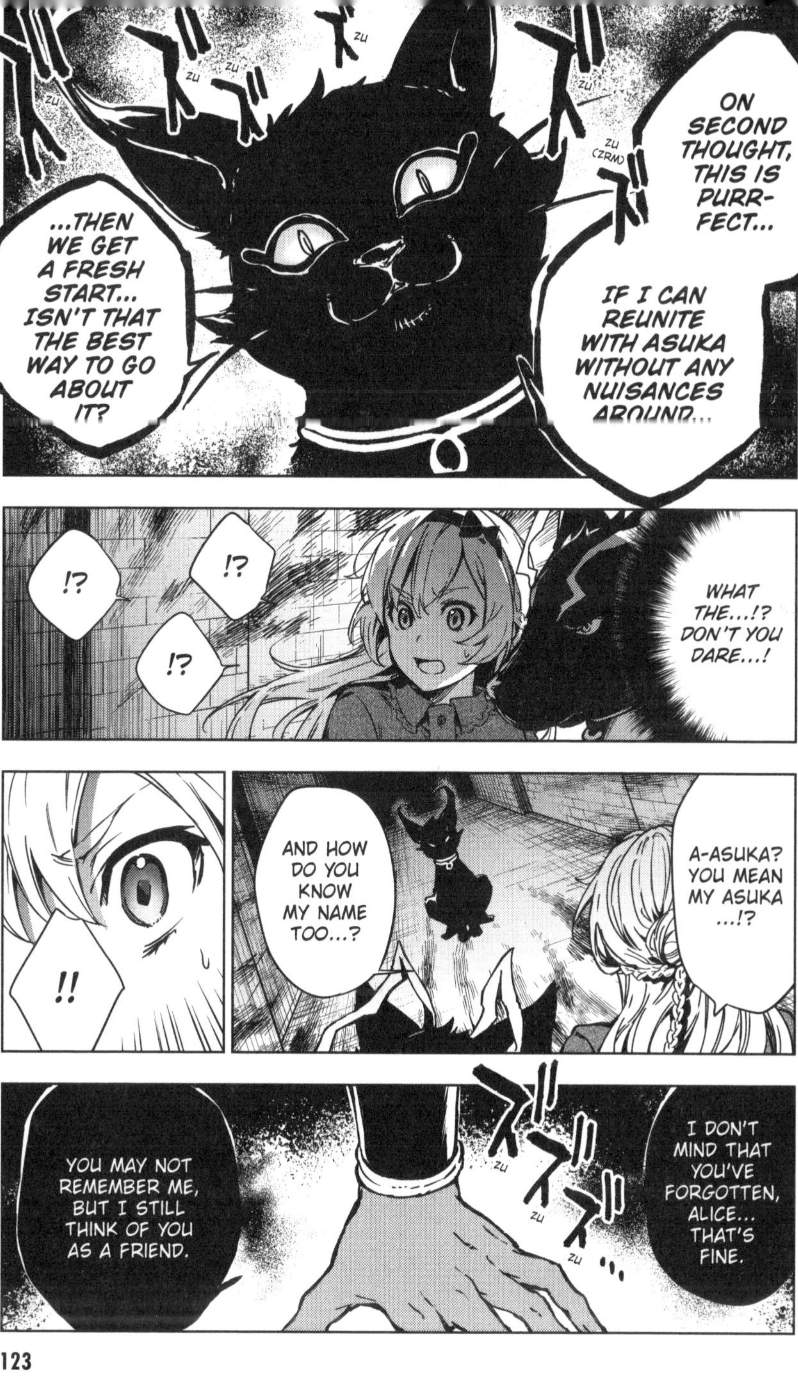
ZU
ZU (ZRM)
ON SECOND THOUGHT, THIS IS PURRFECT...
IF I CAN REUNITE WITH ASUKA WITHOUT ANY NUISANCES AROUND...
...THEN WE GET A FRESH START... ISN'T THAT THE BEST WAY TO GO ABOUT IT?
WHAT THE...!? DON'T YOU DARE...!
!?
!?
!?
A-ASUKA? YOU MEAN MY ASUKA ...!?
AND HOW DO YOU KNOW MY NAME TOO...?
!!
I DON'T MIND THAT YOU'VE FORGOTTEN, ALICE... THAT'S FINE.
ZU
YOU MAY NOT REMEMBER ME, BUT I STILL THINK OF YOU AS A FRIEND.

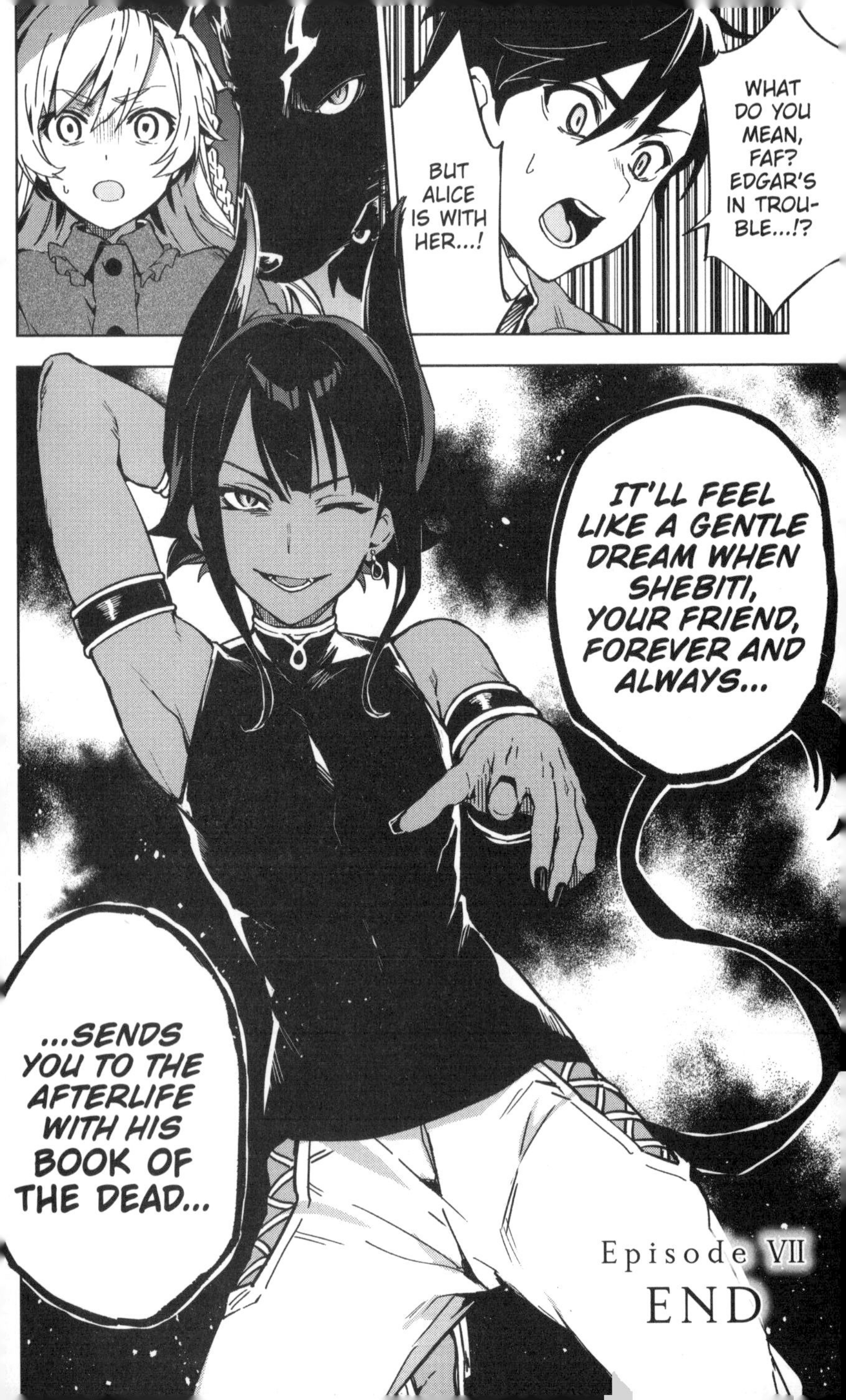
WHAT DO YOU MEAN, FAF? EDGAR'S IN TROUBLE...!?
BUT ALICE IS WITH HER...!
IT'LL FEEL LIKE A GENTLE DREAM WHEN SHEBITI, YOUR FRIEND, FOREVER AND ALWAYS...
...SENDS YOU TO THE AFTERLIFE WITH HIS BOOK OF THE DEAD...
Episode VII
END

BESTIA

MAKOTO SANDA MIYAKOKASIWA ACO ARISAKA

BES TIA

MAKOTO
SANDA

MIYAKOKASIWA

ACO
ARISAKA

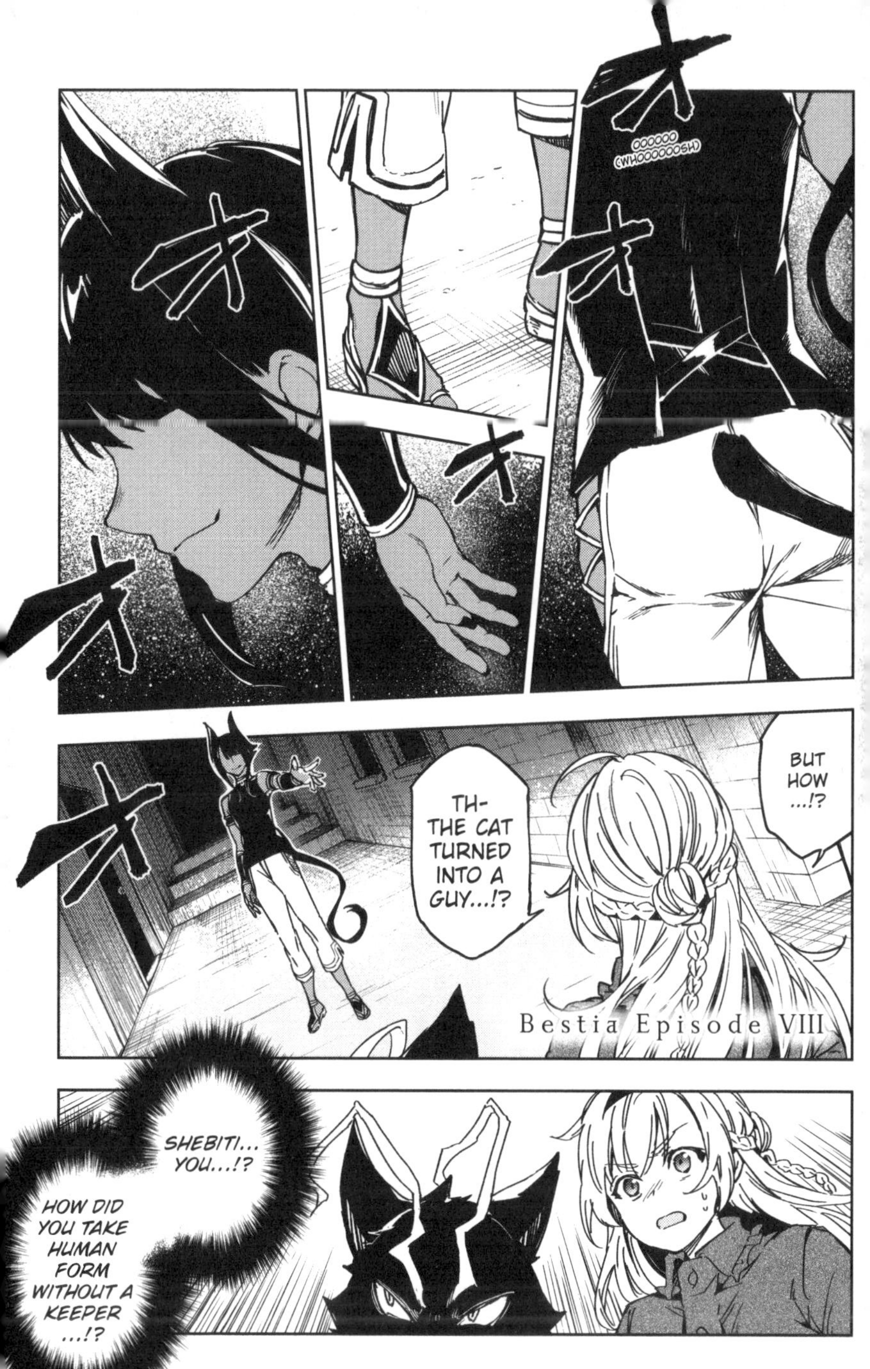
OOOOOO (WHOOOOOOSH)
BUT HOW ...!?
TH- THE CAT TURNED INTO A GUY...!?
Bestia Episode VIII
SHEBITI... YOU...!?
HOW DID YOU TAKE HUMAN FORM WITHOUT A KEEPER ...!?

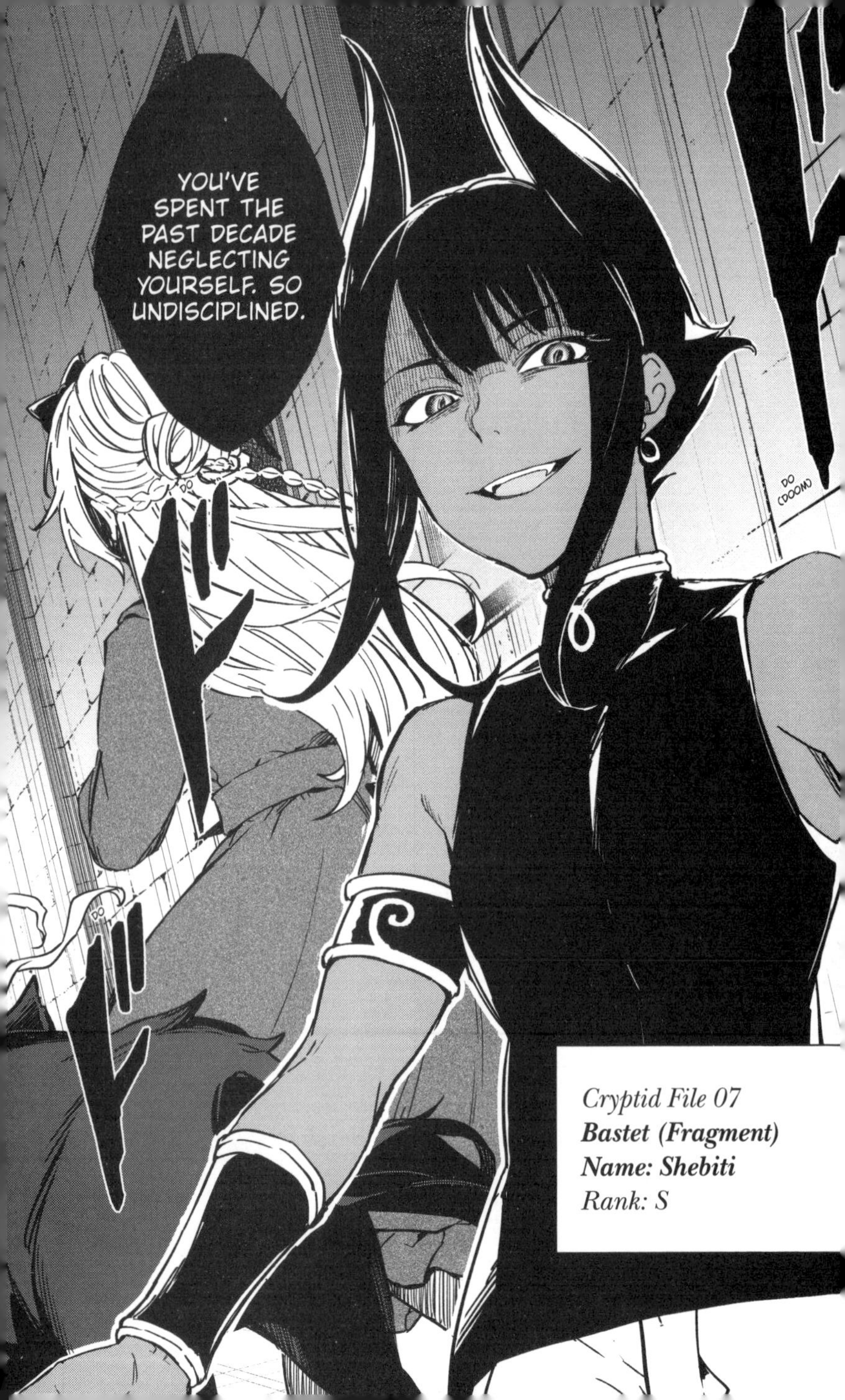
YOU'VE SPENT THE PAST DECADE NEGLECTING YOURSELF. SO UNDISCIPLINED.
DO (DOOM)
DO
DO
Cryptid File 07
Bastet (Fragment)
Name: Shebiti
Rank: S

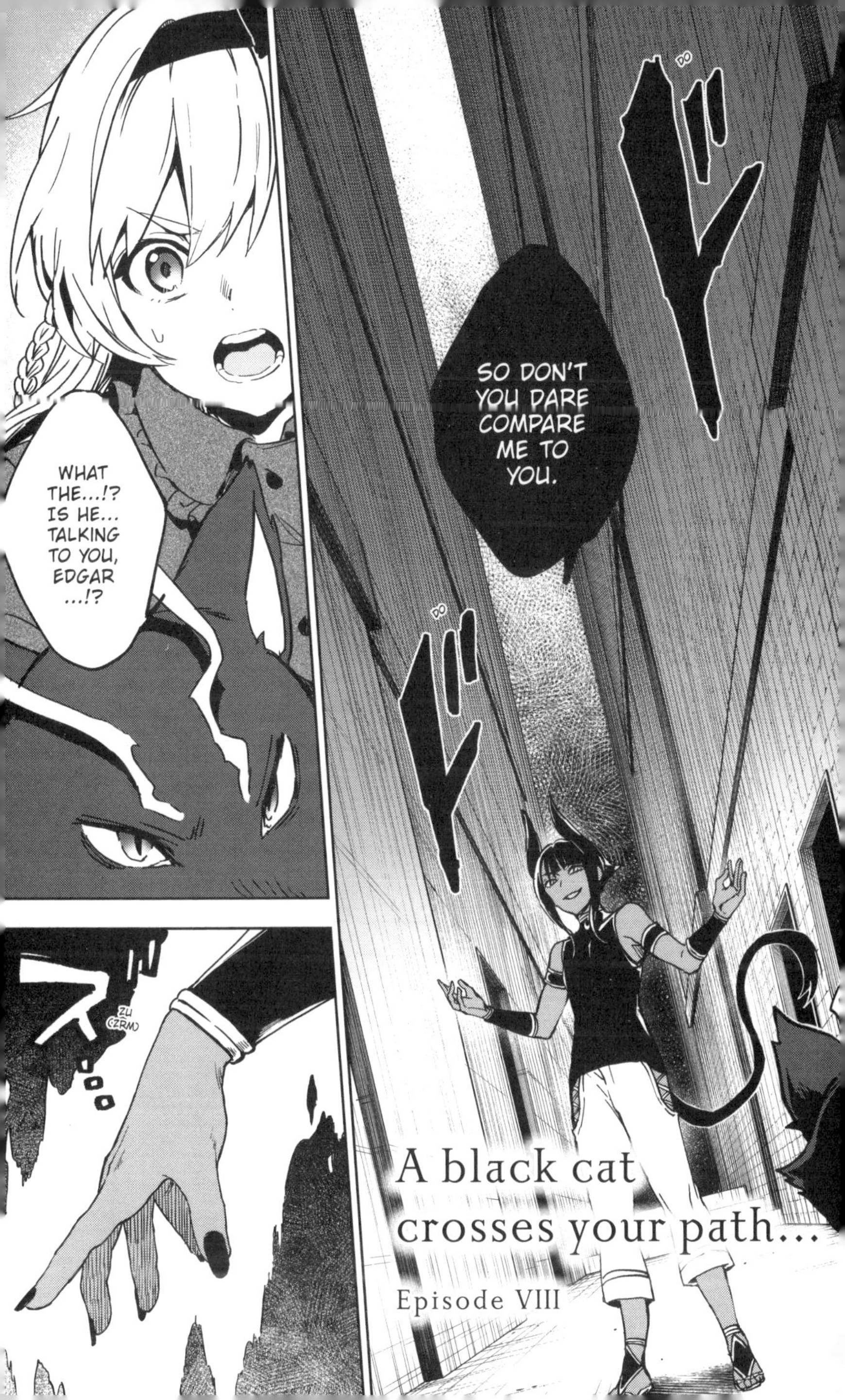
DO
SO DON'T YOU DARE COMPARE ME TO YOU.
DO
A black cat crosses your path...
Episode VIII
WHAT THE...!? IS HE... TALKING TO YOU, EDGAR ...!?
ZU (ZRM)

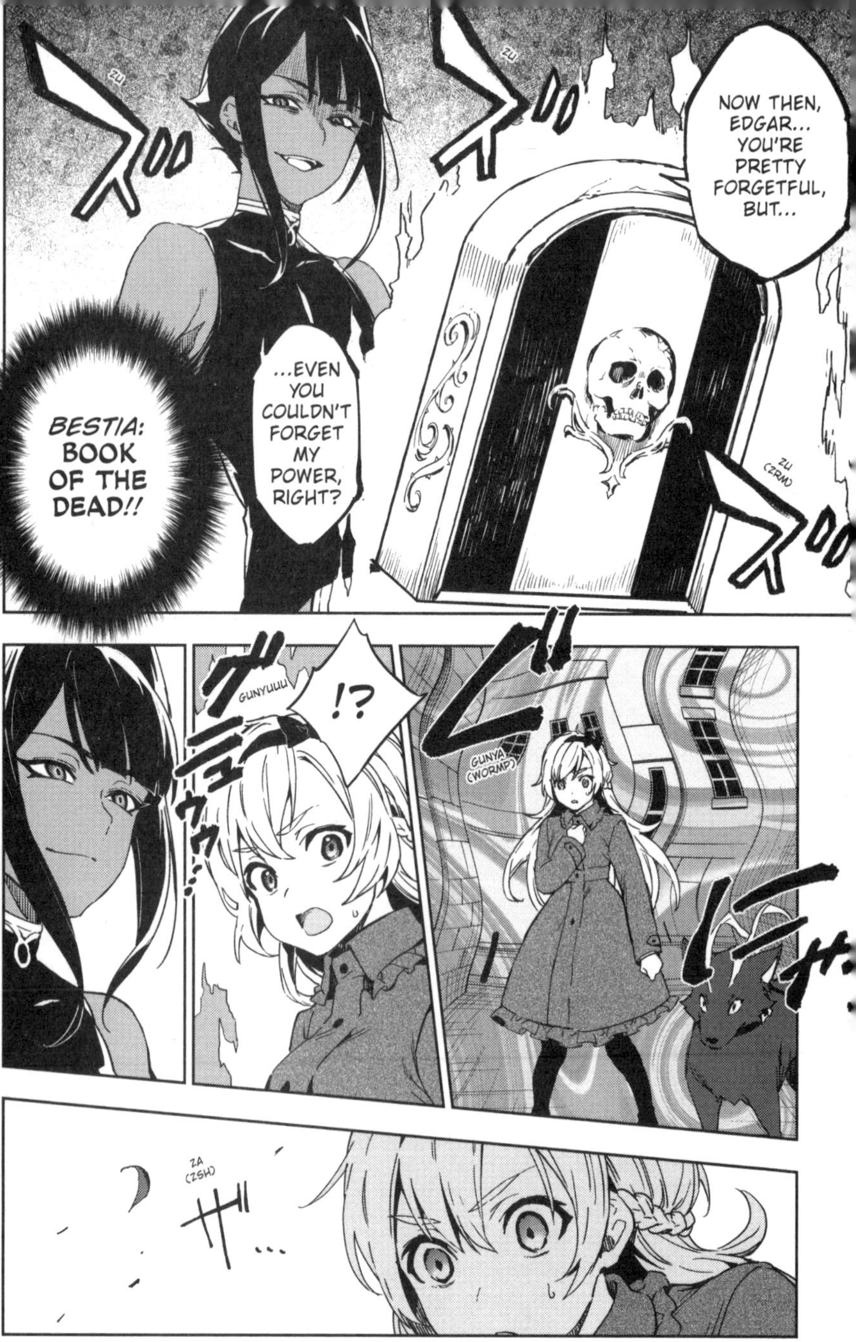
NOW THEN, EDGAR... YOU'RE PRETTY FORGETFUL, BUT...
ZU
ZU (ZRM)
...EVEN YOU COULDN'T FORGET MY POWER, RIGHT?
ZU
BESTIA: BOOK OF THE DEAD!!
GUNYA (WORMP)
!?
GUNYUUU
ZA (ZSH)
...

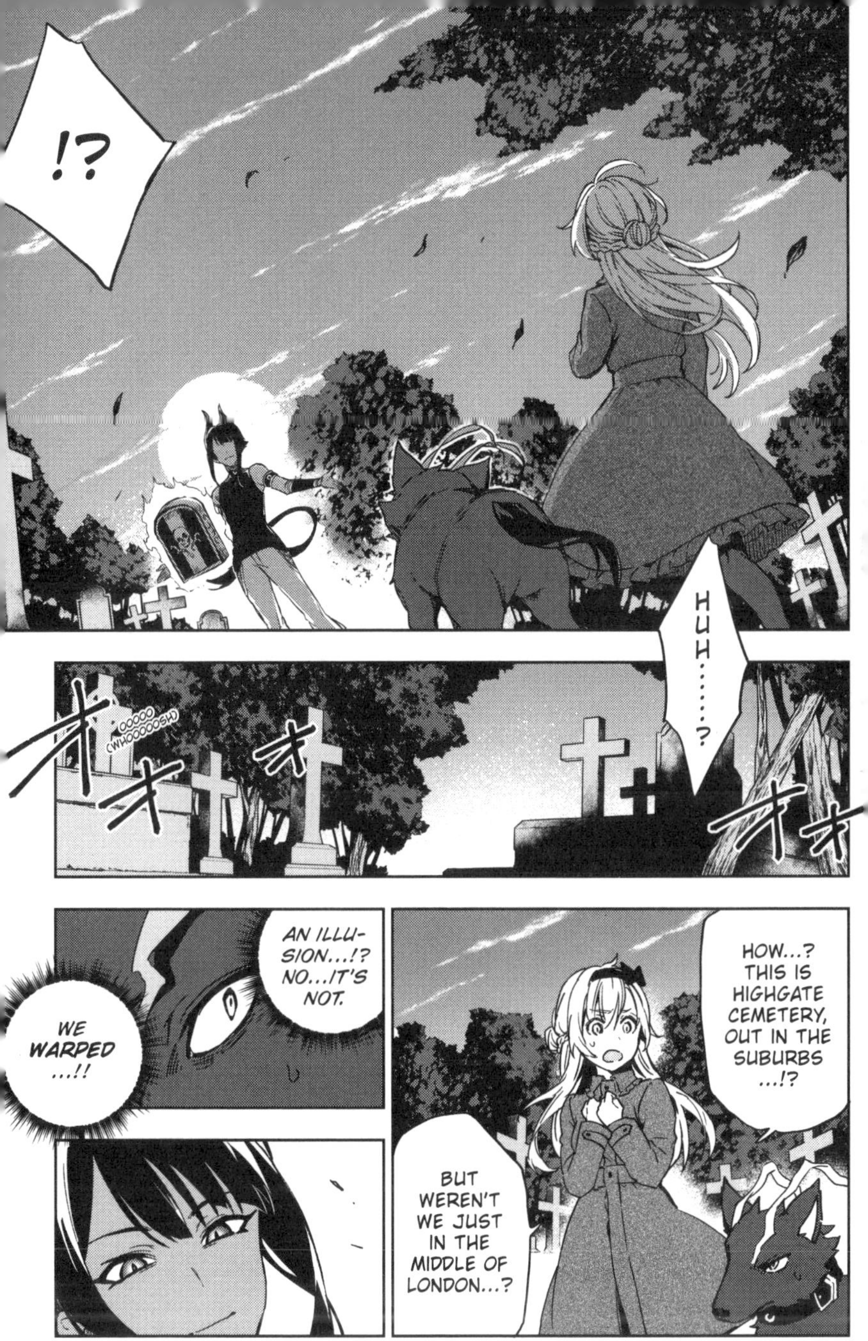
!?
HUH.....?
OOOOO (WHOOOOOSH)
HOW...? THIS IS HIGHGATE CEMETERY, OUT IN THE SUBURBS ...!?
BUT WEREN'T WE JUST IN THE MIDDLE OF LONDON...?
AN ILLUSION...!? NO...IT'S NOT.
WE WARPED ...!!

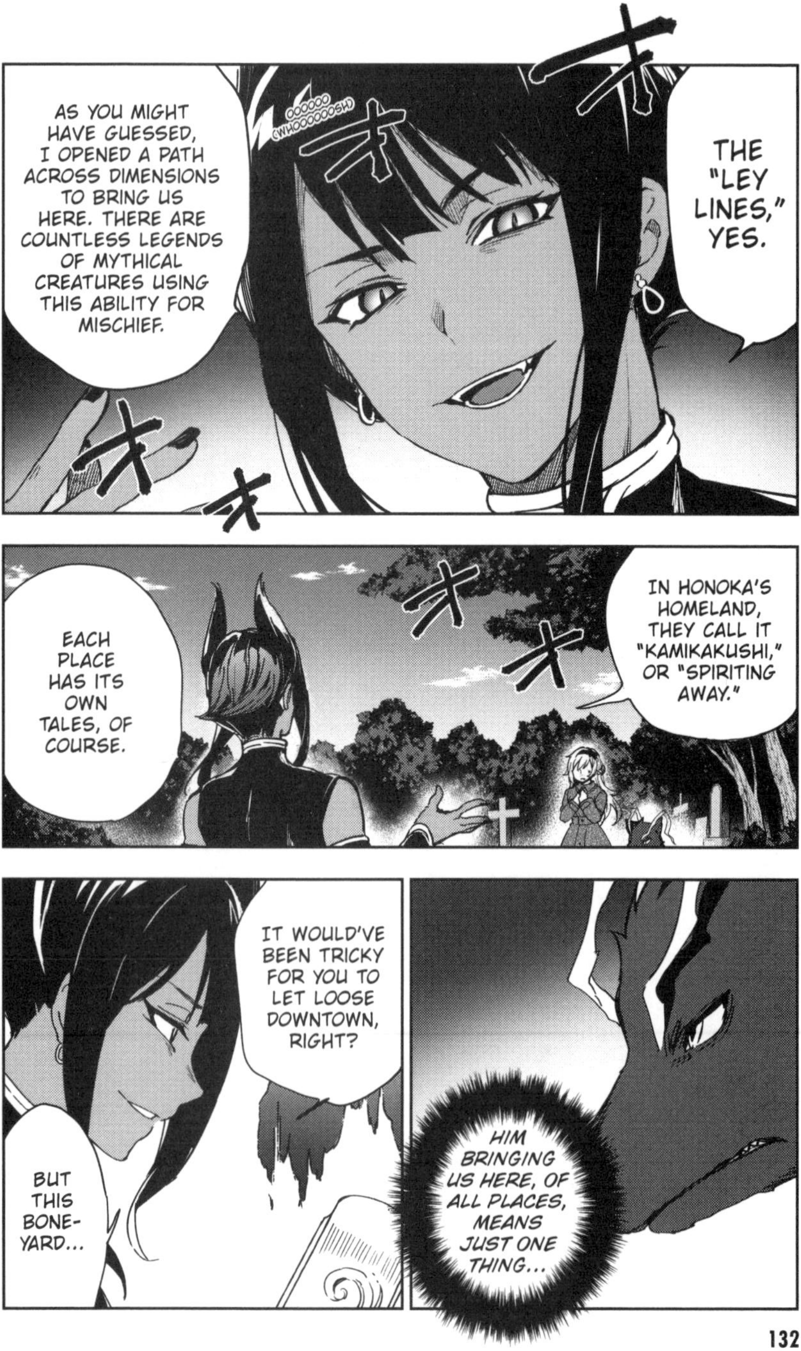

OOOOOO (WHOOOOOOOSH)
THE "LEY LINES," YES.
AS YOU MIGHT HAVE GUESSED, I OPENED A PATH ACROSS DIMENSIONS TO BRING US HERE. THERE ARE COUNTLESS LEGENDS OF MYTHICAL CREATURES USING THIS ABILITY FOR MISCHIEF.
IN HONOKA'S HOMELAND, THEY CALL IT "KAMIKAKUSHI," OR "SPIRITING AWAY."
EACH PLACE HAS ITS OWN TALES, OF COURSE.
HIM BRINGING US HERE, OF ALL PLACES, MEANS JUST ONE THING...
IT WOULD'VE BEEN TRICKY FOR YOU TO LET LOOSE DOWNTOWN, RIGHT?
BUT THIS BONE-YARD...

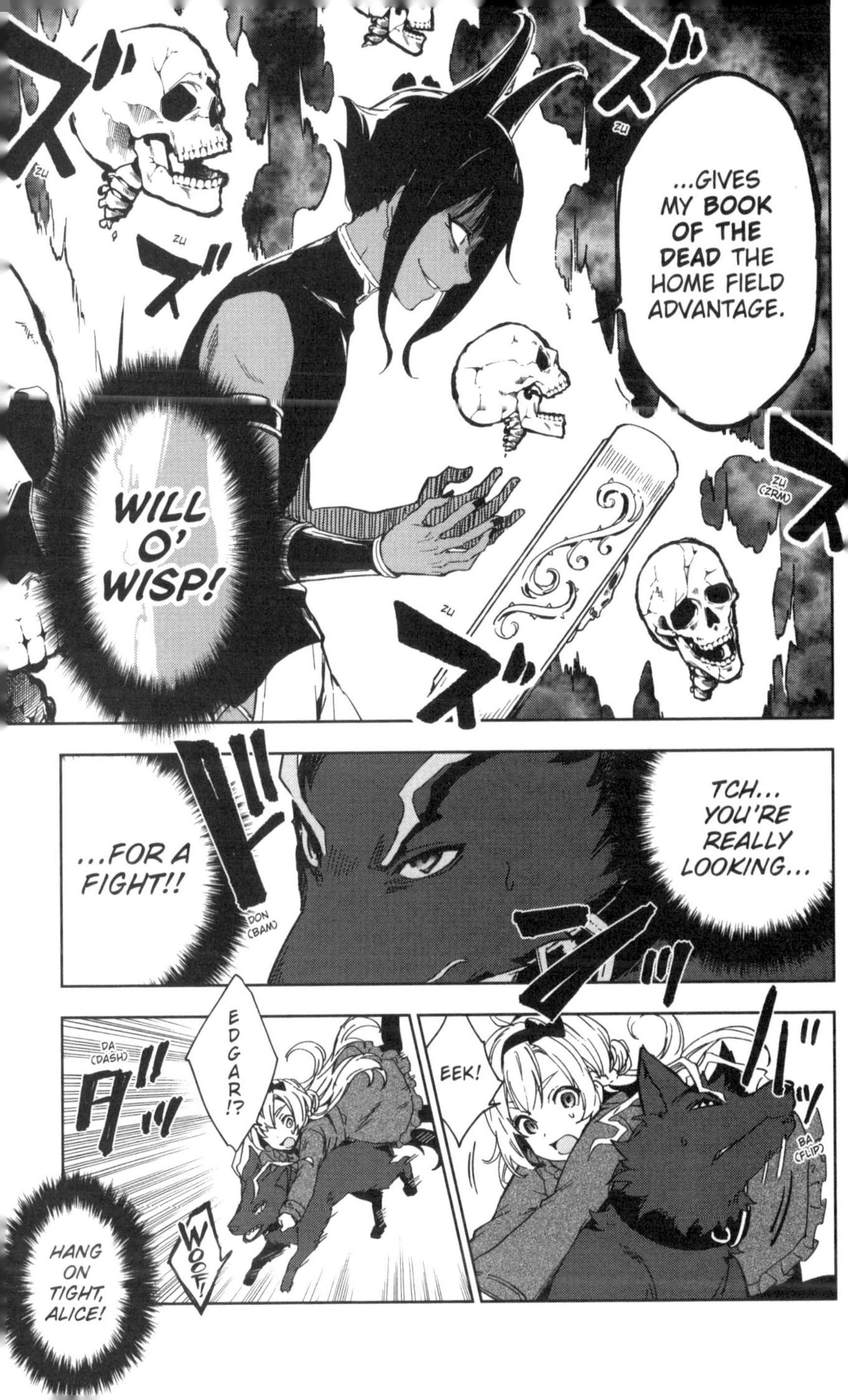
ZU
...GIVES MY BOOK OF THE DEAD THE HOME FIELD ADVANTAGE.
ZU (ZRM)
ZU
ZU
ZU
WILL O' WISP!
TCH... YOU'RE REALLY LOOKING...
...FOR A FIGHT!!
DON (BAM)
BA (FLIP)
EEK!
EDGAR!?
DA (DASH)
WOOF!
HANG ON TIGHT, ALICE!

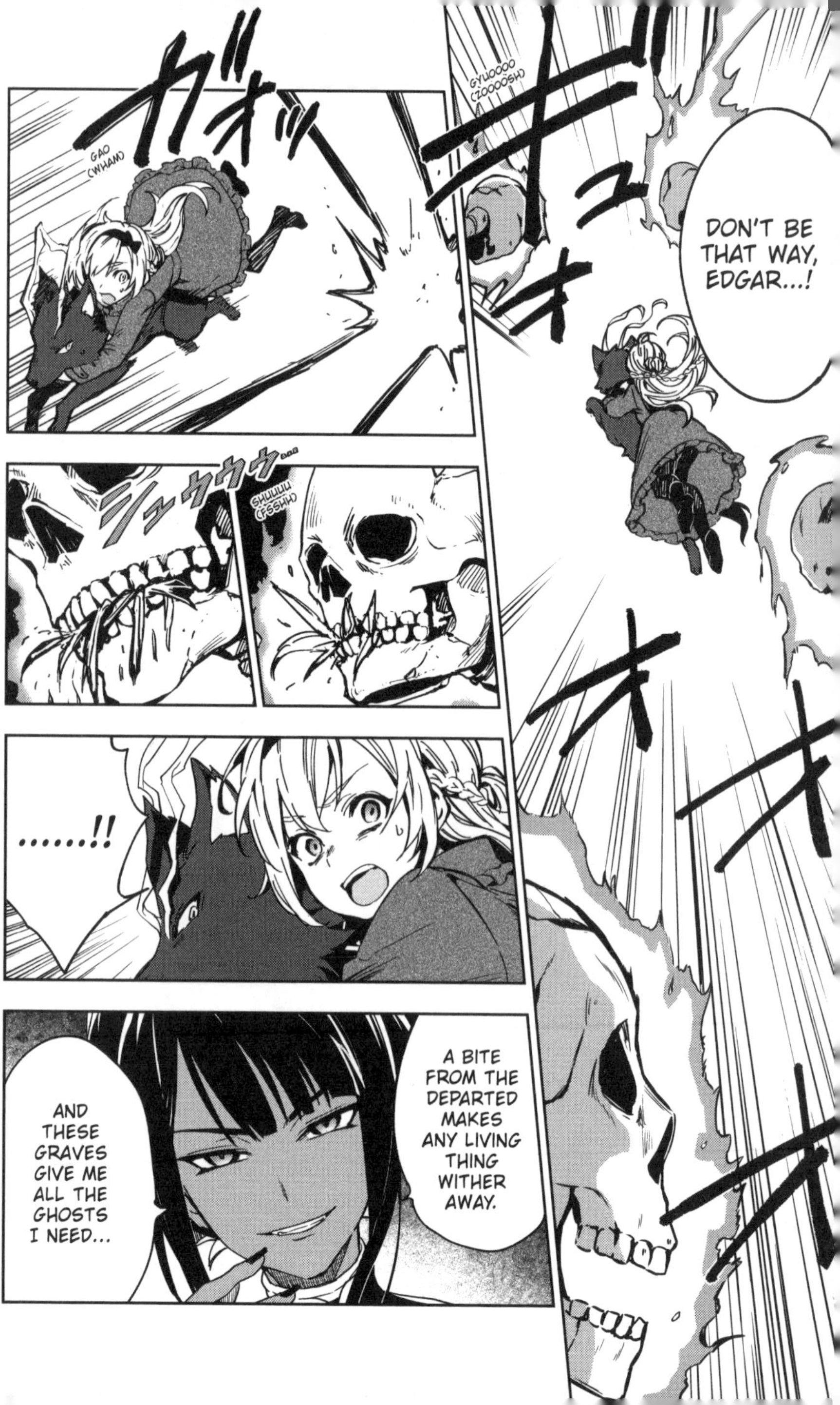
GYUOOOO (ZOOOOSH)
DON'T BE THAT WAY, EDGAR...!
GAO (WHAM)
SHUUUUU (FSSHH)
......!!
A BITE FROM THE DEPARTED MAKES ANY LIVING THING WITHER AWAY.
AND THESE GRAVES GIVE ME ALL THE GHOSTS I NEED...

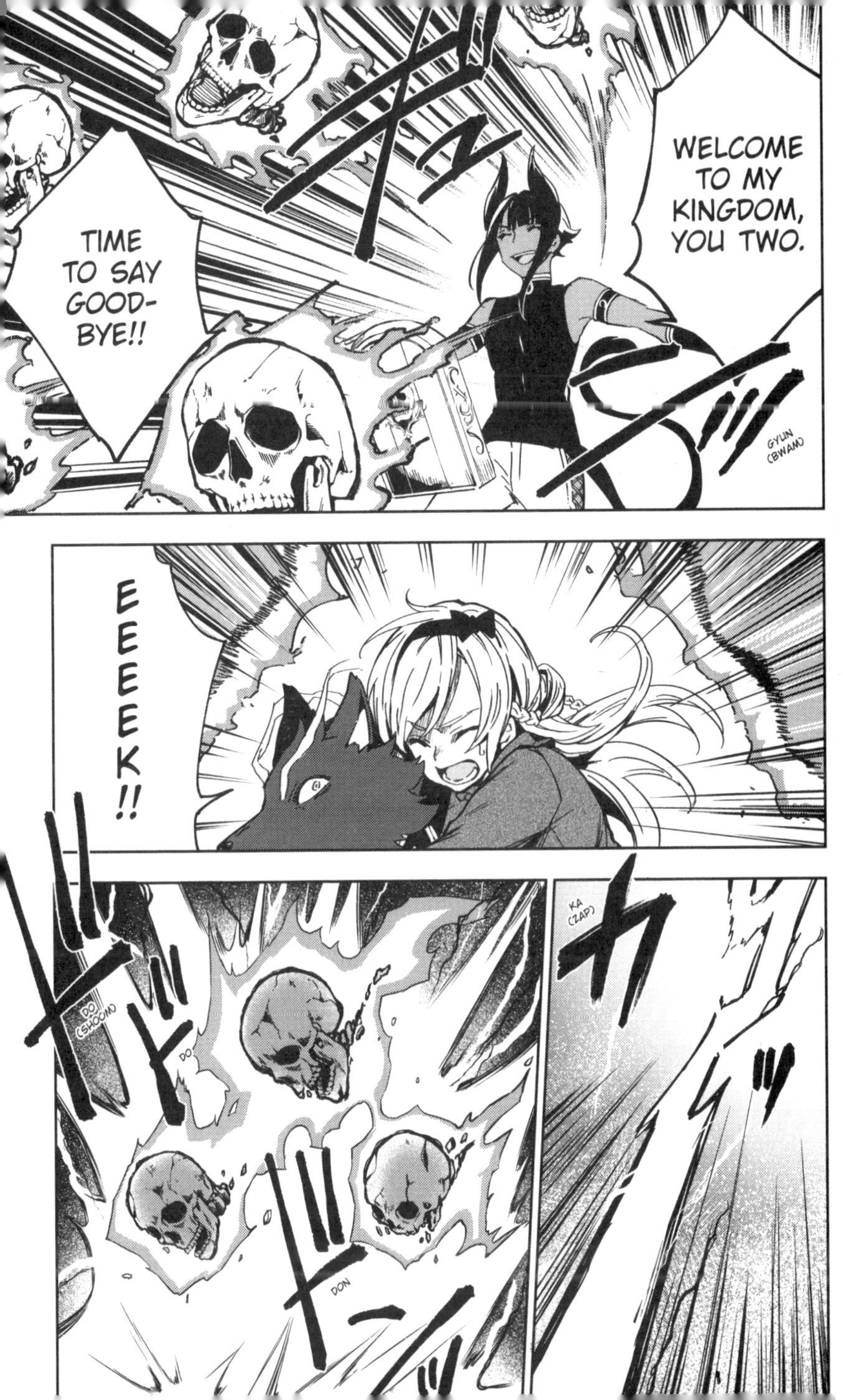
WELCOME TO MY KINGDOM, YOU TWO.
TIME TO SAY GOOD-BYE!!
GYUN (BWAM)
EEEEEK!!
KA (ZAP)
DO (SHOOM)
DO
DON

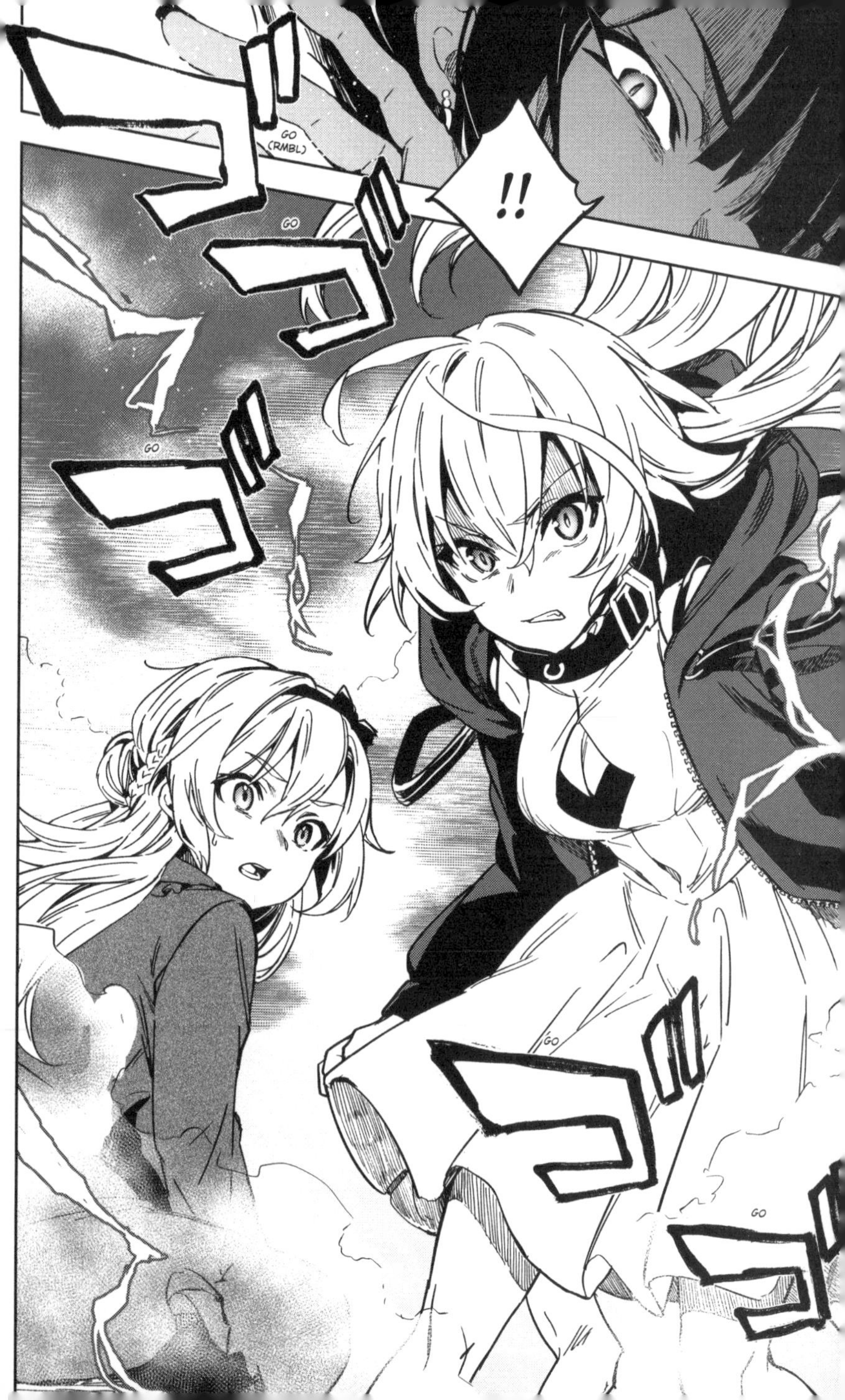
!!
GO
(RMBL)
GO
GO
GO
GO

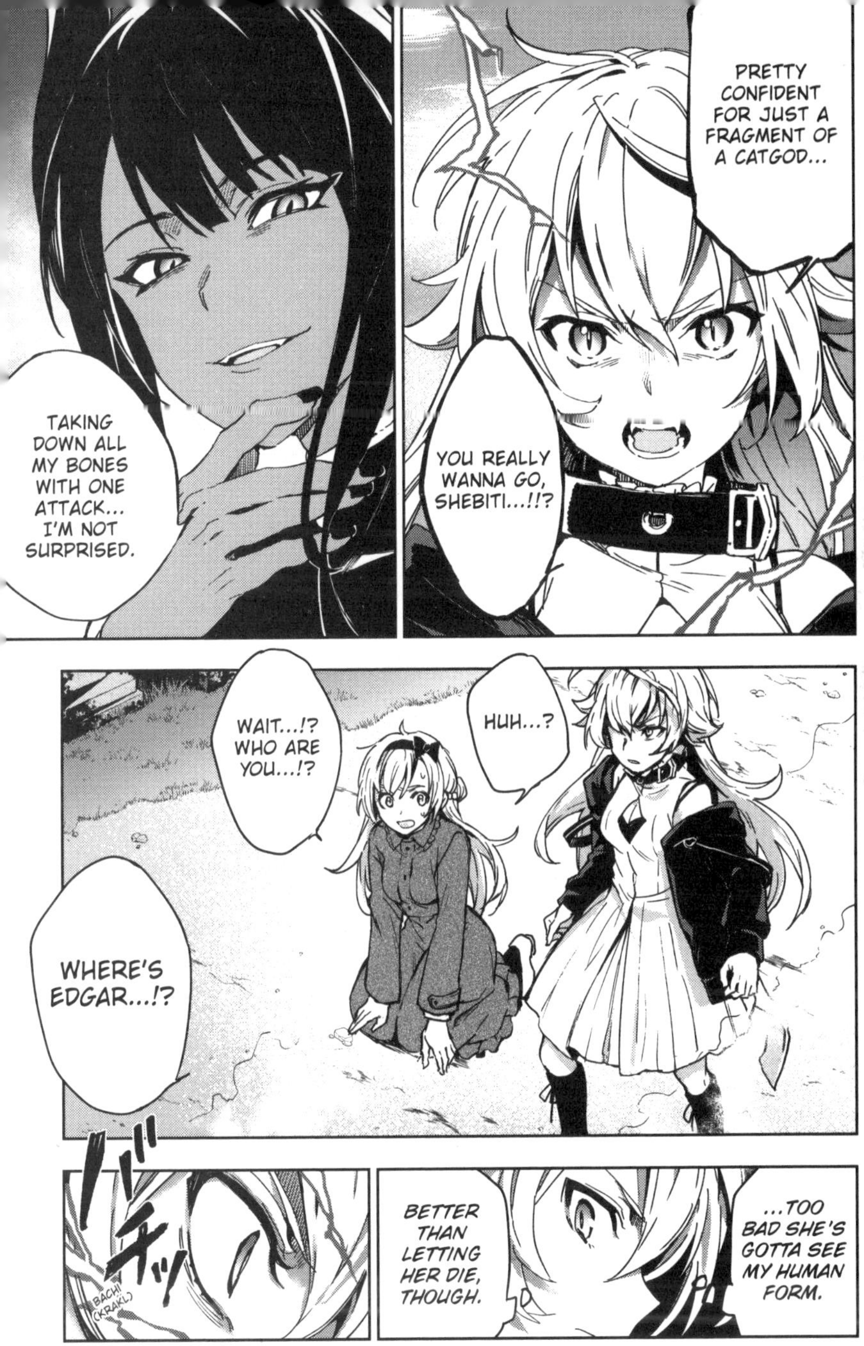
PRETTY CONFIDENT FOR JUST A FRAGMENT OF A CATGOD...
YOU REALLY WANNA GO, SHEBITI...!!?
TAKING DOWN ALL MY BONES WITH ONE ATTACK... I'M NOT SURPRISED.
HUH...?
WAIT...!? WHO ARE YOU...!?
WHERE'S EDGAR...!?
...TOO BAD SHE'S GOTTA SEE MY HUMAN FORM.
BETTER THAN LETTING HER DIE, THOUGH.
BACHI (KRAKL)

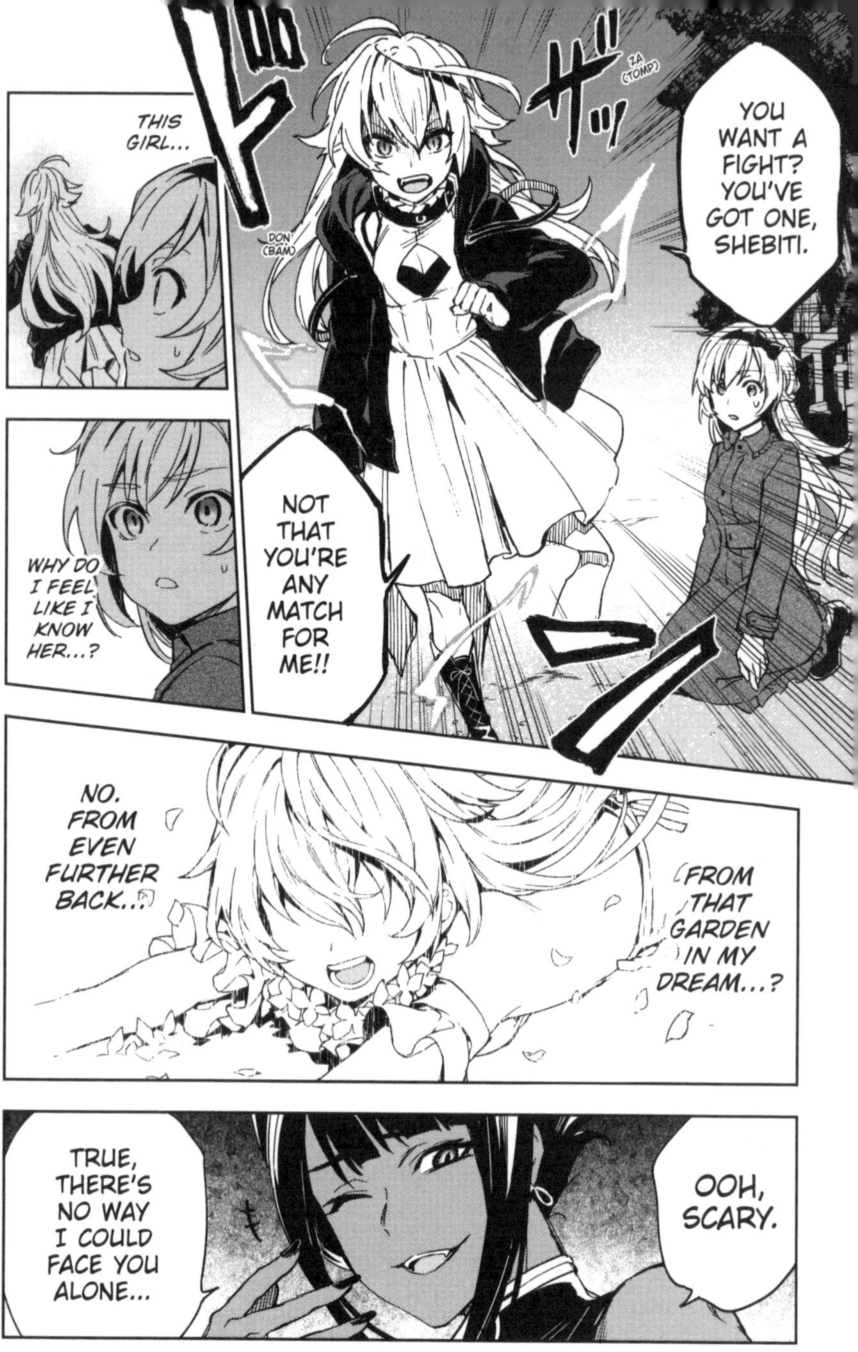
ZA (TOMP)
YOU WANT A FIGHT? YOU'VE GOT ONE, SHEBITI.
DON (BAM)
NOT THAT YOU'RE ANY MATCH FOR ME!!
THIS GIRL...
WHY DO I FEEL LIKE I KNOW HER...?
FROM THAT GARDEN IN MY DREAM...?
NO. FROM EVEN FURTHER BACK...
OOH, SCARY.
TRUE, THERE'S NO WAY I COULD FACE YOU ALONE...

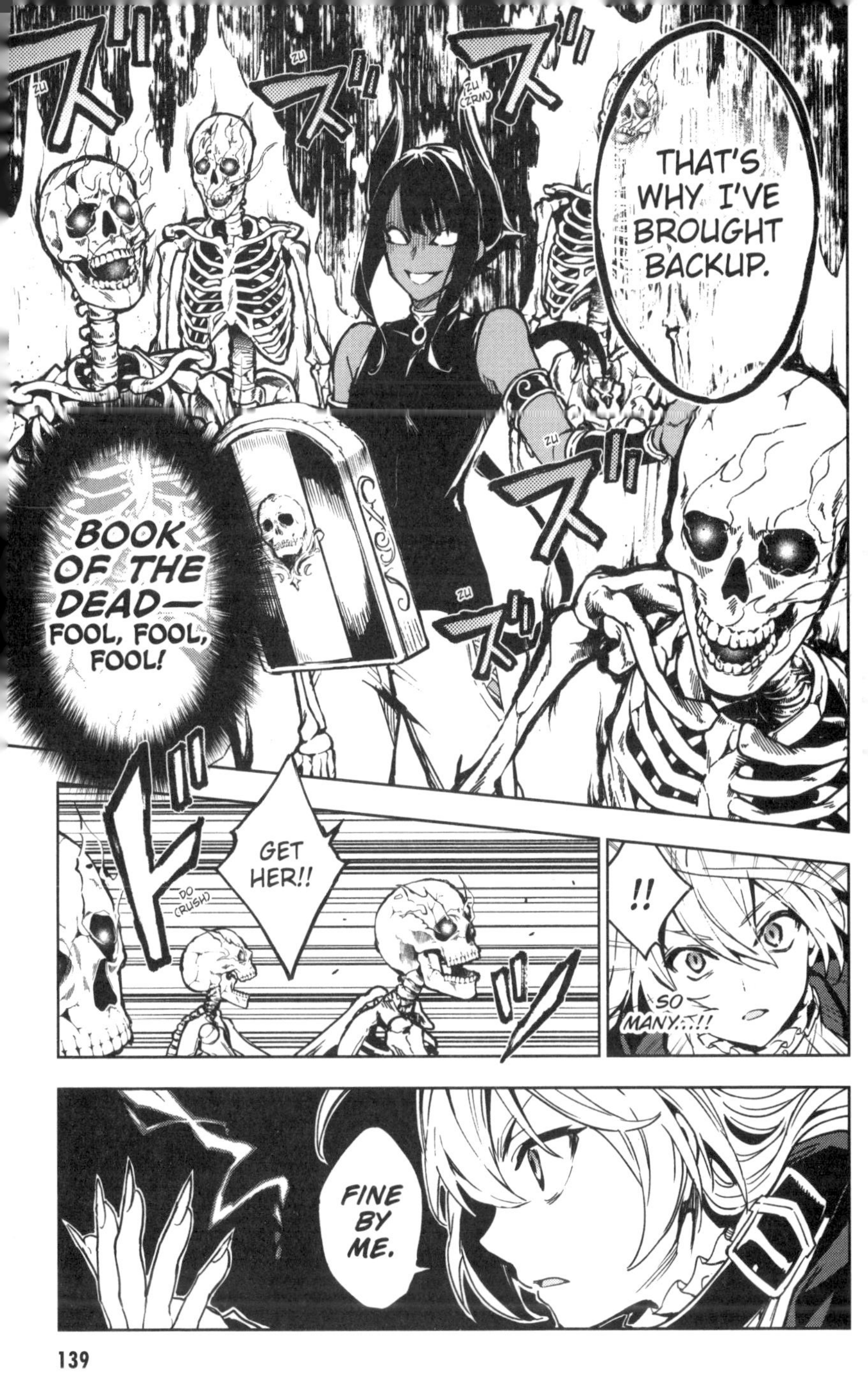
ZU (ZRM)
ZU
ZU
THAT'S WHY I'VE BROUGHT BACKUP.
ZU
ZU
BOOK OF THE DEAD—FOOL, FOOL, FOOL!
!!
SO MANY...!!
GET HER!!
DO (RUSH)
FINE BY ME.

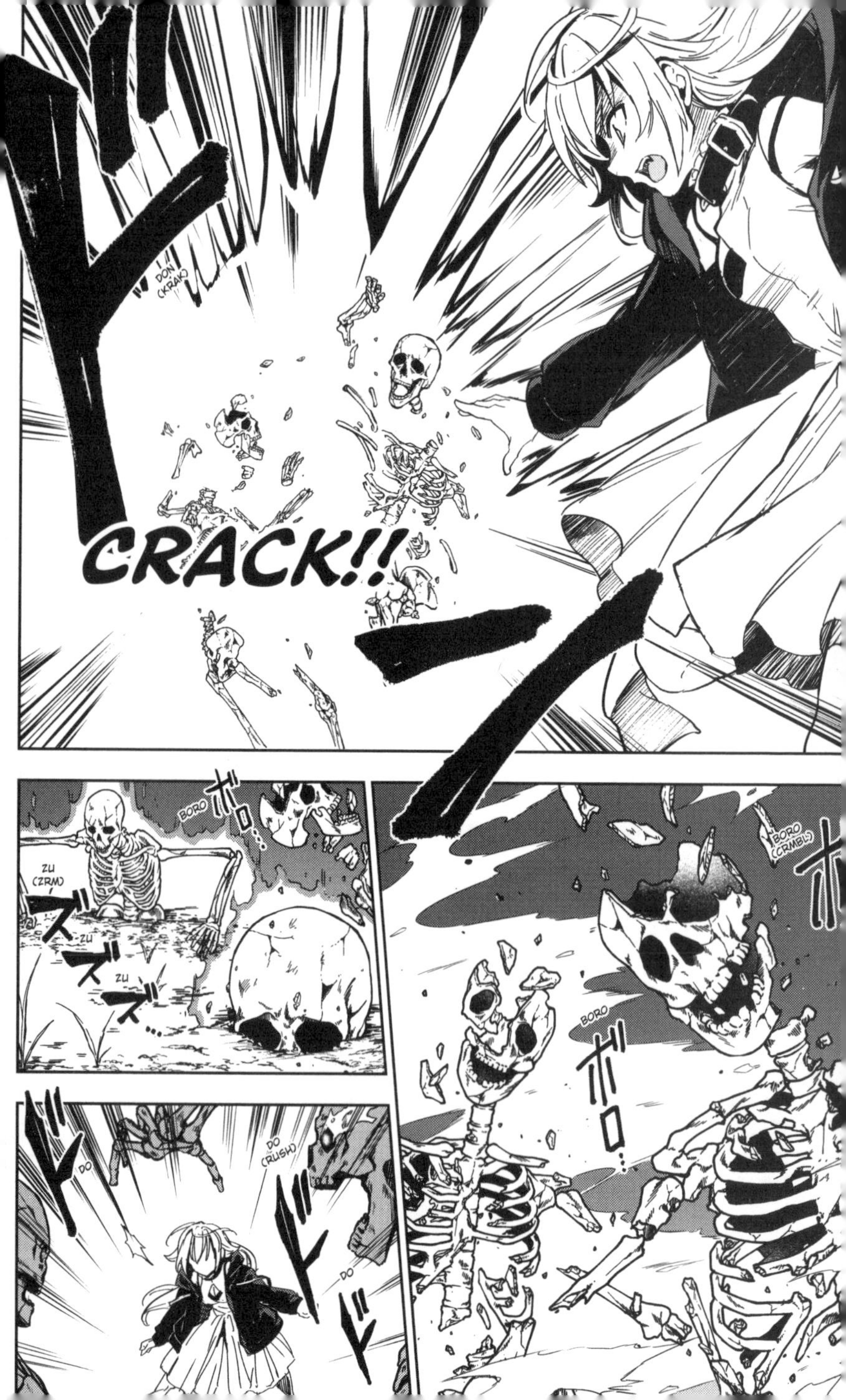
DON (KRAK)
CRACK!!
BORO (CRMBL)
BORO
BORO
ZU (ZRM)
ZU
ZU
DO
DO (RUSH)
DO

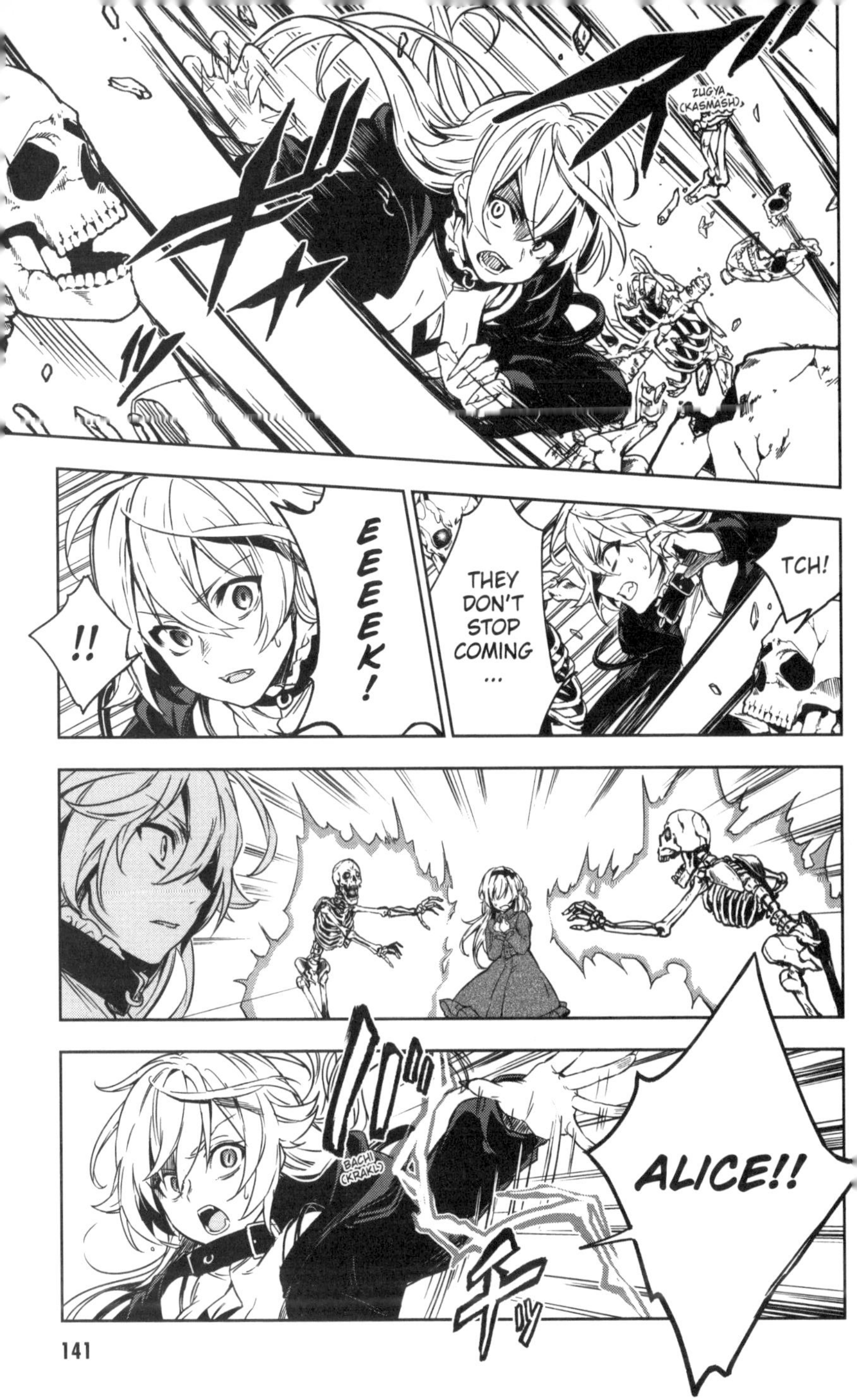
ZUGYA (KASMASH)
TCH!
THEY DON'T STOP COMING ...
EEEEEK!
!!
ALICE!!
BACHI (KRAKL)

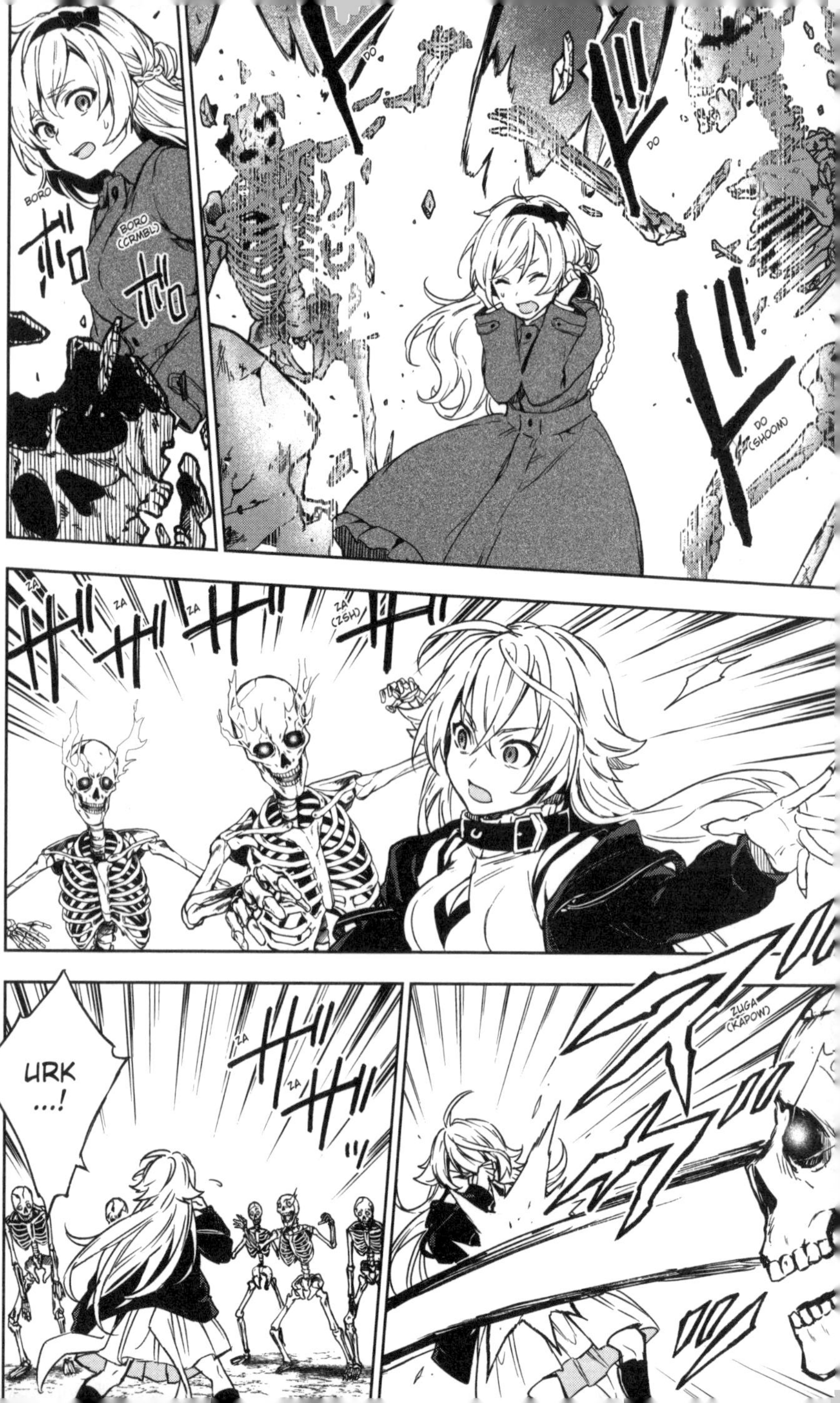
DO
DO
DO (SHOOM)
BORO
BORO (CRMBL)
ZA (ZSH)
ZA
ZA
ZA
ZUGA (KAPOW)
ZA
ZA
URK ...!

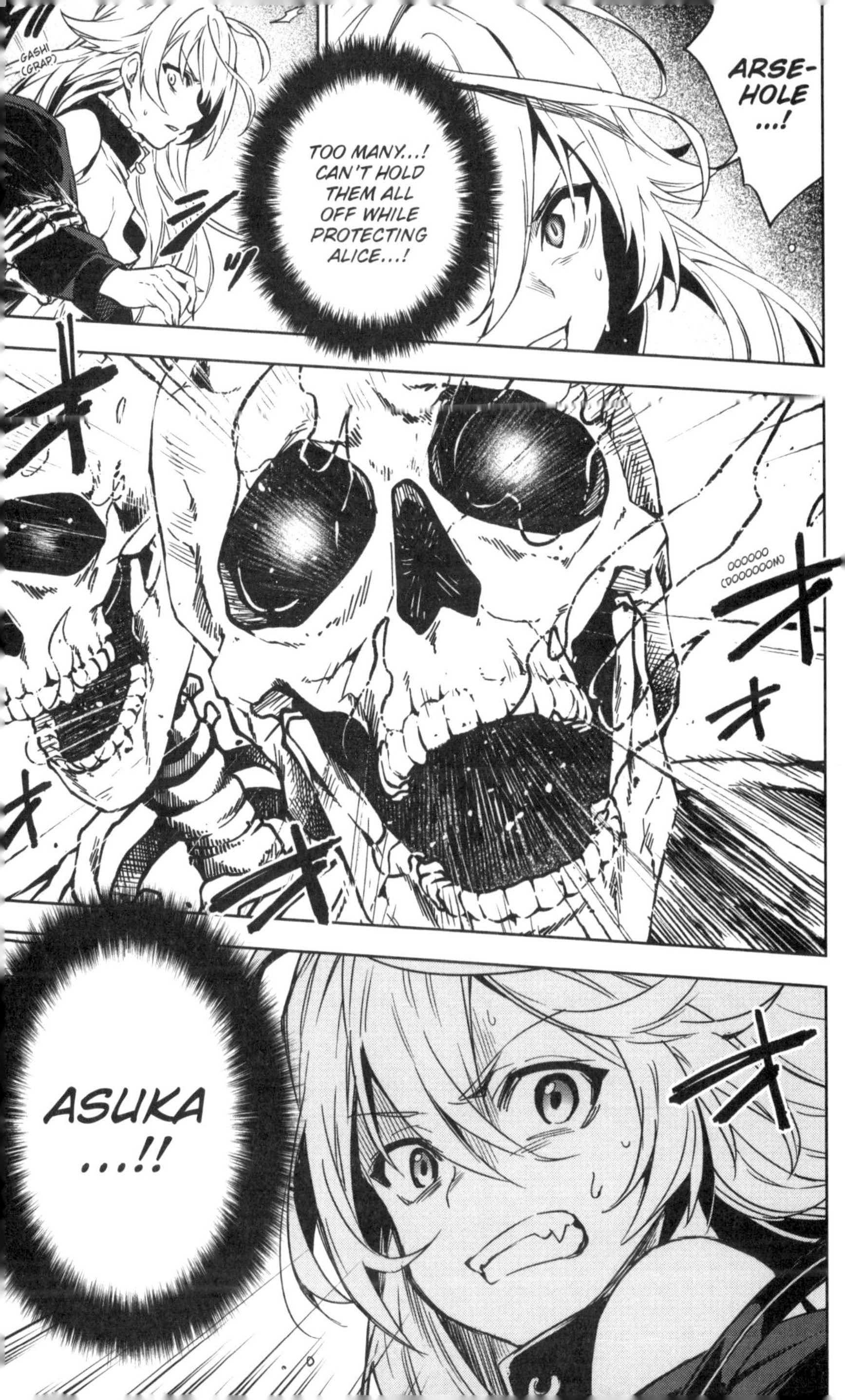

ARSE-HOLE...!
TOO MANY...! CAN'T HOLD THEM ALL OFF WHILE PROTECTING ALICE...!
GASHI (GRAP)
OOOOOO (DOOOOOOM)
ASUKA...!!

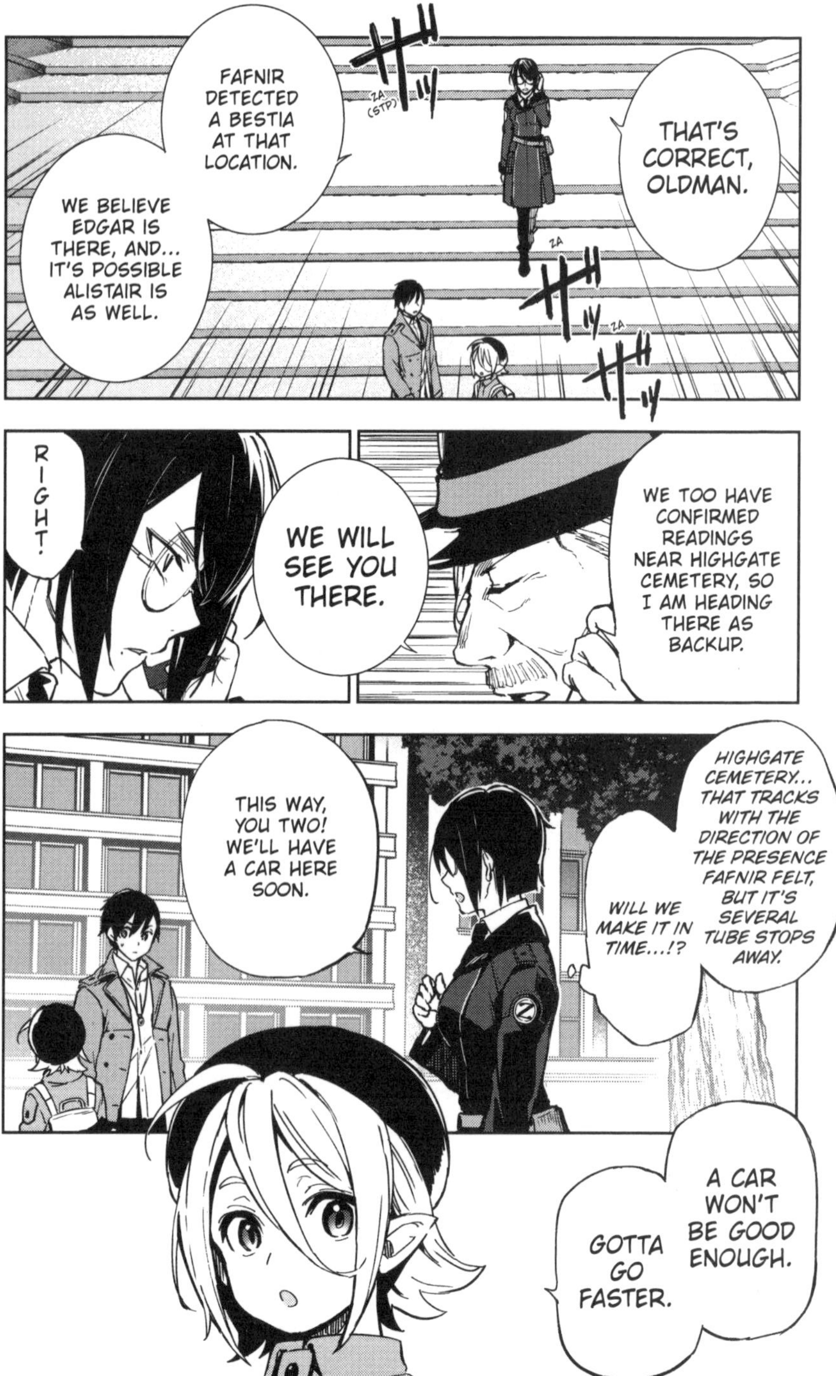
THAT'S CORRECT, OLDMAN.
ZA (STP)
FAFNIR DETECTED A BESTIA AT THAT LOCATION.
WE BELIEVE EDGAR IS THERE, AND... IT'S POSSIBLE ALISTAIR IS AS WELL.
ZA
ZA
WE TOO HAVE CONFIRMED READINGS NEAR HIGHGATE CEMETERY, SO I AM HEADING THERE AS BACKUP.
WE WILL SEE YOU THERE.
RIGHT!
HIGHGATE CEMETERY... THAT TRACKS WITH THE DIRECTION OF THE PRESENCE FAFNIR FELT, BUT IT'S SEVERAL TUBE STOPS AWAY.
WILL WE MAKE IT IN TIME...!?
THIS WAY, YOU TWO! WE'LL HAVE A CAR HERE SOON.
A CAR WON'T BE GOOD ENOUGH.
GOTTA GO FASTER.

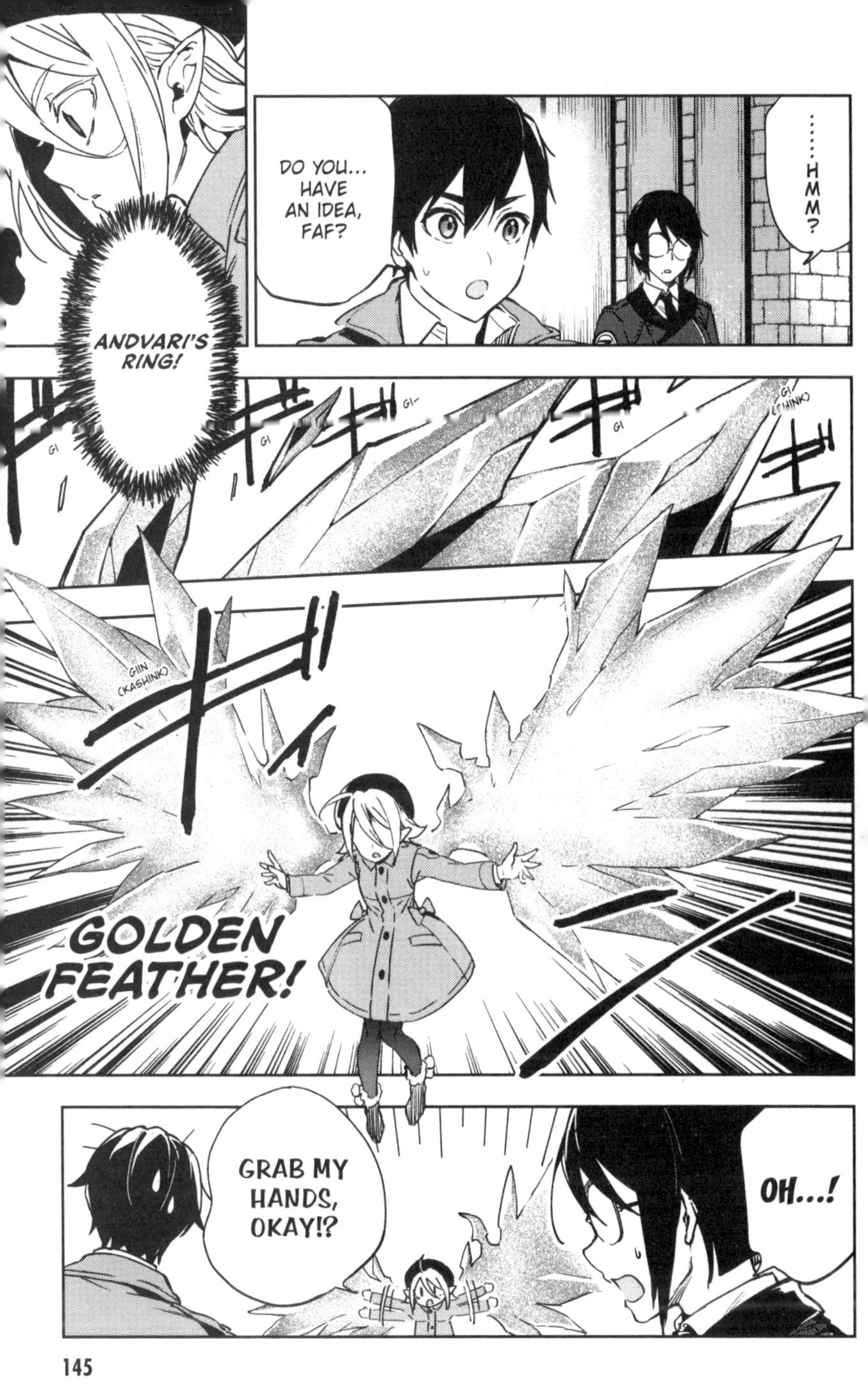
......HMM?
DO YOU... HAVE AN IDEA, FAF?
ANDVARI'S RING!
GI (CHINK)
GI
GI-
GI
GI
GIIN (KASHINK)
GOLDEN FEATHER!
OH...!
GRAB MY HANDS, OKAY!?

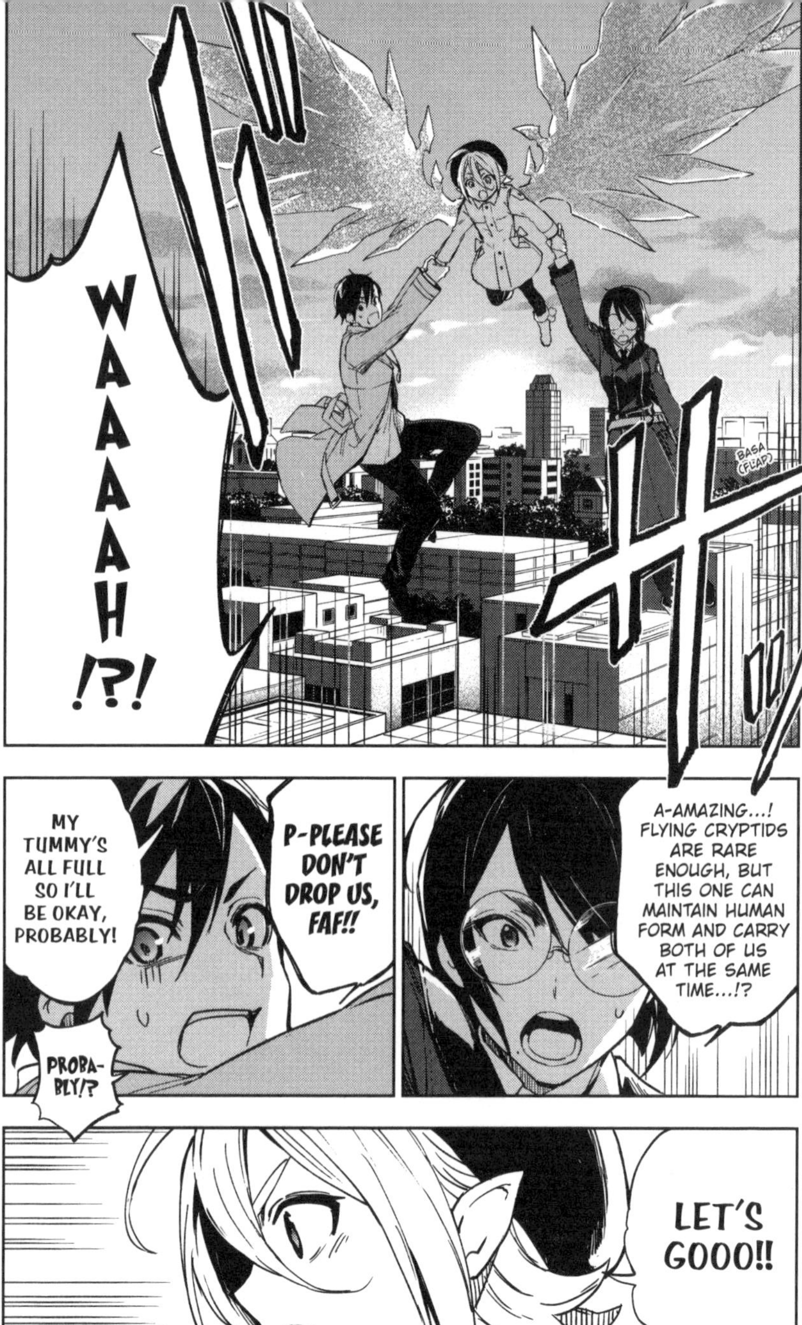
WAAAAAH!?!
BASA (FLAP)
A-AMAZING...! FLYING CRYPTIDS ARE RARE ENOUGH, BUT THIS ONE CAN MAINTAIN HUMAN FORM AND CARRY BOTH OF US AT THE SAME TIME...!?
P-PLEASE DON'T DROP US, FAF!!
MY TUMMY'S ALL FULL SO I'LL BE OKAY, PROBABLY!
PROBA-BLY!?
LET'S GOOO!!

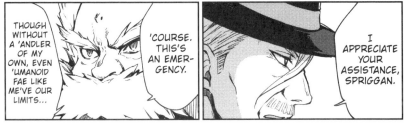

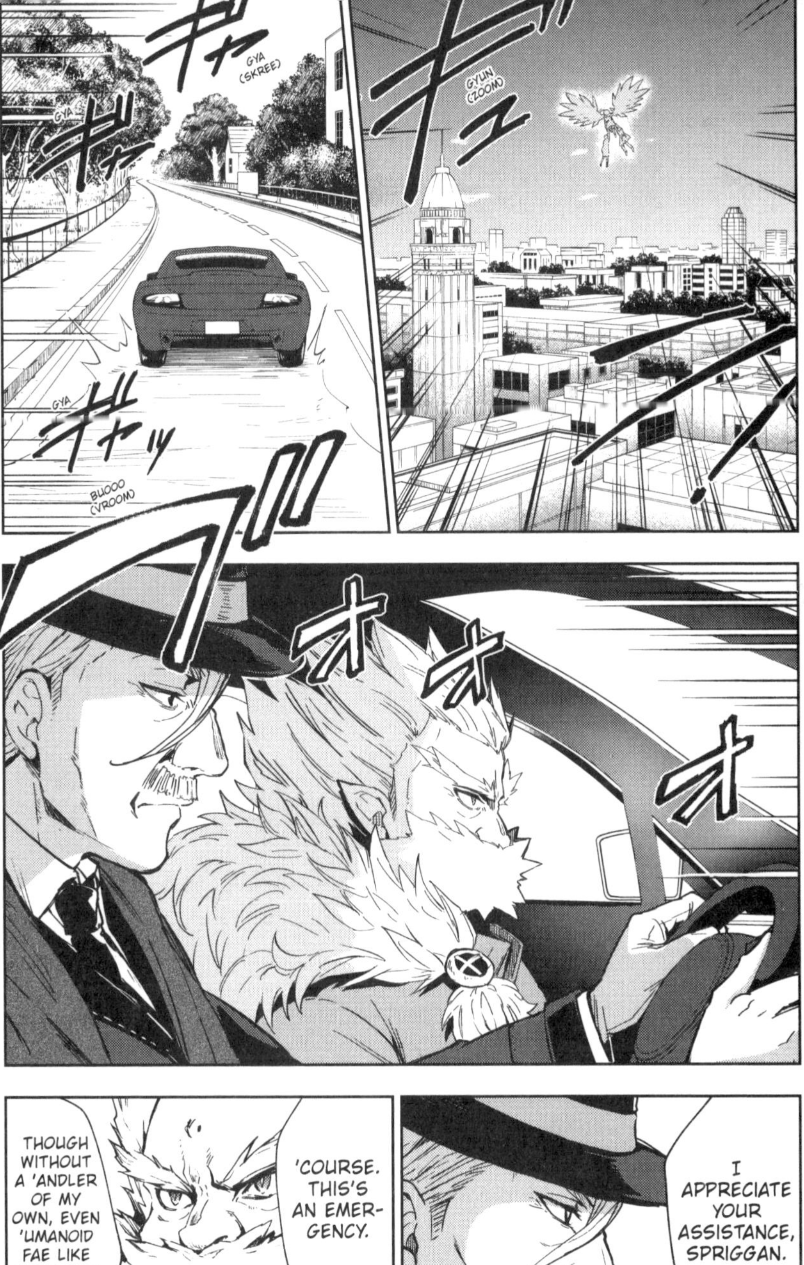
GYUN (ZOOM)
GYA (SKREE)
GYA
GYA
BUOOO (VROOM)
I APPRECIATE YOUR ASSISTANCE, SPRIGGAN.
'COURSE. THIS'S AN EMER-GENCY.
THOUGH WITHOUT A 'ANDLER OF MY OWN, EVEN 'UMANOID FAE LIKE ME'VE OUR LIMITS...

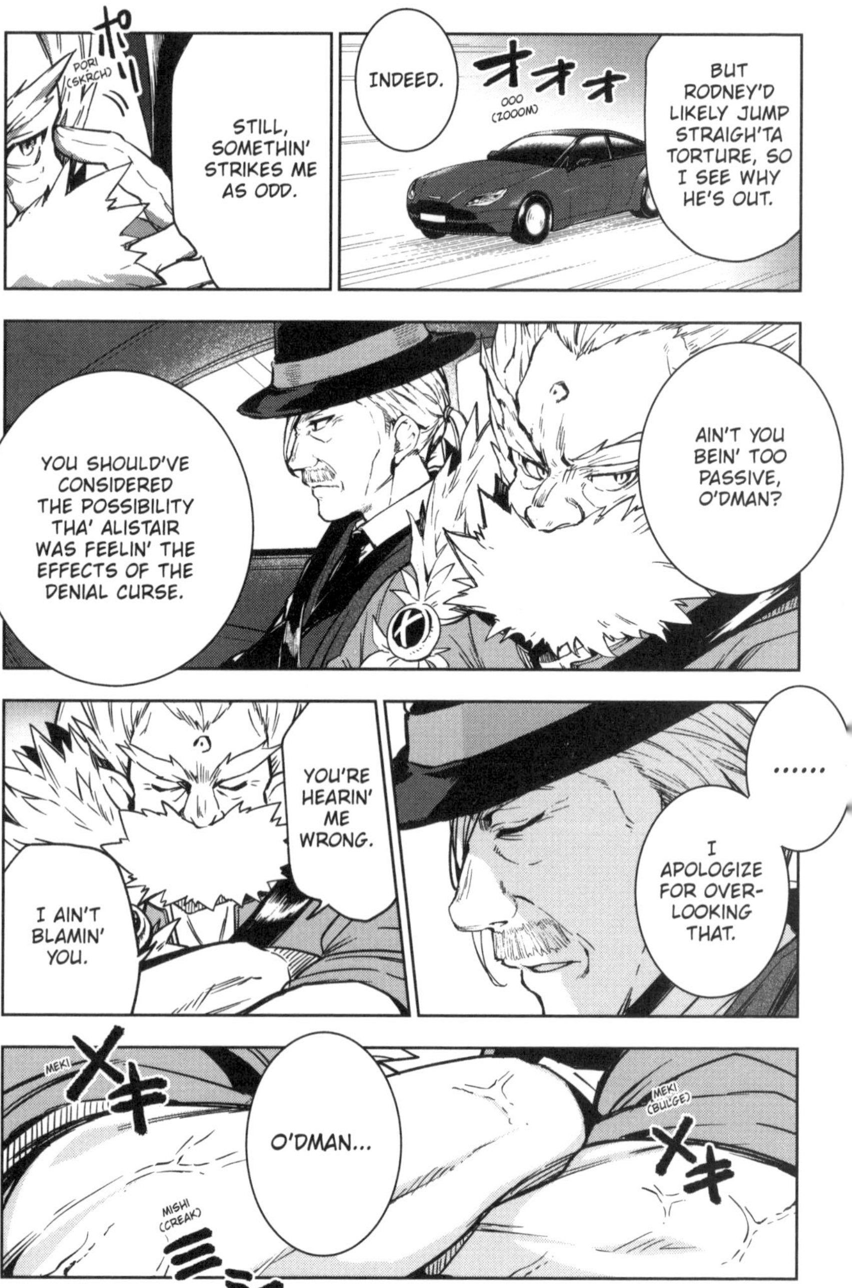
BUT RODNEY'D LIKELY JUMP STRAIGH'TA TORTURE, SO I SEE WHY HE'S OUT.
OOO (ZOOOM)
INDEED.
PORI (SKRCH)
STILL, SOMETHIN' STRIKES ME AS ODD.
AIN'T YOU BEIN' TOO PASSIVE, O'DMAN?
YOU SHOULD'VE CONSIDERED THE POSSIBILITY THA' ALISTAIR WAS FEELIN' THE EFFECTS OF THE DENIAL CURSE.
......
I APOLOGIZE FOR OVER-LOOKING THAT.
YOU'RE HEARIN' ME WRONG.
I AIN'T BLAMIN' YOU.
MEKI (BULGE)
O'DMAN...
MEKI
MISHI (CREAK)

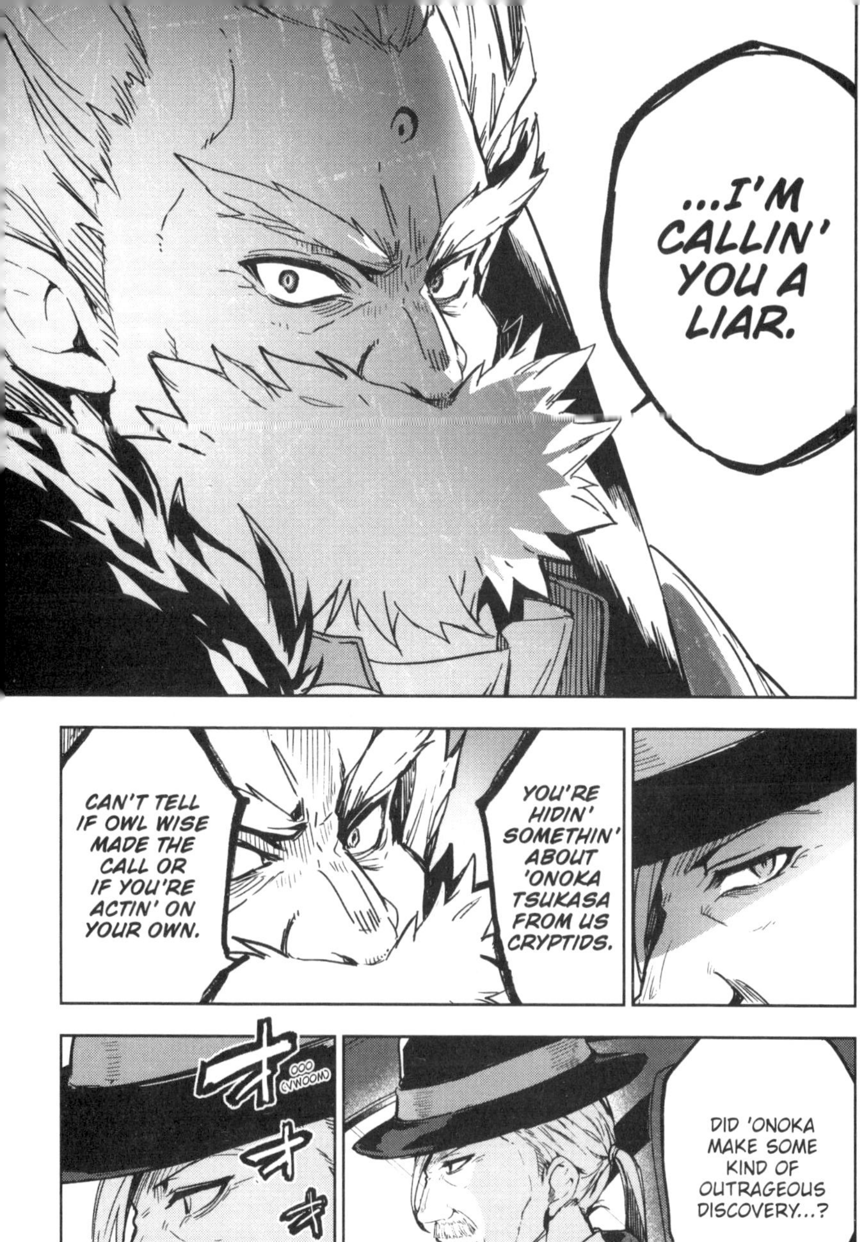
...I'M CALLIN' YOU A LIAR.
YOU'RE HIDIN' SOMETHIN' ABOUT 'ONOKA TSUKASA FROM US CRYPTIDS.
CAN'T TELL IF OWL WISE MADE THE CALL OR IF YOU'RE ACTIN' ON YOUR OWN.
DID 'ONOKA MAKE SOME KIND OF OUTRAGEOUS DISCOVERY...?
OOO (VWOOM)

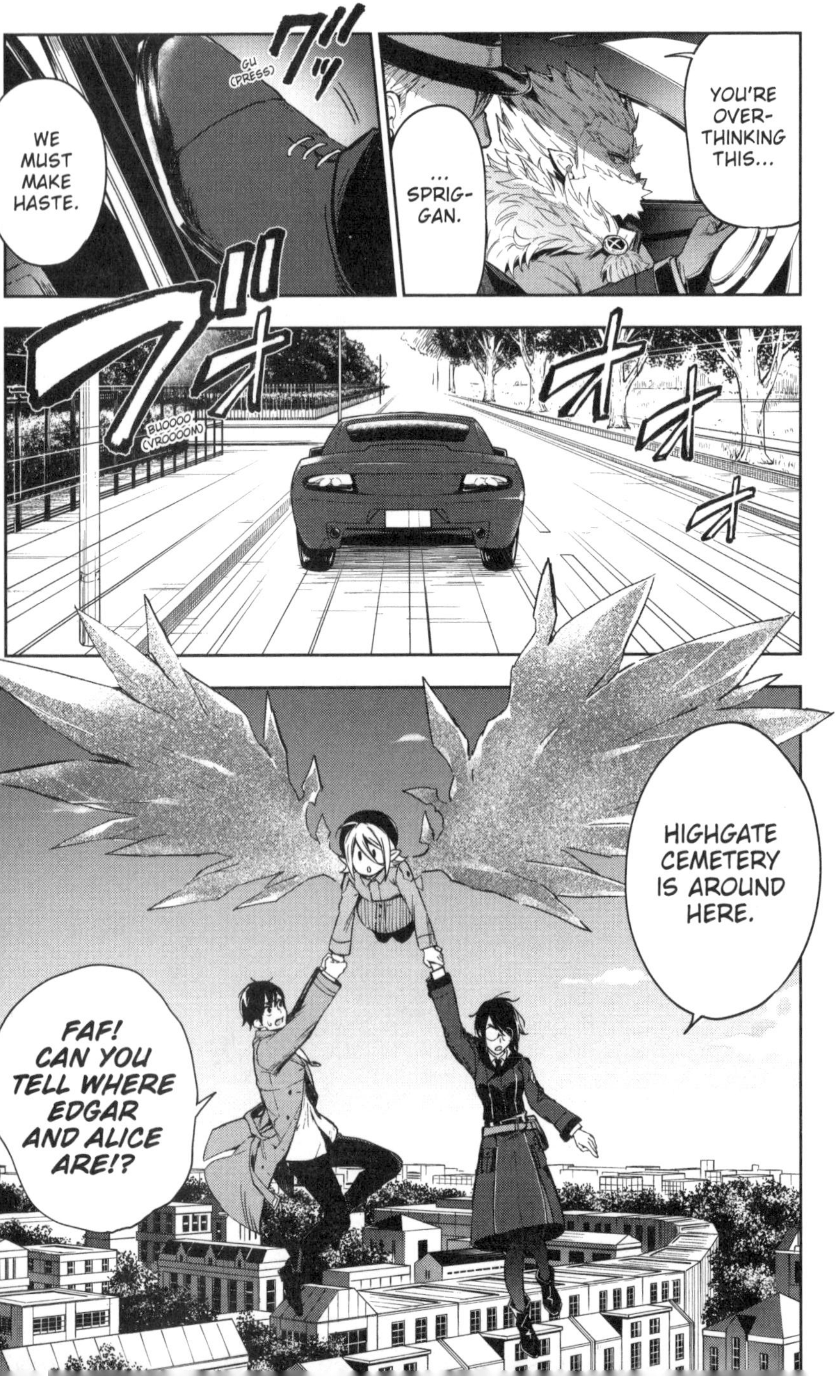
YOU'RE OVER-THINKING THIS...
... SPRIG-GAN.
グッ
GU (PRESS)
WE MUST MAKE HASTE.
ブォオオオ
BUOOOO (VROOOOM)
HIGHGATE CEMETERY IS AROUND HERE.
FAF! CAN YOU TELL WHERE EDGAR AND ALICE ARE!?

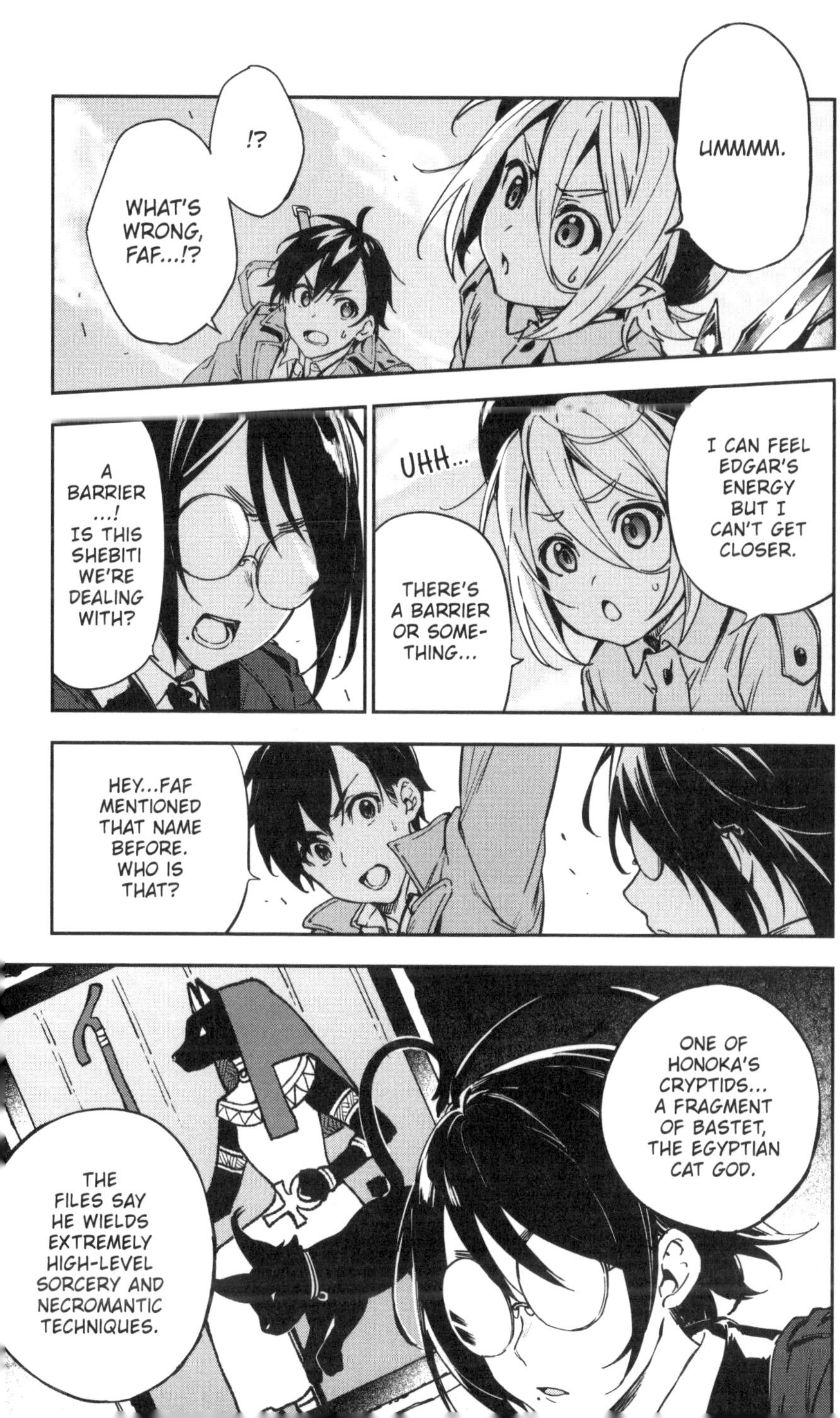
UMMMM.
!?
WHAT'S WRONG, FAF...!?
I CAN FEEL EDGAR'S ENERGY BUT I CAN'T GET CLOSER.
UHH...
THERE'S A BARRIER OR SOME-THING...
A BARRIER ...! IS THIS SHEBITI WE'RE DEALING WITH?
HEY...FAF MENTIONED THAT NAME BEFORE. WHO IS THAT?
ONE OF HONOKA'S CRYPTIDS... A FRAGMENT OF BASTET, THE EGYPTIAN CAT GOD.
THE FILES SAY HE WIELDS EXTREMELY HIGH-LEVEL SORCERY AND NECROMANTIC TECHNIQUES.

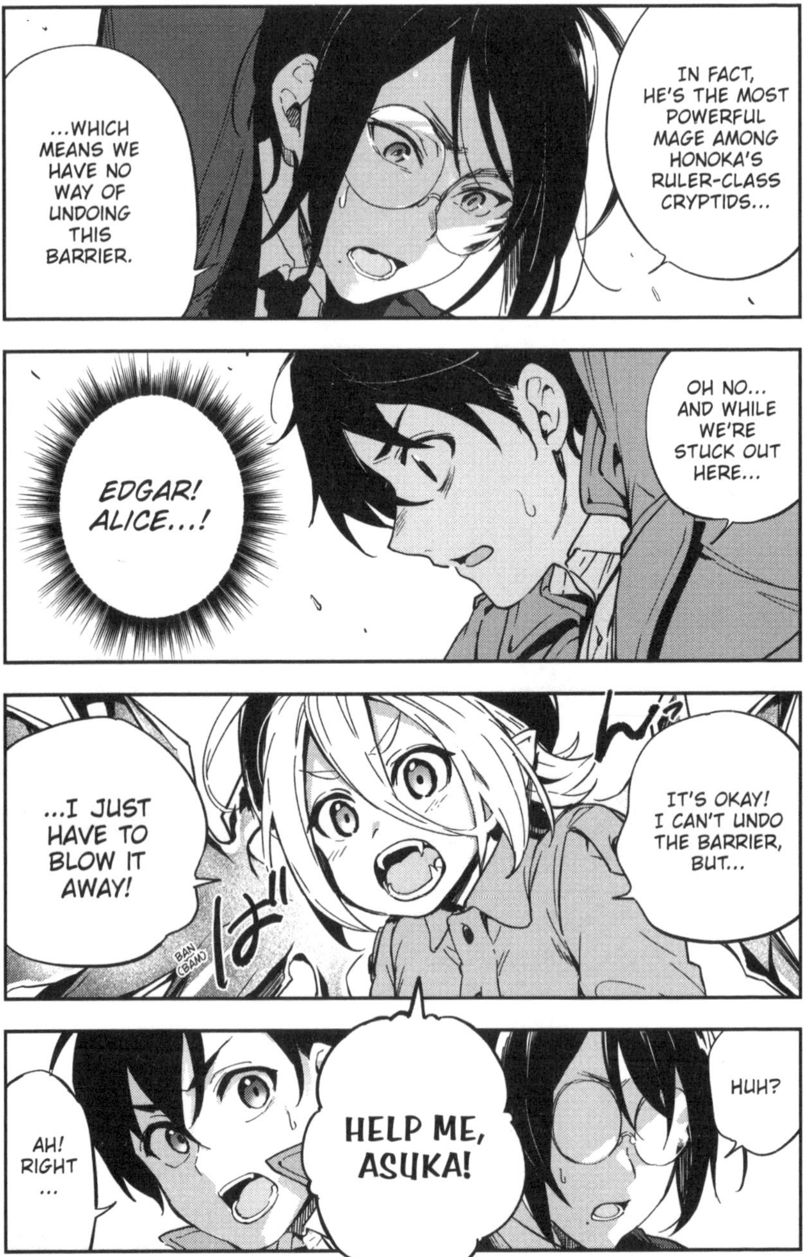
IN FACT, HE'S THE MOST POWERFUL MAGE AMONG HONOKA'S RULER-CLASS CRYPTIDS...
...WHICH MEANS WE HAVE NO WAY OF UNDOING THIS BARRIER.
OH NO... AND WHILE WE'RE STUCK OUT HERE...
EDGAR! ALICE...!
IT'S OKAY! I CAN'T UNDO THE BARRIER, BUT...
...I JUST HAVE TO BLOW IT AWAY!
BAN (BAM)
HUH?
HELP ME, ASUKA!
AH! RIGHT ...

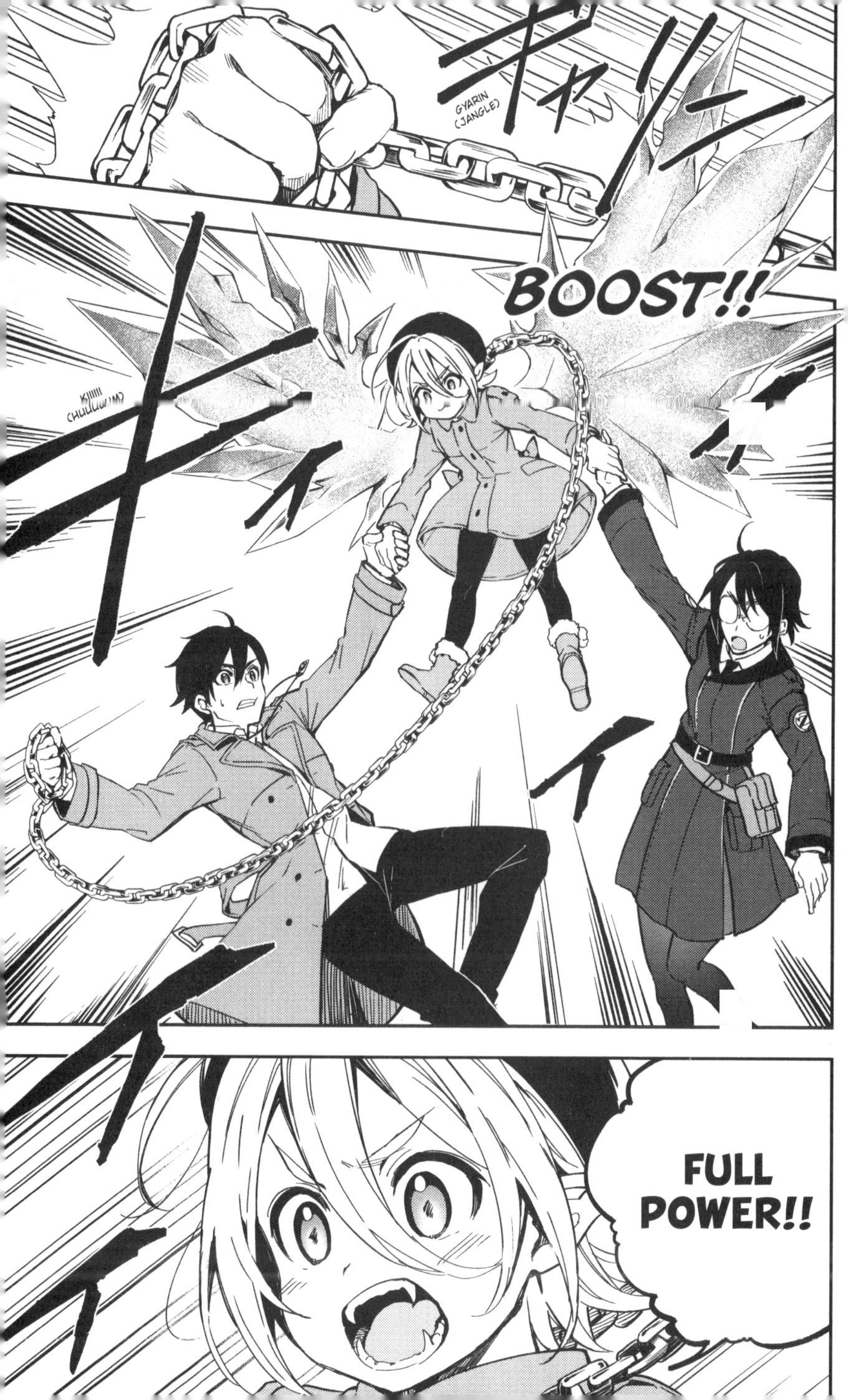
GYARIN (JANGLE)
BOOST!!
KIIIIII
FULL POWER!!

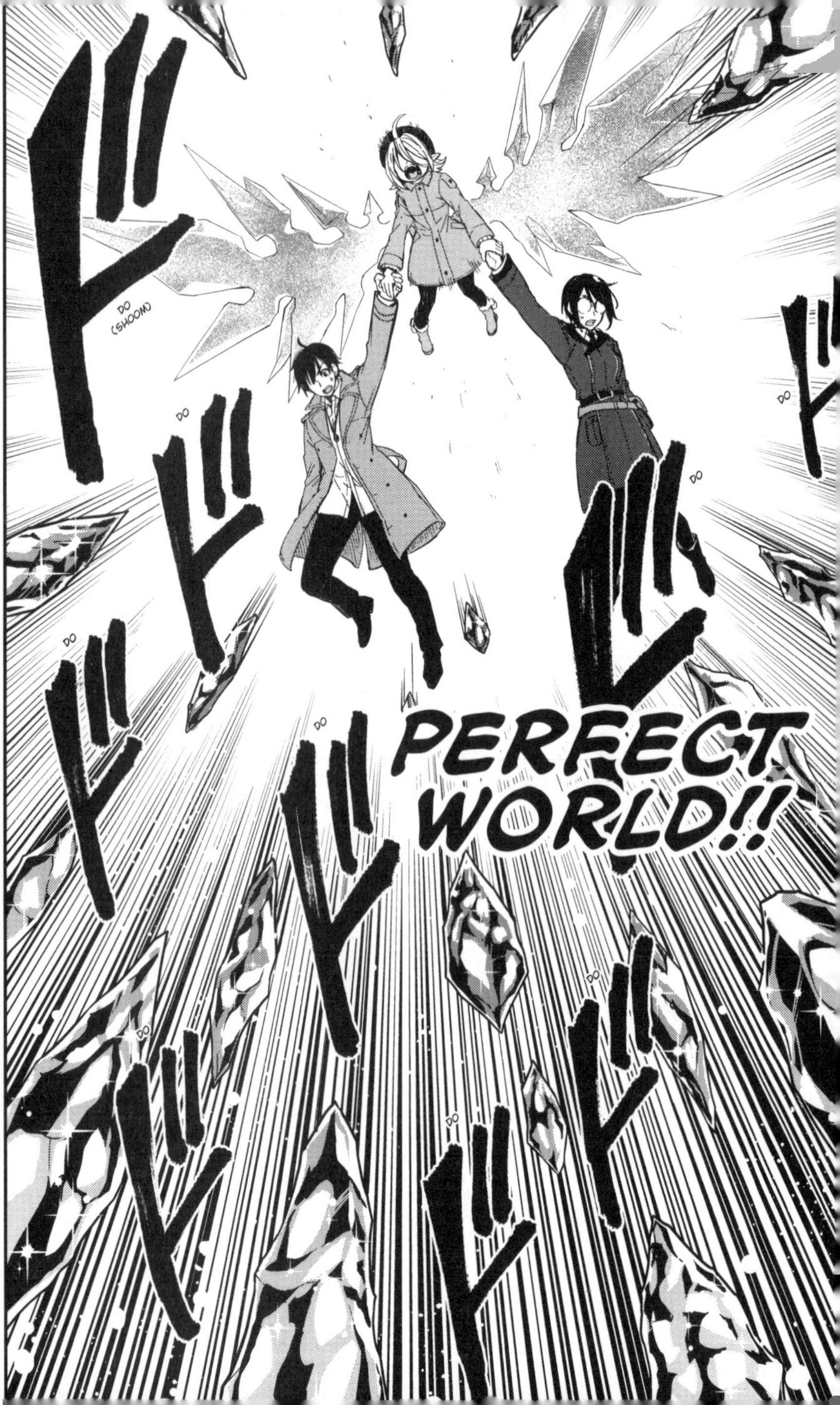
DO
DO
(SHOOM)
DO
DO
DO
DO
PERFECT WORLD!!
DO
DO
DO

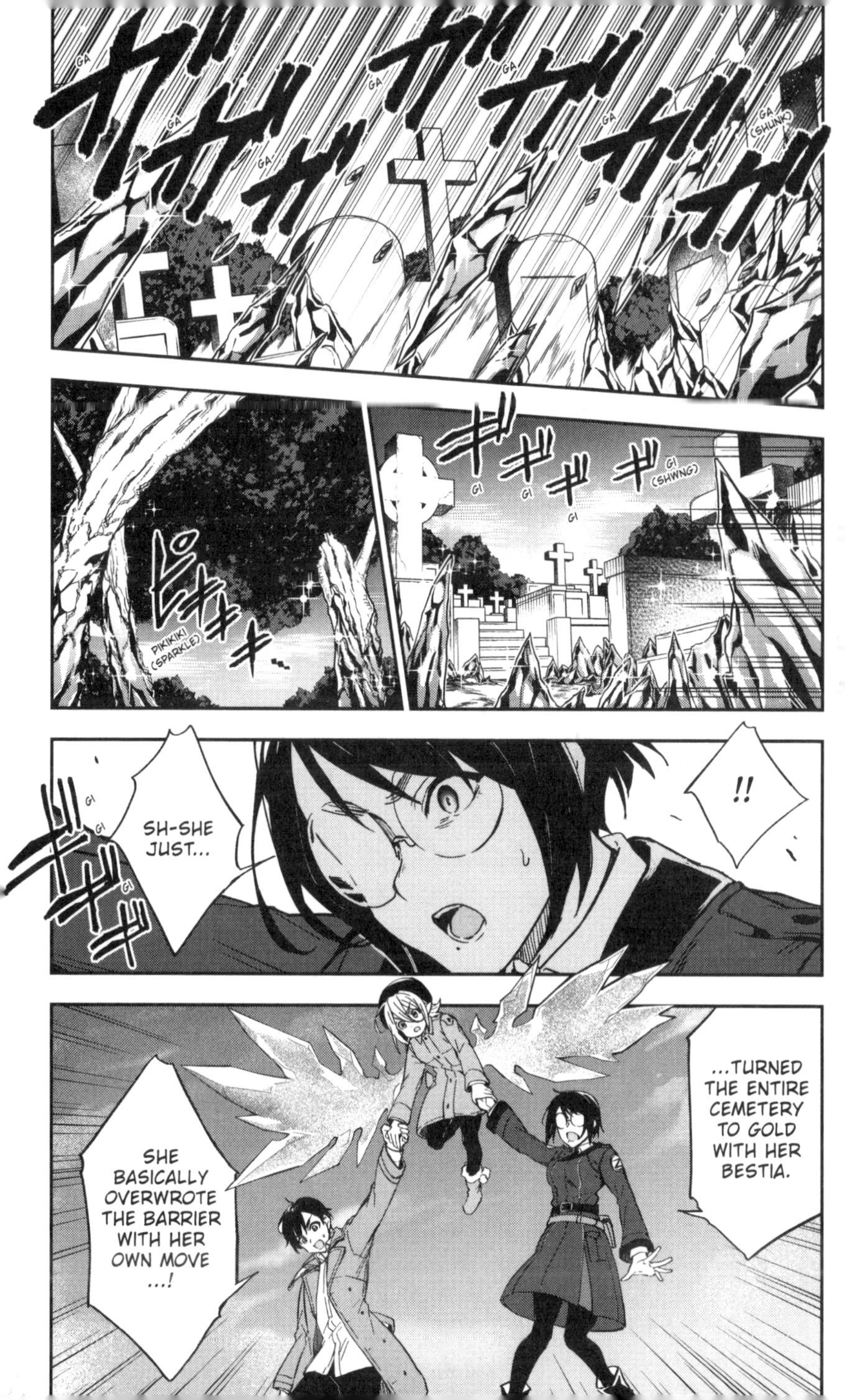
GA (SHUNK)
GA
GA
GA
GA
GA
GI (SHWNG)
GI
GI
GI
PIKIKIKI (SPARKLE)
!!
SH-SHE JUST...
GI
GI
GI
...TURNED THE ENTIRE CEMETERY TO GOLD WITH HER BESTIA.
SHE BASICALLY OVERWROTE THE BARRIER WITH HER OWN MOVE ...!

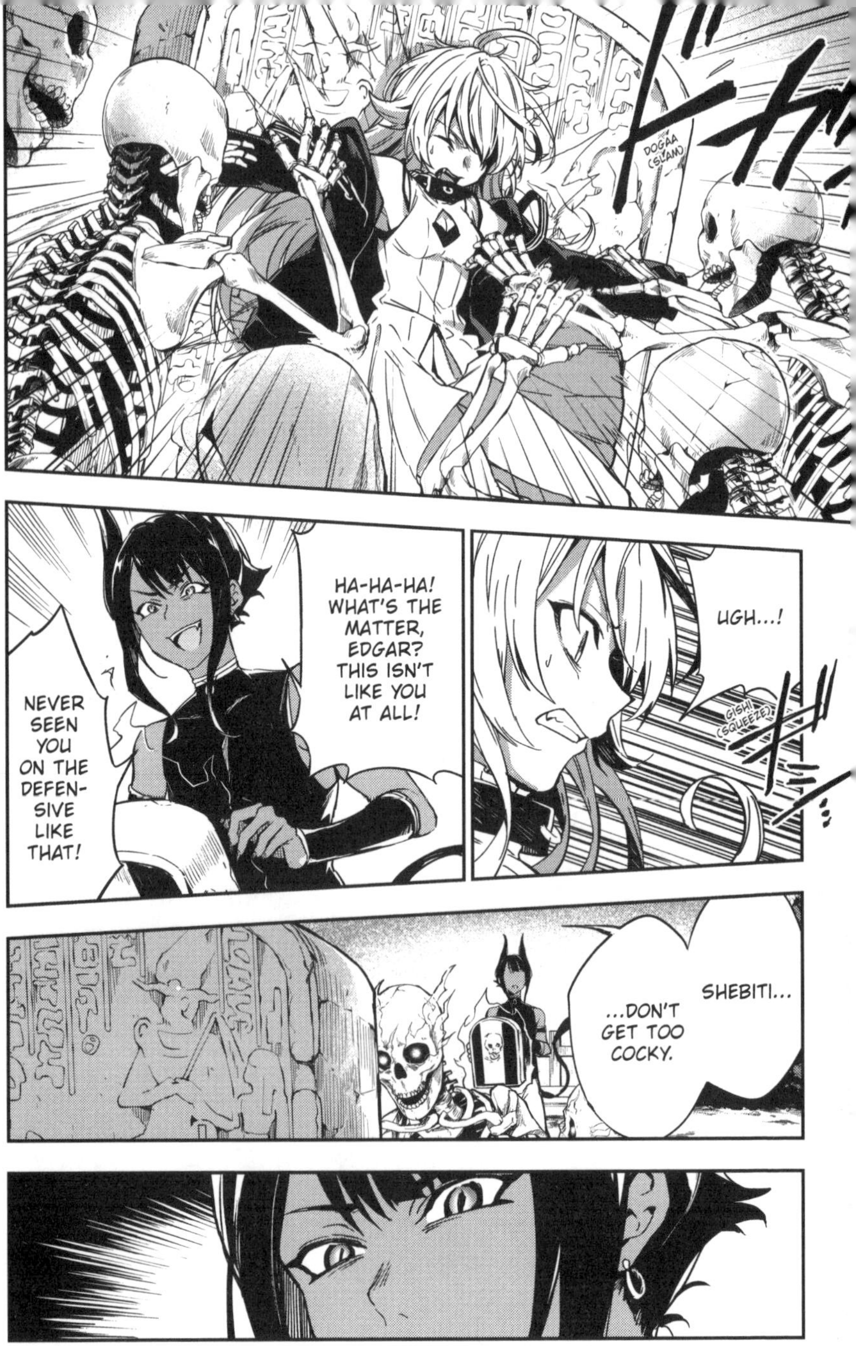
DOGAA (SLAM)
UGH...!
GISH! (SQUEEZE)
HA-HA-HA! WHAT'S THE MATTER, EDGAR? THIS ISN'T LIKE YOU AT ALL!
NEVER SEEN YOU ON THE DEFEN-SIVE LIKE THAT!
SHEBITI...
...DON'T GET TOO COCKY.

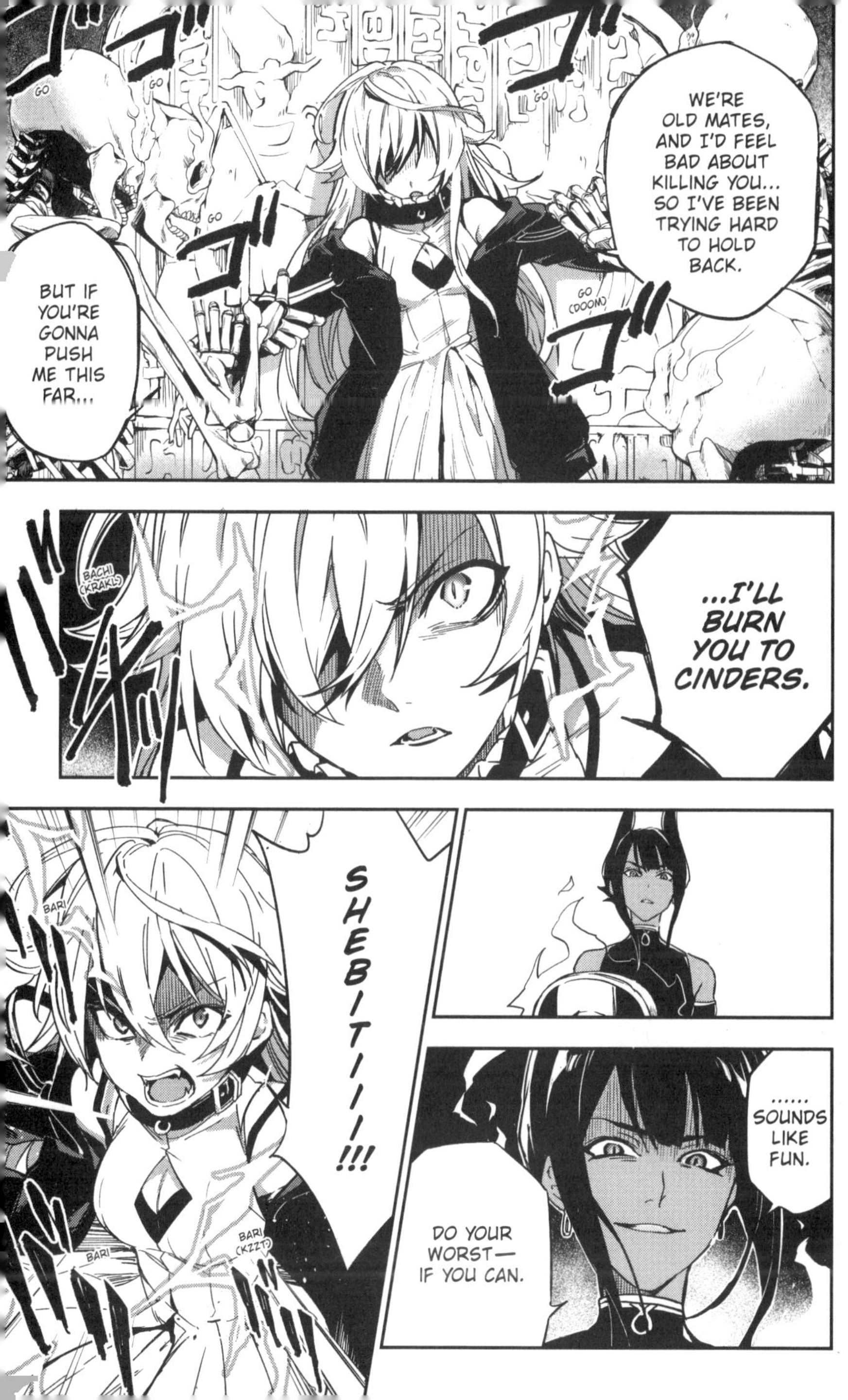
GO
GO
GO
GO
WE'RE OLD MATES, AND I'D FEEL BAD ABOUT KILLING YOU... SO I'VE BEEN TRYING HARD TO HOLD BACK.
GO (DOOM)
BUT IF YOU'RE GONNA PUSH ME THIS FAR...
...I'LL BURN YOU TO CINDERS.
BACHI (KRAKL)
...... SOUNDS LIKE FUN.
DO YOUR WORST— IF YOU CAN.
SHEBIT!!!!!!!
BARI
BARI (KZZT)
BARI

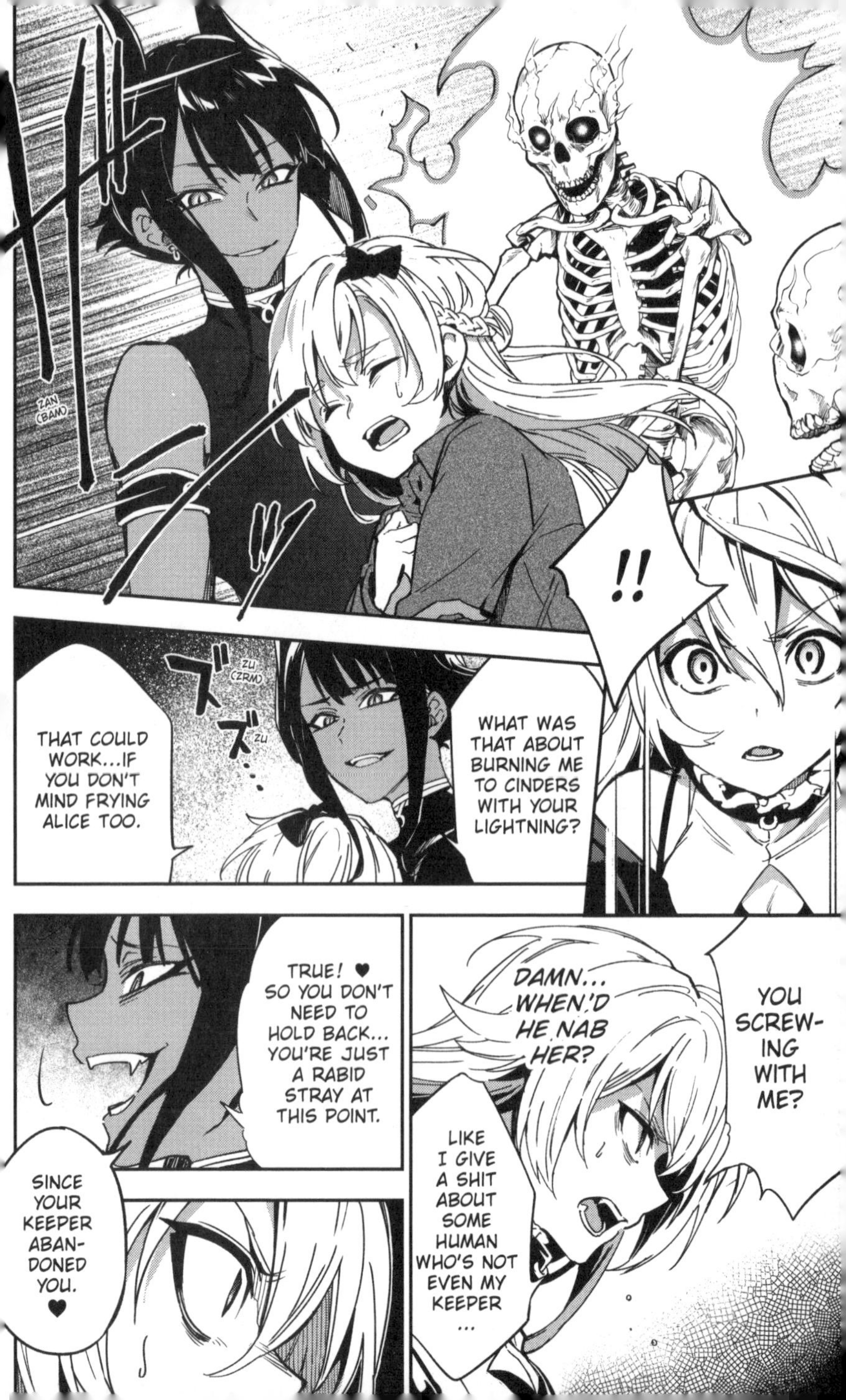
ZAN (BAM)
!!
WHAT WAS THAT ABOUT BURNING ME TO CINDERS WITH YOUR LIGHTNING?
ZU (ZRM)
ZU
THAT COULD WORK...IF YOU DON'T MIND FRYING ALICE TOO.
YOU SCREWING WITH ME?
DAMN... WHEN'D HE NAB HER?
LIKE I GIVE A SHIT ABOUT SOME HUMAN WHO'S NOT EVEN MY KEEPER...
TRUE! ♥ SO YOU DON'T NEED TO HOLD BACK... YOU'RE JUST A RABID STRAY AT THIS POINT.
SINCE YOUR KEEPER ABANDONED YOU. ♥

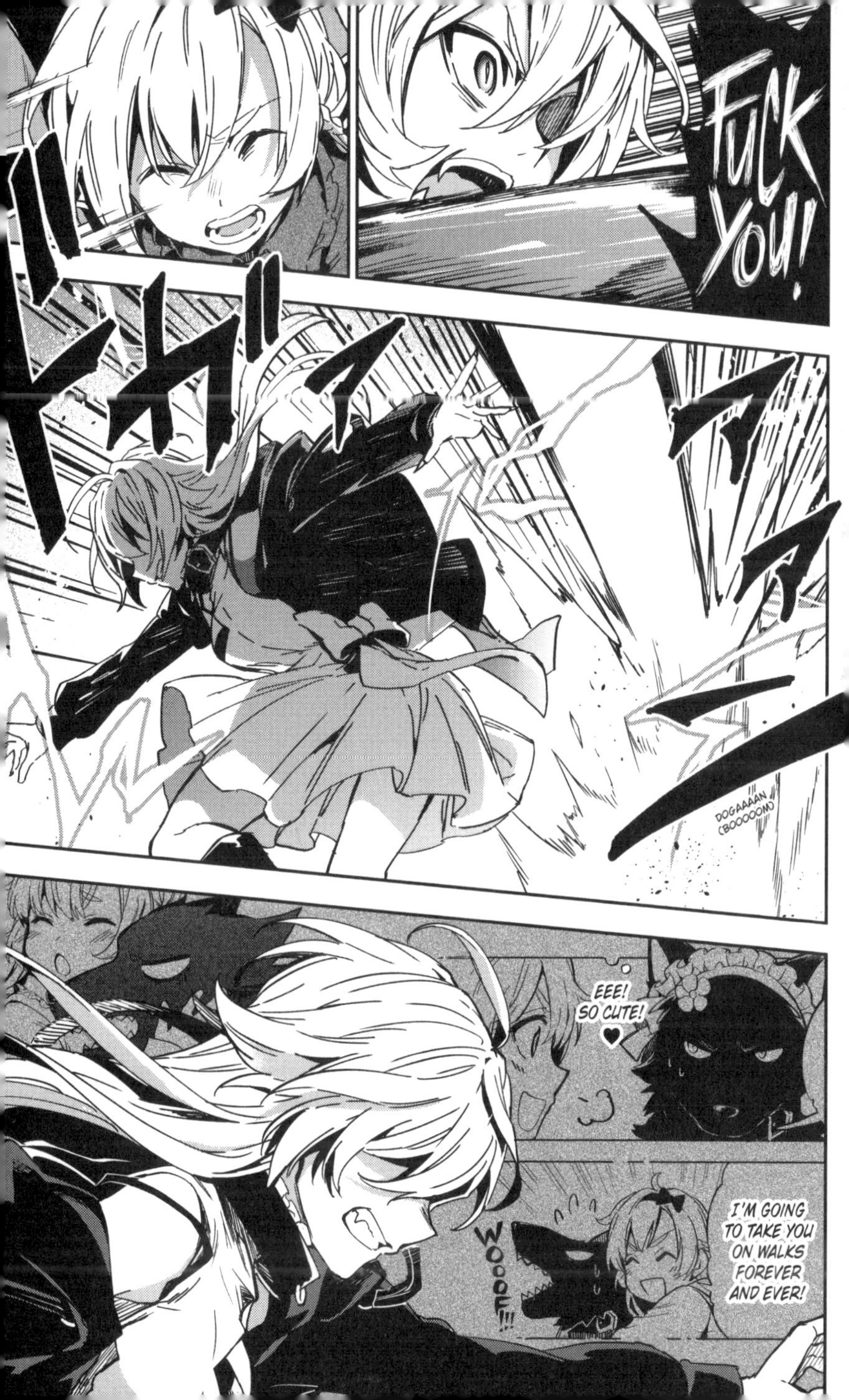
FUCK YOU!
DOGAAAAN (BOOOOOM)
EEE! SO CUTE! ♥
I'M GOING TO TAKE YOU ON WALKS FOREVER AND EVER!
WOOOF!!!

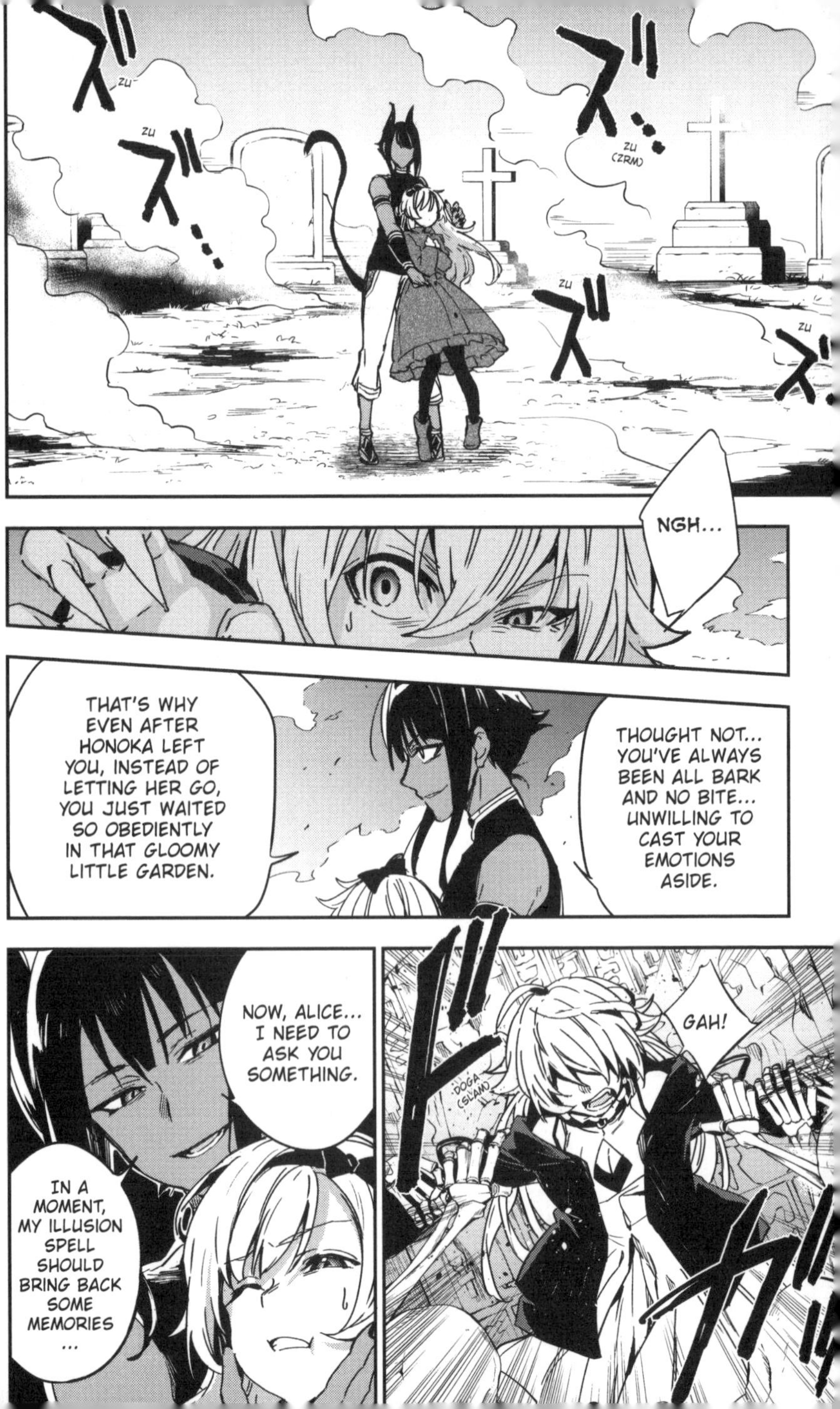
ZU
(ZRM)
ZU
ZU
ZU
ZU
NGH...
THOUGHT NOT... YOU'VE ALWAYS BEEN ALL BARK AND NO BITE... UNWILLING TO CAST YOUR EMOTIONS ASIDE.
THAT'S WHY EVEN AFTER HONOKA LEFT YOU, INSTEAD OF LETTING HER GO, YOU JUST WAITED SO OBEDIENTLY IN THAT GLOOMY LITTLE GARDEN.
GAH!
DOGA
(SLAM)
NOW, ALICE... I NEED TO ASK YOU SOMETHING.
IN A MOMENT, MY ILLUSION SPELL SHOULD BRING BACK SOME MEMORIES...

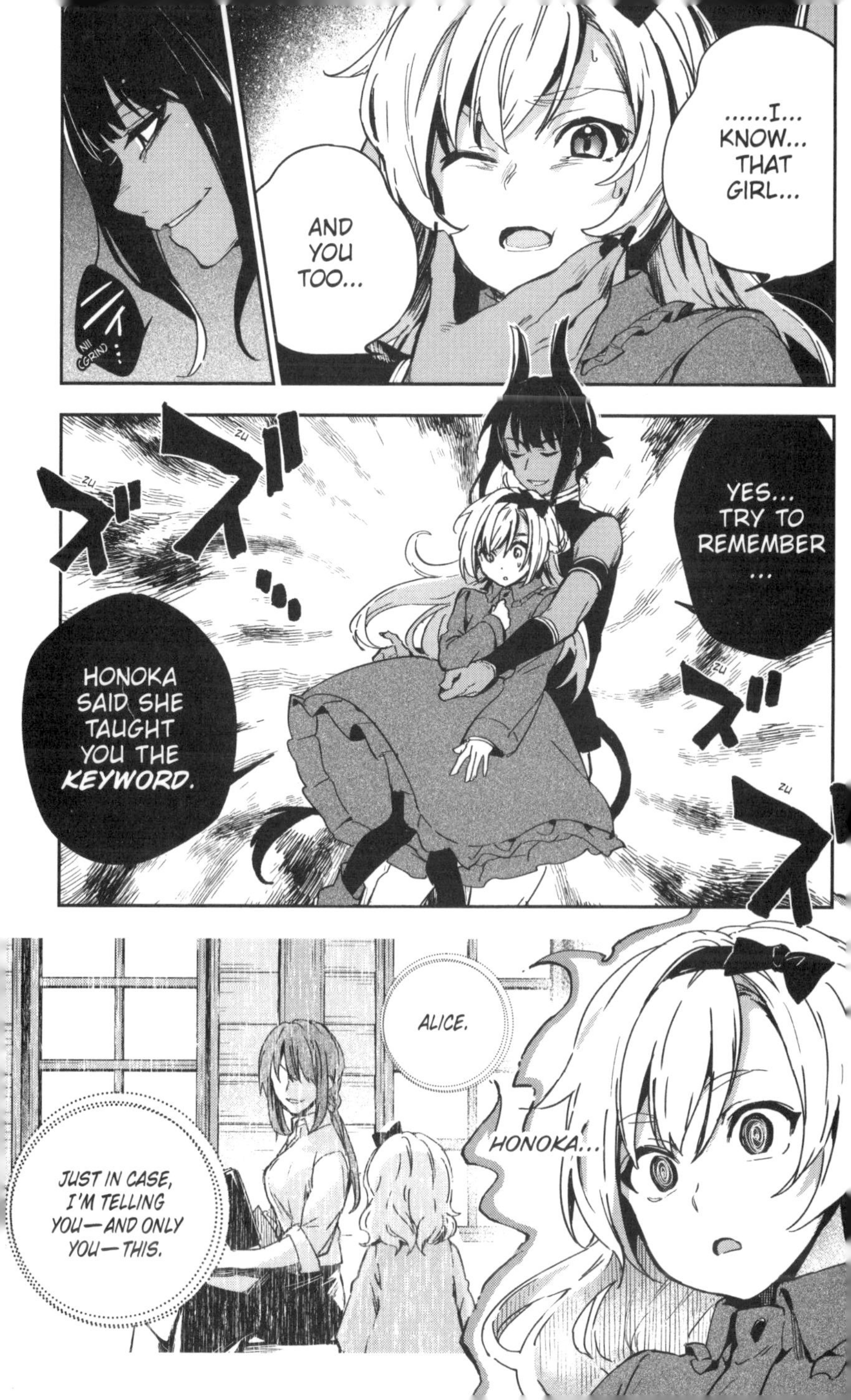

......I... KNOW... THAT GIRL...
AND YOU TOO...
NII (GRIND)
YES... TRY TO REMEMBER ...
ZU
ZU
ZU
ZU
HONOKA SAID SHE TAUGHT YOU THE ***KEYWORD.***
HONOKA...
ALICE.
JUST IN CASE, I'M TELLING YOU—AND ONLY YOU—THIS.

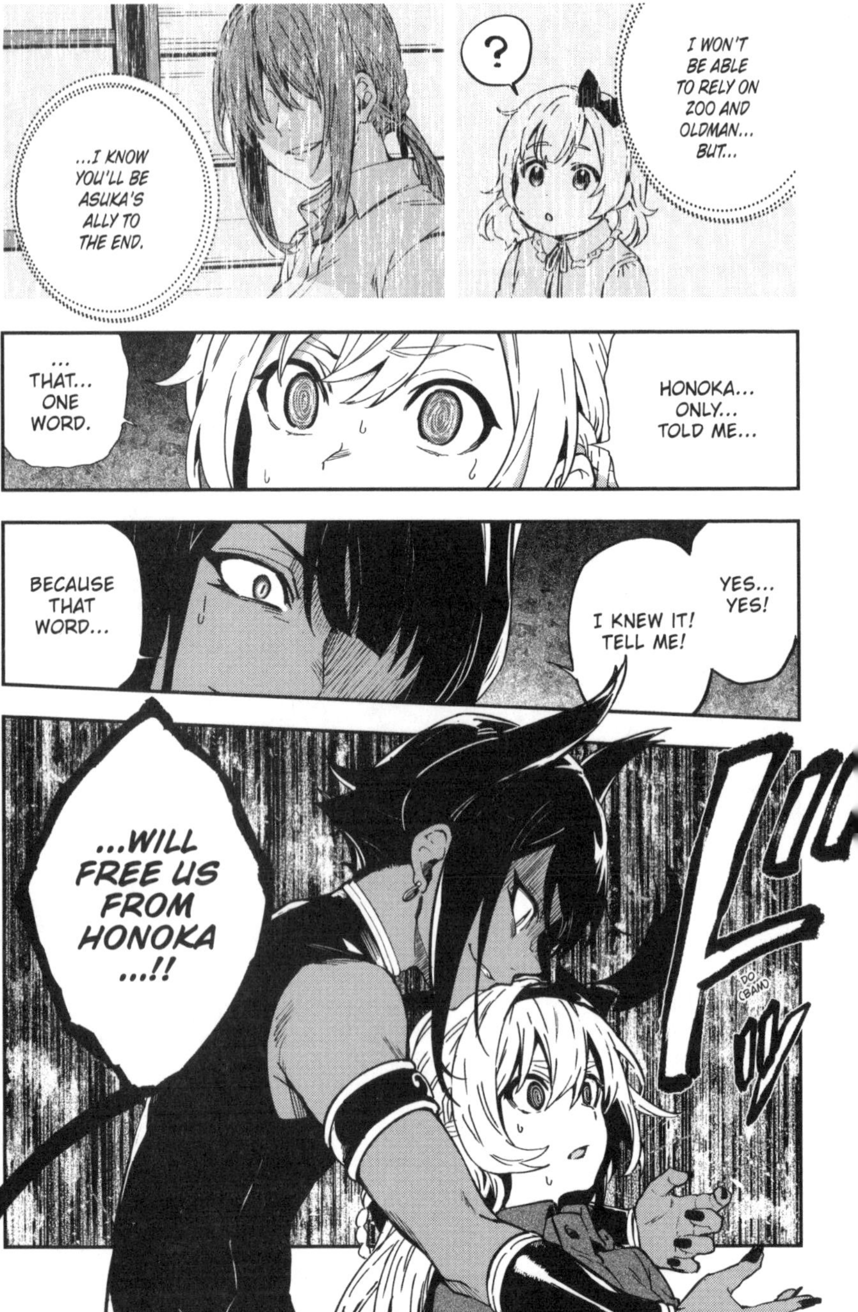
?
I WON'T BE ABLE TO RELY ON ZOO AND OLDMAN... BUT...
...I KNOW YOU'LL BE ASUKA'S ALLY TO THE END.
HONOKA... ONLY... TOLD ME...
... THAT... ONE WORD.
YES... YES!
I KNEW IT! TELL ME!
BECAUSE THAT WORD...
...WILL FREE US FROM HONOKA ...!!
DO (BAM)

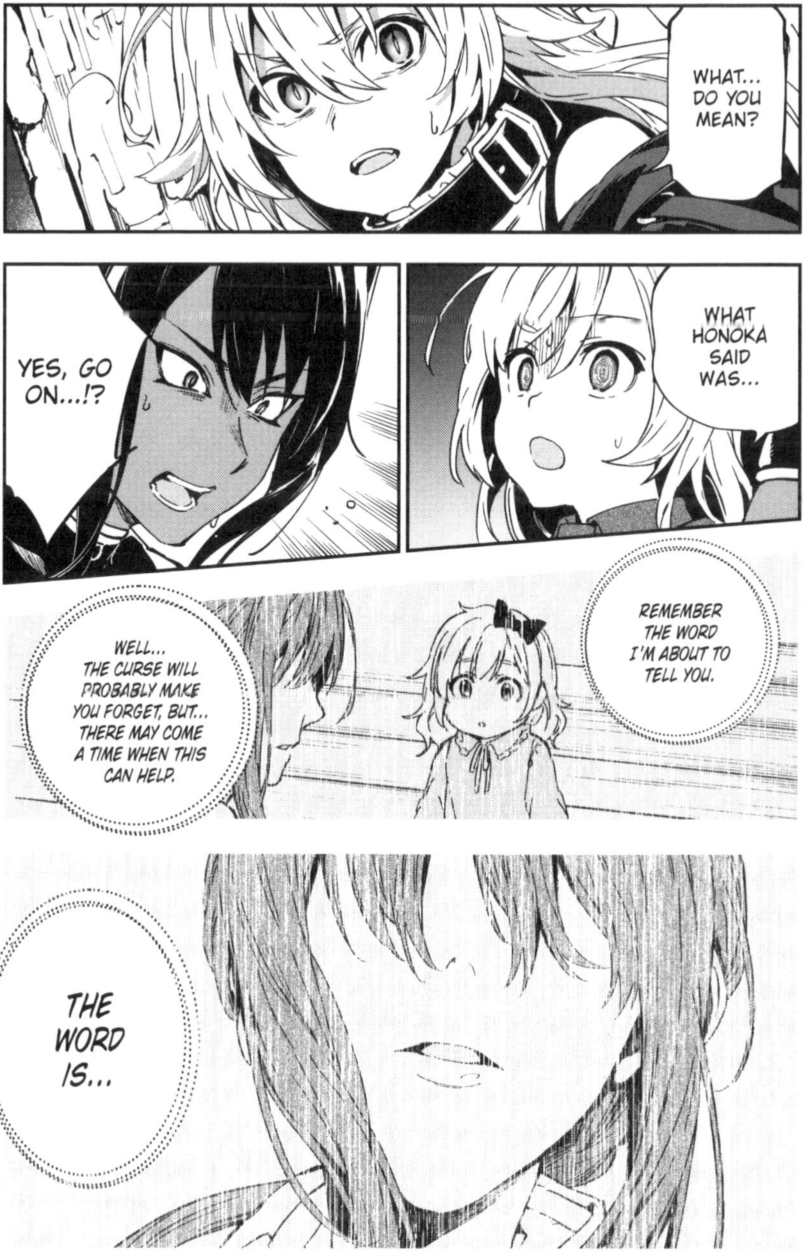
WHAT... DO YOU MEAN?
WHAT HONOKA SAID WAS...
YES, GO ON...!?
REMEMBER THE WORD I'M ABOUT TO TELL YOU.
WELL... THE CURSE WILL PROBABLY MAKE YOU FORGET, BUT... THERE MAY COME A TIME WHEN THIS CAN HELP.
THE WORD IS...

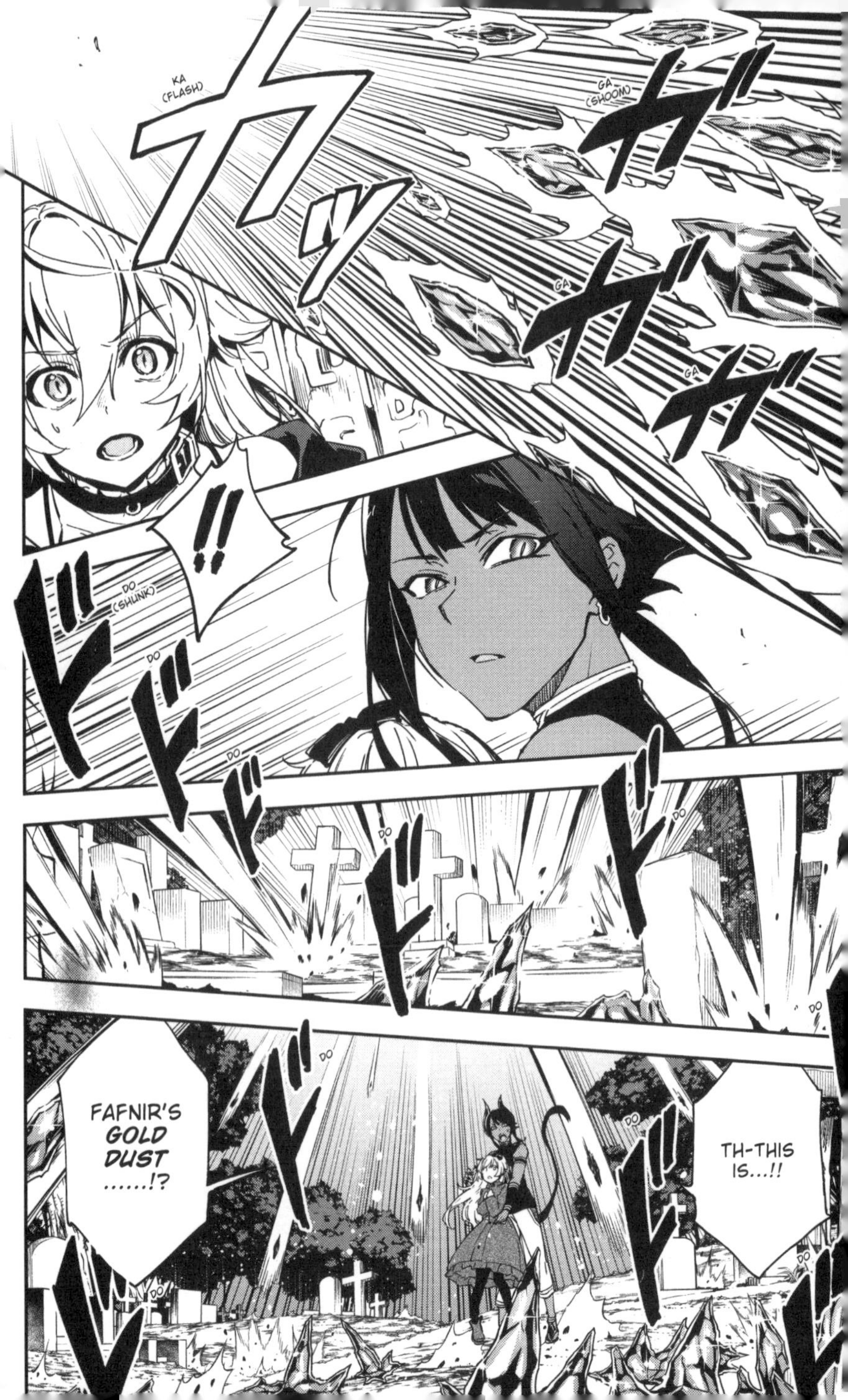
GA (SHOOM)
KA (FLASH)
GA
GA
!!
DO (SHUNK)
DO
DO
DO
DO
DO
TH-THIS IS...!!
DO
DO
FAFNIR'S GOLD DUST ......!?
DO
DO

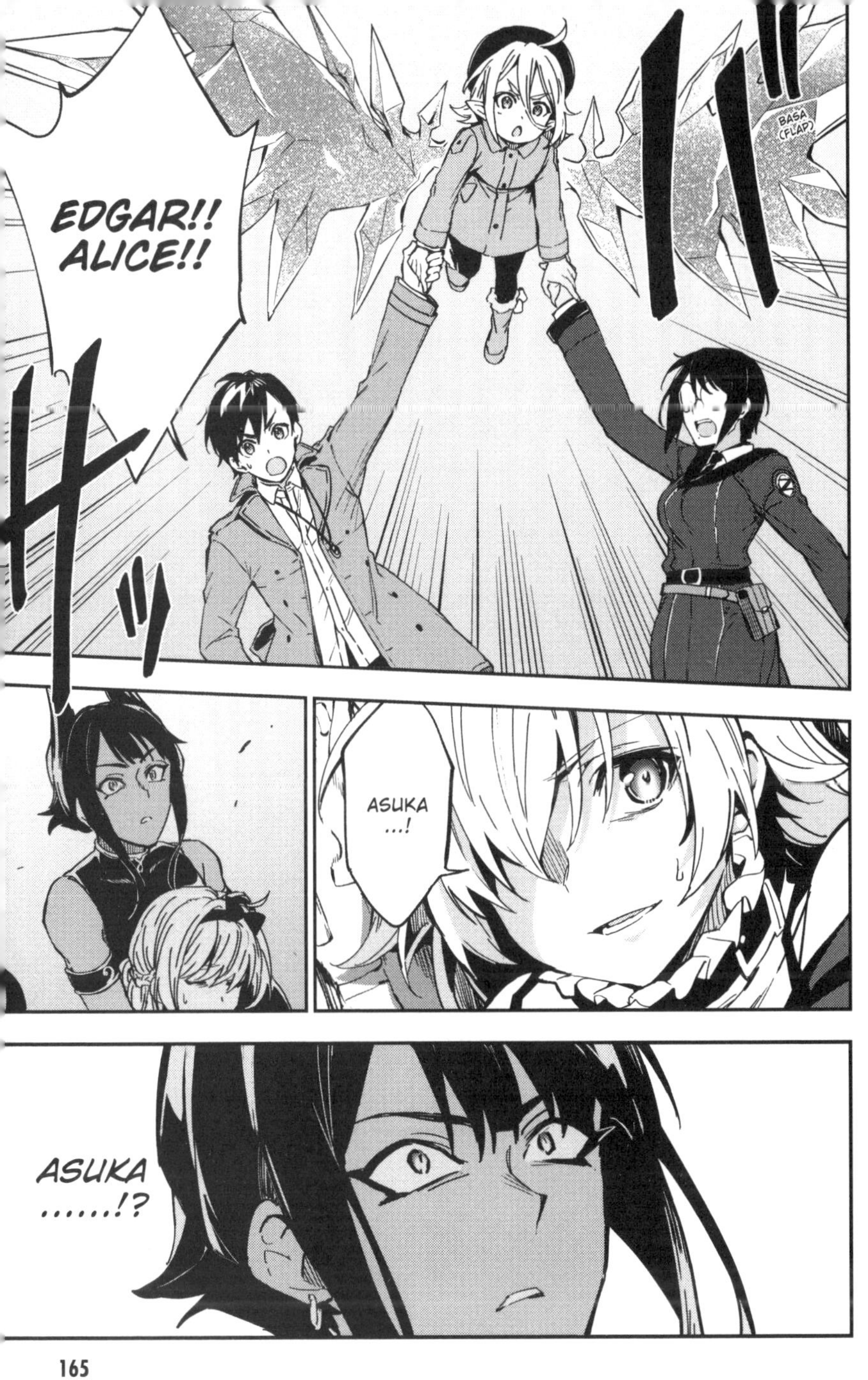
BASA (FLAP)
EDGAR!! ALICE!!
ASUKA ...!
ASUKA ......!?

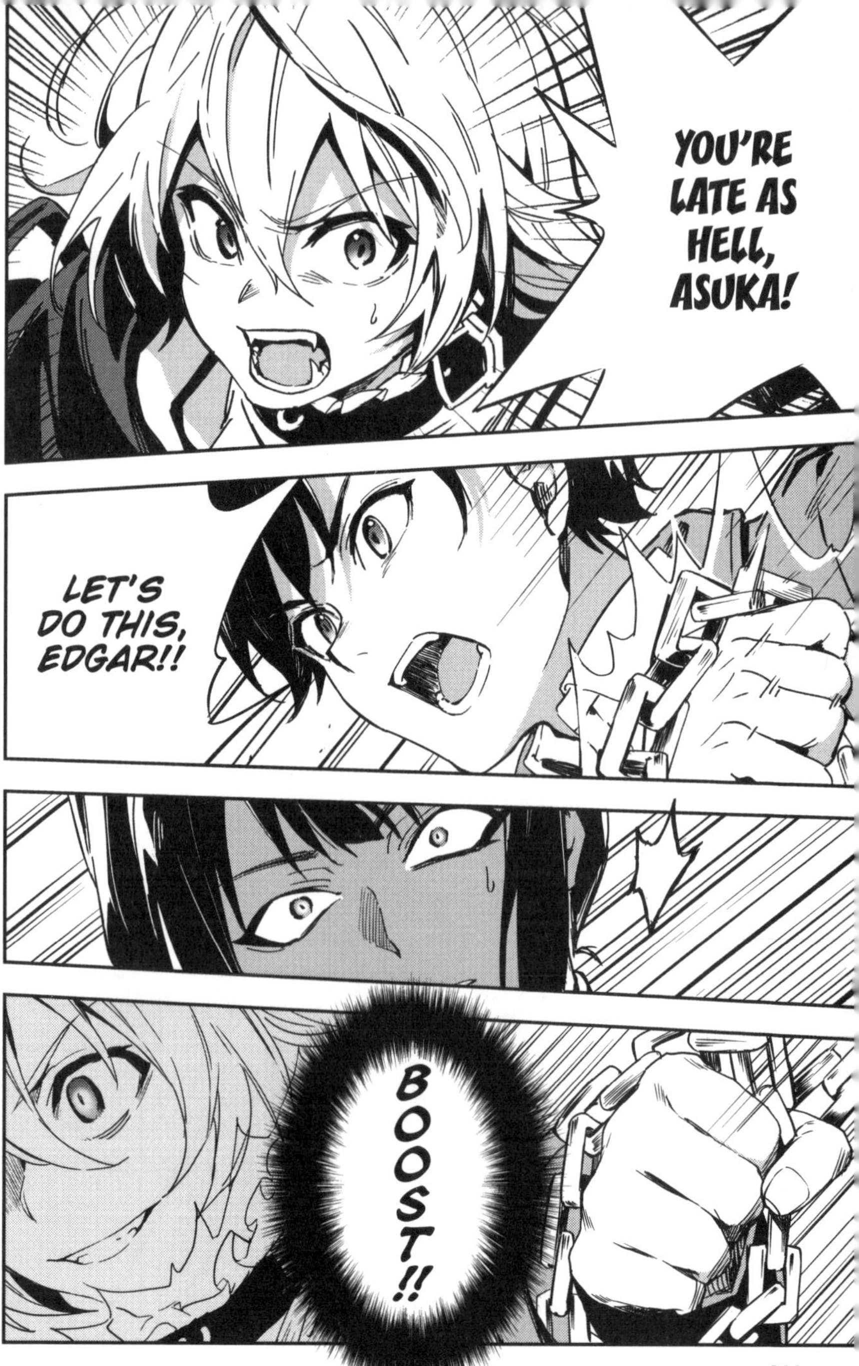
YOU'RE LATE AS HELL, ASUKA!
LET'S DO THIS, EDGAR!!
BOOST!!

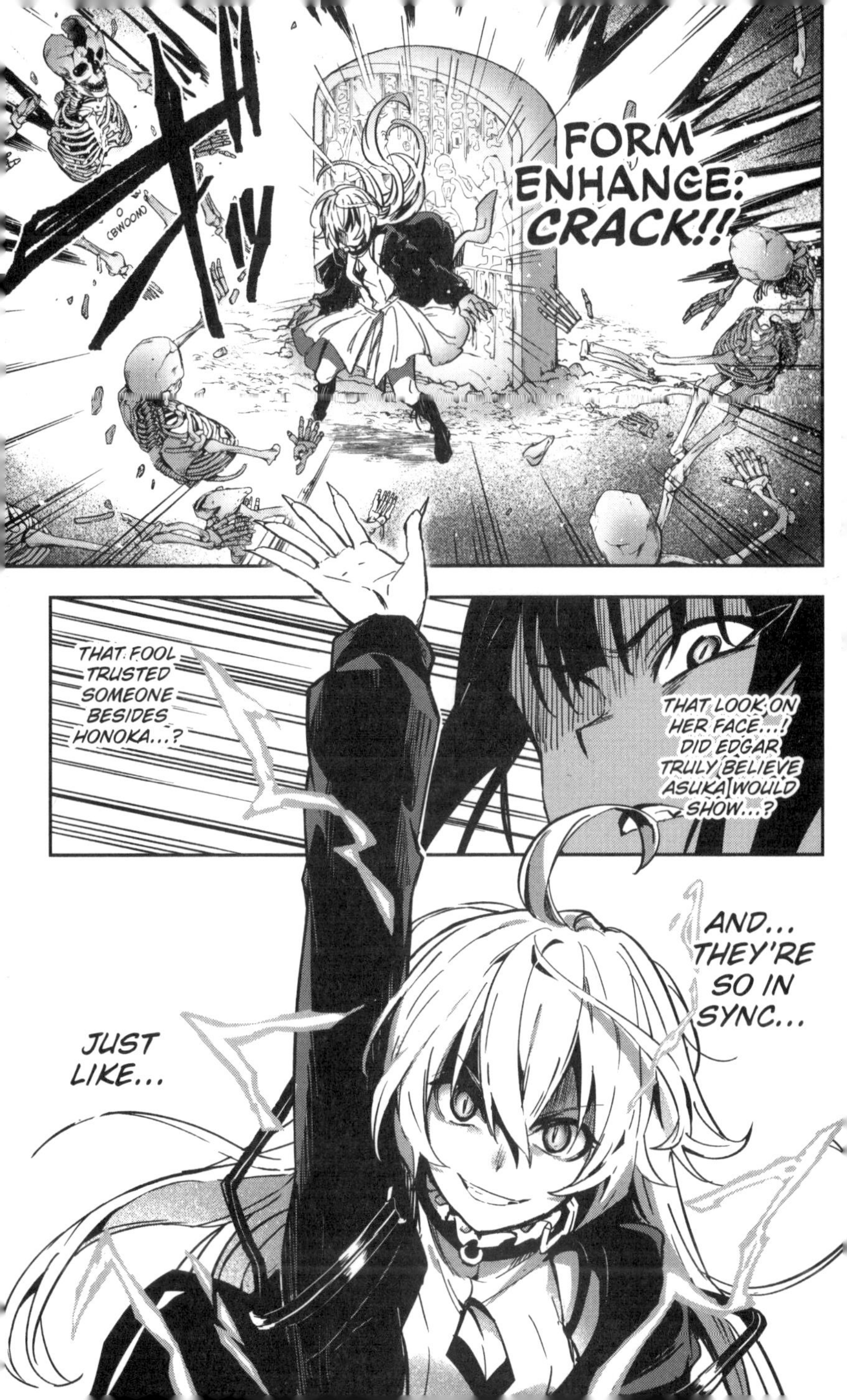
FORM ENHANCE: CRACK!!
(BWOOM)
THAT LOOK ON HER FACE...! DID EDGAR TRULY BELIEVE ASUKA WOULD SHOW...?
THAT FOOL TRUSTED SOMEONE BESIDES HONOKA...?
AND... THEY'RE SO IN SYNC...
JUST LIKE...

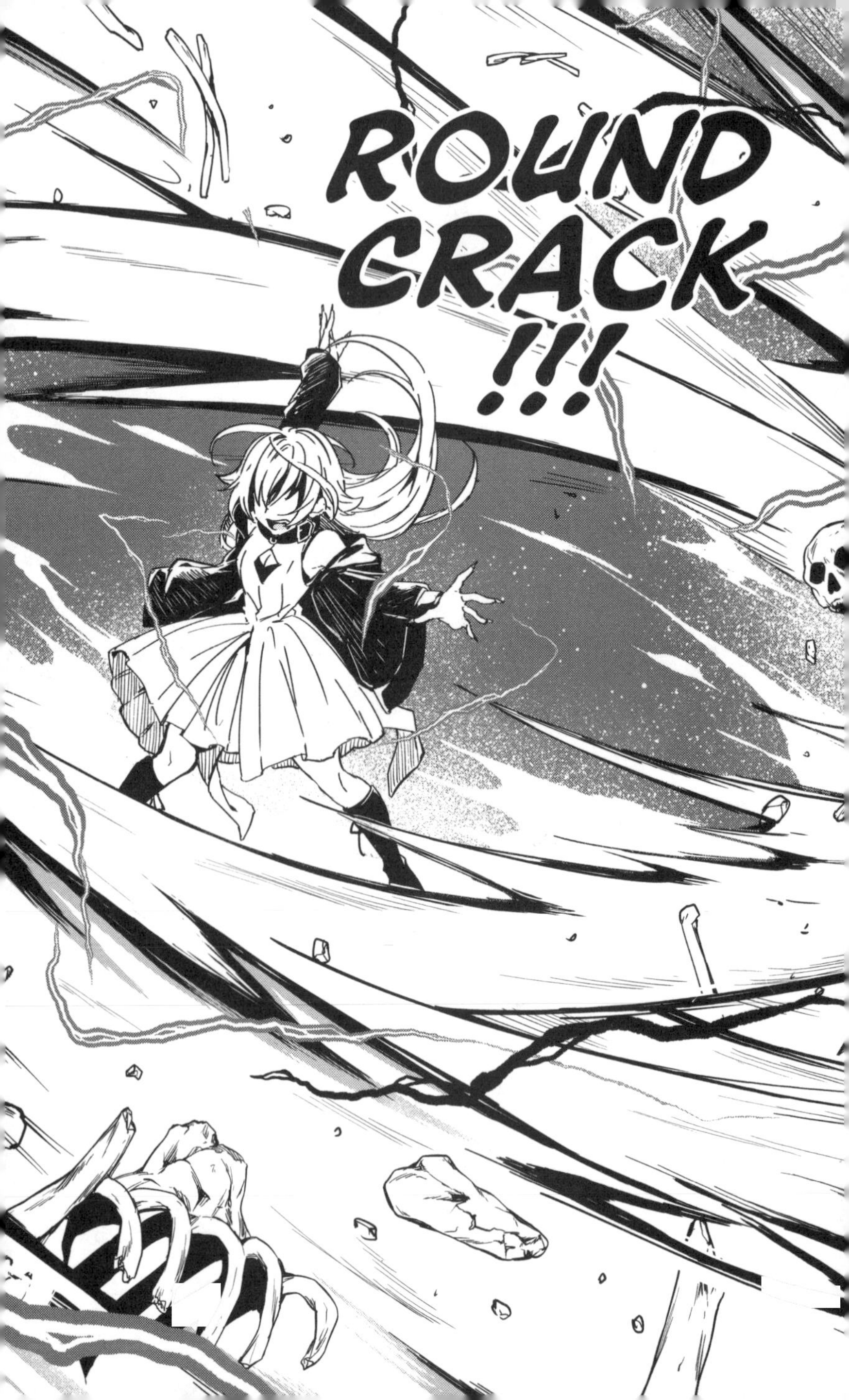
ROUND CRACK!!!

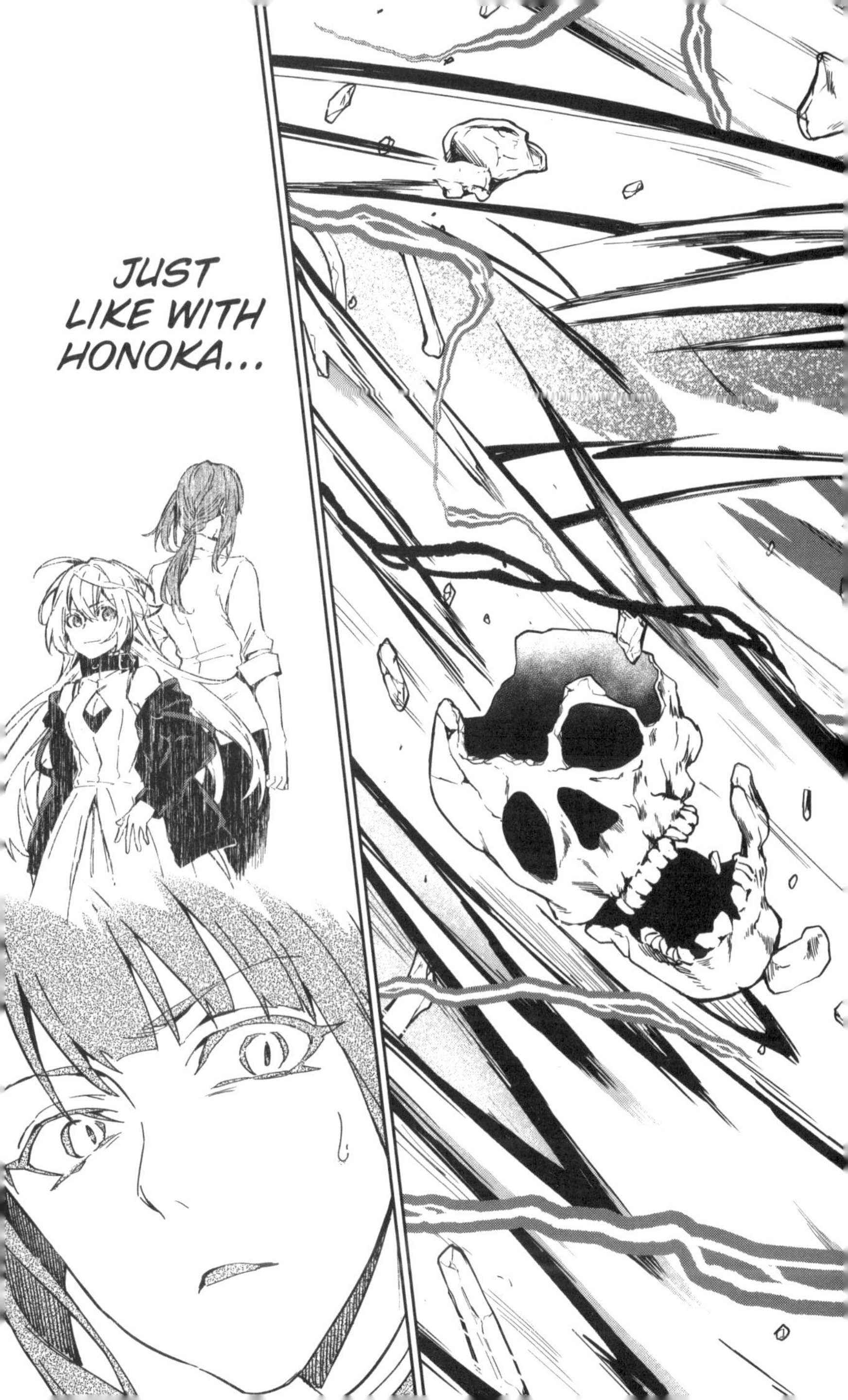
JUST LIKE WITH HONOKA...

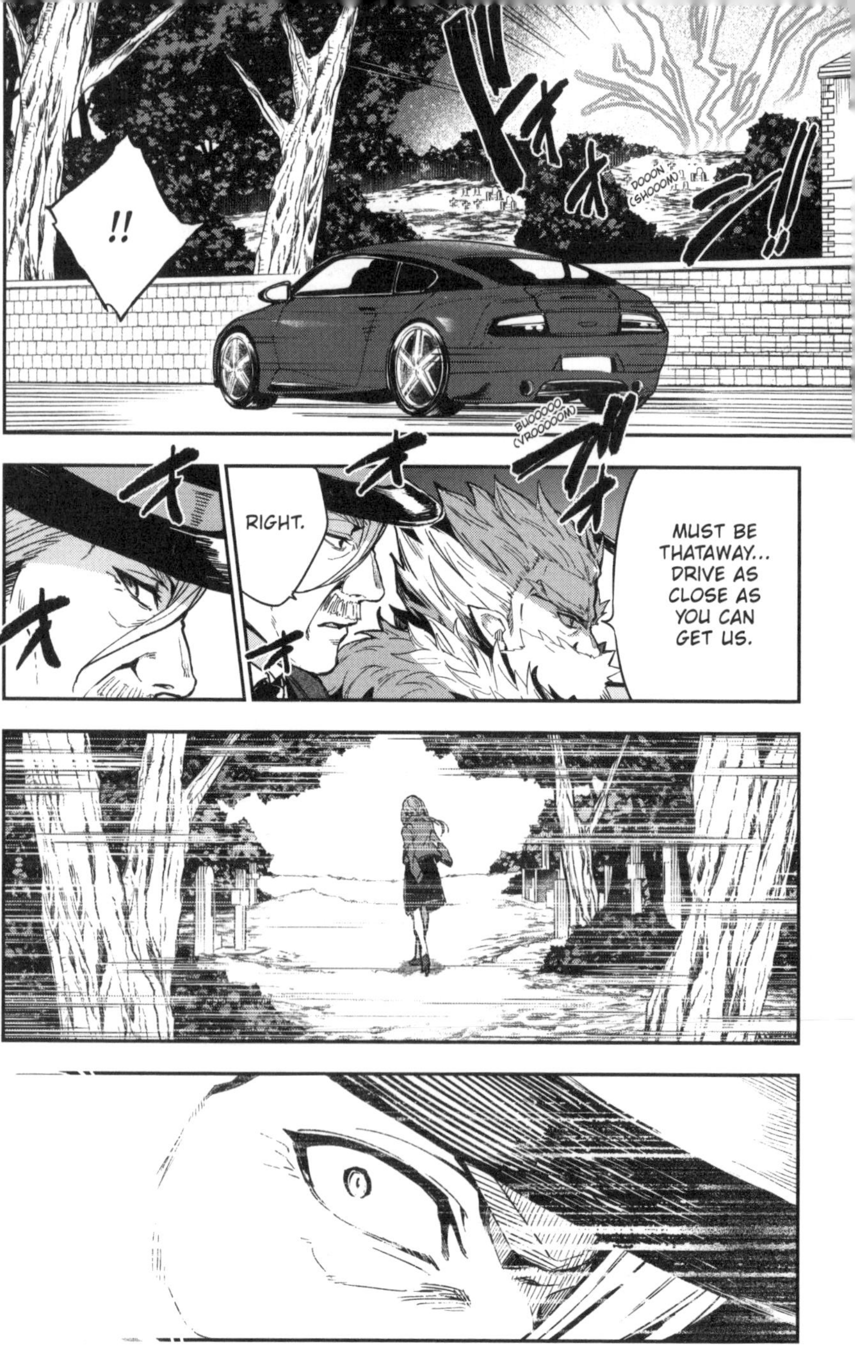
DOOON (SHOOOM)
!!
BUOOOOO (VROOOOOM)
MUST BE THATAWAY... DRIVE AS CLOSE AS YOU CAN GET US.
RIGHT.

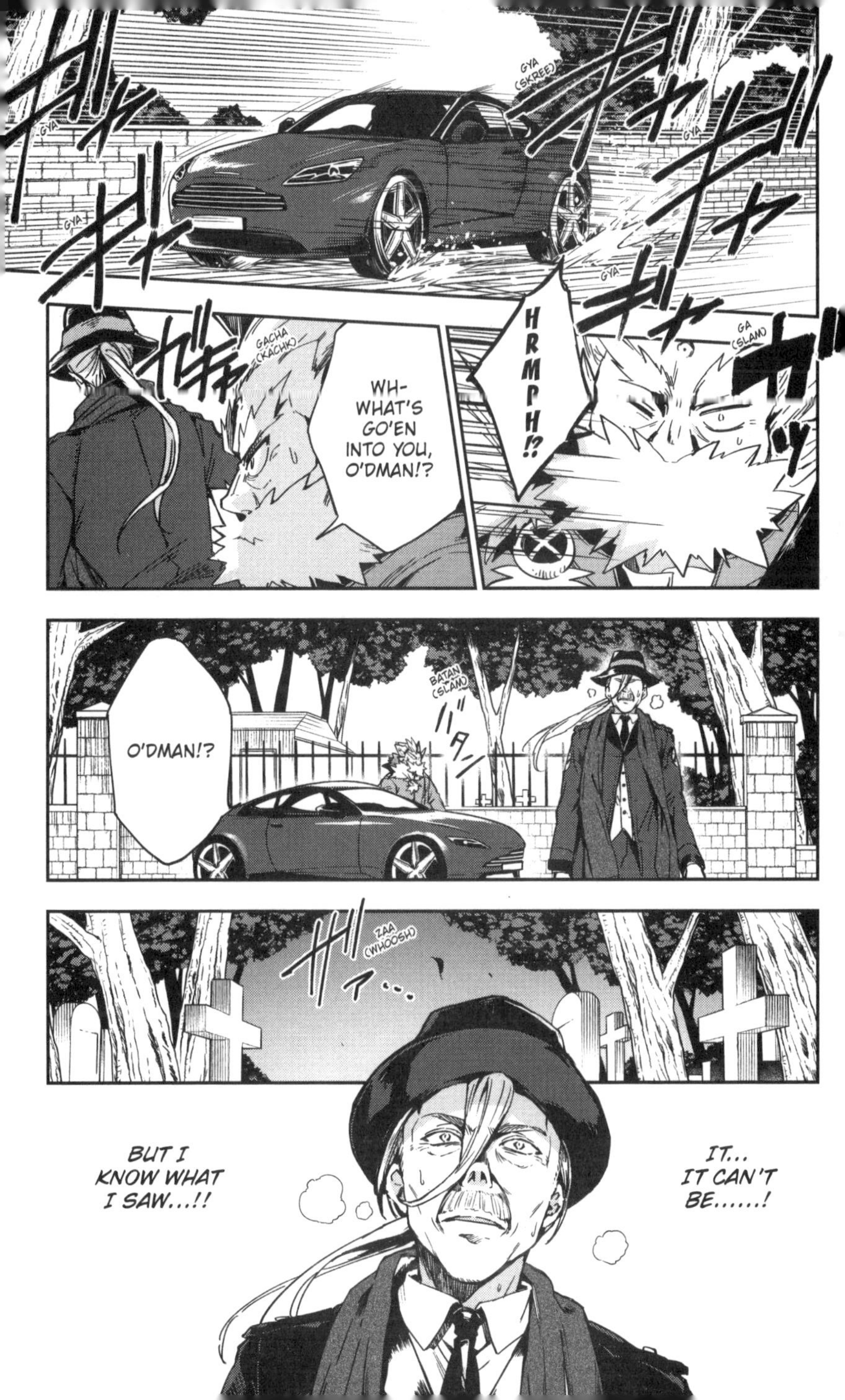
GYA (SKREE)
GYA
GYA
GYA
GYA
GA (SLAM)
HRMPH!?
GACHA (KACHK)
WH- WHAT'S GO'EN INTO YOU, O'DMAN!?
BATAN (SLAM)
O'DMAN!?
ZAA (WHOOSH)
IT... IT CAN'T BE......!
BUT I KNOW WHAT I SAW...!!

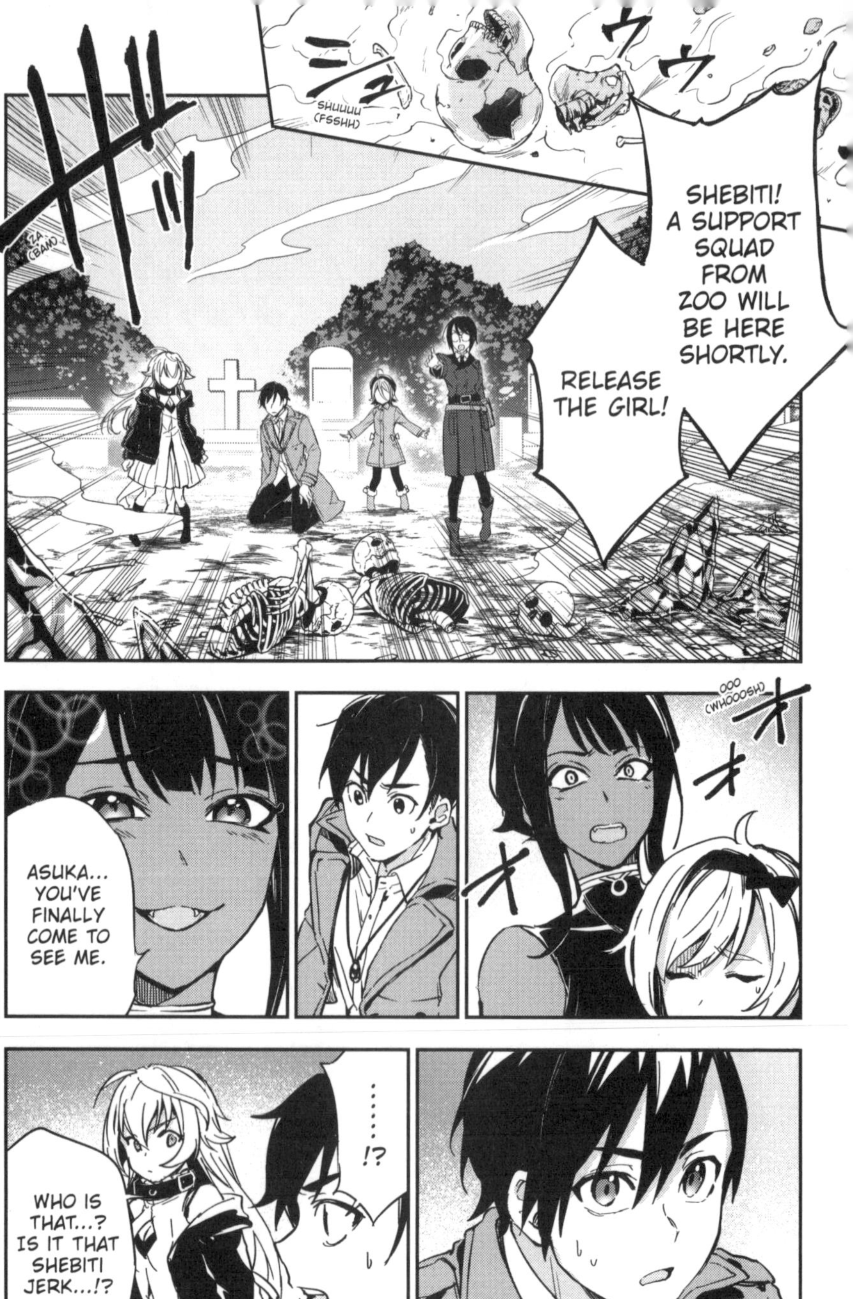
SHUUUU (FSSHH)
SHEBITI! A SUPPORT SQUAD FROM ZOO WILL BE HERE SHORTLY.
RELEASE THE GIRL!
ZA (BAM)
OOO (WHOOOSH)
ASUKA... YOU'VE FINALLY COME TO SEE ME.
......!?
WHO IS THAT...? IS IT THAT SHEBITI JERK...!?

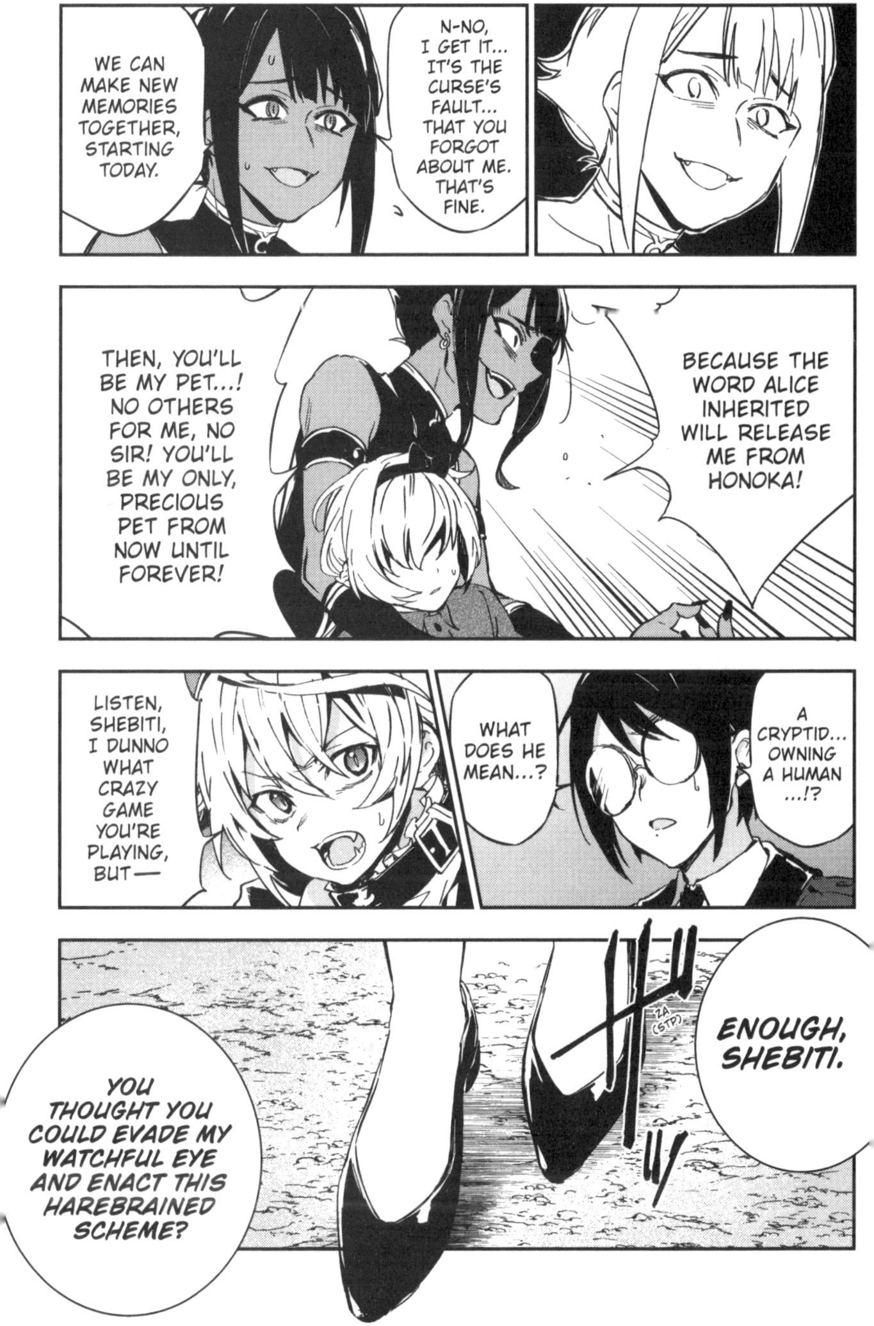
N-NO, I GET IT... IT'S THE CURSE'S FAULT... THAT YOU FORGOT ABOUT ME. THAT'S FINE.
WE CAN MAKE NEW MEMORIES TOGETHER, STARTING TODAY.
BECAUSE THE WORD ALICE INHERITED WILL RELEASE ME FROM HONOKA!
THEN, YOU'LL BE MY PET...! NO OTHERS FOR ME, NO SIR! YOU'LL BE MY ONLY, PRECIOUS PET FROM NOW UNTIL FOREVER!
A CRYPTID... OWNING A HUMAN ...!?
WHAT DOES HE MEAN...?
LISTEN, SHEBITI, I DUNNO WHAT CRAZY GAME YOU'RE PLAYING, BUT—
ZA (STP)
ENOUGH, SHEBITI.
YOU THOUGHT YOU COULD EVADE MY WATCHFUL EYE AND ENACT THIS HAREBRAINED SCHEME?

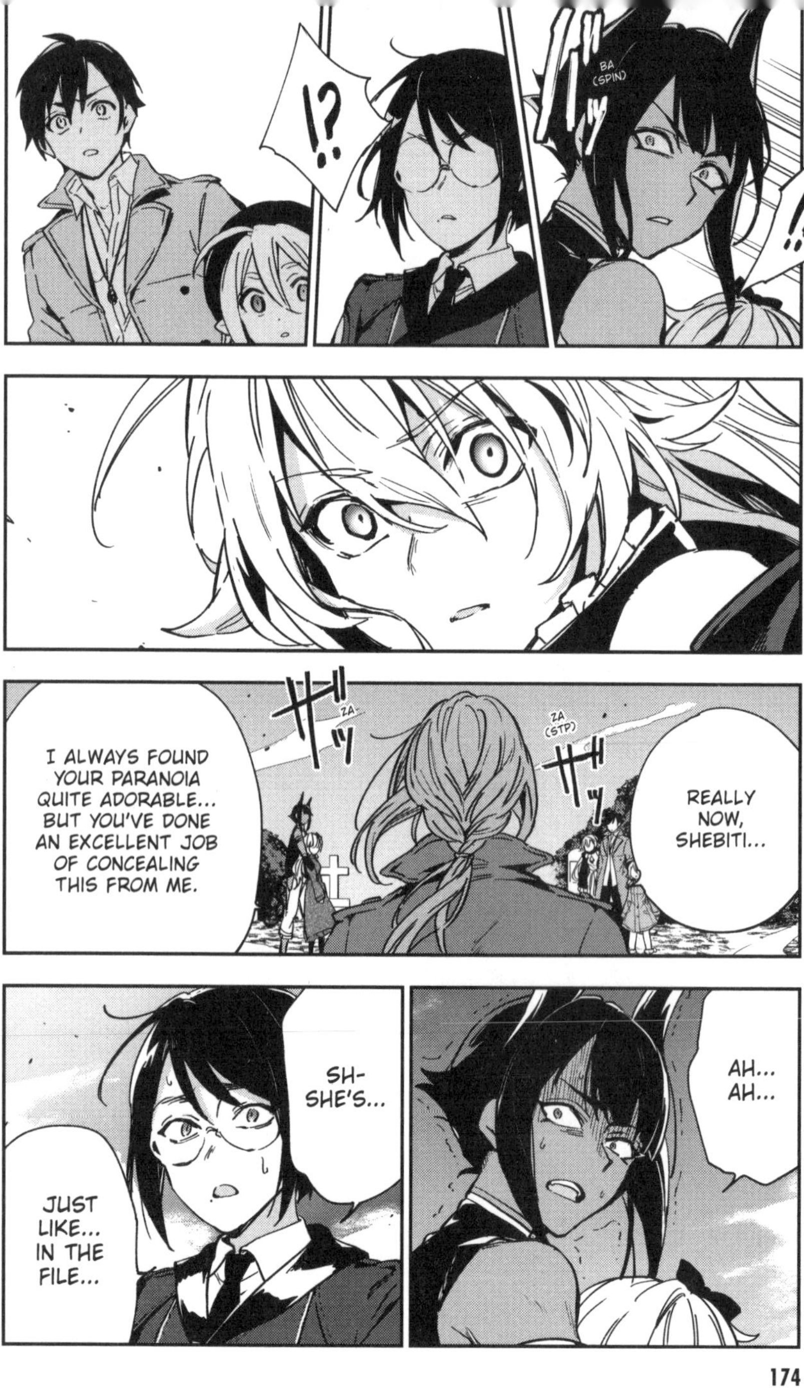
BA (SPIN)
!!
!?
ZA (STP)
REALLY NOW, SHEBITI...
ZA
I ALWAYS FOUND YOUR PARANOIA QUITE ADORABLE... BUT YOU'VE DONE AN EXCELLENT JOB OF CONCEALING THIS FROM ME.
AH... AH...
SH- SHE'S...
JUST LIKE... IN THE FILE...

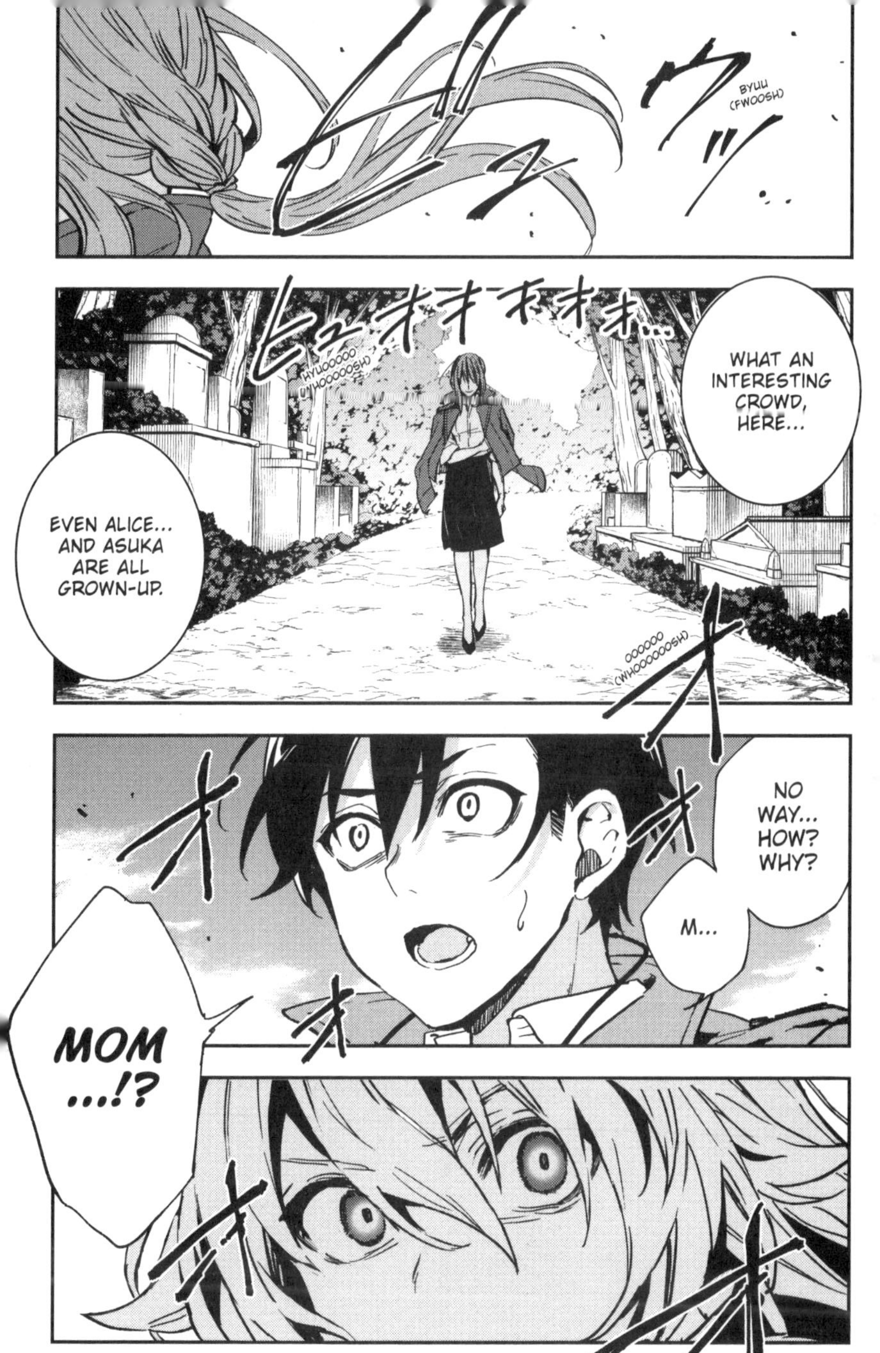
BYUU (FWOOSH)
HYUOOOOO (WHOOOOOSH)
WHAT AN INTERESTING CROWD, HERE...
EVEN ALICE... AND ASUKA ARE ALL GROWN-UP.
OOOOOO (WHOOOOOOSH)
NO WAY... HOW? WHY?
M...
MOM ...!?

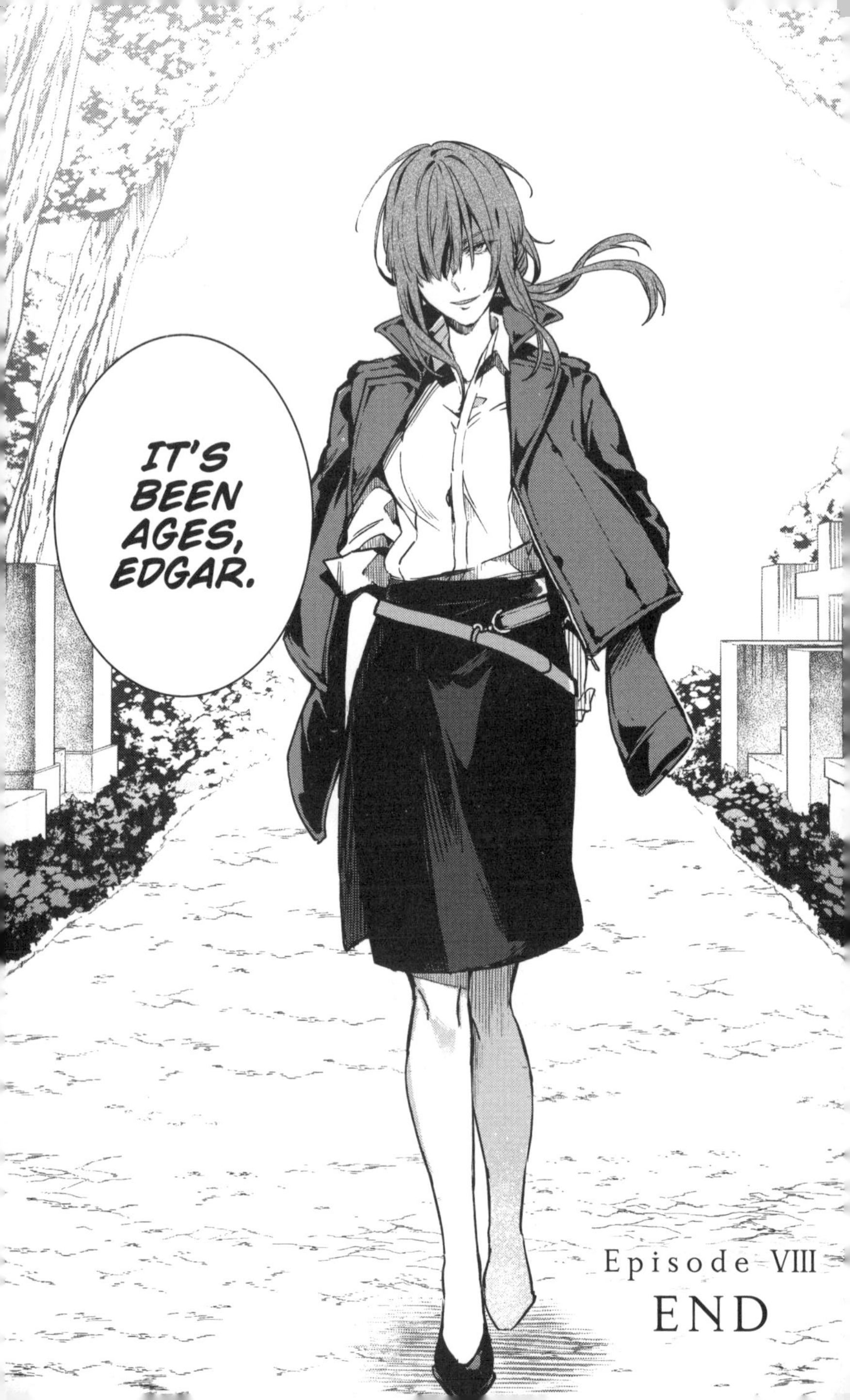
IT'S BEEN AGES, EDGAR.
Episode VIII
END

Translation Notes

Page 20
Sirius is indeed the brightest star in the night sky, and while it is known as the "dog star" due to its prominent position in the constellation Canis Major (the Greater Dog), its name means "scorcher" in Ancient Greek.

Page 57
While both Asuka and Sarai occasionally refer to Oldman as "**Mr. Oldman**," they are saying different things in the original Japanese. Asuka calls him "Oldman-*san*," attaching the default polite honorific -*san*, which is roughly equivalent to the prefix "Mr.," to the end of his name. Sarai, however, says "Mister" in English, as befits an English character (albeit one who is actually speaking Japanese.) This edition makes a distinction between them by spelling Asuka's as "Mr." and Sarai's as "Mister."

Page 76
Alice's Adventures in Wonderland is immensely popular in Japan, so having a character nicknamed Alice who, as a child, falls down a hole into a world filled with magical talking animals is certainly an homage to that book, one which this chapter title makes even more explicit.

Page 90
Spriggans are considered to be the ghosts of giants, ugly and mischievous spirits with the ability to grow to immense size. These legends are native to Cornwall, which is why Spriggan has a Cornish accent.

Page 95
Od, or "Odic force," is a theoretical form of energy emitted by all living things named after the Norse god Odin by Baron Carl von Reichenbach in 1845. Like *qi*, od supposedly creates auras around living creatures and can be manipulated by a few sensitive people to cause various supernatural effects, with the pseudoscientific explanation that it relies on biological electromagnetic fields. The term proved to be short-lived, but since *Bestia* is such a love letter to Western folklore, it makes sense that Sanda-*sensei* would prefer it to *qi*, which is heavily associated with Eastern mythology.

Page 178
The Case Files of Lord El-Melloi II, the anime Sanda-*sensei* was watching, is an adaptation of a light novel series he wrote. The story takes place in the Fate franchise of game developer Type-Moon.

AFTERWORD

Bestia

MAKOTO SANDA MIYAKOKASIWA ACO ARISAKA

Original Story: **Makoto Sanda**

I'm so glad that Volume 2 of *Bestia* has made it to print.

This time, Fafnir joins the battle, Asuka gets a level-up, and the story really starts cranking along.

The scenes where Asuka shouts ***Boost!*** are full of emotion in the original novels, and I'm happy to say that I get just as excited each time I read the drafts Miyako-san and Arisaka-san send me.

I hope you'll keep supporting them too.

Written August 2019, while watching the anime *The Case Files of Lord El-Melloi II.*

Art: **Aco Arisaka**

I'm sorry for the long wait leading up to Volume 2. There are lots of new characters in this one, and the story really begins to unfold. Every one of these characters is so much fun to draw. I even like Shebiti, who, for some reason, is popular among my friends, in a sort of mundane way. That dusky skin! I hope everyone gets a kick out of him—men and women alike.

Thank you to everyone who's sent fan mail following the release of Volume 1! The fan art makes me so happy that I wish I could publish it (assuming I received permission)... In any case, I'd like to return my gratitude in some way!

Thank you for your continued support!

Assistants: Yoshimaru, Takahashi, Nan-chan, cotori, Sakko Amakawa, Mayo Tsuchidome

YEAH, WELL, SORRY FOR BEING A CAT.

BUT YOUR TUFTS KINDA LOOK LIKE THEIR HORNS!

Adaptation: **MIYAKOKASIWA**

When I visited home after the first volume of *Bestia* came out, it turned out that an old friend's kid had read the book and loved it. I said, "Volume 2 is coming out soon, so which new animal do you think we're going to see?" The kid said, "A rhinoceros beetle."

Wrong answer, but maybe Sanda-sensei will introduce a rhinoceros beetle cryptid in the story at some point! Let's hold out hope!

Bestia

2

ORIGINAL STORY: **Makoto Sanda**
ART: **Aco Arisaka**
ADAPTATION: **Miyakokasiwa**

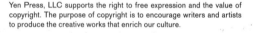

TRANSLATION:
Caleb D. Cook
LETTERING:
Rochelle Gancio

BESTIA Vol. 2
©Makoto Sanda 2019
©Miyakokasiwa 2019
©Aco Arisaka 2019
First published in Japan in 2019 by KADOKAWA CORPORATION, Tokyo. English translation rights arranged with KADOKAWA CORPORATION, Tokyo through TUTTLE-MORI AGENCY, INC., Tokyo.

Yen Press
150 West 30th Street, 19th Floor
New York, NY 10001

Visit us at yenpress.com
facebook.com/yenpress
twitter.com/yenpress
yenpress.tumblr.com
instagram.com/yenpress

First Yen Press Edition: October 2020

Yen Press is an imprint of Yen Press, LLC.
The Yen Press name and logo are trademarks of Yen Press, LLC.

The publisher is not responsible for websites (or their content) that are not owned by the publisher.

Library of Congress Control Number: 2020933613

ISBNs: 978-1-9753-1084-4 (paperback)
       978-1-9753-1083-7 (ebook)

10 9 8 7 6 5 4 3 2 1

WOR

Printed in the United States of America